Indexes to

Seamen's Protection Certificate Applications

and

Proofs of Citizenship

Ports of

New Orleans, Louisiana	1808–1821, 1851–1857
New Haven, Connecticut	1801–1843
Bath, Maine	1833–1868

Additional Ports of

Mobile, Alabama	1819–1859
Middletown, Connecticut	1796–1861
New London, Connecticut	1799–1803
Alexandria, D. C. (now Virginia)	1803–1838
Rockland, Maine	1855–1859
New Bedford, Massachusetts	1801–1826
Salem, Massachusetts	1811 and 1813
Portsmouth, New Hampshire	1813–1827
Newport, Rhode Island	1813–1817

Record Group 36
Records of the Bureau of Customs
National Archives and Records Administration
Washington, D.C.

Compiled by

Ruth Priest Dixon

CLEARFIELD

Printed for
Clearfield Company, Inc. by
Genealogical Publishing Co., Inc.
Baltimore, Maryland
1998

International Standard Book Number: 0-8063-4819-4

Made in the United States of America

Other books by Ruth Priest Dixon:

Index to Seamen's Protection Certificate Applications, Port of Philadelphia, 1796-1823

Index to Seamen's Protection Certificate Applications, Port of Philadelphia, 1824-1861

Sims Settlement, Our Squatter Ancestors, 1806-1818. Northern Alabama Local History and Genealogy.

Contents

Introduction   1

Port	Names	Page
New Orleans, Louisiana	4,428	5
New Haven, Connecticut	3,959	49
Bath, Maine	3,499	88
Mobile, Alabama	865	121
Middletown, Connecticut	851	132
Alexandria, District of Columbia	684	143
Newport, Rhode Island	395	152
Rockland, Maine	130	158
Salem, Massachusetts	115	162
New Bedford, Massachusetts	37	165
Portsmouth, New Hampshire	22	167
New London, Connecticut	18	170

Introduction

Publication of this volume, the third in a series of indexes to early merchant seamen's records, completes the project of indexing all of the Seamen's Protection Certificate applications and related proofs of citizenship held by the National Archives in Washington, D. C. The three volumes make available to researchers a user-friendly finding aide to the names of almost 50,000 seamen who filed for a Seaman's Protection Certificate between 1796 and 1861 in 13 East Coast and Gulf of Mexico ports. This index covers a dozen ports with from 4,400 applications for the Port of New Orleans to 18 proofs of citizenship for the Port of New London, Connecticut. The two previous indexes were to 33,000 applications filed in the Port of Philadelphia. Some of these records are in excellent condition; however, some suffer from neglect, and many are missing.

This volume provides a separate index for each port with those with the largest number of names first. A brief explanation of characteristics of each port and an example of an application or proof of citizenship precedes most indexes. The page numbers are annotated to indicate the port.

The board for The Malcolm H. Stern-National Archives and Records Administration Gift Fund Project approved microfilming Record Group 36, Records of the Bureau of Customs, Seamen's Protection Certificate Applications, as its 1997 Project. When the project is completed, the records for Philadelphia and perhaps other ports will be available. The published indexes will make the microfilm easy to use.

The original intent of Congress in authorizing Seamen's Protection Certificates in 1796 was to protect American seamen from impressment, primarily by the British Navy, a practice which led to the War of 1812. When the seamen were freed and applied for a duplicate protection, they recounted tales of impressment by the British on the high seas and in foreign ports. In reporting the loss of his protection, the seaman often stated, "The British officer tore it up before my very eyes." Genealogists and historians will make exciting finds in these early records.

The 1796 legislation had no sunset clause and the protections apparently continued to be valuable as identification, a sort of passport, for seamen. They were issued long after the British ceased impressing our seamen, right up to the Civil War. Among the highlights of later records are witnesses who are identified as parents or other relatives; names of mothers who have remarried;

naturalization court and date — some naturalization papers are on file; stories of shipwrecks; manumission records, giving the court, date, and name of previous owner; apprenticeship papers with trade, length of service, and name of the master craftsman; church records with place, and date of baptism; military discharge papers; and more.

None of these stories appears, of course, in the index. As is always true, the researcher must see the original document to verify the information in the index and to savor the stories that are told in the original. Names require particular attention. While the handwriting of some notaries is quite legible, others are almost unintelligible. Familiarity with a handbook on early American writing is a great help. Copies of applications or proofs of citizenship can be obtained from the National Archives or by local genealogists.

Seamen were a mobile lot. In each index the researcher will find that while the majority of the seamen is from the area, many apply in a port far from home.

African American genealogists and historians will find the records of some ports rewarding. As many as 37% of the seamen applying in Philadelphia in the 1830s were men of color. In this volume, 7% of the seamen applying in New Orleans, 6% in New Haven, and 3% in Bath were so described. There were 28 in Middletown, 10 in New Bedford, and less than 5 in the other ports. Researchers will find W. Jeffrey Bolster's *Black Jacks, African American Seamen in the Age of Sail,* and Martha S. Putney's *Black Sailors, Afro-American Merchant Seamen and Whalemen Prior to the Civil War,* useful references.

Applications contain more information than the proofs of citizenship. They give the seaman's name, his age when he applied, the city, county, state, or country of birth, and color of skin, eyes, and hair. Many describe tattoos, physical defects, or scars. The applications were witnessed by a person who swore to or affirmed the accuracy of the information. The name of the witness is often a major clue for further genealogical research.

Proofs of citizenship are just that. Some are notarized copies of church or public records. Many give the names of both parents, and the father's trade. Some are statements by a relative or friend as to where and when the seaman was born. Descriptions of the seaman usually are lacking.

Quarterly abstracts and registers, lists of protections issued by the customs collector, are numerous, incomplete, a challenge to research, but very useful. Although many of these records are missing, the extant ones often fill the lacunae in the applications records. They contain the seaman's name, age, place of birth, height, and color of skin. Missing are the witnesses and anecdotes about the seaman and his family.

The National Archives in Washington holds the following registers or abstracts: **Alabama:** Mobile; **Connecticut:** Fairfield, Middletown, New Haven, New London, Stonington; **Delaware:** Wilmington; **District of Columbia:** Georgetown; **Florida:** Fernandina, Key West, Pensacola, St. Augustine, St. Marks; **Georgia:** Darien, Savannah; **Louisiana:** New Orleans; **Maine:** Bath, Belfast, Castine, Frenchman's Bay, Kennebunkport, Machias, Passamaquoddy, Penobscot, Portland-Falmouth, Rockland, Saco, Waldoboro, Wiscasset, York; **Maryland:** Annapolis, Baltimore; **Massachusetts:** Barnstable, Boston & Charlestown, Dighton-Fall River, Edgartown, Gloucester, Ipswich, Marblehead, Nantucket, New Bedford, Newburyport, Plymouth, Salem-Beverly; **New Hampshire:** Portsmouth; **New Jersey:** Newark, Perth Amboy; **New York:** New York City, Sag Harbor; **North Carolina:** Camden, Edenton, New Bern, Plymouth, Washington; **Pennsylvania:** Philadelphia; **Rhode Island:** Bristol & Warren, Newport, Providence; **South Carolina:** Charleston; **Texas:** Galveston; **Virginia:** Alexandria, Cherrystone, Dumfries, East River, Folly Landing, Norfolk & Portsmouth, Petersburg, Richmond; **Wisconsin:** Milwaukee, WI (1861 only).

In addition, the Regional Office in Waltham, Massachusetts, holds some registers for New London and New Haven, Connecticut; Newport, Rhode Island; and Fall River, Gloucester, Marblehead, and Salem, Massachusetts. These are extensive holdings of from two to eighteen volumes each. The Rhode Island Historical Society holds registers for Providence and has compiled an index of about 11,000 names, 1796-1870, published by Genealogical Publishing Company, Baltimore.

One step removed from the registers and two steps removed from the original applications are two card indexes to registers compiled by the WPA. The applications for the port of New York were destroyed but the registers survive. The index to these registers is filed in 18 boxes. The second index of 153 boxes is to the registers of most other east coast ports. Both indexes are in the Archives in Washington, D. C.

Selected References to Merchant Seamen's Records

In the National Archives:
Record Group 36: Seamen's Protection Certificate Applications
          and Oaths of Citizenship.
Record Groups 36 and 41: Crew Lists, Shipping Articles, and Log Books
Record Group 41: Applications for Seamen's Protection Certificates, 1916-1940
Record Group 59: Documents Regarding Impressed Seamen, 1793-1814
          (Archives II)
Microfilm: M1747, *Index to the War of 1812, Prisoner of War Records*
          M2019, *Records Relating to War of 1812 Prisoners of War*
American State Papers, Foreign Relations, and Commerce and
          Navigation, 1790-ca.1815
Printouts of indexes to Seamen's Protection Certificates and Proofs of
Citizenship, compiled by Ruth Priest Dixon, are available in the Textual
Reference Branch.

Publications:
Ruth Priest Dixon, "Genealogical Fallout from the War of 1812," *Prologue,
Journal of the National Archives, 24(Spring, 1992):70-76.*
— "Seamen's Protection Certificate Records for Genealogical Research,"
National Genealogical Society Quarterly 78 (September 1990):204-212.
— *"Grandpa Went to Sea: Merchant Seamen's Records, 1796-1861,"* tape No.
S-197, presented NGS Conference, 1997, Repeat Performance, 2911 Crabapple
Lane, Hobart IN 46342.
— *Index, Seamen's Protection Certificate Applications, Port of Philadelphia,
1796 to 1823, and 1824-1861* (two volumes) (Baltimore: Genealogical
Publishing Company, 1994 and 1995).

Guide to Genealogical Research in the National Archives. Washington, D. C.:
National Archives Trust Fund Board, 1985, pp. 189-191. (Not the new *Guide to
Federal Records,* 1995, which omits Seamen's Protection Certificates.)

Guide to Index Columns

Seaman's name: last, first, middle
Year: year application filed
Age: age at time of application, if given
Color: b = black c = colored m = mulatto
y = yellow I = Indian blank = Caucasian

State: state of birth
Country: country of birth
naturalized = foreign birth, no
country given
Number: protection number for
ports of New Orleans and Bath

On this *Second* — Day of *March*
in the Year of our Lord One Thousand Eight Hundred and *four*
Narcissus Broutin
Before me ~~FRANCIS MUNHALL,~~ Notary Public, dwelling in the City
of New Orleans, personally came *William Beazer*
— — and made Oath — that he

*he has resided in the Territory of
Orleans for upwards of too years and
was here previous to the 30th of April
1803 — and fought in the American Revolution*

and a CITIZEN of the United States that he is aged *forty nine*
Years, of the Height of *five* — Feet *one 8/* Inches
Grey Eyes, *light* Hair, *light* Complexion, *and
India Ink Mark on his right Arm*

Wm Brazier

Police Commander being also duly Sworn
made Oath that he is well acquainted with *William*
Beazer — and verily believes he *above Deposition
to be true* —

Wm Vanander

SWORN as above before me

*Narcissus Broutin
Notry Pub*

Seamen's Protection Certificate Applications

Port of New Orleans, Louisiana

This is an index to 4,428 applications filed in New Orleans between 1804 and 1857. The files are fragmentary: there are no applications for 1808, 1813, and 1817, and there is a long gap between 1821 and 1851. By year, the number of applications on file range from 656 in 1805 to 64 in 1857.

These documents were filed after the Louisiana Purchase was made. Three languages are involved, French, Spanish, and English. Officials and the indexer encountered problems in reading or writing names in languages foreign to them.

It is important to note that the records are not alphabetical by year; they are organized by year and by the number of the protection issued. **To find an application the researcher must find the name in the alpha index, note the year and the number, and locate the application using this information.**

The records show the name and age at time of the application, and most give a physical description and place of birth. As would be expected, many seamen claimed U. S. citizenship by virtue of residence in Louisiana when the Louisiana Purchase was made. Many of these did not give a place of birth.

Seaman's Protection Certificate Applications
Port of New Orleans, Louisiana

Data order: Name, Year, Number, Color, Age, State or Country

Name	Year	Number	Color	Age	State or Country
, Baptiste	1811	48	c	0	Orleans
Abbey, Dennis	1815	54		27	CT
Abby, Obadiah	1812	148		30	CT
Abel, Joseph	1811	99		50	Orleans
Achison, Thomas	1805	634		23	PA
Ackman, John	1855	460		22	NJ
Adail, Robert	1851	1509		22	MD
Adam, Joseph	1805	699		42	
Adams, Alpheus	1851	1188		39	ME
Adams, Frederick	1855	523		31	ME
Adams, George	1811	77		25	MA
Adams, John	1812	139		25	NY
Adams, John B.	1821	145		17	MA
Adams, Joseph S.	1819	101		15	NY
Adams, Leonard	1810	272		23	NY
Adams, Samuel	1821	135	b	35	MA
Adams, Samuel R.	1816	6		25	Ma
Adams, Stephen	1805	903		33	
Adamson, Barnet	1815	137		33	MA
Adde, Laurant	1807	369		36	Orleans
Agarrat, Stephen Bonaventura	1806	1565		44	
Aguino, Philip	1810	60		27	
Agustin, John	1810	209	b	19	
Aiken, David	1819	217	m	0	PA
Ainsley, Zachariah	1807	368		20	MD
Alapunte, Raymond	1805	559		28	Orleans
Albarado, John	1814	155		45	
Albert, Francis	1805	875		21	SC
Albert, Michael	1804	195		23	
Albro, Esek	1814	180		19	RI
Alcedo, Joseph	1805	536		24	Orleans
Ales, Manuel	1810	208		40	
Alexander, Charles	1818	30		33	NY
Alexander, John	1811	153		25	Orleans
Alexander, John	1810	134		44	
Alexander, John	1805	583		40	
Alexander, John	1805	611		40	Orleans
Alexander,JohnJoseph	1819	15		21	
Alexander, Michael G.	1804	257		26	MD
Alfaro, James	1805	839		33	
Allcock, John	1810	326		26	MA
Allcock, Robert	1814	176		22	PA
Allen, Alexander	1804	314		35	VA
Allen, Andrew	1814	194		36	PA
Allen, Caleb Wiley	1811	313		31	RI
Allen, George	1818	168	I	24	
Allen, George	1851	1630		30	PA
Allen, George	1855	217		31	PA
Allen, John	1821	14		26	PA
Allen, John	1814	138		30	MD
Allen, John	1818	6	b	24	PA
Allen, John	1815	17		33	NY
Allen, Thomas	1821	10		24	VA
Allen, Thomas Lee	1819	51		27	MA
Allen, William	1855	525		24	NY
Allen, William	1814	200		22	NJ
Allen, William	1810	190		26	PA
Allen, William	1807	329		26	MA
Alling, Samuel	1821	111		30	CT
Allyn, James	1810	286		44	CT
Allyn, Nathan	1804	140		39	CT
Alome, Louis	1810	266		21	
Alqueste, Adam	1818	273		25	MA
Altemus, Jerman U.	1815	161		30	PA
Ameline, Louis	1805	905		30	
Ames, John	1810	388		17	
Amor, Anil	1812	118		21	
Anderson, Andrew	1851	1671		23	NY
Anderson, Andrew	1805	819		29	NY
Anderson, Benjamin	1805	826	b	33	MD
Anderson, Charles	1851	1424		19	NY
Anderson, Evean	1804	311		18	VA
Anderson, Isaac	1810	176		22	NY
Anderson, James	1811	243		24	PA
Anderson, James	1804	124		28	NY
Anderson, John	1804	46		21	MA
Anderson, John	1804	313		29	MA
Anderson, John	1806	1442		20	ME
Anderson, John	1851	1353		25	NY
Anderson, John	1819	72		17	GA
Anderson, Joseph	1804	90		37	MA
Anderson, Thomas	1805	810		31	PA
Anderson, Thomas	1851	1360		25	PA
Anderson, William	1815	249		19	MA
Anderson, William	1804	213		23	MA
Anderson, William H.	1806	1498		21	VA
Andre, Joseph	1805	920		46	
Andre, Norbere	1805	713	b	20	Orleans
Andrews, Amariah	1810	138		18	MA
Andrews, Anthony	1806	1437		29	SC
Andrews, Asa	1804	236		22	NY
Andrews, B. K.	1855	253		21	CT
Andrews, Howell	1818	181		22	PA
Andrews, Joseph	1805	972	b	45	
Andrews, Robert	1818	111		26	

Name	Year	No.		Age	Place		Name	Year	No.		Age	Place
Andrews, Samuel	1819	86		14 MA			Baam, John B.	1814	134		17 LA	
Annes, Thomas	1812	63		35 PA			Babin, Alexander	1815	271		37	
Ansbey, Charles	1819	102		25 PA			Babin, Mathurin	1814	214		40	
Anselme, Joseph	1805	487		30			Badille, Paul	1811	274		15	
Anson, Benjamin	1804	135		23 NY			Baen, Guillexmo	1805	601		26	Orleans
Anthony, Emanuel	1806	1506		25			Bagley, Charles	1819	203		21 MA	
Anthony, John	1805	672		21 DE			Baguerie, Hipolite	1804	197		29	
Anthony, John	1804	308	b	29 VA			Baham, Pierre	1814	201		42 LA	
Anthony, John	1815	146		39	Portugal		Bahan, Andri	1816	28		28	
Anthony, John, Jr.	1811	318		13 MA			Bailey, Anthony	1805	339		23 MA	
Anthony, Joseph	1821	78		40	Portugal		Bailey, Samuel	1815	80	b	20 DE	
Anthony, Joseph	1805	361		20 LA			Bailey, William	1806	1470		22 VA	
Antoine, Jean	1821	79		25 LA			Baily, Philip	1818	175		22 RI	
Antoine, Joseph	1806	1466		20	Orleans		Baker, Henry	1806	1493		20 MA	
Antony, Joseph	1821	94	y	49 LA			Baker, James M.	1816	96		20 PA	
Appleby, Nathan	1815	188		28 NH			Baker, John	1815	172		36 NY	
Appleton, Charles	1816	46		17 PA			Baker, John	1804	262		24 NY	
Aquilar, Francois	1816	84		23			Baker, Wm.	1855	348		22 MA	
Arden, James	1819	52		16 NY			Bakie, Samuel	1851	1276		47 MA	
Ardisson, Vincent	1805	696		25			Baldwin, John	1851	1635		26 NY	
Armed, Manuel	1805	898		18			Baldwin, Marcus	1815	157		21 CT	
Armstrong, Henry	1851	1680		20 NY			Bales, Edward	1855	456		25 NY	
Armstrong, James	1815	61		28 NY			Ball, John	1810	382		21 NY	
Arnaud, Barthelemy	1812	158		22			Ball, Peter	1805	475		35 NH	
Arnaud, John Baptiste	1810	37		40			Ballard, David L.	1805	545		20 NH	
Arnaud, Rene	1816	89		25			Ballicant, Peter	1805	676	y	24	
Arnold, Alfred	1818	63		21 CT			Ballon, Alexis	1804	2		25	E. Indies
Arnold, John	1804	237		26 MA			Bampfield, George	1816	71	m	45 SC	
Arris, William	1804	110		19 NY			Baptist, John	1805	551		38	
Ashbury, Wm. W.	1855	492		21 CT			Baptist, John	1805	763		28	
Ashwell, Thomas	1855	528		21 MA			Baptiste, John	1805	534	b	14	Orleans
Assemad, Joachim	1819	54	y	28			Baptiste, John	1805	778		30	
Atacho, Joseph	1818	275		24 LA			Baptiste, John	1806	1520	b	23	Orleans
Atherton, Salem T.	1857	134		24 ME			Baptiste, John	1806	1524		32	Orleans
Atkins, John	1815	87		25 VA			Baptiste, John	1815	185		20 SC	
Atkins, Pardon	1818	140		25 MA			Baptiste, Jonh	1819	212	y	34 MD	
Atkins, William	1812	88		29 NC			Baptiste, Joseph Jean	1807	370	b	20	
Atkinson, Henry	1811	185		28 MD			Baranguet, Fransisco	1811	136		29	
Atkinson, William	1812	138		35 MD			Baranguey, Francisco	1806	1801		24	Orleans
Atkinson, William	1805	968		30 NY			Barbet, Robert Adrien	1819	5		28 LA	
Attwood, John	1816	62		26 NY			Barbier, Hiacinthe	1806	1563		0	
Atwell, Edward	1851	1556		23 MA			Barcelo, Pedro	1812	41		28	
Audiben, John	1811	7		30			Barer, Peter	1805	521		14	Orleans
Augier, John Rene	1804	74		0			Bares, Miguel	1805	516		28	
Augusten, Etienne	1811	5	c	26	St. Domingo		Barford, William	1818	314		30 PA	
Augustin, Joseph	1809	224	c	33	Orleans		Bargas, Hermegilous	1805	837		30 IL	
Augustus, Francis	1855	515		23 NY			Barker, Benjamin	1851	1155		31 MA	
Austin, John	1807	394		30 NY			Barker, John	1810	245		18 MA	
Austin, William	1812	166		25 RI			Barker, John	1810	122		18 MA	
Authemant, Joseph	1805	395		24			Barker, John	1810	314		18 MA	
Auville, John Joseph	1805	439		34 LA			Barkle, John	1821	5		38	
Avegne, Pillippo	1815	230		0			Barly, Peter	1812	229		46 LA	
Averell, William	1851	1637		27 ME			Barnes, James	1821	144		21 PA	
Avery, Joseph	1805	906		19 PA			Barnes, Samuel	1805	348		0	

Barnett, Samuel	1805	960		48	
Barney, Joshua,Jr.	1818	347		14 MD	
Barney, Seth	1805	735		18 MA	
Barns, Charles	1810	237	b	25 PA	
Barns, Hill	1810	150		21 NJ	
Baro, Francis	1805	539		30	
Barquet, Louis	1815	5	y	21 LA	
Barrera, Anthony	1810	95		50	Orleans
Barrett,JosephLeonard	1855	480		21 PA	
Barrett, William	1851	1505		26 PA	
Barriere, John	1805	577		19	
Barrio, Francis	1807	401		39	
Barro, Jacques	1807	409		38	Orleans
Barrod, Joseph	1851	1502		36 LA	
Barron, Henry	1851	1275		23 NY	
Barrow, John	1819	127		26	Great Brit
Barry, Edward	1855	285		22 NY	
Barry, Edward	1805	751		40 MA	
Barry, John	1818	53		23 NY	
Barry, Mercein	1855	415		20 NY	
Barston, Frederick O.	1855	173		24 MA	
Barte, Jean	1821	85	m	27	
Barthelemy, Augustin	1819	209		34	
Barthelott, Andres					
(Andrew)	1815	28		0	
Barthole,JohnAnthony	1816	69		0 LA	
Bartholomew, Copall	1805	414		44	
Bartlet, George	1818	241		27 MA	
Barwood, Thomas	1805	855		19 NY	
Baselona, Antonia	1805	651		36	
Basjanand, John	1805	768		26	Orleans
Bass, Wally	1814	178		33 VA	
Bassano, Clement	1851	1669		24 PA	
Bassari, Andre	1812	71		27	
Baston, John	1815	2	c	43 VA	
Batara, George	1818	327		27	
Bates, Benjamin	1818	86		18 CT	
Bates, Richard T.	1855	421		27 NY	
Bates, Thomas	1819	113		30 MA	
Batice, John	1805	575	c	39	
Batice, John	1805	572		18	
Batiste, John Francis	1805	349		0 LA	
Batteck, Wm.	1851	1519		26 NY	
Battle, Timothy	1805	787		21 NY	
Baudy, Charles	1805	709		15	Orleans
Baudy, Charles	1806	1591		17	
Baval, Jacquis	1805	766		25	
Baxter, Bazila	1819	188		17 MA	
Baxter, James	1821	101		25 VA	
Baxter, Obed	1819	94		16 MA	
Baxter, William	1805	723		33 PA	
Bayadores,					
Diego Joseph	1805	594		32	Orleans
Bayard, Antoine	1812	168		22	
Bayard, Arnauld	1811	103	m	20	Orleans
Bayol, Rene	1806	1816		32	Orleans
Beado, Peter	1805	647		16	Orleans
Bear, Andrew	1805	918		25	
Beasley, John	1811	237		23 MD	
Beauvais, Auguste	1819	186		24	
Beazon, William	1811	2		26 SC	
Bebee, Nathan J.	1811	59		14 CT	
Beck, John	1804	165		21 MD	
Becker, Henry	1851	1625		17 WI	
Beckner, Henry	1815	18		23 NJ	
Beckwith, William	1805	631		24 MD	
Bee, Samuel T.	1855	534		21 MA	
Beears, John	1821	84	b	30 MA	
Beecher, James C.	1851	1148		23 MA	
Belase, Mattio	1805	597		34	
Beles, Domingo	1806	1531		24	Orleans
Belfast, Peter	1805	750	b	29 DE	
Belfore, Joseph	1811	122		24	
Belger, Daniel	1818	96	y	21 DC	
Belicave, Francis	1810	115		32	Mississipp
Bell, George	1805	375	c	16	
Bell, George B.	1855	497		38 ME	
Bell, John	1857	143		24 RI	
Bell, John	1805	884		23	
Bell, Joseph	1809	25		27 MD	
Bell, Stewart	1804	132		22 VA	
Bell, Thomas	1855	545		22 PA	
Bellinger, Martin	1810	124		26 NY	
Bello, Christopher	1806	1440		22	Orleans
Bello, Johanna	1804	175		24	
Bellot, Peter	1805	437		21	
Benford, Thomas	1851	1493		24 MA	
Beng/Boney,Selemon	1805	410		22 MA	
Benit, Filipe (Philip)	1816	24		28	
Benjamin, Eliel	1818	213		23 NY	
Benner, Thomas	1851	1490		26 ME	
Bennet, Arben	1812	96		25 PA	
Bennet, George	1805	351		22 NY	
Bennet, Joseph	1810	335		25	Louisiana
Bennet, William	1812	206		21 GA	
Bennett, Alvah	1851	1307		19 ME	
Bennett, Henry	1855	262		21 PA	
Bennett, James	1821	130		25 VA	
Bennett, John	1815	88		24 MA	
Bennett, Joseph	1805	957		28	
Bennett, Manuel	1818	304		21	
Bennett, Reuben	1804	190		27 MA	
Bennison, Leonard	1811	280		23 NY	
Benois, Bernard	1814	202		50	MS Terr.
Benson, Andrew	1809	247		31 MD	
Benson, James	1851	1306		27 NY	
Benson, Jonas	1810	47		18 MD	
Benson, Samuel	1810	380		21 MA	

Benson, William	1816	104	b	39 RI		Blair, Robert	1805	345		23 NJ	
Bensted, Nathaniel	1810	155		34 PA		Blake, Charles	1807	363		51 SC	
Benton, James L.	1851	1286		23 MA		Blake, Ezekiel	1819	87		32 ME	
Benus, Peter	1811	6		20		Blake, John	1855	191		68 NY	
Bera, Joseph Mary	1810	59		24		Blake, Will.	1818	127		45 VA	
Berge, Louis	1811	261		37		Blan, Simon	1805	652		33	
Bericuta, Nicholas	1805	585		16	Orleans	Blanc, Alexander	1806	1530		40	
Berkley, John	1811	163	y	26 PA		Blancard, Remond	1810	64		25	Orleans
Berkley, John	1811	117	y	26 PA		Blanchard, William	1819	128		25 ME	
Bernard, Hestin	1812	34		46		Blanchard, William	1804	98		0	
Bernard, Peter	1812	25	m	28		Blanchard, William P.	1804	98		18 MA	
Bernare, Gaspard	1811	126		52		Blanco, Anthony	1811	316		32	
Berrien, John	1812	85		30 NY		Blanco, Antonio	1812	212		36 LA	
Berrio, Jacques	1815	13		39		Blancq, Peter	1804	0		0	
Berry, Charles	1851	1334		29 NH		Blane, Etienne	1819	29		50	
Berry, Henry	1855	324		22 NY		Blang, Charles	1807	362		45	
Berry, John	1819	100		21 NY		Bleach, George	1807	402		21 MA	
Berry, William	1806	1545		26 NY		Bliven, Erastus, Jr.	1855	267		23 RI	
Berryman, Newton	1810	255		22 VA		Blodget, Harry	1811	232	y	20 RI	
Bertho, Jean	1811	61		30		Bloomfield, John	1805	869		17 PA	
Bertholy, Charles	1809	221		27	Orleans	Blount, William	1805	981		38 PA	
Berto, Joseph	1809	256		21		Blue, Jno. George	1810	334		18 VA	
Bertoli, Nicolas	1821	110		41		Bock, William	1851	1407		24 NY	
Bertram, John	1804	260		0		Bodley, Thomas	1809	44		17 MD	
Bertrand, Francisco	1806	1578		23		Boey, Felix	1818	254		28	
Besely, John	1811	195		25 MD		Bofill, Ramon	1819	218		25	
Besswicks, William	1821	81		39 MD		BoForguez, Pedro	1810	342		30	
Bevan, John	1805	957		25		Bolden, William	1812	26		25 NY	
Beverhaut, Peter	1810	259		30 LA		Bolger, Thomas	1851	1535		22 NY	
Beverhoudt, Peter	1812	198		22 MA		Bond, Thomas	1809	287		32 VA	
Bickfoer, Chandler	1855	247		31 ME		Bond, William	1821	123		24 MA	
Bickford, Jacob S.	1857	116		19 ME		Bonfils, Julien	1804	285		32	Orleans
Bilard, Martin	1805	614		33	Orleans	Bongerdin, Joseph	1805	452		32	
Bill, Robert	1815	184		17 MA		Bonham, Zedekiah	1805	663		28 NJ	
Billard, James	1805	606		21		Booth, George	1818	245		28 MD	
Biller, Jims (James)	1819	13		25 LA		Booz, Christian	1804	145		19 PA	
Binette, Mary	1818	215		23		Boras, Gaspard	1805	764		30	
Binlet, Joseph	1805	657		18	Orleans	Borden, Samuel	1812	0		32 RI	
Biol, Joseph	1805	901		30		Bornier, Charles	1805	705		30	Orleans
Birden, John	1809	305		21 NY		Bortohesi, Antonio	1812	28		30	
Birtwiske, James	1855	250		19 NJ		Borxas, Dionitius	1812	0		26	
Bisbee, Elizah	1818	169		23 MA		Bosley, Samuel B.	1810	243		22 MD	
Bisbee, Isaac	1818	258		24 MA		Bosquet, John	1804	272		29	
Bishop, Joseph	1810	331		24 CT		Boss, James L.	1815	38		26 RI	
Black, Frederick	1812	173		27 PA		Bosse, Barthelemy	1818	0		11 LA	
Black, James	1855	472		28 ME		Bosse, Francis	1811	96	c	27	
Black, William	1815	121	b	35 PA		Bosse, Francois	1810	125	c	27	
Black, William	1812	7		24 RI		Bossier, John Lewis	1810	372		38	
Blackburn, William	1812	27		24 GA		Bostick, Philip	1810	202		28	
Blackwood, Bilbe	1815	90		30 NJ		Boswell, Peter	1812	131		33	
Blactot, Joseph	1811	94		18	Orleans	Botina, Gio. Battista	1810	226		30	
Blaine, Ephraim Roland	1810	289		27 PA		Boucher, John	1804	79		23	
Blaine/Bler, Thomas	1814	181		22	Miss Terr	Boud, Antoine	1806	1590		45	
Blair, James	1805	346		21 PA		Boudeau, Jean	1821	39		26 LA	

Name	Year	No.		Age/State	Origin	Name	Year	No.		Age/State	Origin
Boudreau, Hipolite	1805	486		16	Orleans	Brien, Lawrence	1851	1420		24 NY	
Bouisson, Joseph	1806	1574		31	Orleans	Brieze, Jeofroy	1804	136		24	
Boulger, James	1851	1203		21 MA		Briggs, Jotham	1818	137		36 MA	
Boune, Jean Jacques	1814	151		38		Briggs, Thomas	1821	120		15 MA	
Bourbon, Jean	1805	707		26	Orleans	Briggs, William	1819	150		36 RI	
Bouteiller, Thomas	1815	2		45 LA		Brignell, George	1818	16		21 NY	
Bowden, Oliver	1821	129		23 ME		Brignon, Joseph	1807	377		36	
Bowding, James	1812	128		51 MA		Brignon, Joseph	1805	900		36	Sicilia
Bowditch, Bass	1810	246		28 MA		Bringier, Louis	1805	369		21 LA	
Bowditch, J. B.	1851	1376		24 NY		Bringloe, Richard	1815	213		21 SC	
Bowen, James	1818	66		20 RI		Briscoe, Wm.	1851	1549		18 ME	
Bowen, John	1804	171		0		Brisson, Jacques	1814	211		26 LA	
Bowering, John	1855	220		26 MA		Bristol, Moses	1814	215	b	30 MD	
Bowers, Jonas	1812	95		23 MA		Broad, Richard	1810	309		17 PA	
Bowling, Thomas	1851	1186		22 NY		Bronson, Alden	1857	68		26 NY	
Bowman, Frederick R.	1851	1529		29 ME		Brookes, James	1804	263		29 PA	
Bowman, John	1811	27		24 PA		Brooks, Joseph	1805	897		30 PA	
Boyd, Edward	1851	1443		49 NY		Brooks, Russell	1811	271		30 CT	
Boyd, George M.	1851	1588		21	Ireland	Brooks, Samuel	1805	734	b	25 PA	
Boyde, Wm. H.	1855	417		19 CT		Browen, Benjamin P.	1821	86		20 NY	
Boyer, James	1818	362	c	22 LA		Browm, Joseph	1819	48		26 NH	
Boyer, John	1804	182		45		Brown, B.	1855	256		23 RI	
Boyes, Samuel	1810	49		16 MD		Brown, Charles	1851	1193		17 ME	
Boyk, George	1851	1430		29 PA		Brown, Charles	1855	529		25 PA	
Boyla, Francis	1815	167		25 MD		Brown, Charles	1851	1351		28 PA	
Boyle, Edward	1809	307		31 PA		Brown, Charles	1805	445	y	25	
Boyrie, Maralin	1816	56		28	Cuba	Brown, Daniel A.	1819	117		32	
Brackenridge,Samuel	1810	154		33 PA		Brown,					
Bradford, Mickle	1855	500		32 MA		Daniel Alexander	1819	118		33 CT	
Bradford, William	1851	1408		19 NY		Brown, David D.	1851	1619		31 ME	
Bradley, Henry	1851	1670		21 MA		Brown, George	1805	971	b	25 VA	
Bradley, Michael	1804	164		19 MA		Brown, Henry	1855	484		29 PA	
Bradway, Ebenezer	1811	62		22 MA		Brown, Isaac S.	1851	1674		35 ME	
Brady, Maguire	1810	198		26 PA		Brown, James	1819	111		29 MD	
Brague, William	1804	293		29 VA		Brown, James	1855	561		25	Ireland
Braham, George	1851	1686		22 MA		Brown, James	1812	144		27 CT	
Bramble, Asa	1806	1468		27 VA		Brown, James	1815	145		26 MA	
Branette, Francesco	1805	407		27 LA		Brown, James	1812	91	b	43 DE	
Brannagin, Felix	1805	541		25 MD		Brown, Jesse	1810	18	c	21 GA	
Brannon, William	1819	84		21 NY		Brown, John	1810	238	y	34 PA	
Brant, Christopher	1816	51		25 MA		Brown, John	1810	193		18 MD	
Brard, Francis	1819	44		30	Cape Franc	Brown, John	1811	328		29 MD	
Braton, Charles	1806	1815		0 RI		Brown, John	1815	248		21 MA	
Braune, Charles	1855	289		26 LA		Brown, John	1816	106	n	25 SC	
Brazier, Nathl.	1810	21		18 MA		Brown, John	1851	1366		33 NY	
Brazier, William	1805	406		49		Brown, John	1851	1358		36 NY	
Brece, John	1804	184		28		Brown, John	1851	1558		32 MA	
Bremere, George	1857	95		38	Sweden	Brown, John	1821	41	m	28 DE	
Bremond,						Brown, John	1851	1539		32 NY	
Joseph Lewis	1810	144		38		Brown, John	1819	45		17 LA	
Brewnning, Andrew	1804	300		36		Brown, John	1806	1798		21 MD	
Briard, Jean	1810	360		42 IL		Brown, John	1805	966		32 PA	
Brickhouse, George	1818	34	m	26 MD		Brown, John	1805	499		24 PA	
Bricknell, Henry	1855	243		21 MA		Brown, John	1805	806		28 NY	

Brown, John	1806	1428		44	
Brown, Joseph	1806	1572	b	31 NJ	
Brown, Joseph	1806	1534	b	31 NJ	
Brown, Joseph T.	1811	148		23 VA	
Brown,					
Nashan Volontine	1821	131		45 NY	
Brown, Nathan	1805	641		0 MD	
Brown, Nicholas	1804	271		23	Orleans
Brown, Peter	1804	334		26	
Brown, Philip	1811	178		18 MD	
Brown, Preserve	1805	464		25 NJ	
Brown, Reuben	1818	69	b	32 MA	
Brown, Sawyer	1810	174		33 NY	
Brown, Thomas	1810	391		25 NY	
Brown, Thomas	1810	390		23 NY	
Brown, Thomas	1851	1665		22 NY	
Brown, Thomas	1851	1542		28 NY	
Brown, Thomas	1804	43		35 VA	
Brown, William	1809	35		22 MD	
Brown, William	1855	265		21 NY	
Brown, William	1851	1329		21 NJ	
Brown, William	1821	25		0 PA	
Brown, William	1810	316		23 PA	
Brown, William	1818	130	b	25 CT	
Brown, William	1816	30		37 CT	
Brown, William	1815	10	m	19 MD	
Brown, Wm.	1811	331		23 NY	
Browne, Benjamin	1818	138		26 ME	
Browning, John	1811	273		26 MA	
Bruden, James	1818	269		21 VA	
Brue, Lorenzo	1818	92		42	
Brulee, Similion	1819	53	y	22 NO	
Brullon, Pierre	1805	618		33	Orleans
Brumage, John	1804	44	b	21 SC	
Brumley, John	1812	159		31 CT	
Brun, Guillaume	1818	134		36	
Brun, John					
Baptiste Alexis	1816	95		24 LA	
Brunel, Philip	1805	922		46	
Brunet, Francis	1805	818		0	
Brunston, David	1811	199	b	28 MA	
Brushell, William	1810	236		55 RI	
Bryan, James C.	1855	575		30 NY	
Bryan, Sharrard	1810	277	y	24 NC	
Bryer, Stafford	1818	174		20 RI	
Buck, John	1812	130		22 PA	
Buck, Swaine	1816	15		0	
Buckley, Mathew	1809	318		25 NY	
Buckley, Phineas W.	1818	113		27 PA	
Buckway, Jacob	1811	165	b	28 MA	
Buckway, James	1812	149	b	26 MA	
Bud, Thomas	1806	1809		28 NJ	
Budd, Thomas	1812	32		29 CT	
Bullett, Wilson	1805	747		22 PA	

Bunker,					
William Franklin	1819	200		29 MA	
Buole, Joseph	1805	938	y	30	
Burbank, Bobert	1811	255		32 CT	
Burbank, Charles H.	1855	207		16 MA	
Burch, John	1804	76		24 VA	
Burch, John D.	1821	142		18 NJ	
Burdy, John	1804	155		17 VA	
Burele, Clement	1805	823		40	
Burgen, Gabriel	1810	63		15 MD	
Buriez, Peter	1804	284		21	
Burk, Joseph	1818	101		25 LA	
Burke, John Mathias	1810	113		34 GA	
Burkman, Joseph	1819	114		19 MA	
Burman, Carl	1804	269		33	
Burnel, Alexander	1819	214		22	
Burnell, Thomas	1855	312		30 NY	
Burnham, William	1814	140		22 MA	
Burns, Joseph	1805	571		20	
Burns, Me/" sic.	1851	1551		24 NY	
Burns, Nathan	1806	1490		20 OH	
Burns, Thomas	1810	121		24 MA	
Burrell, John	1805	914		26 MA	
Burridge, John	1851	1508		24 NY	
Burrill, Charles	1815	265		33 RI	
Burton, William	1851	1676		21 MA	
Bussia, William	1809	206		33	Orleans
Butell, Denis	1810	26		22 PA	
Buther, Henry	1851	1475		21 LA	
Butiero,					
Francisco Patricio	1810	270		27	
Butler, James	1815	170		23 NY	
Butler, John	1855	344		23 NY	
Butler, JosephWarner	1803	801		16	US
Butler, Philip	1815	205		40 NY	
Butler, Thomas	1818	33	b	34 MD	
Butler, Thomas	1810	23		23 MD	
Butler, Thomas	1819	97	b	37 MD	
Butler, William	1814	192		24 NY	
Butterfield, William	1811	162		24 MD	
Butterworth, Thomas	1805	503		35 NY	
Buxton, James H.	1855	538		22 NY	
Byrn, David	1818	62		29 NY	
Byrne, Nathan	1804	129		18 MD	
Cabre, John	1811	1		27 SC	
Cacasson, Peter	1811	123		40	
Cade, George	1855	526		22 LA	
Cady, Parley	1806	1492		21 MA	
Caesar, Simon	1806	1589	c	25	
Caeser, Simon	1806	1426	b	25	Orleans
Cafot, Marcos	1805	645		40	
Cain, James	1855	556		25	Ireland
Cain, Joseph	1819	34		24	
Caldwell, George	1804	336		26	

Callender, John	1809	245	28 NY	
Camaret, Donatien	1805	447	28	
Camartel, Vincent	1805	983	45	
Camas, Francois	1805	548	30	
Cameron, John	1815	34	20 NY	
Cameron, William	1855	422	23 ME	
Cameson, Archibald	1818	75	26 MA	
Campbell, Alexander	1812	187	33 NY	
Campbell, Benjamin	1804	163	18 PA	
Campbell, George H.	1815	96	31 NY	
Campbell, James	1816	105 y	30 SC	
Campbell, James	1812	0	22 PA	
Campbell, James	1804	205	20 PA	
Campbell, James	1806	1527	29 NY	
Campbell, John	1804	47	25 PA	
Campbell, John	1811	219	15 NY	
Campbell, John	1855	508	24 NY	
Campbell, John	1819	77	19 MA	
Campbell, John	1851	1516	29 NJ	
Campbell, Lewis	1821	37	27	
Campbell, Robert W.	1855	513	28 ME	
Campbell, William	1818	246	32 NJ	
Camper, Richard	1818	27 b	15 MD	
Campfield, Edward	1810	0	25 CT	
Cana, Dimitry	1810	103	34	
Ca nacanos, John	1805	928	20	
Cane, John	1805	828	34 NJ	
Cane, William	1810	82	23 NY	
Canello, John Baptist	1810	67	25	
Canfield, Benjamin	1805	538	20 NY	
Cannon, John	1804	119	23 PA	
Cannut, Charles	1805	454	36	
Canovas,				
Joseph Charles	1818	185	25 LA	
Capdebo, Bernard	1809	2	36	Mao
Carbonel, Joseph	1818	139	50	
Carbonell, Antonio	1818	255	30	
Card, John	1819	125	22 NH	
Carkane, Antoine	1805	448	35	
Carlaw, Nathaniel	1814	191	24 MA	
Carllos, Luis	1805	387	20	
Carmalt, John	1809	295	32 NC	
Carmatt, John	1815	254	39 NC	
Carne, John	1810	393	18 Ny	
Carney, Mark	1806	1481	32	Orleans
Carpentier, Nicholas	1812	110	17	
Carr, Francis	1805	427	23 SC	
Carr, James	1805	894	23 PA	
Carrales, Joseph	1805	977	19	
Carrere, John	1811	259	40	
Carrick, James	1804	0	0	
Carrol, James	1809	243	27 PA	
Carroll, John	1812	121	30 PA	
Carroll, William	1855	268	21 OH	

Carston, William	1851	1200	19 FL	
Carter, Charles	1818	161	28 VA	
Carter, Henry	1810	276 b	20 Va	
Carter, John M., Jun.	1821	98	16 NH	
Carter, Thomas	1810	363	23 MD	
Carver, Caleb F.	1855	419	18 ME	
Carvin, Nicholas	1855	264	20 NY	
Casaneuve, Gravier	1818	64	45	
Casey, Thomas, Jr.	1806	1491	30 NY	
Cash, Howard	1806	1505	38 VA	
Cassaignan, Ambrose	1818	46	37	
Cassibry, John	1814	207	27	
Casson, Thomas	1804	202	34 PA	
Castain, Lewis	1805	440	24 LA	
Castain, Peter	1805	441	22 LA	
Casten, Saml.	1818	125	22 RI	
Castian, James	1810	158	38	
Caston, Peter	1851	1687	21 MA	
Caty, Francis	1811	222	30	
Caulbert, John	1855	554	31	Ireland
Cavanaugh,WilliamV.	1851	1628	32 PA	
Cavelier, Lenon	1804	0	0	
Cavelier, Pere,				
Anthony	1804	0	0	
Caverlot,				
Jean Baptiste	1810	272	45	
Cavie, Francois	1819	215 y	23	
Caxares, Joseph	1805	624 b	18	Orleans
Cayton, Jesse	1812	99	25 PA	
Cemp, John	1815	160	38 NY	
Cenestar, Lewis	1805	512	42	
Chabana, Manuel	1818	283	33	
Chace, David Bowers	1818	14	17 MA	
Chace, John	1810	89	19 MD	
Chalmers, William E.	1819	32	18 NY	
Chamberg, Peter	1806	1820	33	
Chamberlin, John	1811	279	24 MA	
Chammings, Thomas	1815	169	21 MA	
Chamoron, Joseph	1818	257	43	
Champlin, Silas	1812	33	25 CT	
Chandler, Thomas	1818	109	25 NY	
Chandler, William D.	1855	192	45 VA	
Channing, Joseph	1811	245	25 RI	
Chany, Samuel	1818	203	20 CT	
Chaplin, John	1805	679	44 NY	
Chaplin, Thimothy E.	1810	306	22 CT	
Chapman, Daniel	1815	166	42 MD	
Chapo, Francisco T.	1812	1	30	
Chappe, Felix B.V.	1819	142	24	
Charie, Baptiste	1805	769	35	Orleans
Chasena, Joseph	1809	313	28	
Chasse, Stephen	1816	22	34	Italy
Chateau, William	1805	494	42	
Chaudurie, John	1811	100	20	

Name	Year	No.		Age	Place
Chaumette,					
Francis Joseph	1804	106		21	Orleans
Chavarria, Joseph	1805	598	y	21	
Chazel, John Peter	1810	32		29	
Chess, Jacque	1805	742		45	Orleans
Chevalier, John	1809	259		31	
Chevalier, Nicholas	1806	1497		23	Orleans
Chichester, Richard	1855	357		23 NY	
Chickering, Sameul	1815	238		23 MA	
Child, Samuel Sterry	1819	110		31 CT	
Chirez, Francisco	1805	400		18	
Choinet, Rene R.	1818	142		36	
Choppin, Paul	1815	16		17	
Chora, Manuel	1812	217		37	
Chreighton, John	1805	816		20 NY	
Christain, Hans	1804	258		26 VA	
Christian, Adam	1811	138		22 MA	
Christian, Charles	1855	115		0	
Christian, Daniel	1812	11		28	
Christian, Henry	1809	244		25 SC	
Christian, Levi H.	1811	73		20 NY	
Christie, Gurdon	1809	36		21 CT	
Christie, William	1818	249		18 NY	
Christmas, Noel	1804	331		25	
Church, Peter	1811	121	y	24 MD	
Church, Rufus	1819	98		20 MA	
Cirron, Monplaisir	1810	201		20	Orleans
Claiborne, Thomas	1810	45		26 VA	
Clane, Jacob	1810	91		31 NY	
Clarine, Nicolas	1811	321		36	
Clark, Archibald	1821	125	m	32 PA	
Clark, Baily	1806	1513		26 PA	
Clark, Birdsey	1816	47		19 NY	
Clark, Charles	1818	145		40	
Clark, Danl	1818	346		32 PA	
Clark, David	1809	316		23 NY	
Clark, Elijah	1805	537		26 NJ	
Clark, George	1811	84		26 NC	
Clark, George	1815	78		19 NC	
Clark, George	1851	1629		25 GA	
Clark, Henry	1855	249		35 PA	
Clark, Hiram	1815	244		0	
Clark, Isaac	1855	282		36 MA	
Clark, James	1818	146		29 NJ	
Clark, John	1805	669		22 RI	
Clark, John Sular	1804	127		23 CT	
Clark, Joseph	1855	323		30 NY	
Clark, Richard	1809	233		31 VA	
Clark, Robert	1804	107		19 NY	
Clark, William	1804	275	y	25 NY	
Clark, William	1815	20		25 MA	
Clark, William	1815	245		29 MD	
Clark, William	1818	267		29 MA	
Clark, William	1812	103		32 PA	
Clarke, John	1810	364		23	
Clarke, Richard	1815	240		45	
Clarke, Robert	1818	341		21 NY	
Clauson, Henry	1855	239		29 NY	
Clavie, Andre	1804	0		0	
Clay, James	1851	1656		46 NY	
Clay, John	1815	108		20 MA	
Cleansey, Alexander	1818	77		49 VA	
Clement, Louis E.	1851	1383		25 NY	
Clennan, Robert	1805	846		23 RI	
Cler, Esteven	1806	1515		38	Orleans
Coast, John	1806	1461		35	
Coates, John	1811	141		17 CT	
Coats, John	1810	68		21 NY	
Coats, Russel	1812	210		27 MA	
Cochain, John	1818	278		26	
Coe, James N.	1855	491		19 CT	
Coffin, Daniel	1810	13		25 MA	
Coffin, Dominick	1821	15		28 LA	
Coffin, Hiram	1819	147		28 NH	
Coffrey, Fredrick	1805	381		26 NY	
Coggeshall, Charles	1805	798		20 MA	
Cogshell, Rowland	1818	126		22 RI	
Coil, Antonio	1805	522		33	
Colachi, Nicholas	1810	212		17	
Colbert, Christian	1807	334		25 MD	
Colbert, John	1815	18	b	17 MA	
Colby, Benjamin S.	1855	212		21 ME	
Colcock, William	1804	281		21 VA	
Coldridge, Elkanah F.	1819	92		26 CT	
Cole, Elijah	1806	1554		29 CT	
Cole, James	1810	375		22 MD	
Cole, John	1811	69		24 PA	
Cole, Peter	1812	64	b	25 NJ	
Cole, Peter	1804	80		23 NY	
Cole, Robert	1804	120		21 DE	
Cole, Robert	1819	221		21 MA	
Colgin, James	1805	556		23 NY	
Colley, William	1811	217		19 MA	
Collins, David	1804	38		14 GA	
Collins, John	1812	209		26 MA	
Collins, John	1812	74		19 MD	
Collins, William	1815	261		18 MA	
Colsson, Frederick	1804	229		17	Orleans
Colter, James	1810	304		34	
Comb, Samuel	1809	252		16 MA	
Combs, Henry	1811	272		37 SC	
Combs, John	1810	223		22 MD	
Combs, Roland S.E.	1857	107		21 ME	
Combs, William	1818	123		22 NY	
Compiane, Jean	1812	205		32	
Con, Daniel	1811	51	b	35 MA	
Condon, H. H.	1857	136		35 ME	
Conklin, William	1810	312		30 NY	

Conn, John	1818	309		26 MD	Coux, William	1805	947		25
Connand, John Mary	1805	442		37 LA	Coverturt, Joseph	1806	1555		28
Conner, Thomas	1805	832		0	Cowan, William	1807	331		25 NY
Conner, William	1805	809		20 MD	Coward, Henry A.	1816	26		20 MD
Connor, Casar	1818	72	b	25 MA	Cox, Henry B.	1819	160		17 NY
Connor, James	1818	259		17 MD	Cox, Stephen	1804	158		23 NC
Connor, John	1804	337		38 PA	Cox, Thos.	1818	68		26 MA
Connor, Thomas	1805	391		23 VA	Cozanet, Nicolas	1818	144		23
Conrod, Fredrick W.	1805	892		39	Cracklou, William	1815	195		23 PA
Conroy, Philip	1805	673		36 RI	Craig, Robert	1855	539		28 NH
Constant, Jean	1805	568		19	Orleans	Craig, William	1810	273		20 NY
Constant, Michael	1805	926		28	Craighton, Samuel	1811	231	y	45 SC
Constantini, Francis	1821	100		33	Craigie, Augustus	1851	1356		20 NY
Conway, Peter	1851	1371		26 NY	Cramer, George	1851	1632		28 NY
Cooley, Abraham	1805	893		17 SC	Crandall, John	1810	102		26 NY
Coomb, William	1804	91		26 NY	Crandall, John	1816	91		30 NY
Cooper, George	1855	553		26 MA	Crane, William	1851	1524		20 ME
Cooper, Lodowick	1819	71		21 RI	Crangle, William	1851	1430		18 LA
Cooper, William	1805	879		25 NY	Crate, Jean Nicolas	1807	392		19 La
Cope, William	1851	1604		26	England	Crawford, Andrew	1816	103		16 MA
Copeland, Elisha	1809	38		33 NC	Creguez, Miguel	1810	119		33
Copeland, James	1811	9		22 PA	Creighton, William	1805	876		22 MA
Copp, Daniel	1805	845		31 NH	Cresse, Aaron	1816	17		18 NJ
Copp, James	1821	8		19 NH	Cresson,JohnAndrew	1806	1423		22	Orleans
Corales,Joseph Maria	1818	329		30	Creswell, Robert	1815	6		27 GA
Corbet, Ollet	1821	31		30 MA	Crismaes, Jean				
Corbit, Jonathan	1816	27		29 DE	(John) Charles	1816	72		34 LA
Corchel, Augustin	1812	37		25	Cristy, Edward	1811	188		29 PA
Corke, James	1810	99	b	36 PA	Crocker, John	1818	151		19 MA
Cornelis, Henry	1855	85		41	Belgium	Cromwell, Hugh	1807	400		31 PA
Cornelius, Charles	1818	43		0 PA	Crosley, Nathan	1812	59	l	26 CT
Cornell, William	1819	136		22 NY	Cross, George	1818	119		25 MA
Cornick, Henry K.	1811	221		25 VA	Crow, John	1811	172		25 MD
Corrales, Joseph	1806	1797		21	Crowley, John	1815	84		24 DC
Correll, Phillip	1821	68		26 MA	Cruddin, Henry	1851	1394		24	Europe
Corrigan, Patrick	1804	67		49	Ireland	Cruix, Jacob Leonard	1810	260	y	44
Corrigan, Peter	1818	209		25 PA	Cujol, Bartholomew	1805	565		27
Cortelyou, Martin	1815	50		19 NY	Cullen, James	1851	1381		21 NY
Cosley, Thomas	1812	115		28 MD	Cullin, Andrew	1806	1503		30	Orleans
Cosse, Barthelmy	1818	291		11	Cumming, John	1819	12		32 MA
Coster, Philip	1806	1424		15 NY	Cummingham,Mathew	1855	237		22 NY
Cotter, John Michaael	1814	146		15 PA	Cummings, Charles	1811	79		33
Cotton, Joseph	1818	266		15 NH	Cummings, Edward	1855	278		26 PA
Cottrell, Henry	1851	1348		21	Cumpiano, Lazaro	1818	262		35	Gene
Coulson, Jacob	1810	140		21 KY	Cunning, Samuel	1815	232		19 MA
Courardy,					Cunningham, Edward	1855	240		28 NY
Bartholomew	1805	687		25	Cunningham, George	1855	201		21 NY
Courdeasio, Celestine	1805	844	y	32	Cunningham, James	1855	572		37	Ireland
Courletto, Francis	1816	25		23	Cunningham, John	1811	4		45 SC
Courtney, Jeremiah	1815	74		22 NY	Cunningham, Patrick	1851	1570		25	Ireland
Courtney, Thos.	1818	29		32	Ireland	Curhy, Thomas	1851	1489		38 RI
Coustan, Joseph	1805	579		33	Curiel, Isaac	1809	314	y	24	Orliens
Coustant, John	1805	745		28	Orleans	Curran, Charles	1851	1589		20
Couteillere, Thomas	1805	382		38 LA	Curran, James	1818	89		32 MA

Name	Year	No.		Age/State	Place
Currie, James	1819	85		23 RI	
Currie, Sampson	1812	86	n	35 MA	
Curry, Peter	1851	1477		37 ME	
Curry, William R.	1806	1502		41	US
Cutler, James	1810	161		27 DE	
Cutter, Charles	1815	164		26 MA	
Cuzac, William	1811	143		44	
d"Orange, Joseph	1804	283		23	
D'Acosta, Samuel	1811	109	b	26 RI	
D'Aincibieru,	1807	412		48	
da Roza, Manuel	1812	24		0	
Daggett, Robert	1818	132		25 RI	
Dailey, James	1818	19		21 NY	
Dailey, Thomas	1811	241		23 NC	
Dakin, William	1815	116		31 PA	
Daly, Aneas	1819	151		18 PA	
Daly, William	1851	1547		21 NY	
Dames, Harry	1809	213		23 PA	
Dana, Jonathan G.	1819	140		21 RI	
Danden, Peter	1804	306		26 VA	
Dane, Pum	1814	148		40	Louisiana
Daniel, Henry	1807	386		20 NJ	
Daniel, James	1805	737		28 PA	
Daniel, Jean	1815	258		38	
Daniel, Lewis	1806	1806		32	
Daniel, Peter	1814	137		30 LA	
Danston, Oliver	1805	789		25 NY	
Dargeles,PeterAndrew	1818	333		21	
Darneand, Francois	1815	214		41	
Darramat, Francis	1810	189		24	New Orlean
Darward, Thomas	1855	266		20 NY	
Dassen, Allen	1804	185		21 MA	
Daumas, Jean Louis	1818	73		29 LA	
Dauphini, Franc	1805	542		42	
Dauston, Henry	1855	321		22 ME	
Dautrieul, John B.	1818	356		60	
Daux, Francois	1810	345		26	St. Doming
Davais, Thomas	1819	17		47 MD	
Davey, Peter	1807	391		24 NY	
David, Anthony	1818	261		30	
David, Frederick	1812	6		32	
David, John	1812	42		27 CT	
David, John	1804	295		36	
David, Morris	1818	287		22 PA	
Davids, Augustus	1855	479		23	
Davidson, Benjimain	1805	482		20 NY	
Davidson, James	1805	513		18 MA	
Davidson, James	1811	146		20 PA	
Davidson, John	1807	380		37 SC	
Davidson, Samuel	1805	748		19 PA	
Davidson, Thomas J.	1814	183		38 NC	
Davies, Daniel	1806	1474		20 MA	
Davirou,Bartholomeco	1805	593		34	Germany
Davis, David	1804	108		25 NY	
Davis, Eben	1818	191		25 MA	
Davis, George	1851	1639		28 NY	
Davis, Henry	1857	124		28 MA	
Davis, Henry	1857	128		29 NY	
Davis, James	1807	459		33 NY	
Davis, James	1811	252		22 NJ	
Davis, James	1812	172		25 MA	
Davis, John	1811	329		32 MA	
Davis, John	1819	164		35 MD	
Davis, John	1855	257		23 NY	
Davis, John	1809	11		28 MD	
Davis, John E.	1855	205		19 ME	
Davis, Richard	1812	94	b	23 NJ	
Davis, Samuel	1812	194	m	23 PA	
Davis, Samuel	1801	962		20 MA	
Davis, Samuel B.	1804	0		0	
Davis, Stephen	1812	119	b	20 NY	
Davis, Thomas	1809	10		39 MD	
Davis, William	1805	489		28 RI	
Davis, William	1811	149		21 MD	
Davis, William	1851	524		19 MD	
Davis, William	1819	235	b	30 PA	
Dawson, Andrew	1851	1357		27 NY	
Dawson, James	1821	147		30 MD	
Dawson, John	1819	146		22 PA	
Dawson, John	1809	236		27 NJ	
Day, James	1809	250		31 CT	
de Biera, Joseph	1805	472		0	Orleans
de la Coste, Francois	1806	1558		23	Orleans
de Malaga, Juan Ros.	1805	531		20	
de Santos, John	1805	485		24	Orleans
Deacon, Wm. E.	1855	506		24 LA	
Dean, Charles F.C.	1816	4		14 NY	
Dean, Henry	1811	46		14 NY	
Dean, Henry	1851	173		22 VT	
Dean, James	1855	467		32	Scotland
Dean, Jonas	1804	153		30 MA	
Dearing, Elihu	1821	112		28 NH	
Debascual, John	1810	132		27	
DeBerge, John B.Vincent	1819	16		37	
Deblet, John Baptist	1810	163		19	Orleans
DeBordeau, Charles Joineau	1805	912		42	
Debuys, Laspard	1804	0		0	
DeCastro,JohnAntonio	1805	911		32	
Decayme, Francis	1806	1817		14	Orleans
Dechant, Jean	1805	703		24	Orleans
Dede, Francis	1810	181		36	Orleans
Deegan, Matthew	1851	1521		25 MA	
Degrass, Recall	1815	22	m	35 MA	
Delano, Lindor	1818	311	b	21	St.Domingo
Delany, John	1816	65	b	21 MD	

Name	Year	No.	flag	Age/State	Place
Delarue, John Alfred Niel	1812	9		10 SC	
Delaune, John Baptiste	1810	228		23	
Delbore, John	1805	716		40 NC	
deLemos, Antoine Fernando	1806	1460		0	Orleans
Delhonmaux, Nicolas	1818	141		19	
Delino, Francis	1811	278		20	
Delivera, Anthony	1805	979		29	
Dellino, William H.	1851	1634		30 DE	
Delmas, Valantin	1814	208		24 LA	
Delony, Emanuel	1804	114	b	35	Orleans
Deming, John	1818	85		17 CT	
DeMohy, Joseph Rene	1810	24		23	Orleans
DeMouline, August	1805	899		16	
Demprey, Patrick	1805	843		28 MD	
Deneyra, Joseph	1805	653		26	
Denick, Cornelius	1812	15		18 NY	
Denike, John	1818	45		22 NY	
Denio, John	1805	635		21 OH	
Denis, Jeanne (John)	1816	55		26 LA	
Denis, John	1810	36		18 Guadeloupe	
Dennin, William	1851	1638		27 NY	
Dennis, John	1806	1542		22 SC	
Dennisten, Robert	1804	194		29 PA	
DeOjeda, Sebastien	1807	390		29	Orleans
Depas, H. Chs	1851	1318		27 LA	
DePazo, JosephGabriel	1805	989		38	
Depiane, Bartholomew	1805	770		34	
Deponise, Jacques	1815	4	m	26 LA	
Dermody, Peter	1851	1584		26	
Desarme, Peter	1811	159	y	38 StDomingo	
deSousie, John Batiste	1804	178		33	
Devereux, Charles	1855	181		16 ME	
Devier, Henry	1821	56		19 CT	
Devine, Richard	1851	1605		20 NY	
Devino, Joseph	1812	35		25	
Devo, Charles	1811	145		24 NY	
Devo, Charles	1809	319		27 NY	
DeWageneere, Francis	1851	1411		24 NY	
Dewetter, William	1806	1526		23 PA	
Deykin, Samuel	1851	1547		31 NY	
Dias, Joseph	1806	1579		19	Louisiana
Dias, Juan	1818	3		25 LA	
Dias, Vincente	1811	191		0	
Dickens, Richard	1851	1585		35	
Dickson, Robert	1855	347		21 MA	
Dickson, William	1809	272		29 NY	
Dienett, Frank	1851	1506		22 PA	
Dieu, Francis	1816	2		40 LA	
Diven, John	1857	126		19 CT	
Diviney, John	1812	16		23 KY	
Dixon, Thomas	1804	317	m	28 NJ	
Doane, John	1816	77		21 MA	
Dobbin, Hugh	1804	126		19 PA	
Dobson, William	1855	445		25 MA	
Dodd, John	1804	82		21 MD	
Dodge, Charles A.	1855	517		16 ME	
Dodge, Jonathan	1810	93		22 MA	
Dodgson, Oliver	1819	165		21 NY	
Doherty, John	1851	1551		33 NY	
Doimick, Guiseppi	1818	115		25	
Dolbow, George W.	1855	231		23 NJ	
Dolliole, Pierre	1819	56	m	30	
Domingo, Thomas	1805	824		16	
Domingo, Thomas	1805	923		17	
Donaldson, John	1855	481		23 NY	
Donaldson, Joseph	1821	104		25 NY	
Donatien, Charles	1812	112	c	28	Orleans
Donavan, Richard	1802	862		26	
Donis, John	1807	385		35	Orleans
DonKrgue, John B.Michile	1805	913		29	
Donnalls, James	1810	348		22 PA	
Donnel, William	1805	790		19 PA	
Donneld, James	1810	362		19 NY	
Donohue, Timothy	1818	107		37 NJ	
Dorell, John	1811	88		21 MA	
Dorman, William B.	1805	937		35 MD	
Dorr, William	1857	105		19 ME	
Dorval, Charles	1805	958	m	24	
Douben, Henry	1811	19		29 NY	
Douns, Nesse	1814	150		23	
Dove, John	1810	397		41 PA	
Dow, Francis	1805	761		23	
Dow, John	1810	96		19 MA	
Downes, Richard	1811	213		34 KY	
Downey, John	1818	253		21 MA	
Downing, George A.	1857	142		36 RI	
Downing, John	1851	1429		23 DE	
Downs, Isaac	1816	76		27 MA	
Downs, John	1818	173		23 MA	
Doyle, Luke	1811	42		28	
Doyle, Thomas	1804	245		50 NY	
Doyle, Will. E.	1818	24		21 NY	
Doyle, William	1805	456		20 PA	
Drago, Esteva	1806	1484		24	Orleans
Draper, James	1810	287		24 RI	
Draper, Wm.	1818	339		20 NY	
Draw, Christopher	1812	57		16 MD	
Drew, James	1811	182		31 NJ	
Drew, John	1815	123		45 PA	
Dring, John	1811	167		10 CT	
Driscoll, John	1851	1397		20 MA	
Drole, Jean Joseph	1806	1547	b	24	
Drummond, Richard	1805	420		20 VA	

Name	Year	No.	Flag	Age	Place	Origin
Dryden, Hamilton	1815	175		22 MD		
Duart, Zacaria	1812	156		23 PA		
Dubeur, Varrie	1805	578		26		
DuBoy, John	1815	97		38		
Dubuisson, Eugene	1814	157		30 LA		
Dubuisson, Silvain	1814	147		25 LA		
Ducas, John	1810	328		25		
Ducos, Jean Baptiste	1818	163		42		
Ducost, Francis	1806	1448		30	Orleans	
Ducros, Louis Vincent	1818	118		31 LA		
Dudden, Samuel	1810	105		18 PA		
Dudgeon, Moses	1809	6		22 NY		
Dudley, John H.	1851	1350		20 NY		
Dudley, Luke	1811	45		26 MD		
Dudley, Richard	1814	172		26 VA		
Dufau, Dominique	1804	103		0		
Dufourd, Peter	1806	1436		19	Orleans	
Dulbecco, Vincent	1810	227		33		
Dulin, Gerard	1815	177		21 DC		
Dumas, Pierre	1809	216		24	Orleans	
Dun, Robert	1821	2		27 NY		
Dunan, John	1806	1426		24	Orleans	
Dunbar, William	1812	191		24 MA		
Dungan (Duncin), David C	1819	2		0		
Duningham, Thomas	1815	67		42 MA		
Dunklebury, John	1804	37		28 PA		
Dunlop, William	1855	316		38 NY		
Dunman, Charles	1855	485		36 NY		
Dunmore, Abraham	1815	25	y	32 MD		
Dunn, William	1805	858		22 PA		
Dunwell, Tennant	1819	23		17		
Dupes, John	1805	767		36		
Dupin, Pierre Felix	1812	116		14		
Dupont, Nicholas	1818	326		20 LA		
Dupouy, Pierre	1804	58		23		
Dupre, Joseph	1805	644		20	Orleans	
Duprey, Louis	1812	57		27		
Dupui, Pierr	1804	51		22		
Dupuy, Peter	1805	569		23		
Dupuy, Peter	1819	161		25		
Dupuy, Pierre	1814	219		37		
Dupuys, Pierre	1804	64		20		
Durand, Andrew	1805	677		30		
Durand, John	1816	82	m	36		
Durant, Jacob	1810	405		29 NY		
Durhum, Thomas	1812	153	y	37 DE		
Dutil, John	1815	220		31 LA		
Dutour, Jean	1806	1450		48		
Duvant, Gilbert	1806	1508		30		
Duvant, John	1815	181		24 MA		
DuVerge, Sanon	1811	95	b	24		
Duvignau, Francis	1810	197		24	Orleans	
Dyer, Benjamin	1806	1516		18 MA		
Dyer, Ebenizer	1812	18		27 MA		
Dyne, Martin	1804	88		32 PA		
Eadman, Gustavus	1806	1568		36 PA		
Eagleson, James	1804	305		45 PA		
Eagleston, Abraham	1815	156		21 MD		
Easterbrooks, Jeremiah H.	1818	298		23 MA		
Easterbrooks, Thomas Gorham	1815	41		21 MA		
Eastman, Alonzo S.	1816	32		17 NY		
Easton, William	1805	457	b	21 VA		
Eaton, John	1811	317		38 MD		
Eben, William	1851	1499		24 MA		
Echeto, Martin	1818	82		44	France	
Echevert, John	1805	688		31		
Edgar, William	1805	772		38	Britain	
Edlur, Louis	1807	415		22	Orleans	
Edwards, Abel	1819	226		21 CT		
Edwards, DavidJones	1812	186	c	26 NY		
Edwards, David Nye	1815	251		16 MA		
Edwards, Francis	1815	215		22 MA		
Edwards, John	1815	86		31 PA		
Edwards, Samuel	1851	1194		25 MA		
Edwards, Standish F.	1821	105		34 PA		
Edwards, Thomas	1819	163		28 ct		
Edwards, Thomas,Jr.	1821	122		33 MA		
Edwards, Will.	1818	21		33 NY		
Edwards, William	1810	117		17 MA		
Eells, Nathan	1821	74		44 CT		
Egbert, David	1804	73		21		
Eitinne, Richard	1818	318		21		
Eldridge, James	1855	473		18 RI		
Eldridge, Joseph B.	1855	260		31 ME		
Eldridge, William M.	1851	1627		25 MA		
Elka, Roswell B.	1812	0	b	25 MA		
Ellenick, George	1805	733		21 PA		
Elliott, Albert	1855	183		22 NY		
Elliott, James	1851	1393		26 NY		
Elliott, William	1818	135		17 MD		
Ellis, Francis	1815	117		20 MA		
Ellis, Peter	1810	187		36	Prussia	
Ellison, Joseph	1815	52		18 NY		
Elsey, Thomas	1815	31		18 MD		
Elwell, Abraham	1810	39		26 MA		
Elwell, David	1821	62		24 ME		
Emerso, George T.	1851	1184		28 MA		
Emery, William	1819	27		33 PA		
Emit, George	1818	157		24 RI		
Emory, John W.	1851	1160		30 MD		
England, William	1814	141		19 PA		
English, Edward	1812	22		22 NY		
English, John	1815	105		22 MD		
English, John	1805	827		37 NY		
English, John	1804	172		36 NY		

Enns, Archibal	1819	211		22 VA	Farrell, Lawrence L.	1815	73		21 MA
Enright, John	1804	96		28 MD	Farrell, Thomas	1805	666		23
Eodra, Vantail	1805	483		27	Farris, Daniel	1857	117		22 ME
Erguene, Niclise	1814	195		32	Faure, Peter	1804	0		0
Ermer, Joseph	1804	286		39	Fauriedo, Joseph	1804	0		0
Errera, Juaguin	1805	921		19	Faver, James	1805	874		36
Erskine, Charles	1851	1354		22 MA	Favier, Lewis	1809	229		48 Orleans
Ertman, Jacob	1805	507		20 NY	Fax, James	1818	71	b	25 MD
Ervin, John E.	1855	175		22 ME	Fayard, James	1814	170		26 Miss. Terr
Erwin, William Henry	1810	396		26 NY	Fearne, William	1851	1668		32 NY
Esmete, Antonia	1807	383		22	Fearr, Henry	1811	166		29 SC
Espanett, Louis	1805	338		36	Feek, William	1811	326		24 NY
Espinosa, Felipe	1805	517		21 LA	Feernandes, Anthony	1812	146		17 Orleans
Estamp, Peter	1805	814		44	Feinhour, Stephen	1804	152		21 PA
Estasmecrine, Pierre	1811	129	y	26	Fell, John Gardiner	1821	108		10 LA
Estaugh, William	1815	92		23 NJ	Felt, William	1811	239		24 MA
Esteba, Joseph	1805	840		53	Felter, Jacob	1810	149		23 NY
Estrada, Antonio	1811	74		22 Orleans	Fenera, Francisco Jn.	1855	423		27
Etene, Ambroase	1805	399		40	Ferdon, Peter	1818	122		32 NY
Etienne, Pierre	1814	135		40	Ferdyth, William	1855	486		21 ME
Etwood, John	1809	46		31 MD	Feres, Cerille	1806	1473		22 MA
Eustis, Henry	1855	198		41 MA	Feret, Louis	1805	529		32
Evans, Hugh	1855	251		27 PA	Ferguson, David	1851	1433		19 NY
Evans, Moses	1812	136	b	25 VA	Ferguson, Edward	1851	1213		22 NY
Evans, Pascal	1811	285		27 VA	Ferguson, Henry	1851	1607		20 PA
Evans, William	1812	196		28 MD	Ferguson, James	1815	89		24 PA
Evans, William	1811	179		48 PA	Ferguson, John	1818	70		17 NY
Evans, William	1855	505		26 NY	Fernand, Francis	1805	505		33
Evens, Samuel	1809	326		22 MD	Fernand, Francis	1805	690		29 LA
Evens, Thomas	1809	317		23 DE	Fernandez, Emanuel	1807	345		20 Valenzuela
Everett, John	1804	210		46 MD	Fernandez, John	1806	1557		40 Orleans
Everitt, Thomas	1818	52		23 VA	Fernandez, Joseph	1806	1522		30
Ewell, Charles D.	1855	516		20 ME	Fernandez, Joseph	1810	87		16
Ewer, Ebenezer, 2nd	1812	207		25 MA	Fernandez, Joseph	1812	79		31
Exley, William	1815	1		35 DE	Fernandez, Manuel	1805	885		33
Ezern, Bontura	1805	659		35	Fernandez, Manuel	1805	625		19 Orleans
Faber, Joseph	1811	44	y	18 RI	Fernandez, Peter	1821	24		44 LA
Fabregas, Benito	1818	94		45 LA	Femate, Samuel D.	1819	67		16 NH
Faggart, James	1809	3		17 PA	Feron, Peter	1805	992		36 Orleans
Faharty, Michael	1811	190		26 MD	Ferraire, Felix	1811	101		30
Faherty, Thomas	1804	39		38 MD	Ferrand, Francis	1821	132		32
Faitevas, Henry	1805	780		33	Ferrand, Pierre	1815	32		45
Falconet, John	1810	218		26	Ferrandez,				
Falkner, John	1851	1437		23 NY	Jose(Joseph)	1815	43		28
Fanco, Francis	1805	574		30	Ferre, Peter	1805	384		0
Fandress, JohnBatist	1805	895		16	Ferre, Pierre	1811	330		48
Fanning, James	1821	143		26 CT	Ferrer, Charles	1809	298		29
Faranto, Angelo	1805	678		32 LA	Ferrer, Francisco	1806	1549		31 Orleans
Fargaro, Agostin	1819	152		28	Ferrer, Josef	1811	131		23
Fargues, Charles	1804	0		0	Ferret, Bertrand	1804	49		15 Orleans
Fariary, Ryno	1807	408		22	Ferret, Cadet	1805	736		28
Farnam, Chauney	1815	9		21 CT	Ferrier, John	1818	87		32 NY
Farnan, James J.	1812	98		19 NY	Ferrino, John	1818	7		40
Farnsworth, Charles	1811	56		25 MA	Ferts, Cevill	1805	426	b	22 MA

Name	Year	No.		Age/Place	Name	Year	No.		Age/Place
Feyler, Godfrey	1857	64		25 ME	Fonce, George	1818	49		0
Fiander, Thomas	1811	242		38 VA	Fonce/Founce,George	1805	385		28 PA
Fichard, John	1810	379		40	Fontain, John	1805	925	b	38 VA
Field, Joseph	1804	223		26	Fontaine, Antoine	1855	254		32 Italy
Field, William	1804	324	b	19	Fontenille, Thomas	1805	623		36
Field, William	1855	182		27 MA	Fonvergne, Renaud	1805	848	y	0
Fillet, Pierre	1810	173		38	Foradino, John	1805	596		34 Orleans
Fine, John, Jr.	1816	78		23 NY	Forbes, Nathaniel	1812	0		27 PA
Fink, John	1818	194		32 VA	Forbes, Simon	1806	1439		25 MA
Finlay, Robert	1855	569		30 England	Ford, David	1821	1		43 MA
Finn, John	1810	199		44 MD	Ford, Francois	1806	1585		24
Finten, Thomas	1815	94		38 DE	Ford, Timothy G.	1809	303		26 US
Fipalo, Charles	1857	88		23 Sardina	Forest, Peter	1804	115		24 PA
Fischer, John	1807	377		34 PA	Forrest, Robert	1811	234		21 NY
Fisher, Charles	1851	1663		29 PA	Forrester, Henry	1819	133		38 MA
Fisher,JamesAbsalom	1804	326		36 MA	Forstall, Francois	1815	104		21
Fisher, John	1805	683		32 SC	Forster, Joseph	1810	318		23 NY
Fisher, John	1805	626		26 LA	Forsythe, Alexander	1809	8		22 SC
Fisher, John	1809	30		29 PA	Forteau, Pierre	1811	137		36
Fisher, Richard D.	1812	78		25 PA	Fortin, Michael	1810	66		31
Fisher, Thomas	1818	217		20	Fortur, John Michael	1804	0		0
Fisher,ThomasWebber	1851	1181		16 NC	Fortur, Michael, Jr	1804	0		0
Fisher, Walter	1855	537		23 NY	Foss, Jeremiah C.	1851	1533		29 NH
Fisher, William	1805	917		17 MA	Fosset, James	1814	143		26 DC
Fiske, Edmund	1819	75		30 RI	Foster, Abram	1812	152		35 MA
Fithian, Thomas	1806	1475		24 NY	Foster, George	1806	1544		36 NY
Fitz, Jos. L.	1855	219		36 MA	Foster, Hatherley M.	1815	15		20 NY
Fitzgerald, William	1851	1445		22 ME	Foster, James	1804	159		36 MA
Fitzgerald, Wm.	1809	215		35 NY	Foster, Josh	1851	1684		28 VA
Fitzpatrick, John E.	1812	203		25	Foster, Ralph	1815	60		23 PA
Flamborough, William	1805	686		45	Foster, Samuel	1821	64		32 NJ
Flanders, Charles	1851	1442		24 MA	Foster, William	1804	226		24 NY
Flatt, Robert	1815	252		38 NC	Fou, Jodi	1806	1551		20 Orleans
Flecher, John R.	1810	175		29 PA	Fouger, Louis	1805	942		23
Fleet, Chalres	1809	26		26 MD	Fournois, Stephen	1806	1571		29 Orleans
Flemming, James	1855	4		28 MA	Foutaine, Jean	1806	1575		29 Orleans
Flemming, James	1851	1524		24 NY	Foutenait, Francia	1812	154		23 LA
Fletcher,PaulRaymond	1819	95		31 MA	Fowler, James	1812	68	b	22 MA
Fleury, Benjamni	1809	322		18 Orleans	Fowler, John	1812	142		23 CT
Fleury, Wm. J.	1851	1480		23 NY	Fowler, Thomas	1807	357		21 NY
Fliguan, Pierre	1812	113		19	Fowles, Joseph	1851	1319		22 NY
Flint, Robert	1811	76		18 NY	Fox, Harvey	1810	325		21 CT
Floch, Francis	1805	609		34	Fox, Jacob	1815	114		26 NC
Florence, John	1805	466	b	40	Fox, John	1810	7		19 MD
Flores, Joseph	1805	415		30 LA	Fozer, Samuel	1810	401		29 PA
Florimon, Lewis	1812	93	m	23 LA	Frabregas, Benedict	1809	225		34
Flowers, Lambert	1816	29		31 MA	Frame, John	1804	332		19 NY
Flynn, James	1855	222		23 MA	Franc, Joseph	1805	636		34 Orleans
Flynn, Peter	1851	1531		19 MA	Francis, Charles	1819	61		26 MA
Foale, Edward	1851	1427		25 NY	Francis, John	1805	759	b	20 Domica
Fogg, Eleazar	1815	208		22 MA	Francis, William	1805	558		20 NJ
Folger, PeterBenjamin	1811	37		15 NY	Francisca, Samuel	1821	139		24 NY
Folk, Francis	1805	973		22 Orleans	Franco, Antonio	1809	16		25
Foller, Peter	1810	319	m	25 MA	Francois, Jean	1814	220	y	20

Name	Year	No.		Age	State/Origin
Frank, Anthony	1805	752		30	Orleans
Frank, George H.	1821	83		22	
Franklin, Edward	1809	241		37 SC	
Franklin, Ismy	1819	210		28 MD	
Franklin, James	1810	239		20	
Franklin, John	1804	151		48 PA	
Franklin, Thomas	1811	325		27 NY	
Franklin, William	1804	186		25 DE	
Franz, Joseph	1805	592		54	Orleans
Frauvegal, Manuel	1806	1514		22	
Frazer, J.	1819	8		0	
Frazer, John	1806	1504		28 MA	
Frazer, John	1806	1486		26 NY	
Frazier, John A.	1855	271		22 RI	
Frazier, William	1807	358		25 PA	
Frederick, Matthew	1804	169		39	
Fredericks, William	1807	354		29 NY	
Freeborn, Joseph	1814	187		25 PA	
Freeman, Charles	1851	1309		23 MA	
Freeman, Francis	1818	207	b	25 CT	
Freeman, George	1816	3		23 NY	
Freeman, Joshua	1855	299		20 MA	
Freeman, Joshua	1855	279		20 MA	
Freeman, Peter	1818	225	b	30 CT	
Freeman, Richard	1809	28		20 PA	
Freeman, Thomas	1804	296	m	20 MD	
Frelet, Pierre	1805	567		19	
French,CharlesFranklin	1855	184		17 NH	
French, John Walker	1818	312		33 MA	
Frey, Jacob	1810	118		23 PA	
Frizell, John D.	1810	194		22 MD	
Froment, Jacque Francois	1815	216		27	
Fromme,CordtHenrick	1804	319		47	
Front, William	1855	429		18 LA	
Frost, Benjamin	1810	282		25 MA	
Frotters, Phillip	1805	462		34	
Fulcher, John	1821	20		31 NC	
Fullard, John	1815	253		30 NY	
Fuller, Thomas	1815	209		21 MA	
Fulton, Adam	1812	150		21 NY	
Furtion, John Baptiste	1811	275		21	
Fury, Samuel	1851	1603		24	
Gabrielle, Francois	1811	226		30	
Gaff, Calvin W.	1851	1655		30 CT	
Gage, Isaac	1818	331		28 MA	
Gallaro, Raimon	1810	268		20	Orleans
Galliot, John	1810	267		18	
Gamble, Robert P.	1815	179		22 MD	
Garces, Pedro Juan	1806	1552		40	Orleans
Garcia, Alonzo	1818	95		51	Spain
Garcia, Anthony	1809	222		28	Orleans
Garcia, Antoine	1811	53		28	
Garcia, Antonio	1805	570		20	
Garcia, Antonio	1805	540		25	
Garcia, Antonio	1804	0		0	
Garcia, Balthasar	1805	422		20 LA	
Garcia, Gregory	1809	226		32	
Garcia, Jose	1818	338		33	
Garcia, Joseph	1805	740	c	28	
Garcia, Joseph	1806	1564		0	
Garcia, Juan	1805	725		23	
Garcia, Manuel	1805	562		32	
Garcia, Manuel	1818	271		29	
Garcia, Michael	1818	219		25 LA	
Garcie, Francis	1810	17		36	Orleans
Gardener, Charles	1851	1527		21 NY	
Gardiner, Job	1804	208		23 RI	
Gardiner, Matthew	1815	148		25 MA	
Gardiner, Niles	1821	49		23 RI	
Gardiner, William B.	1819	181		36 RI	
Gardner, Bezaleel	1807	403		24 MA	
Gardner, Edward	1851	1517		23 PA	
Gardner, Gilbert A.	1851	1608		57 NY	
Gardner, James	1805	640		20 NY	
Gardner, Joseph	1818	290	b	33 RI	
Gardner, William	1819	105		18 MA	
Gardon, Peter	1810	404		37	Sardinia
Gardy, James	1810	1		24 PA	
Garland, Wm. G.	1804	0		0	
Garnett, Edmund	1851	1428		29 NC	
Garo, Manuel	1806	1553		0	Orleans
Garrison, Richard	1811	16		14 VA	
Garrison, Richard	1818	369		24 VA	
Gashiot, John	1805	460		39 LA	
Gaspar, Nicholas	1810	4		31	
Gaston, John	1806	1519		0	
Gates, William	1818	183		22	
Gattes, John W.	1821	32		23 NJ	
Gaubile, Vincent	1810	234		32	
Gaugac, Jean	1804	60		20	
Gautier, Francis	1805	753		33	Orleans
Gawl, John	1805	889		45	
Gay, Isaac J.	1819	83		25 MA	
Geddes, Robert	1819	21		22 MA	
Gee, Thomas	1818	198		31 PA	
Gego, Nicholas	1806	1587		35	
Gellet, Yves	1810	298		0	
George, Jacob	1809	296	b	36 PA	
George, John	1818	112		28	
Gerald, Samuel	1804	212	c	28 PA	
Gerard, Caleb	1821	18		26 CT	
Gerard, Samuel	1855	309		27 NY	
Gerbaut, Pierre	1811	119		35	Orleans
Germon, Auguste	1815	129		20	
Germon, Peter	1818	106		30 LA	
Geroge, John	1810	61		24	
Gerome, Coussaint	1816	8		35	

Name	Year	No.		Age	Origin
Getchell, Sewell	1857	122		25 ME	
Geterhill, Josiah	1821	48		29 ME	
Gibbon, James	1811	183		23 MD	
Gibbs, John F.	1821	90		40 RI	
Gibbs, Russel	1819	106		19 MA	
Gibson, David	1811	284		32 PA	
Gibson, Hugh	1804	128		22 PA	
Gibson, James	1851	598		31 NY	
Gibson, Peter	1857	66		62 NY	
Giddean, John	1805	693		18 VA	
Giddens, Thomas	1812	4		23 VA	
Gill, James	1805	803		27 MD	
Gilley, Isaac F.	1851	1492		43 ME	
Gilmore, John	1818	211		25 SC	
Gilson, Peter	1805	573		23	
Gilstone, George	1811	305	b	31 NJ	
Gioppo, Domenico	1811	64		29	
Giot, John	1818	323		22 LA	
Girand, Joachin	1805	591		30	Orleans
Girandeau, Anthony	1805	581		15	
Girandel, John	1805	358		29	
Girod, John Baptiste	1810	350		30	
Gladding, Joseph H.	1821	30		21 CT	
Glance, Frederick	1805	501		24 MD	
Glancy, Edward	1857	103		20 PA	
Glasier, John	1804	270		32 MA	
Glidden, Loth	1851	1365		23 ME	
Glidden, William	1819	123		13 ME	
Glover, Samuel	1815	197		27 PA	
Glynn, Stephen M.	1812	83		32 PA	
Godberry, Thomas	1810	224		18 NC	
Godefrey, Daniel	1809	27	m	14 SC	
Godfrey, William	1811	35		25 NC	
Golden, James	1805	488		30	Orleans
Gomes, Jose	1805	363		25 LA	
Gomez, Juan	1810	279		22	
Gomez, Juan	1812	216		34	
Gonsales, Martin	1805	523		27	
Gonzales, Domingo	1806	1434		37	Orleans
Gonzales, Ignacio	1818	0		38	
Gonzales, Ignacio	1818	296		39	
Gonzales, John	1818	196		35	
Gonzales, JohnVincente	1806	1435		30	
Gonzales, Joseph	1806	1819		18	
Gonzales, Manuel	1818	5		36	Portugal
Gonzalez, John Anthony	1805	741		19	
Gonzana, Joseph	1805	588		28	Orleans
Goodman, Peter	1857	104		18	Ireland
Goodrich, Phineas	1821	82		16 NH	
Goodwin, John	1821	97		32 MA	
Goodwin, John	1806	1538		22 MA	
Goold, Ruben H.	1851	1578		32 NY	
Gordon, James	1818	365		22 MA	
Gordon, Louis	1811	324		18 VA	
Gordon, Nathaniel	1814	175		19 PA	
Gorham, Allen	1819	184		21 MA	
Gorham, Francis F.	1855	313		24 MA	
Gorton, William	1819	79		39 RI	
Goss, Henry F.	1815	130		21 NY	
Gott, John J.	1855	576		28 NY	
Goudran, Rock	1810	116		35	
Goula, John	1821	54		23 MD	
Gould, Peter	1810	288		55 NY	
Gouldin, Thomas	1804	238		31 PA	
Goushe, John	1805	985		40	
Gousset, Peter	1816	14		41	Francia
Gouzalez, Anthony	1807	321		15	
Goxdi(George), Juan	1805	782		22	
Gracias, Onofre	1810	54		23	
Gracy, William	1805	695		19 PA	
Grafton, William	1805	514		41 RI	
Graham, George	1851	1554		24 MA	
Graham, John	1855	549		35 PA	
Graham, John	1811	198		27 CT	
Gramer, George	1814	182		32 PA	
Grandjean, Joseph MaryMalfroy	1805	760		32	
Granet, William	1855	200		26 MA	
Grant, James	1810	223		28 NY	
Grant, Robert	1821	17		21 NY	
Grant, William	1857	133		21 NY	
Graval, Adrian	1804	309		34	Orleans
Graves, William	1821	126		23 ME	
Gray, Andrew	1819	96		34 VT	
Gray, James	1811	210		30 DE	
Gray, James	1810	130	y	28 MD	
Gray, Rufus	1855	470		23 MA	
Gray, Thomas	1814	205		32 NY	
Grayson, Lawewnce	1812	208		30	
Greaves, Anthony F.	1821	27		30 PA	
Grec, Jean	1818	295		33	
Gree, Joseph	1810	354		30	
Green, Charles	1812	14	m	23 PA	
Green, Henry	1805	674		27 MD	
Green, Jacob	1805	496		34 PA	
Green, James	1819	129		22 PA	
Green, James K.	1857	91		28 MA	
Green, Jeremiah	1819	168	b	25 MA	
Green, John	1815	17	y	51 MD	
Green, John	1851	1596		31 NY	
Green, John	1855	149		26 OH	
Green, Robert	1818	116		28 MA	
Green, Robert	1804	303		18 NY	
Green, Samuel	1821	23		38 MA	
Green, Wm	1855	434		22 NY	
Greene, Simon	1818	15	b	14 GA	

Greenland, Edward	1851	1385		27 MA	
Greenleaf, Samuel	1815	226		23 MA	
Greenleaf, Stephen	1811	55		20 MA	
Greenwood, Henry	1810	44		32 MD	
Gregory, Alexander	1851	1210		45 NY	
Gregory, Francis H.	1810	170		20 CT	
Gregory, John	1805	717		31 PA	
Grenotte, Pierre	1821	133		25	
Griffin, Moses	1815	7	c	29 MA	
Griffin, William	1814	198		20 NC	
Griffith, James	1815	100		24 MA	
Griffith, William H.	1851	1688		56 MA	
Grimes, John	1807	376		29 VA	
Grimms, Christian	1804	33		24 PA	
Gringier, James	1805	552		50	
Grinnalds, Henry	1815	180		20 VA	
Griseman, Jacob	1804	215		17 VA	
Grisues, Juan	1812	2		26	
Gros, Joseph	1806	1425		26	Orleans
Grover, Robert	1855	248		23 ME	
Groves, Robert	1812	13		28 PA	
Groves, William	1809	282		21 DE	
Grozier, William	1814	186		24 NY	
Grumman, Aaron	1821	29		39 CT	
Gueret, Charles	1809	246		30	Orleans
Guerin, Nicolas	1811	319		28	
Guerry, James Alexis	1810	51		45	
Guest, Anthony	1805	969		25	Orleans
Guest, John	1851	1315		32 NY	
Guetry, Jean	1816	38		39 LA	
Guillonet, John	1811	36		35	
Guine, Louis	1810	90		33	
Guinnis, Benjamin	1851	1314		19 GA	
Guivernau, Francisco	1805	776		24	
Gullager, William M.	1810	109		21 MA	
Gunby, Wm. H.	1851	1441		23 MD	
Gunnell, James	1809	9		31 VA	
Gunnet, Stephen	1805	924	y	17	
Gunsal, Joseph	1805	762		26	
Gurney,OliverSamson	1815	162		18 MA	
Gurnt, Sevastain	1807	325		14	Orleans
Guthrie, James V.	1806	1456		28 PA	
Gutiers, Lewis	1819	145		26 MA	
Guverno, Francis	1806	1811		25	Orleans
Guy, Robert	1818	0	b	27 PA	
Guy, Robert	1818	270	b	27 PA	
Guyar, Joseph	1811	236		33	
Gwilt, Richard	1851	1185		22 NY	
Hackerman, Henry	1812	40		31 NJ	
Halaes, Francis	1805	786		30	
Hale, Christopher	1810	101		26 VA	
Hale, Joel Williamson	1815	102		26 VA	
Hale, Shadrack	1814	193	y	31 MD	
Haley, Nathan	1821	33		22 CT	
Hall, Charles	1851	1328		41 NY	
Hall, Daniel	1818	32	b	25 CT	
Hall, Emest	1855	413		19 LA	
Hall, Ezekeil	1811	115		23 PA	
Hall, George	1805	692		22 MD	
Hall, James	1821	128		26 ME	
Hall, Lachariah	1819	219	c	34 NY	
Hall, Thomas	1855	259		29	Gr.Britain
Hall, Waterman	1855	504		24 ME	
Hallett,Samuel W.Jr.	1857	101		25 MA	
Hallock, William F.	1855	204		17 ME	
Hally, James	1851	1577		25	Ireland
Halpin, Thomas	1851	1347		24 NY	
Hamba, John	1812	185		28 VA	
Hambleton, William	1811	283		24 MA	
Hamilton, Christopher	1812	61		22 PA	
Hamilton, George	1810	177		30 PA	
Hamilton, William	1851	1404		20 NY	
Hammon, John	1804	150		21	
Hancock, James	1811	246		22 NC	
Handy, Jacob	1818	13	b	17 RI	
Hanegreef, John	1818	74		26 NC	
Hanford, Isaac	1811	26		26 NY	
Hanger, Joseph	1805	970	y	17	Orleans
Hanrang, Peter	1804	52		23	Orleans
Hansford, Stephen	1811	40		24 VA	
Haper, Abel	1810	129		23 MA	
Harby, Levy Chas.	1851	1362		23 SC	
Hardey, William	1811	174		18 MD	
Harding, Gamaliel	1818	61		21 MA	
Harding, John	1804	216	b	19 PA	
Harding, Mathew	1851	1616		24 MA	
Hardy,Herbert James	1855	206		27 CT	
Hardy, Peter	1805	432		22 LA	
Hardy, Resdon	1818	153	b	32 DE	
Hareaux, John	1812	70		29	
Hareraux, John	1812	213		29 LA	
Harker, John	1806	1422		27 RI	
Harkness, George P.	1855	546		52 CT	
Harley, John	1809	1		26 MA	
Harman, Cyrus	1804	248	b	18 PA	
Harman, John	1810	71		25	
Harper, William	1855	521		32 MA	
Harragan, Jeremiah	1807	348		26 MD	
Harrington, John	1805	831		26 MA	
Harrington, homas J.	1851	1391		0	Great Br.
Harris, John	1815	23	m	28 NY	
Harris, John	1805	808		25 NY	
Harris, John M.	1818	235		22 CT	
Harris, Nathaniel S.	1851	1355		16 MA	
Harris, Thomas	1807	361		19 PA	
Harris, Thomas	1807	336		19 PA	
Harris, Thomas D.	1821	118		35 CT	
Harris, Thomas R.	1851	1419		22 ME	

Name	Year	No.		Age/State	Note
Harris, William	1810	34		28	
Harrison, David	1851	1312		42 NY	
Harrison, Harry	1810	16		25 NY	
Harrison, John	1819	191		29 SC	
Harrison, Joseph	1818	184		29 PA	
Harrison, Joseph	1811	155		18	
Harrison, Samuel	1814	171		25 NC	
Harrison, William	1806	1471	b	32 PA	
Harry, David	1810	216		25	Mishegon
Harry, James	1807	372		20	
Harry, John	1806	1458		26 PA	
Hart, John	1821	16		21 PA	
Hart, John	1855	499		22 PA	
Hartnett, James	1855	489		24 NJ	
Harvey, James	1811	294		30 RI	
Harvey, John	1812	188		22 MD	
Harvey, John	1812	3		23	
Harvey, John	1804	101		11	Orleans
Harvey, William	1855	246		26 NY	
Harvey, William	1851	1523		24 NY	
Haskell, Robert	1818	250		36 MA	
Haskins, Robert	1810	159		23 VA	
Hasloun, Charles E.	1855	478		32 MA	
Haslund, Niels C.	1851	1652		30 NY	
Hat, William	1855	218		33 ME	
Hatton, John	1809	271		28 VA	
Hauziere,JeanThomas	1810	340		40	
Haven, Wm. S.	1851	1576		20 NY	
Havens, Benjamin	1804	146		25 NJ	
Havey, Samuel	1810	139		20 MA	
Hawkins, Edwin	1855	263		21 NY	
Hawkins, Samuel	1804	131		21 VA	
Haws, Elithan	1811	39		37 NC	
Hay, Edward	1805	721		22 VA	
Hay, William	1819	190		27 NH	
Hayes, Adam	1857	110		30 NY	
Hays, Joseph	1814	206		26 NH	
Hays, William H.	1818	306		20 CT	
Hayward,JamesHenry	1804	83		20 SC	
Hazard, Silas H.	1819	41		15 CT	
Heath, John	1815	243		34 NY	
Heath, Perry	1807	374		29 MD	
Hector, Peter	1810	43	y	50	
Hedge, John	1818	294		41 MA	
Helderson, Charles	1851	1317		24 MD	
Helm, Charles	1816	63		37 PA	
Helm, Charles	1810	106		31 PA	
Hembrow, John	1814	168		31 NY	
Henoricks, John	1810	361		24 NY	
Henrie, Antoine	1811	102		48	
Henry, Charles	1815	42	b	35 MD	
Henry, Daniel	1807	0		29	
Henry, John	1811	209		29 SC	
Henry, John	1812	67		27 PA	
Henry, John	1819	197		28 NY	
Henry, Joseph	1816	57		25 LA	
Henry, Joseph	1810	327		21	
Henry, Robert Jenkins	1815	3		21 MD	
Henry, Thomas G.	1855	172		17 MI	
Herbert, Louis	1816	59		28 LA	
Herbert, Peter	1816	73		0	St. Doming
Hemandes,Dominique	1811	258		41	
Heron, William	1804	329		27 MA	
Herouard, Philipe	1804	167		30	
Heroward, Philip	1807	359		33	
Herrara, Peter	1818	57		41 LA	
Herredia, Antonio	1806	1803		19	Orleans
Herrington, James	1819	158		26 NJ	
Herron, James	1804	198		23 MD	
Hervieu, JeanBaptiste	1804	56		24	Orleans
Hery, Martin	1811	180		53	
Hesketh, James	1805	940		21 NY	
Heslop, John L.	1851	1439		23 MA	
Hewing, George	1811	54		19 NY	
Hewit, Mitch	1805	783		22 NY	
Hewlett, L. Florsan	1855	440		24 LA	
Heymer, John	1819	228		22 NY	
Hibbens, John	1806	1537		26 NY	
Hickey, John	1851	1426		30 NY	
Higinbotthom,George	1807	351		39 MD	
Hildebrandt, Christian	1855	476		24 PA	
Hill, James	1818	354		16 PA	
Hill, John	1816	85		39 PA	
Hill, Robert	1811	161	b	18 MA	
Hill, Thomas	1851	1392		23	Scotland
Hill, William	1857	132		26 PA	
Hill, Wm.	1804	310		19 MD	
Hiller, Thomas, Jr.	1818	31		22	
Hilman, George	1804	328		26 PA	
Hilton, Winthrop	1818	208		23 NH	
Hincox, Moses	1812	189		19 KY	
Hinds, John	1809	306		34 MA	
Hines, Samuel	1815	139		23 MD	
Hinks, Elisha A.	1855	461		27 ME	
Hintz, Anthony	1818	229		33	
Hiriart, Joseph	1810	340		26	
Hisnard, John	1805	480		29	Orleans
Hizard, Manto	1806	1580		30	Louisiana
Hoare, James	1818	222		28 NY	
Hobkirt, James	1805	430		25 MD	
Hochen, Henry	1812	122		40 MA	
Hodgdon, Asa	1819	148		17 NH	
Hodge, John	1815	277		19 MA	
Hodgman, Hiram	1819	222		21 MA	
Hodgskins, John	1805	830		34 MA	
Hogan, Patrick	1811	216		38 NY	
Hogg, James	1810	221		30 PA	
Holbrook, Benjamin	1805	854		24	

Name	Year	No.		Age/State	Origin
Holden, John	1851	1382		21 CT	
Holey, William	1809	217		33 MD	
Hollidge, Richard	1805	500		22 VA	
Hollywood, Richard	1851	1372		30 MA	
Holmes, Alfred C.	1855	411		26 MA	
Holmes, James	1810	224		21 NJ	
Holmes, Peter	1804	40		51 PA	
Holmes, Philip	1811	315		23 PA	
Holroid, William	1810	367		30 NY	
Homes, John	1855	287		21 NY	
Homes, William	1810	192		25 VA	
Honore, Joseph	1806	1543		35	Orleans
Hood, Edwin H.	1855	446		23 NY	
Hook, Samuel	1804	176		19 MD	
Hooper, Hiram	1857	118		18 ME	
Hopkins, Caleb	1819	35		32 MA	
Hopkins, Edmund	1821	9		42 MA	
Hopkins, Elisha	1818	300		23 MA	
Hopkins, Henry	1804	78		20 VA	
Hopkins, James	1806	1476		29 PA	
Hopper, Jacob	1818	154		22 NY	
Hored, Joseph	1805	357		20 LA	
Hornsby, Joseph	1805	773		24 VA	
Horstman, David	1819	192		25 MD	
Horton, David	1812	204		33	
Hosford, Othniel	1816	20		29 CT	
Hoskin, James	1815	235		21 RI	
Hosten, Jeremiah	1811	170		23 MD	
How, John	1811	205		16 NY	
Howard, George Washington	1855	211		15 PA	
Howard, Henry	1811	228		19 NC	
Howard, James	1810	171		23 NY	
Howard, John	1811	175		17 MD	
Howard, Reuben	1815	186		15 MA	
Howard, Robert	1804	121	m	24 MD	
Howe, Lot	1807	350		22 MA	
Howell, Benjamin	1804	280		29	
Howell, Elijah	1805	817	b	26 NC	
Howell, Thomas	1812	19		23 MA	
Howes, Nathan	1812	69		27 NJ	
Howland, John	1810	383		25 MA	
Hoyt, Ebenizar	1819	131		20 MA	
Huan, Simon	1804	323		28	
Hubbard, John	1812	44		28 PA	
Huber, Jacob	1812	223		28 PA	
Hucke, James	1805	711		39	
Hudson, John	1811	249		26 NC	
Hudson, Samuel	1821	71		44 CT	
Hue, P. Emanuel Dominiegues	1818	221		25 LA	
Huff, Josiah	1809	283		24 MA	
Hughes, Edward	1851	1640		22 NY	
Hughes, Erin	1855	170		34 NY	
Hughes, Henry	1818	152		21 VA	
Hughes, James	1812	64		30 NY	
Hughes, John	1851	1683		21 VA	
Hughes, Thomas	1819	132		23	England
Hughes, Thomas	1804	192		32 PA	
Hughy, John	1812	106		22 MD	
Hulant, John Francis	1814	158		31	
Hull, Geroge E.	1857	144		21 RI	
Hull, Ozias	1818	84		21 CT	
Hull, William	1819	68		39 NY	
Hull, William Fox	1815	8	b	23 CT	
Hume, Nicholas	1819	36		27 LA	
Hunt, Charles H.	1818	251		38 MA	
Hunt, Henry	1810	41		40 NY	
Hunt, John	1819	196		23 NJ	
Hunt, Joseph	1851	1549		22 NY	
Hunter, William W.	1819	194		17 PA	
Hurd, Henry W.	1809	31		28 CT	
Hurler, Charles	1810	211		32 MD	
Huston, John	1805	524		23 DE	
Hutchins, Edward	1811	31	m	21 MD	
Hutchins, James	1810	337		22 MD	
Hutchinson, Hugh	1851	1582		25	Scotland
Hutchinson, JamesD.	1851	1438		29 VT	
Hutchinson, William	1804	141		29 PA	
Hutchinson, William	1805	909		0	
Hyde, Horace P.	1810	385		24 MA	
Hyer, C. L.	1855	258		33 MA	
Ichegaray, Martin	1806	1525		20	Orleans
Ignacio, Jose	1805	444		38	
Inger, Joseph	1810	188		41	
Ingram, Edward	1805	710		24 PA	
Inkster, John	1816	101		30 NY	
Innis, Joseph	1804	69		0	
Iordy, Manuel	1805	604		30	Orleans
Irish, Isaac	1806	1511		24 RI	
Irvin, James	1805	915		22 PA	
Irwin, William	1851	1305		27 NY	
Ishen, George	1818	162		21 VA	
Israel, Joseph	1805	518		43 DE	
Ives, Samuel	1815	0		25 CT	
Jack, Antoine	1805	497	y	33	Orleans
Jackno, Peter	1804	325		27	Orleans
Jackson, Francis	1816	50		27 NY	
Jackson, Henry	1804	304	b	42 VA	
Jackson, James	1810	97		26 MA	
Jackson, James	1851	1559		31 NY	
Jackson, John	1821	141	b	30	
Jackson, John	1819	159		22 MA	
Jackson, Robert	1851	1599		32 NY	
Jackson, Samuel	1804	211		19 PA	
Jackson, Thomas	1815	21	b	25 NY	
Jacobs, Francis	1818	200		35 PA	
Jacobs, George	1804	113		19 NY	

Name	Year	No.		Age/Place	Origin
Jacobs, Morris	1812	145		25 NY	
Jacobson, William	1805	392		25 CT	
Jacops, Thomas	1816	102	c	25 MA	
Jacquette, Peter	1821	146		17 MD	
Jadot, Lewis	1811	3	b	27	Orleans
Jadwin, Robert	1806	1813		34 NY	
James, Edward	1805	341		24	
James, John	1810	295		19 MD	
James, John	1811	304		25 NJ	
James, John	1816	34		25 NY	
James, John	1816	86		40 MD	
James, John	1855	210		28 MD	
James, John M.	1819	225		20 CT	
James, John, 3rd.	1816	8		27 MA	
James, Maldie	1804	352		28 NY	
James, Noble	1818	78		40 DE	
James, Richard	1811	47	b	19 NY	
James, Thomas	1810	62		27 MD	
James, Thomes	1812	175		28 MD	
James, William	1804	70		32 VA	
Jameson, Arthur	1851	1645		22 MA	
Jameson, Matthew	1811	15		31 MA	
January, John	1804	149		22	
Japlace, Lorence	1804	287		32	
Jardela, Joseph	1806	1807		20	Orleans
Jarvis, John	1810	48		24 VA	
Jeantete, Peter	1810	292		34	
Jeantt, Antoine	1811	23		18	
Jefferson, George	1806	1465		26 PA	
Jeffries, David	1811	276		19 PA	
Jenkins, Charles	1857	99		23 NY	
Jenkins, John	1857	111		38 MD	
Jenkins, William	1811	306	b	24 PA	
Jenkinson, John	1855	168		35 MD	
Jennings, George H.	1821	63		14 NY	
Jessop, Samuel	1855	217		27 ME	
Jewett, Joseph H.	1821	69		28 MA	
Jewitt, Jonathan	1815	53		26 MA	
Jilson, Amos	1819	237		27 MA	
Jlores, Joseph	1805	359		30	
Joachim, Antonio	1818	17		26	Portugal
Jobona, Lorenzo	1807	367		25	Orleans
John, Peter	1805	627		25	
Johns, Benjamin	1809	209		29 MA	
Johnson, Charles	1821	26		20	Sweden
Johnson, Charles	1815	9	m	25	
Johnson, David	1814	190		39 NJ	
Johnson, David	1815	29		32 NJ	
Johnson, David	1851	1678		28 NY	
Johnson, Frederick	1851	1564		23 NY	
Johnson, Frederick	1804	217		23 MA	
Johnson, George A.	1855	302		26 VA	
Johnson, Henry	1851	1606		23 NJ	
Johnson, Henry	1855	188		25 NY	
Johnson, Henry	1821	55		35 VA	
Johnson, Henry	1821	19		30 NY	
Johnson, Henry	1804	137		0	
Johnson, Jacob	1810	160		24 PA	
Johnson, James	1818	367	c	20 MA	
Johnson, James	1851	1370		26 NY	
Johnson, John	1851	1344		24 GA	
Johnson, John	1818	51	b	19 MA	
Johnson, John	1811	147	l	32 MD	
Johnson, John	1811	207	b	22 PA	
Johnson, John	1804	157		28 IT	
Johnson, Joseph	1804	299		60	
Johnson, Joseph	1804	204		23 VA	
Johnson, Lewis	1811	114	y	38 NY	
Johnson, Marck	1812	54		23 MD	
Johnson, Michael	1818	244		30	Scotland
Johnson, Nels	1809	290		33 PA	
Johnson, Obadiaher	1814	203		20 VA	
Johnson, Onno	1851	1364		23 NY	
Johnson, Peter	1851	1307		43 PA	
Johnson, Richard	1804	244	b	29 NY	
Johnson, Robert	1805	964		0	
Johnson, Stephen	1807	393		19 NY	
Johnson, Thomas	1804	34		32 VA	
Johnson, Tom	1851	1198		17 MA	
Johnson, William	1814	1		20 SC	
Johnson, William	1805	374	b	25 MA	
Johnston, Henry	1806	1459		48	
Johnston, James	1815	149		21 MA	
Johnston, James	1819	88		35 MD	
Johnston, John	1818	313	b	22 NY	
Johnston, John	1805	510		0	
Johnston, Robert	1804	301		23 VA	
Johnston, Thomas	1806	1432		25 SC	
Johnston, Zeanas	1811	302		31 NY	
Joice, Samuel	1811	196		27 MD	
Joitz, Pablo	1810	230		28	
Jokin, Manuel	1818	41		0	
Jole, Dominick	1805	873		35	
Jones, Charles	1819	38		22 MD	
Jones, Charles	1851	1615		26 NY	
Jones, Daniel	1814	189		50 NY	
Jones, David	1810	242		24 VA	
Jones, David	1855	559		25	Wales
Jones, Edward	1851	1192		52 MD	
Jones, Edward	1807	399	b	28 VA	
Jones, Francis	1855	348		35 MA	
Jones, Francis V.	1816	5		23 MA	
Jones, George	1815	143		20 Md	
Jones, Hiram	1818	28		18 NY	
Jones, James	1818	170		26 MD	
Jones, James	1810	38		21 MA	
Jones, John	1805	857		42 MD	
Jones, John	1804	77		21 VA	

Jones, John	1804	118		37 PA	
Jones, John F.	1851	1575		23	England
Jones, John H.	1855	461		0	
Jones, Joseph	1810	186		23 DE	
Jones, Levi	1804	30		29 PA	
Jones, Nathan H.	1811	192		39 CT	
Jones, Nathen	1810	168		19 NH	
Jones, Richard	1816	44	m	29 MA	
Jones,Richard Robert	1851	1395		23 PA	
Jones, Robert	1818	40		25	
Jones, Samuel	1821	75		21 NH	
Jones, Thomas	1815	182		21 CT	
Jones, Thomas	1812	134		42 MD	
Jones, Thomas Howard	1855	436		21	England
Jones, William	1815	33		24 VA	
Jones, William	1819	230		21 NY	
Jones, William A.	1855	252		19 CT	
Jones, Wm. Henry	1855	317		23 MA	
Jordan, John	1804	266		26 MD	
Jordan, William	1806	1583	m	20 VA	
Jordon, John	1805	453		35	
Jose, Antonio	1819	233		25	
Joseph, Anthony	1806	1451		25	
Joseph, Antony	1818	324		34	
Joseph, Candido	1806	1507		25	
Joseph, Collin	1851	1339		18 NY	
Joseph, John	1806	1588		16	Orleans
Josselyn, Judson	1815	64		25 MA	
Joubin, Denisie	1815	29	b	19	
Jourdan, Joseph	1818	242		29 LA	
Jourdan, Peter	1806	1454		18	
Joure, Jean Louis	1814	161		46	
Joy, Samuel	1805	681		25 MA	
Joze, Victorino	1807	410		20	
Judisse, Antono	1814	136		40 LA	
Julien, Andrew	1819	6		30 LA	
Julien, Andrew	1810	148		22	
Julien, Francois	1816	53	b	16 LA	
Julien, Lazar	1815	266		55	
Jurette, Laurens	1811	8		31	
Kane, Hores	1812	89	m	19 MD	
Kane, John	1851	1334		24 NY	
Kargorr, Aldui	1805	397		27 LA	
Karns, Jesse J.	1815	189		24 PA	
Karr, William	1811	215		33 MA	
Kasche, Frederick	1805	714		24 PA	
Kean, Henry	1821	76		37 PA	
Kearin, Edward	1805	781		24 MA	
Kearney, James	1818	199		23 NJ	
Kearney, James	1855	448		25 MA	
Keefer, Henry	1855	577		24 NY	
Kees, Benjn.	1806	1576		23	Orleans
Keg, Philip	1804	246		26 PA	
Kegg, William	1819	43		21	England
Keiniston, Samuel	1851	1620		19 ME	
Keith, Kingman	1851	1646		38 ME	
Keller, Amariah	1855	543		22 ME	
Keller, Jocob	1807	353		25 PA	
Kelley, George K.	1855	418		22 NH	
Kelley, Wm. H.	1855	270		22 NY	
Kelly, James	1804	265		25 NY	
Kelly, John	1804	277		51 PA	
Kelly, Joshua	1810	280		22 PA	
Kelly, Thomas	1819	76		21 MA	
Kelly, William	1804	230		37	
Kemp, Henry	1855	527		36 ME	
Kendrick, James	1809	277		25 MA	
Kennedy, Alexander	1851	1374		24 MA	
Kennedy, Henry D.	1812	133		33 NY	
Kennedy, Jacques (Jack)	1816	88		22	
Kennedy, John	1815	228		21 NY	
Kennedy, Thomas	1818	117		22 NY	
Kennedy, William	1809	5		33 PA	
Kenny, Ehphalet G.	1819	220		24 MA	
Keoff, Joseph	1804	87		20 NH	
Kergoit, Aldrie	1805	872		0	
Kerns, James	1815	133		27 NY	
Kerns, John	1810	341		32	
Kerr, David	1851	1352		26 NY	
Kerr, Samuel	1810	315		32 PA	
Kerry, John S.	1855	487		27 ME	
Kesler, Ralph	1810	248		23 NJ	
Keysor, Joseph	1812	228		24 PA	
Kheo, Thomas	1851	1503		26 MA	
Killingsworth, John	1818	11		23 DE	
Kimball, Benjamin	1819	109		27 MA	
Kimball, Joseph	1818	178		15 MA	
Kimball, Samuel	1811	17		20 RI	
Kincaid, William R.	1857	121		46 NY	
King, Edward	1851	1633		22 NY	
King, John	1851	1552		19 NY	
King, Leonard	1805	470		26 MD	
King, Orvis	1809	311		13 MA	
King, Solomon	1810	200		23 NY	
King, William	1809	12		27 NY	
Kingsland, John	1818	20		24 NY	
Kingston, John Picton	1851	1205		24 MA	
Kinney, Robert	1855	433		28 PA	
Klee, Charles Gotlieb	1811	248		48	
Kling, Charles	1855	245		23 NY	
Klyne, Bamard D.	1815	11		23 MA	
Knab, William	1815	36		25 MD	
Kneben, John	1809	312		37 NY	
Kneber, John	1809	312		37 NY	
Knight, Abner	1818	234		21 PA	
Knight, Alexander	1855	234		35 ME	

Knight, John	1816	66		21 GA		Landreau, Peter	1816	36		39 LA
Knight, Joseph	1818	25		20 NY		Landreesher, Victor	1804	322		15
Knight, Simeon	1805	774		31 VT		Lane, Amos	1818	363		27 MA
Knight, William	1851	1545		26 ME		Lane, James	1851	1211		49 CT
Knoll, Pierre Poul	1855	511		55 TX		Lane, John	1819	104		26 MA
Knowles, Amos	1810	146		27 CT		Lane, Solomon	1810	136	b	30 NJ
Knox, James	1811	218		23 VT		Lang, Willis	1815	85		22 SC
Kollberg, Christian	1805	502		21 MD		Lange, Marie	1805	756		30
Krebs, Antoine	1814	209		28	MS Terr.	Langlace, Antoine	1805	902		30
Kurlin, John L.	1806	1592		22 PA		Langlace, Antonio	1815	264		42
L'egriel, Nicholas	1805	390	y	32		Langmaid, Samuel	1805	463		23 MA
Labarde, John	1806	1533		56	Orleans	Lankester, Samuel	1805	633		28 MA
Labat, John Batiste	1814	163		38 LA		Lanman, James M.	1812	31		27 MA
Labatus, Peter	1805	702		18		Lanrence, Alexander	1806	1463		19 NJ
Labla, John	1806	1539		23		Lans, Vincent	1806	1799		28	Orleans
Labsen, Hindrick	1811	262		34 PA		Lanusse, Paul	1804	0		0
Lacassaigne,Armand	1818	277		42		LaPauze, John Lewis	1804	138		0
LaCasta, Francisco	1806	1802		24	Orleans	Lapsley, James	1851	1323		21 IL
LaCave, Peter	1806	1570		0	Orleans	Laranto, Angelo	1805	821		0
LaChiapella, Gerome	1804	0		0		Lardret, Charles	1811	125		30
LaChiapella, Stephen	1804	320		23		Larken, Gilbert C.	1855	574		39 NY
Lackington, Wm.	1851	1389		23 NY		Larkin, Wm.	1818	320		27 MA
Lacktune, Batist	1805	888	b	21		LaRock, Framcos	1805	867		42
Laclotte, Pierre	1811	303		0		Larsen, Henry	1855	288		23 NY
Laconte, Andre	1816	87		26		LaRume, Peter	1810	2		34
Lacost, M. A.	1805	951		11		Lary, John	1806	1500		45 NH
Lacosta, Francisco	1805	727		22		Lasbeth, William	1851	1579		27	at sea
Lacroix, Jean	1812	46		28	New Orlean	Lasson, Bernard	1805	953		33
Lacroix, Pierre	1804	156		15		Latham, James	1810	275		20 MA
Lacy, Edward	1815	59		26 MA		Latham, William	1810	81		41 CT
Ladenaixe, Baptiste	1812	0		23		Laudasino, Salvador	1805	822		28	Sicilia
Ladmir, Cugire	1815	119	m	24		Laudeman, Jacob	1819	156		22 MD
Lafaille, Bernard	1812	90		35		Laudry, Joseph	1810	311		36	Orleans
Lafite, Joseph	1811	132	c	20	Orleans	Laughlin, James	1855	542		28 NY
Lafont, Nicholas	1806	1561		23	Orleans	Laurouet, Jean	1805	425		31
Laforgue, Gabriel	1818	281		30		Laurouet,				
Lafosse, Bernard	1804	105		55		Jean Baptiste	1821	28		38
Lagois, John	1812	218		0		Lavanz, Francisco	1805	602		17
Lakeman, Asa	1819	154		33 MA		Lavrille, Paul	1805	934		19
Lalle, Henri	1851	1380		21 MD		Lawrence, Joseph	1809	284		21	Orleans
Lamant, Charles	1818	243		37 LA		Lawrence, Joseph H.	1851	1447		21 ME
Lamar, George	1811	186		26 PA		Lawson, James	1816	35	m	28 RI
Lamarlerett, Joupt	1811	43		13 MD		Lawton, Jeremiah	1815	163		35 RI
Lamb, William	1815	103		24 MA		Layfield, George	1819	155		20 VA
Lambert, Henry	1811	164		28	Hanover	Leaming, Allison	1810	252		24 NJ
Lambert, John	1811	142	y	22	Orleans	Leandre, Lewis	1818	343		31	Corse
Lambert, William B.	1815	115		15 MA		Lear, John	1818	297		55	DK?
Lambson, Martin	1805	511		25 NJ		Leard, Jesse	1851	1649		19 MA
Lament, Joseph	1818	35		41 LA		Leary, Daniel	1818	282		25 NY
Lamont, Joseph	1855	510		50 ME		Leavitt, Samuel	1804	112		25 MA
Lamoureux,						Lebergh, John	1818	121		25 NY
Jean Francis	1821	6		40		Lebon, Lewis	1806	1569		25
Lampman, Divid	1810	264		23 NY		Lebon, Louis	1805	443		22
Lancaster, Richard	1818	288		18 RI		Lebopain, Francis	1804	170		24

Name	Year	No.		Age/State	Place
LeBriu, Joseph	1811	99	y	30	
Lechere, JeanBaptiste	1815	219		42	
LeClere, LewisJoseph	1804	282		26	
Ledes, Francis	1810	241		31 PA	
Lee, George	1811	300		25 PA	
Lee, Henry	1810	112		19 MA	
Lee, John	1810	274		25 MD	
Lee, John	1811	116		19 VA	
Lee, Richard	1810	111		25 MA	
Lee, Thomas	1809	268		16 MD	
Leeds, Joseph C.	1855	384		22 MA	
Lees, John W.	1810	92		35 PA	
Lefavour, William	1818	179		20 MA	
Lefort, Alexis	1806	1447		29	Orleans
Leganger, John	1805	434		34 LA	
Legrand, Germain	1816	79		40	
Lehmann, John	1857	109		27	Germany
Leigh, George					
Washington	1805	804		24 VA	
Lema, Joseph	1818	47		30	
Lemon, John	1805	580		25	
Lemon, William	1810	225		24 NY	
Lemont, Adam	1805	670		31 MA	
Lenine, John	1819	62		26 NY	
Lenox, Abraham	1810	128		21 MD	
Lens, Bernable	1810	215		20	
Lent, William	1810	265		36	Orleans
Leon, Joseph	1815	262		55	
Leorrobee,					
Alexander S.	1855	229		21 ME	
Lepage, Henry	1805	987		28	
Leprestre, Jean					
Baptiste Emeli	1806	1548		0	
LeQuesne, Phillip	1807	339		20 OH	
Lerain, Gerard	1811	264		38	
Leroux, Francois M.	1811	322		0	Orleans
LeRoux, Jacque	1809	248		22	
Leroy, Marien	1805	642		40	
LeRoy, Marier	1805	689		40	Orleans
LeSage, Henry	1805	416		13 LA	
LeSassier, Vincent	1810	196		18	
Leslie, John	1805	813		36 NY	
Lesperance, Joseph	1810	399		27	
Lespinas, Bernard	1809	278		45	
Lester, William	1812	181		25 CT	
Levreau, Lewis	1804	209		30	
Lewis, Antoini	1811	57		25	
Lewis, Conklin	1815	204		0 NY	
Lewis, Ebenezer	1810	394		30 MA	
Lewis, Frederick	1811	139		27 MD	
Lewis, George	1811	112	b	22 NY	
Lewis, George	1807	328	y	22 NY	
Lewis, Jack	1810	377	b	20 MD	
Lewis, Jacob	1805	853		30 NY	
Lewis, John	1810	213		34	Orleans
Lewis, John	1809	45	b	35 MD	
Lewis, John	1806	1443		21 VA	
Lewis, John	1804	161	m	41	
Lewis, John	1810	320	y	22 CT	
Lewis, John	1812	8	b	24 NY	
Lewis, John	1818	350		26 NY	
Lewis, John W.	1855	544		24 MA	
Lewis, Joseph	1804	116	m	28 PA	
Lewis, Robert	1851	1341		19 SC	
Lewis, Thomas	1807	373		25 MA	
Lewis, William	1804	143		34 VA	
Libby, Soloman	1815	233		32 MA	
Libby, William	1857	63		17 ME	
Liddle, Michael	1815	76		18 Md	
Liddle, William	1809	300		35 PA	
Liddy, Michael	1851	1618		16 ME	
Lightfoot, John	1851	1444		28 NY	
Lightfoot, Timothy	1815	159		23 NY	
Lightner, George	1811	229		22 PA	
Likens, Parker	1812	100		26 PA	
Lilly, Robert	1804	255		19 PA	
Linares, Raphael	1805	554		60	
Lind, Peter	1815	82		28 NY	
Lindbergh, Jacob	1807	404		37 MD	
Lindsey, Joseph	1815	178		36 MA	
Linn, David	1804	279		25	
Linnott, John	1810	347		21 PA	
Lionnet, William	1804	54		28	Orleans
Litle, James	1811	312		29 NY	
Little, Francis	1805	825	m	21 MD	
Little, Jacob T.	1819	82		27 MA	
Littlefield, Lyman	1810	9	b	20 RI	
Livier, Peter	1812	0		0	
Livimore, Arthur	1818	38		28 NH	
Llorens, Francisco	1809	231		40	Orleans
Lloyd, Archibald T.	1857	119		24 ME	
Lobrano, Joseph	1807	388		22	
Lockwood, David	1810	29		30 NJ	
Logan, William	1810	27		23 MD	
Loiseau, Louis	1816	94		24 LA	
Loison, Baptis	1805	932		24	
Lollot, Marshall	1809	286		27	
Lombard, Eugene	1855	443		18 LA	
Lombard, Hezekiah	1811	82		32 MA	
Lombard, Jacques	1810	299		23	
Lombard, Louis	1819	30		30	
Lone, Jacques	1819	166		34	
Loney, William	1819	208		0 NJ	
Long, Beaty	1805	342		25 NC	
Long, Henry	1851	1491		39	St Thomas
Long, John	1855	420		36 PA	
Long, Lawrence	1855	441		50 NY	
Long, Peter	1812	137		29 MA	

Name	Year	No		Age/State		Name	Year	No		Age/State	
Long, Samuel	1818	319	b	52 PA		Lyons, Robert	1855	439		21 PA	
Lonnick, George	1810	386		26		Lyons, William	1814	169		24 SC	
Lonsausee, Joseph	1805	664		40		Macarty, Juand	1804	0		0	
Loomis, Henry Lewis	1855	424		16 LA		Mack, John	1819	26		32 MA	
Lope, John	1805	779		48		Mackay, John	1806	1433		26 SC	
Lopez, Antoine	1805	535		35	Orleans	MacKenzie,Alexander	1819	202		23 NY	
Lopez, Francis	1805	615		26	Orleans	Mackintosh, Simon	1805	739		20	
Lore, William	1811	194		22 MD		Macwell, Wm.	1855	174		24 ME	
Lorens, John Antonio	1805	495		30		Madison, Malcolm	1851	1197		20 MA	
Lorenzo, Peter	1806	1501		26	Orleans	Madran, Joseph	1807	366		32	
Lorget,JohnTranquille	1804	278		36		Magana, Jose Miguel	1811	49		24	
Loring,Francis Mobec	1855	304		18 ME		Mage, Pascale	1810	344		25	
Loring, Henry	1815	256		22		Mahoney, Maurice	1855	286		21 NY	
Loring, Rufus	1816	10		17 MA		Main, Joseph	1804	298	b	25 GA	
Lorte, Charles	1809	219		22 DE		Main, William	1815	194		27 PA	
Lorton, William	1812	49		0 NY		Maine, Alexander	1851	1390		26 NY	
Losada, Vicente	1805	613		31		Mainner, Henry	1815	192		24	
Lothrope, John	1819	167		16 MA		Maire, Lonzo	1816	100		22	Europe
Loud, Daniel M.	1819	42		41 PA		Maizen, David	1811	200		23 CT	
Loud, Thomas O.	1818	366		25 NH		Malabar, John	1810	244		19	
Louderback, John	1816	9		21 NJ		Malander, George	1809	34		33 PA	
Loughlin, Michael	1805	944		31		Malbert, Antoine	1805	706		42	Orleans
Louis, Jean	1812	30		34		Maldie, James	1804	35		28 NY	
Louis, Jno. Baptiste	1805	533	b	22		Mallol, Miguel	1811	50		24	
Louis, John	1804	294	b	23		Malow, Henry P.	1857	125		32 ME	
Louis, Pierre	1812	47	m	22		Malthe, Antoine	1816	83		25	
Louis, Vinsun	1805	948		12		Maltman, James	1855	202		28 NY	
Lounsbery,						Mana, Peter	1804	63		30	
William W.	1812	0		25 CT		Mann, James	1851	1324		22 IL	
Love, James	1806	1482		24	Orleans	Manuel, Jean	1811	130		36	MS Terr.
Lovefree, Levi	1812	75	b	25 NY		Manuel, Lewis	1806	1509		27	Orleans
Lovett, John	1810	346		37 NY		Maquire, John	1816	7		52	
Lowder, Joseph	1814	177		22 PA		Marchand, Joseph E.	1812	10		14 LA	
Lowe, William	1819	223		53 MD		Marchand,					
Lowman, Adam	1805	694		22 PA		Peter Eugene	1811	106		18	Orleans
Lowman, John	1805	871		26 PA		Marchand, Barnard	1819	39		23 NY	
Lowry, James	1805	700		26		Marchant, Elijah	1809	7		43 VA	
Loyd, Charles	1801	800		27	US	Marck, Peter	1807	416		24	Orleans
Loyd, James	1851	25		27		Mardenburrough,					
Luanes, Francois	1806	1810		21		Malbro	1815	13	m	24 RI	
Lucas, Chalres	1851	1626		25 MA		Maria, Jean Joseph	1812	36		25	
Lucus, John M.	1851	1367		23 MA		Maria, Joseph	1810	269		25	
Lumbard, Ansel	1810	165		30 MA		Marich, Stephen	1807	414		35	
Lumbert, William	1819	120		38 NY		Marie, Francois	1809	280		35	Orleans
Lunber, Mathew	1805	793		25 VA		Marie, John	1806	1495		17	Orleans
Luscombe, William F.	1851	1195		25 NY		Marie, Joseph	1807	379		16	Orleans
Lyeget, Henry	1810	297		26 NY		Marie, Paul John	1810	74		36	
Lynch, John	1806	1499		28 MD		Marien, Antonia	1805	933		26	
Lynmire, Elison B.	1855	230		45 NJ		Marle, George C.	1855	447		23 MA	
Lynn, Charles	1851	1679		25 NY		Marque, Antonio	1805	976		22	
Lyon, Isaac	1810	137		28		Marques,John Baysta	1818	212		21	Andalousia
Lyon, James	1811	323	b	35 NJ		Marsden, John	1819	121		27 NY	
Lyon, William	1805	436		27 NY		Marsh, John	1805	877		39 PA	
Lyons, John	1810	322		16 PA		Marsh, William	1855	431		32	England

Marshal, Joseph	1851	1400	23 NY	
Marshall, John	1855	214	24 RI	
Marshall, Nahum	1821	116	24 ME	
Marshall, Ralph	1810	381	22 NC	
Marshall, William S.	1851	1190	21 MD	
Marsher, Henry	1810	357	16 MA	
Marston, William H.	1851	1647	28 ME	
Martin, Anthony	1806	1577	40	
Martin, Daniel	1804	292	b 24 MA	
Martin, Edward	1812	135	26 NJ	
Martin, Edward	1851	1330	21 PA	
Martin, Geroge	1815	267	19 NC	
Martin, James	1805	697	26 NY	
Martin, JamesBernard	1805	396	53 MA	
Martin, Jeremiah	1805	715	29 PA	
Martin, Jeremiah	1815	138	46 NY	
Martin, John	1851	1311	28 KY	
Martin, John	1819	117	32 NY	
Martin, John	1855	171	28 NY	
Martin, John	1805	365	36 LA	
Martin, John	1806	1479	21 PA	
Martin, John	1809	22	26 MD	
Martin, Joseph	1815	260	36	
Martin, Manuel	1806	1800	25	
Martin, Peter	1804	261	18	
Martin, Peter	1810	365	24	
Martin, Pierre Dupoy	1805	975	26	
Martin, Samuel J.	1851	1346	20 DE	
Martin, William	1818	189	24 NY	
Martin, William	1816	97	26 NY	
Martin, William	1815	176	18 NY	
Martin, William	1851	1147	30 MA	
Martinau, Augustin	1805	850	42	
Martines, Manuel	1805	532	29	
Martines, Rafael	1805	595	36	Orleans
Martinez,JoseYgnacio	1819	171	18 LA	
Martinez, Peter	1811	75	21	Orleans
Martinich, John	1818	368	34	
Martten, Gian	1804	85	0	
Mary, Davis	1818	351	26	
Mary, John	1811	214	18 MA	
Mason, Hanney, Jr.	1818	317	m 29	
Mason, William	1811	68	21 PA	
Massicot, Pierre	1818	315	37	
Massy, James	1810	333	32 MD	
Mather, Jean Baptiste	1819	55	y 23	
Mathews, Cornelius	1819	64	30 NY	
Mathews, Thimothy	1812	21	30 GA	
Mathews, Thomas	1805	738	42 MD	
Mathier, Boyer	1815	24	21	
Mathieu, Rock	1804	218	43	
Mathieus, John	1811	204	22	
Matthews, Corneilus	1806	1469	16 PA	
Matthews, George	1806	1573	22 SC	
Matthews, John	1810	368	y 18 PA	
Matthews, John	1855	306	47 MA	
Matthews, John	1851	1553	24 NY	
Maughan, John	1805	584	19 MA	
Maura, Ignacio	1818	114	27 LA	
Maurant, L. A. D.	1814	133	17 LA	
Maurel, Peter	1805	755	27	Orleans
Maxarette, Joseph	1806	1567	14	Orleans
May, John	1810	263	25 PA	
May, Joseph	1815	268	28 LA	
May, Nicloas	1812	123	21 NJ	
Mayer, Nicholas	1811	97	24 PA	
Mayire, Jacob	1819	216	29 LA	
Mayor, Andrew	1851	1369	42 MA	
Mays, Charles	1851	4	25 PA	
Mazanti, Giousanni	1809	309	32	
Mazille, Pierre	1815	118	44	
McAdams, Robert	1855	193	22 MO	
McAllister, David	1809	41	20 PA	
McAllister, Edward	1805	743	43 GA	
McArdel, Aquila	1809	14	23 PA	
Mcarthur, John	1804	219	23 NY	
McArthur, Neol	1811	289	35 NY	
McBride, Edward	1807	341	39 MD	
McBroom, Henry	1855	462	23 MD	
McCabe, Levi	1812	105	26 MD	
McCabe, Michael	1851	1574	19 NY	
McCahan, Griffith	1810	371	0 PA	
McCain, Joseph	1809	294	20 PA	
McCammen, Joseph	1805	428	40	
McCarragher, James	1804	193	21 PA	
McCarter, Samuel	1814	196	18 MD	
McCarthy, James	1851	1157	25 NY	
McCarthy, Timothy	1851	1425	30 MA	
McCellean, William	1810	5	27 PA	
McCland, James	1815	66	23 NY	
McCleary, Edward	1851	1689	21 RI	
McClish, Archibald	1815	26	25 VA	
McCloud, John	1804	189	45 PA	
McCollum, James W.	1855	512	29 ME	
McComber, Richard	1810	100	28 RI	
McConnel, John	1805	730	22 PA	
McConnell, Hans	1855	567	33	England
McConnell, William	1810	204	27 PA	
McCormack, John	1851	1549	22 NY	
McCormick, Allen	1851	1158	24 NY	
McCoy, Daniel	1811	118	25 PA	
McCoy, Peter	1851	1601	24 PA	
McCulley, James	1811	309	21 NJ	
McCurdy, James A.	1810	80	22 MA	
McCutchen,				
Lewis Jones	1818	98	21 VA	
McDonald, David F.	1819	189	23 NY	

Name	Year	No.	Age	Origin
McDonald, William L.	1821	3	20	Jamaica
McDonnell, James	1821	53	48 VA	
McDougall, Robert	1855	457	27 NY	
McDougell, John	1818	1	21 PA	
McDougla, John	1851	1150	19 NY	
McGee, Charles	1804	134	25 PA	
McGee, Chas	1804	333	0	
McGee, Joseph	1855	918	35 PA	
McGinnes, Peter	1855	560	40	Scotland
McGlenning, Edward	1851	25	28 MA	
McGrath, William	1805	936	26 NC	
McGregor, James	1851	1285	19 ME	
McGregor, Robert	1855	414	30 NH	
McIntire, Jesse	1818	131 b	23 NY	
McIntire, Pelletia	1821	95	35 ME	
McIntyre, Francis J.	1855	547	25 NY	
McKee, Alex	1805	746	33	
McKee, John	1804	173	25 DE	
McKeever, Isaac	1806	1462	21 DE	
McKenna, John	1851	1432	23 NY	
McKennon, Francis	1809	260	29 PA	
McKenzie, Donald	1851	8	36 OH	
McKenzie, James	1851	1672	25 NY	
McKenzie, John	1821	61	20 NY	
McKeon, James	1855	318	37 NY	
McKinley, John	1851	1624	27 MA	
McLane, John	1851	1342	25 SC	
McLane, John	1815	19 m	31	St. Doming
McLarron, John	1811	134	40 PA	
McLaughlin, James	1857	89	45 NY	
McLean, Richard	1851	1368	24 NY	
McMichael, Isaac	1821	109	22 DE	
McMin, James	1811	107	26 NY	
McMitchel, James	1821	149	0 MA	
McMullen, Alexander	1851	1555	18 NY	
McMullen, John	1809	320	25 PA	
McNair, Samuel	1804	81	28 PA	
McNear, Baker, II	1855	475	20 ME	
McNeely, Isaac	1821	127	48	Ireland
McNickel, John	1851	1580	35	Ireland
McQue, John	1805	886	28 DE	
McQueen, James	1811	244	27 SC	
McQuen, Rory	1851	1648	23 NY	
Meader, Timothy	1818	50	27 MA	
Medina, Anthony	1805	945	26	
Mefoy, Daniel	1811	193	21 DE	
Megon, Henri	1805	619	22 NY	
Mehegan, George	1855	564	21	Ireland
Meisto, Thomas	1804	31	28 VA	
Mellaerts, Guillaum	1821	140	22	
Mellon, Phillip	1807	371	30 MD	
Melvin, John	1809	275	17 MA	
Menard, Gabriel	1818	272	25	
Merchand, Francis	1807	375	34	Orleans
Meredith, Thomas	1851	1394	27	England
Meridith, James S.	1815	30	17 PA	
Merieult, John Francis	1804	0	0	
Merit, William	1810	133	25 NY	
Merithew, Arleney	1805	792	28 MA	
Merkins, John	1811	80	17 NY	
Merle, Baptist	1805	549	25	
Merle, John	1804	59	0	Orleans
Merriet, William	1804	203	23 NY	
Merritt, William	1811	287	29 PA	
Merry, Nicholas	1812	214	27 LA	
Mesle, Pierre	1818	182 m	32	
Mesponiet, Alexander	1818	263	50	
Messick, Clemons	1815	47	22 DE	
Metcalf, John	1815	199	22 MD	
Meyboom, Christopher	1821	89	19	
Meyer, Charles	1811	89	24 MD	
Meyers, Henry	1812	160	28 PA	
Michaels, Anthony	1815	122	15 PA	
Michel, James	1811	34	30	
Michel, Jean Louis	1804	321	29	
Michel, Joseph	1812	109	29 LA	
Mickel, Peter	1805	865	21 DE	
Middlesex, Perkins	1819	4 n	22 MA	
Mier, Lawrence	1804	111	34	Orleans
Migon, Peter	1810	52	25	
Miguel, Louis	1805	949	29	
Miles, Abner	1806	1487	21 MA	
Miles, Charles	1851	1595	23 NY	
Millar, James	1805	506	21	
Millar, John James	1855	540	45 MA	
Millard, Charles F.	1855	468	22 LA	
Miller, Daniel	1810	258	25 NY	
Miller, Enoch	1805	675	27 MD	
Miller, Frederick	1811	266	34 MD	
Miller, George	1851	1304	29 NY	
Miller, Henry	1810	164	31 NC	
Miller, James	1811	181	28 NY	
Miller, John	1816	13	42 NJ	
Miller, John	1812	190 b	35 MD	
Miller, John	1818	210	33 NY	
Miller, John	1851	1412	31	none given
Miller, John	1809	302	23 VA	
Miller, John	1810	195	32 MA	
Miller, Micheal	1807	349	25 VA	
Miller, William	1855	509	26 PA	
Milliken, F.	1855	221	33 ME	
Millson, John	1809	43	25 NY	
Milton, William	1809	4	22 MA	
Milwright, James	1851	1495	22 NY	
Minitre, John	1804	214	24 MD	
Minor, Richard	1851	1586	32	England
Minor, William	1810	293	21 C	
Minot, Anthony	1810	180	32	Orleans

Name	Year	No.	Age/State	Extra
Minot, Etienne	1805	910	40	
Miske, John	1818	334	30	
Mistoche, Matthew	1805	639	24	Orleans
Mitchele, David	1811	13	30 PA	
Mitchell, Andrew, Jr.	1816	41	30 NY	
Mitchell, Charles	1851	1532	20 PA	
Mitchell, George	1810	65	24 PA	
Mitchell, Isaac	1818	103	18 CT	
Mitchell, Jeremiah	1855	305	16 ME	
Mitchell, John	1811	173	43 NY	
Mitchell, John	1810	42	26 CT	
Mitchell, John	1805	372	20 LA	
Mitchell, John Louis	1810	359	48	
Mitchell, Joseph	1811	286	22 NY	
Mitchell, Nathan	1812	199	26 MA	
Mitchell, Robert	1811	71	0 NH	
Mitchell, Stephen	1810	278	26	
Mitchell, William	1810	121	37 NY	
Mitchell, William	1804	330	26 MA	
Mobeck, Augustin	1806	1594	25	Orleans
Moffatt, John	1819	139	18	England
Moffit, James	1815	241	38	
Mogon, Jean Baptisto	1805	708	32	Orleans
Moie, John	1810	25	21 PA	
Molin, John	1851	1327	19 PA	
Moline, Selzing	1811	250	19 PA	
Monclin, Silvain A.	1819	124	29	
Mondier, Frances	1818	172	24	
Money, William	1851	1316	21 ME	
Monfaun,				
Joseph Merci	1805	429	23 LA	
Monogert, John	1812	29	30	
Monplaisir, Etienne	1815	6	m 22	
Monroe, William	1810	254	31 VA	
Monsherdin, Joseph	1810	352	37	
Montagne, John	1805	993	20	Orleans
Montague, George	1806	1536	b 36 NY	
Monteith, Alexander	1851	1387	25 NY	
Montes, Manuel	1806	1550	33	
Montgomery, amuel	1805	386	20	
Montrose, Nicolas	1812	111	c 27	Orleans
Moodelius, John	1810	284	33	
Moor, James	1816	52	26 NY	
Moore, Ambrose	1806	1421	19 NJ	
Moore, Andrew	1809	304	32 MD	
Moore, Andrew	1851	1413	22 NY	
Moore, Anthony	1818	80	b 28 NY	
Moore, Benjamin	1818	303	28 NY	
Moore, Charles	1855	187	30 NY	
Moore, David	1805	655	21 NH	
Moore, John	1805	860	b 33 PA	
Moore, John	1806	1562	19 MD	
Moore, John	1819	173	26 NC	
Moore, Thomas	1805	630	27 PA	
Moore, Thomas T.	1818	120	21 MD	
Moore, William	1815	93	31 DE	
Moore, William	1815	250	31 NY	
Moors, John	1805	474	25 NJ	
Morales, Anthony	1805	758	22	
Morales, Joseph	1807	364	20	Orleans
Moran, Samuel	1851	1422	23 ME	
Moran, William	1819	126	38 MD	
Morant, Joseph	1805	950	21	
More, William	1809	274	24 PA	
Moreau, Clement	1811	281	31	
Moreau, Peter	1806	1560	32	
Moresco, Francisco	1819	213	29	
Moreto, George	1812	224	20	
Morey, Silvenus	1818	289	33 MA	
Morgan, Ebenezer	1811	120	26 NY	
Morgan, James	1815	99	24 MA	
Morgan, James	1805	812	31 DE	
Morgan, Morgan	1805	811	20 Ma	
Morgan, Patrick	1804	0	0	
Morgan, William P.	1819	130	30 NY	
Morin, Domingo	1805	393	30	
Morin, Peter	1810	303	36	
Morin, Simon	1805	771	27	
Moro, John B.	1809	255	18	Orleans
Moron, William	1815	49	21 MA	
Morrell, Abraham L.	1819	183	26 ME	
Morris, Abraham	1805	842	21 NY	
Morris, Cadet	1805	404	15 PA	
Morris, David E.	1816	48	25 NJ	
Morris, Frank	1855	578	27 NY	
Morris, George	1851	1512	23 ME	
Morris, Hendrick	1811	227	32 DE	
Morris, Leander	1815	5	y 26 NY	
Morris, Nath	1805	662	32 NJ	
Morris, Peter	1809	249	y 20	Orleans
Morris, Robert	1815	112	24 NC	
Morrison, John	1851	1337	27 TX	
Morrison, John	1806	1430	26	
Morrison, Thomas	1851	1388	44 NY	
Morrison, William	1804	104	25 VA	
Morrison, Wm.	1818	164	20 PA	
Morry, Lewis	1815	212	38 MA	
Mors, William	1814	152	23 PA	
Morton, John M.	1812	200	25 NY	
Morton, Samuel	1815	79	29 NY	
Morton, William	1812	127	18 MA	
Moss, Charles	1810	387	26 DE	
Mossop, Joseph	1810	22	33 MA	
Mottran, William	1804	249	19 PA	
Mouchot, Etienne	1809	279	19	Orleans
Mouillie, Pierre	1814	210	24	
Moulente, Peter	1810	169	32	
Moulton, Joseph	1819	122	30 MA	

Mountain, John	1851	1631		29 PA		Newcamp, Philip	1815	247		15 PA
Mountany, Nicholas	1809	267		28 NY		Newell, Francis	1816	61		18 MD
Moutar, John	1812	73		38		Newhall, Augustus	1818	124		15 MA
Mulford, Enos	1857	131		27 NJ		Newhall, George	1855	283		22 MA
Mulharren, John	1805	794		35 PA		Newman, William	1815	113		31 MD
Mumford, James	1851	1550		26 NY		Newton, Albert	1857	130		29 NY
Munn, George	1851	1189		31 MD		Nichol, James	1805	788		21 PA
Murch, Geroge E.	1857	135		23 MA		Nicholas,Christopher	1814	188		26 RI
Murchant, William	1851	1613		22 NY		Nicholas, John	1818	223		36
Murduck, John,Jr.	1815	62		28 PA		Nicholas, John	1805	930		26
Murphy, Daniel	1857	62		17 ME		Nichols, James W.	1855	495		22 ME
Murphy, Joseph	1855	571		33	Ireland	Nichols, Nathaniel	1855	242		45 ME
Murphy, William	1815	39		20 PA		Nicholson, John	1818	321	y	55 MA
Murray, Charles	1855	498		36 MA		Nicholson, John	1805	851		23 NY
Murray, David	1804	251		21 NY		Nicholson, Joseph	1855	255		24 NY
Murray, John	1804	276		21 NY		Nicholson, Philip	1805	833		25 MA
Murray, John	1819	69	m	25 PA		Nickels, Amos	1855	490		20 ME
Murray, John	1818	236		0		Nickerson, David P.	1851	1643		19 MA
Murray, Thomas	1812	87		23 NY		Nickerson, Philip	1804	297		23 MA
Murry, Henry	1851	1538		24 NY		Nickerson, Varanus	1855	533		17 MA
Murry, James	1810	84		19 MD		Nicolas, John	1806	1494		35	Orleans
Murtha, Thomas	1851	1196		17 NJ		Nicolas, Joseph	1810	19		30 PA
Musket, William	1821	40		38 PA		Nicoles, Louis	1814	160		23 LA
Muxo, Joseph	1805	566		30		Nicolls, Stephen B.	1818	167		37 NY
Myatt, Edward	1810	183		21 SC		Nieba, Andres	1805	378		24 LA
Myers, Henry	1821	114		45		Nixon, Jacob	1857	129		25 NJ
Myers, James	1818	108	b	55	Africa	Noble, Anthony	1819	49		50	Corunna
Myers, John	1809	207		28 PA		Noble, Nicholas	1805	446		47
Myers, John	1804	335		21		Noland, Perry	1815	12		39 MD
Nabb, John	1819	157		19 MD		Nordike, Benoni D.	1819	103		23 NJ
Narcissus, Peter	1805	459	b	19 LA		Norman, Elijah	1806	1812		31 MD
Nartisse, John	1811	240		32		Norris, Henry, Jr.	1818	8		22 CT
Naud, Lewis	1804	48		37		Norris, Howes	1811	267		39 MA
Nauran, Peter	1805	605		33		Norton, James	1815	221		14 SC
Navarre, Francois	1821	134		40		Norton, Nathanial	1819	179		28 MA
Nay, John	1812	126		27 PA		Norton, Thomas	1851	1583		25	Ireland
Neafus, William G.	1855	381		17 LA		Norwood, Charles	1804	0		0
Neal, John	1821	137		22 MA		Nott, John C.	1855	488		16 MA
Neally, Saml.	1818	349		27 NH		Nove, Nicholas	1805	988		48
Neil, John	1819	107		17 DC		Novera, Pedro	1805	617		34	Orleans
Neil, Robert	1810	338		29 MA		Nowlan, James	1815	25		22 NY
Neilly, William	1805	868		52 PA		O'Brien, Peter	1855	194		21 MA
Nelder, John	1855	465		32 NJ		O'Connor, Roderick	1805	939		28 MA
Nelson, Charles	1851	1566		22 PA		O'Neill, Daniel	1851	1401		28 NY
Nelson, Mark	1809	37		35 SC		O'Niel, James	1851	1592		25
Nepo, Joseph	1812	161		38 NJ		Oakley, William	1855	444		24 MA
Ner, Geronimo	1806	1478		20	Orleans	Obeix, Jean	1805	409		52
Neto, Francis	1819	234		33	Minorca	Obey, Francis	1805	354		29 LA
Neumayr, James	1804	181		19 MD		Ocano, Anthony	1805	377		26 LA
Nevan, Matthew	1821	11		17 NY		Odiome, John	1818	240		34 MA
Neven, John	1806	1521		42	Orleans	Ogal, John	1805	360		54
Neville, Thomas	1812	104		24 NY		Ogier, Joseph W.	1819	116		23 ME
Newberry, John F.	1818	206		35	Sweden	Ogier, William C.	1851	1518		23 ME
Newby, Miles	1810	6	b	24 PA		Ogilvie, Peter L	1804	95		23 VA

Name	Year	No.	Flag	Age	Place
Ogreda, Joseph	1818	48		37	NY
Olivar, Lorenzo	1806	1523		26	
Olivas, Joachin	1818	280		31	
Olive, John Peter	1818	214		22	
Oliver, David	1857	65		26	ME
Oliver, James	1818	247	b	20	MD
Oliver, John	1815	95		22	NJ
Oliver, John	1810	306		30	
Oliver, Lazarus	1809	211		31	Orleans
Oliver, Theodosia	1805	484		30	
Oliviate, Joseph	1805	612		36	Orleans
Oltmann, Wm.	1851	1326		39	NY
Oneto, Francis	1805	935		26	
Ons, John	1809	310		25	
OReilly, James T.	1851	1602		23	Ireland
Ormea, Nicholas	1810	251		44	
Orne, Josiah, Jr.	1818	260		32	MA
Orsdil, George John	1812	193	b	23	
Ortega, Juan Baptiste	1818	4	y	26	
Ortis, Mariano	1810	126		31	
Osbom, Frederick	1855	438		34	
Osbom, John	1819	153		33	NY
Osbom, Robert	1819	135		31	MA
Oscar, Lewis	1855	451		28	SC
Ottey, Joseph	1815	203		21	CT
Otto, Henry	1805	967		20	PA
Otto, John Gastavus	1805	492		36	RI
Otway, Nicholas	1805	852		21	MD
Owens, Abraham	1804	100		26	NY
Owens, John W.	1851	1151		24	ME
Owens, Joseph	1805	791		24	NH
Owens, Peter	1805	543		25	NY
Owens, Thomas	1819	198	b	24	PA
Pacheco, Joseph	1814	162		29	
Paddison, John	1804	232	b	27	MD
Page, Charles E.	1857	114		19	ME
Page, Henry	1804	312	y	25	
Page, Solomon	1810	20		17	
Page, William	1851	1560		23	MA
Page, William	1855	335		23	ME
Paignand, Joseph	1804	0		0	
Palanque, Mathais	1816	74	m	30	LA
Palao, Antoine	1814	174		24	
Palma, Joachim	1806	1805		23	
Palmer, G. F.	1855	474		35	ME
Palmer, James A.	1815	196		24	CT
Palmer, John	1818	268		29	NY
Palmer, Nicholas	1812	219		34	LA
Palmer, Robert	1818	232		17	NY
Palmer, William	1805	955		26	VA
Palmer, William, Jun.	1821	121		23	NY
Palome, Nicolas	1812	72		36	
Pamneino, Marco	1805	582		30	
Pantof, Nicholas	1812	197		44	SC
Parfait, Rene	1811	104	y	21	
Parfait, Rene	1814	218	y	23	
Paris, Juan Antonio	1805	376		25	LA
Park, John	1819	134		25	PA
Park, Thomas P.	1851	1375		22	MA
Parker, Cornelius	1855	552		18	CT
Parker, George	1855	320		32	NY
Parker, Henry	1815	51		23	NC
Parker, Hugh S.	1814	204		28	VA
Parker, Jacob	1809	315		26	
Parker, James	1851	1345		30	MA
Parker, John	1816	45		21	NH
Parker, Solomon	1811	150		38	CT
Parker, William	1815	126		28	PA
Parker, William	1851	1514		28	PA
Parnell, Frederick	1855	261		21	PA
Parsons, Austin	1811	224		23	MA
Parsons, John	1806	1595		21	CT
Parsons, Samuel	1815	109		33	MA
Parsons, Samuel	1818	197		26	MA
Parsons, Thomas	1818	307		31	PA
Pasaman, Jean	1804	0		0	
Pascale, Francis	1819	205		28	Toulon
Pascole, Joseph	1805	481		25	
Passament, John Baptiste	1804	0		0	
Passano, Manuelde	1821	136		44	
Passerow, William	1815	71		18	MA
Passons, Joseph	1805	984		24	
Patch, John E.	1857	115		19	ME
Paterson, Samuel	1812	43		25	MA
Patey, Philip	1819	40		26	MA
Patrick, Timothy	1804	142		56	VA
Patron, Francis	1805	461		30	
Patte, Peter	1805	820		36	
Patten, Parker	1857	106		18	ME
Patterson, John	1805	467		29	NY
Patterson, John	1821	115		34	NH
Patterson, Joseph	1815	70		12	LA
Patterson, Robert	1807	355		33	PA
Patterson, Thomas	1809	17		39	NY
Patterson, William	1804	133		21	SC
Patton, Robert	1818	37		42	LA
Patton, Thomas	1805	629		20	PA
Patton, William	1805	423		24	NY
Pauachie, Pascal	1805	643		33	
Paul, Jeremiah	1811	158		33	Italy
Paul, Juan	1811	124		23	Orleans
Paulin, George	1818	227		23	LA
Payne, Joseph	1851	1617		24	MA
Payne, Richard	1818	81		33	NY
Peabody, George W.	1819	176		19	
Peace, Thomas	1806	1540		0	
Peachy, William	1857	96		52	ME

Name	Year	No.		Age/State		Name	Year	No.		Age/State	
Pearse, William	1811	156		27 NY		Peters, Anthony	1812	53		23 MA	
Pearson, Henry	1818	279		42 DE		Peters, John	1810	253		30 PA	
Pease, Francis	1815	275		24 MA		Peters, John,	1818	56		29 LA	
Peck, David	1818	342		22 NJ		Peters, Nathan	1812	45		20 NJ	
Peck, Lyman	1811	66		19 MA		Peters, Peter	1821	7		21 CT	
Pedrick, James	1804	109		16 NC		Peterson, Andrew	1805	864		34 VA	
Pedro, Michael	1805	526		28		Peterson, David	1809	308	b	23 NY	
Peince, John	1811	298		28 MD		Peterson, John	1809	288		28	
Peirce, George P.	1816	70		28 MA		Peterson, John	1805	722		24 RI	
Peirce, Stephen	1804	45		20 RI		Peterson, John	1811	223		30 NY	
Pelas, Antoine	1805	450		18		Peterson, Nicolas	1809	212		51 PA	
Pelegrin,JohnBaptiste	1805	350		30		Peterson, Peter	1810	389		29 NY	
Pelicier, John	1811	60		43		Peterson, Thomas	1812	192		30 MA	
Pell, John	1815	12	m	24 CT		Peterson, William	1815	257		23 PA	
Pelman, David	1818	284		27 NY		Peterson, William	1812	195		28 NY	
Pender, Henry	1814	164		19 NJ		Petis, John	1805	405		24 VT	
Peney, Simon	1810	167		53 MA		Petit, Honore	1807	395	y	17	Orleans
Penn, William	1815	272		38 PA		Petre, Jean Francois	1812	55		24	
Penn, William	1815	81		38 PA		Peustis, Francis	1805	883		28	
Peno, Francis	1805	394		25 LA		Phenix, John	1815	101		32 NY	
Penson, John	1851	1182		20 NY		Philipe, Bernardo	1819	232		39	
Pepper, Knowles	1806	1445		33 MA		Philippe, Laban	1811	220		24 MD	
Perarra, Manuel	1807	352		25		Philips, Richard	1851	1377		33 NY	
Percy, Henry	1855	281		20 KY		Phillimore, James	1851	1644		35 MA	
Peres, John	1819	162		36		Phillips, Benjamin	1855	531		19 MA	
Perez, Anthony	1809	227		45		Phillips, Bertrand	1815	68		32	
Perez, Antonio	1811	297		16		Phillips, James D.	1851	1572		14 NY	
Perez, Antorni	1812	162		39		Phillips, James D.	1851	1398		42 NY	
Perez, Bernardo	1805	719		21	Orleans	Phillips, John	1821	65		31 NJ	
Perez, John	1805	834		21		Phillips, John	1812	120	b	25 PA	
Perez, John	1805	836		30		Phillips, Pierre	1818	230		26	
Perez, Ramon	1818	110		20 LA		Phillips, Robert F.	1857	139		17 MA	
Perin, Peter Gabriel	1810	376		30	Orleans	Phillips, Thomas	1819	47		21 MA	
Perkins, Asher	1821	38		35 CT		Phillips, William	1811	257		35 NY	
Perkins, Harry	1819	169		21 MA		Phillips, William	1810	231		33 NY	
Perkins, John	1810	408		20	Orleans	Piacentiny, Giuseppe	1810	240		26	
Peron, Peter	1804	289	m	15	Orleans	Picaluga, Anthony	1819	14		35	
Perry, Joseph	1815	75		32 LA		Picar, Antonio	1810	70		32	Orleans
Perry, Samuel	1811	90	b	22 MD		Pickens, Daniel	1804	191		17 MA	
Perry, Stephen	1819	93		24 MA		Pierce, Earl	1818	176		19 MA	
Perry, Thomas Bates	1855	176		33 NY		Pierce, Henry A.	1855	311		25 MA	
Perry, William	1811	105		21		Pierce, James	1815	158		29 MD	
Persons, Absolam	1810	10	y	22 RI		Pierce, Peter	1818	299		31 NH	
Peter, John	1810	262		26	Orleans	Piersons, John	1821	113		20 ME	
Peter, John	1805	418		21		Pile, John	1818	328		23 MA	
Peter, John	1804	147		27		Pilot, Anthony	1810	53		22	
Peter, John	1805	608	b	35		Pimontel, Manuel	1812	39		0	
Peter, Joseph	1805	576		26		Pinatel,AntoineLazard	1811	127		49	
Peter, Joseph	1810	378		32		Pinder, John	1810	343		25 NY	
Peter, Manuel	1806	1510		23	Orleans	Pinkney, Josiah	1818	18		0	
Peter, Peter	1805	607	c	19		Pinlotz, John	1805	389		24 LA	
Peter, Phillip	1805	478		20 LA		Pino, Peter	1805	880		31	
Peter, Simon John	1805	527	b	22		Pinto, Antonio	1805	622		26	
Peters, Albert	1851	1511		48 ME		Pinto, John	1805	637		25	

Name	Year	No.	b/m	Age	Place
Pintro, Antonio	1805	799		25	
Piscay, Charles W.	1855	466		24 FL	
Pitre, Thomas	1805	638		27	
Platt, George	1812	12		31 MD	
Plumb, Daniel	1806	1586		27 MA	
Plumby, George	1855	190		46 MA	
Plumer, James	1818	202		24 GA	
Plummer, James	1806	1480		16 NY	
Polistina,AnthonyRoco	1809	281		27	
Polk, Antonio	1805	498		22	Orleans
Poll, John	1804	180		19	
Pollard,WilliamJames	1815	237		20 VA	
Polliner, Joseph	1806	1483	b	17	Orleans
Pollock, Thomas	1805	943		22	
Polou, Louis Joseph	1815	44		26	
Pomard, JohnMaturin	1805	628		23	
Pomet, Leonards	1818	186		0	
Ponson, John	1805	712		13	Orleans
Poole, Edward	1818	133		30 PA	
Poole, John	1811	233	b	21 RI	
Poole, Laurens W.	1855	346		21 ME	
Poole, Samuel G.	1815	210		20 MA	
Pope, Frederick	1812	60		20 MA	
Pope, Isaac	1805	724		44	
Poppoche, John	1810	384		38	
Porche, John	1818	352		25	
Porie, Charles	1809	230		28	Orleans
Porter, Isaac	1809	208		22 MA	
Porter, Joseph	1818	340		25 MD	
Porter, Peter	1816	19		27 MD	
Porter, Thomas	1811	310		21 NY	
Porter, Thomas	1811	263		33	
Portz, George	1851	1338		24 NY	
Posey, James	1818	44	m	27 VA	
Posole, John	1806	1818		0	Orleans
Poterin, Daniel	1804	196		26	
Potier, All Saints	1805	468		38	
Potter, Howard	1805	424		25 CT	
Potter, Thomas Jefferson	1815	276		15 RI	
Potter, Vinces	1811	18		35 SC	
Potter, Wm. E.	1855	420		22 MA	
Potter, Zelas	1819	143	b	28 RI	
Poulain, Louis	1814	139		16	
Pounell, John	1811	28		27 VA	
Pousset, Toussain	1805	479		38	Orleans
Powell,PeterEusebius	1851	1415		21 NY	
Power, Pierce	1851	1507		23 MA	
Power, William	1804	123		21 PA	
Powers, David	1805	965		39	
Pradel, Jean	1819	193		29	
Prado, Manuel	1805	493		25	Orleans
Prats, Joseph	1805	563		23	
Pray, William Fernald	1855	195		32 ME	
Prean, John	1806	1489		17 NY	
Prentis, Lodowick	1818	105		30 CT	
Pretely, Maximilien	1805	684		18	Orleans
Preve, Joseph	1816	98		29	
Prevost, Francois	1806	1556		26	
Price, Bernard	1810	302		33 SC	
Price, John	1819	29		0 MA	185
Price, John	1819	185		29 MA	
Price, John	1851	1479		26 PA	
Price, Samuel	1809	214		0 VA	
Price, Thomas E.	1819	58		21 MD	
Prieto, Andrew	1805	621		24	
Pritchard, Elias	1812	230		38 PA	
Pritchard, James	1811	254		28 PA	
Proeda, Peter	1805	667		28	
Provatons, Antoine	1814	197		56	
Provatore, Nicol	1810	355		50	
Prudent, Julien	1804	75		0	
Prudent, Julien	1804	75		0	
Pugol, Raimond	1818	330		45 LA	
Pumarino, Bernabe	1806	1467		0	
Purnell, Thomas	1811	269		27 MD	
Pursell, Archibald	1814	199		20 NC	
Putman, John	1851	1497		19 MA	
Quackenbush,William	1812	65		32 NY	
Quagen, George	1815	274		22 PA	
Quarice, Peter	1806	1814		33	Orleans
Quen, Michael	1819	18		21 PA	
Quere, John	1806	1532		24	
Quernier, Augustin	1818	76		54	France
Questiz, John	1807	413		27	
Quidiniae, Jean	1805	490		27	Orleans
Quillet, James H.	1851	1515		0 NY	
Quinbero, Jose	1805	603		36	Orleans
Quinlan, Thomas	1851	1567		26 MA	
Quinn, Malachi	1855	568		28	Ireland
Quinones JohnBaptiste	1804	315		22	Orleans
Quinot, Pierre	1812	174		30	
Quintane, Francis	1805	650		27	
Quinton, Thomas	1851	1436		24 PA	
Rabasson, John	1814	159		18 LA	
Rabaya, Benoit	1811	277		30	
Racy, John	1805	600		36 NY	
Radish, Antonio	1805	610		48	
Raffaille, Nicholas	1805	449		48	
Rafit, Bernard	1806	1485		36	Orleans
Rafo, Thomas	1811	92		25	
Ragor, Burket	1804	147		21 PA	
Raiba, Phillip	1807	344		28	
Raine, William	1807	340		22 PA	
Rains, Charles	1812	220		31 NH	
Rambo, Gabriel	1805	956		37 NJ	
Rameris, Joseph	1805	765		22	
Ramiras, Joseph	1805	728		22	

Name	Year	No.		Age	Place	Name	Year	No.		Age	Place
Ramsey, David C.	1818	155		23	CT	Reynolds, James	1811	308		25	VA
Randall, Wm. A.	1855	437		21	ME	Rhen, John	1805	451		26	
Randell, John Martin	1804	241		30		Rhodes, John R.	1821	117		20	CT
Raney, William	1811	202		29	MA	Rhodes, William	1805	555		24	NY
Ranier, George	1810	351		28		Riba, Agustin	1805	841		35	
Rassell, William H.	1851	1435		28	NY	Riba, Sebastian	1805	946		18	
Rati, Paul	1818	143		33		Ribas, Manuel	1805	838		25	
Raura, Rogue	1805	401		20		Rice, William	1812	20		11	MA
Ravenscroft, William	1804	259		19	KY	Richard, John	1812	23		0	
Rawson, George	1811	256		25	MA	Richards, John	1810	308		24	Orleans
Ray, Isaac	1821	50	y	0	NJ	Richards, Joseph	1815	132		21	SC
Ray, Will	1805	726		27	PA	Richards, William	1819	19		18	NY
Ray, William	1804	125		18	PA	Richards, William	1804	79		28	MA
Raymond, Jasent	1805	931		28		Richardson, Fisher	1806	1446		35	MA
Raymond, Jean	1812	50		22		Richardson, Henry	1851	1483		38	MA
Raymond, John	1805	974		20	Orleans	Richardson, John	1805	815		29	PA
Raymond, Pierre	1810	203		18	Orleans	Richet, Peter	1804	53		25	Orleans
Rea, William	1815	217		23	RI	Richmond, Samuel	1851	1351		23	NY
Read,JosephAgustus	1855	224		28	MA	Richmore, David	1805	829		24	NY
Redden, Paul	1821	58		50	Sweden	Richter, John	1811	327		49	
Reddon, Hiram L.	1855	550		22	PA	Rickards, John	1851	1386		21	MA
Redick, Samuel	1805	797		47	PA	Rickes, Charles	1851	1310		30	ME
Redmond, James	1811	41		28	MA	Ricks, William	1811	52		30	NY
Redonda, Dominick	1806	1593		51		Ride, Francis	1804	273		27	NY
Reed, Hawes Y.	1855	343		29	ME	Rideout, Rodman D.	1851	1361		23	ME
Reed, Jesse	1815	15	b	15	MA	Riere, Peter	1805	530		20	
Reed, John	1855	277		26	PA	Riley, John	1851	1404		21	England
Reed, John	1810	407		0		Rimker, Alexir	1804	290		18	
Reed, John	1804	220		38	RI	Ringent, John	1807	354		38	
Reed, Payson	1857	113		22	ME	Riordan, Michael	1855	562		31	England
Reed, Robert	1851	1540		30	NC	Riou, Francis	1810	302		33	
Reed, Washington	1812	176		19	PA	Ripley, Henry	1818	361		15	NY
Rees, William	1821	45		36	MD	Rivar, Andrea	1806	1532		18	Orleans
Rees, William	1804	154		27	PA	Rivera, Joseph	1805	835		35	IL
Reight(Wright),Bristol	1805	904	b	28	VA	Rivero, Pedro	1818	193		28	LA
Reiley, John	1855	483		35	PA	Rivierre, Joseph	1811	260		27	
Reilly, Patrick	1855	563		20	Ireland	Roach, Samuel	1805	863		15	NY
Reily, George	1818	188		0		Robb, Charles	1851	1449		23	NY
Reines, Peter	1805	649		24		Robbins, Thomas	1821	42		32	MA
Remon, Jasinte	1807	382		27		Robbins, William	1804	264		20	SC
Renal, Joseph	1812	141	m	23	LA	Robbinson, George	1851	1653		24	MA
Renand, John	1815	37		36		Robens, George	1805	340		28	MA
Renauld, John	1804	250		27	Orleans	Robert, Jean Louis	1814	144		36	
Rengrose, John	1804	42		32	PA	Robert, John	1804	240		29	
Renier, Auguste	1815	3	y	23	LA	Robert, Joseph	1805	362		24	LA
Renoullauz, Jacques	1807	323		30	Orleans	Robert, Nicholas	1809	240		17	
Renstrom, Johnan	1819	99		28	MA	Robert, Pierre	1818	238		34	
Requis, James	1815	211		45		Roberts, Charles	1804	302		21	VA
Revelle, John Louis	1810	214	m	26	New Orlean	Roberts, James	1855	555		23	NewBrunswk
Reveson, John	1810	57		34	Orleans	Roberts,JamesJones	1818	83		18	CT
Rey, Charles	1851	1543		19	NY	Roberts, John	1811	175		23	PA
Rey, John A.	1812	215		23	Ny	Roberts, John	1804	231		19	MD
Rey, Ramon	1810	250		40		Roberts, John	1810	110		33	MA
Reynal, John	1805	927		42		Roberts, John	1810	98		22	SC

Roberts, Joshua	1809	232		25 MA	
Roberts, Peter	1851	1476		22 PA	
Roberts, William	1818	325		25 MA	
Roberts, William	1851	1685		55 MA	
Robertson, James	1815	26	b	15 PA	
Robertson, James	1806	1431		42	
Robertson, James	1805	546	m	19 NY	
Robertson, John	1807	330		43 CT	
Robertson, Thomas	1818	218		29 MA	
Robeson, James	1851	1557		22 MA	
Robins, Charles	1857	120		26	Canada
Robinson, Abner	1810	166		20 MA	
Robinson, Charles	1815	269		14 PA	
Robinson, Charles H.	1851	1179		36 MA	
Robinson, Daniel	1855	342		47 MA	
Robinson, Francis	1821	47	m	13 VA	
Robinson, Henry	1804	148		27 NY	
Robinson, James	1818	88	m	38 SC	
Robinson, James	1815	24		30 CT	
Robinson, Jaques	1812	101		21	
Robinson, John	1819	66		25 VA	
Robinson, John	1804	227		21 MD	
Robinson, Joseph	1815	19		25 MA	
Robinson, Richard	1851	6		23 NY	
Robinson, Samuel	1816	49		17 RI	
Robinson, Samuel	1805	616		0 SC	
Robinson, Silas	1815	27	m	32 NC	
Robinson, Thomas	1815	242		18 NY	
Robinson, William	1851	1528		21 CT	
Robinson, YoungLove	1806	1808		22 NJ	
Roch, Edmand	1851	1675		25 NY	
Roch, Joseph	1805	658		36	
Roch, Joseph	1805	589		30	Orleans
Rochar, Thomas	1805	754		26	Orleans
Roche, Juan	1805	731		46	
Roche, Pierre	1806	1535		15	
Rocher, Peter	1805	383		20 LA	
Rocket, Andrew	1810	217		20	
Rockwood, Amos	1810	205		25 CT	
Roco, Phillis	1805	364		40 LA	
Rode, William	1818	102		0 MD	
Roderick, Peter	1804	288		20	
Rodgers, John	1851	1520		23 MD	
Rodgers, John	1851	1690		19 NY	
Rodgrigues, Antonil	1818	201		21 LA	
Rodier, James	1805	471		51 LA	
Rodney, John	1818	216		38 PA	
Rodolph, John	1815	63		22 PA	
Rodrick, Joseph	1810	157		30	Orleans
Rodrigues, Anthony	1805	553		23	
Rodrigues, Antonio	1805	718		40	Orleans
Rodrigues, Peter	1811	235		24	
Rodriguez, Firmin	1810	55		26	
Rodriguez, Ignacio	1809	220		37	

Rodriguez, Jose Antonio	1810	271		31	
Rodriguez, Joseph	1812	0		34	
Rodriguez, Simon	1812	163		26	
Roe, Isaac H.	1818	237		19 NY	
Roffatte, Francisco	1811	238		30	
Roger, John Batiste	1806	1582		28	Orleans
Roger, Louis	1805	704		25	Orleans
Rogers, Ami	1851	1440		47 NY	
Rogers, Andrew S.	1815	106		29 MA	
Rogers, Asa	1818	10		30 NY	
Rogers, Daniel	1805	691		23 NY	
Rogers, Edward	1818	265		17 OH	
Rogers, Francis	1811	24		21 RI	
Rogers, Philip	1804	166		31 NY	
Rogers, William	1806	1517		23 PA	
Roget, PatrickCharles	1818	256		20	
Rogue, James	1805	866		22	
Rogue, Michel	1812	80		34	
Roker, William	1805	411		19	
Roland, Francis	1805	368		25	
Roland, Francis	1807	321		26	
Roland, Vinzan	1811	206		22	
Role, Thomas	1804	61		32 NY	
Roles, John	1818	23		25	
Rolet, Francis	1804	256		39	
Rolfe, Richard H.	1811	152		34 NY	
Rolland, Peter	1805	528		23	
Roman, John	1806	1559		30	
Romanek, John F.	1809	257		33	Orleans
Rommior, Michel	1810	179		30	
Roncey, LouisThomas	1810	184		40	
Rosa, John	1805	366		28	
Rosacrantz, Phillip	1810	229	b	28	
Rose, David W.	1851	1423		30 OH	
Rose, Henry	1857	96		31 OH	
Rose, Jacob	1855	223		21 NY	
Rose, James	1815	131		44 RI	
Rose, William	1851	1379		20 MA	
Rose, William	1804	72		26 NY	
Roseberry, George	1806	1457	y	28	Orleans
Rosetto, Peter	1855	453		22	none given
Rosillon, Anthony	1805	923		39	
Rosin, Peter	1811	291		0	
Ross, Benjamin F.	1811	108		0 RI	
Ross, Daniel	1815	120		25 PA	
Ross, Daniel	1821	88		22 MA	
Ross, John	1855	315		20 NY	
Ross, Joseph	1821	138		21 LA	
Ross, William	1851	1667		21 NY	
Rossetter, David	1815	255		21 CT	
Roswell, Charles	1815	14	b	23 NH	
Roussel, Louis	1816	92		45	
Rousset, Jean	1805	550		25	

Name	Year	No.		Age/Place	
Rousset, Joseph	1805	438		16	
Roux, Joseph	1811	93		46	
Rowan, Samuel W.	1815	46		26 TN	
Rowe, Moses	1811	65		26 NH	
Rowland, Thomas	1857	98		22 NY	
Rowley, James	1818	67		23 VA	
Rowley, James	1816	39		0	
Rubin, Yves Joseph	1816	93		30 LA	
Rudd, Saml.	1806	1455		22 NY	
Ruddock, John	1804	254		23 MA	
Rudolph, Benjamin	1804	228		25 PA	
Rudolph, John	1811	86		23 VA	
Ruos, Jose	1809	218		31	
Rushet, John	1805	896		33	
Russel, George	1811	10		22 NJ	
Russel, Joseph	1805	929		27	
Russell, John	1806	1477		23 NY	
Russell, John	1851	1522		23 NY	
Russell, Joseph	1808	28		24	
Russell, Robert	1819	90		22 VA	
Russell, Samuel	1815	142		25 NY	
Rutten, Richard	1855	463		27 MA	
Ryan, John	1818	337		39 NY	
Ryan, Michael	1819	180		19 NY	
Ryrie, James L.	1855	422		28 MA	
Ryrie, James S.	1855	275		28 MA	
Sadler, Isaac	1810	249	y	27 MD	
Sadler, Lewis	1804	160		22 MD	
Sadler, Thomas	1819	137		23 PA	
Sadler, William	1816	40		20 NY	
Sadler, William	1815	111		32 MD	
Saget, Auguste	1811	29		21	Louisiana
Sahn, Dominick	1805	356		24	
Salas, Anthoy	1805	784		40	
Salgado, Miguel	1807	411		40	Orleans
Salisbury, Daniel	1810	14		37 RI	
Salsburg, John	1821	36		34 NY	
Salter, Richard	1815	141		24 NY	
Sampson, John	1806	1441	b	21 MD	
Sampson, Thomas	1818	355	m	31 VA	
Sanches, Joseph	1805	367		22	
Sanchez, Joseph Anthony	1806	1464		40	Orleans
Sanchez, Peter	1810	88		22	
Sanders, Isaac	1855	339		22 MA	
Sanders, Jacob	1805	661		22 RI	
Sanderson, Aaron	1819	177		24 MA	
Sanderson, Benjamin	1818	148		13 MA	
Sanderson, Joseph	1819	178		22 MA	
Sandmessur, George	1818	305		42	
Sans, Pedro	1818	93		41	
Santos, Pedro	1812	38		25	
Sapia, Giovani	1805	685		21	Orleans
Sassanis, Antonio	1805	413		29	
Saunier, Peter	1812	48	m	25	
Sauvage, Laurent	1812	84		24	Orleans
Savage, Aaron R.	1815	168		21 CT	
Savage, William	1855	224		38 VA	
Savage, William W.	1855	274		26 CT	
Savere, Lawrence	1805	504		53	Orleans
Savery, William	1816	16		25 MA	
Sawnddry, John	1815	83		21 MA	
Sawtell, Hollis	1815	22		24 MA	
Scannell, Edward	1855	469		23 MA	
Schneidan, G. A.	1857	94		16 LA	
Scipion, Pierre	1810	353		0	
Scott, Alexander	1815	154		23 NY	
Scott, Henry	1811	189		21 MD	
Scott, James	1815	153		29 MA	
Scott, James	1809	40	y	43 VA	
Scott, John	1818	195		32 MA	
Scott, Joseph	1851	1274		23 NY	
Scott, Louies	1851	1206		24 MD	
Scott, Robert	1855	452		40	Sweden
Scour, Peter	1804	97		42 PA	
Seaman, Prince	1815	28	n	25 NY	
Searcy, Archibald	1810	185		28 NC	
Searle, George	1851	1557		27 NY	
Seely, Charles	1855	435		28 NY	
Seguin, Constantine	1805	986		44	
Segure, Guillauinine	1807	326		33	
Seiders, Joseph H.	1857	61		21 ME	
Seines, Joseph	1810	31		33 NH	
Seldon, Wilson Carcy	1811	320	b	22 MD	
Semony, Jacob	1809	323		18 MD	
Semson, Joseph	1815	202		28 MA	
Sena, Joseph	1805	660		32	
Senter, Prince	1805	795	b	32 NJ	
Sequin, John	1816	33	b	12 NY	
Serche, Vincent	1810	206		38	
Serreng, Antoine	1815	45		52	
Sewell, John	1810	235		21 MD	
Sewens, Thomas	1819	22	b	28 MD	
Seymour, Joseph	1810	294		18 MA	
Shaddle, John	1815	48		22 NY	
Shalmer, Jacob	1810	71		34	
Shanks, Solomon	1819	119		25 NY	
Shapley, Albert	1819	141		12 NH	
Sharon, William	1805	355		25 PA	
Shaw, Charles	1819	10	b	22 MA	
Shaw, Eben A.	1855	518		21 ME	
Shaw, Isaiah	1809	21		27 NJ	
Shaw, Leonard D.	1821	44		18 ME	
Shaw, William	1816	31		23 NH	
Shawman, John	1812	180		20 PA	
Sheafe, Augustus W.	1816	43		16 NH	
Shearwood, Stephen	1807	347		30 NY	
Shedford, William	1805	433	b	46 NY	

Sheerson, William	1855	455		19 NY		
Sheffield, Robert	1810	12	b	20 RI		
Sheper, Henry	1815	110		21 MD		
Sheperd, John	1815	187		19 MA		
Shepherdson, Elijah	1810	290		22 RI		
Shepperd, James	1851	1398		0 NY		
Sherburn, Henry	1821	52		20 NH		
Sherer, John L.	1855	337		23 PA		
Sheridan, James	1809	39		23 MD		
Sheriff, Geroge	1810	152		21 NY		
Sherondel,						
Etienne Robert	1805	344		32		
Sherwin, Edward	1805	891		35 NY		
Shives, Alexander	1818	158	m	32 SC		
Shorpley, Samuel	1855	551		27 VA		
Short, James	1812	143	b	30 MD		
Shorter, Jesse	1811	91	b	30 MA		
Shurlock, Simond	1851	1571		32	Ireland	
Sibley, Horace	1818	292		20 MA		
Sicara, Bartholomew	1804	239		23		
Sicard, Bart Solomon	1810	400		23		
Sicared, Nazawe	1805	590		26	Orleans	
Siffas, Richard	1819	25	b	38 MA		
Siglton, Benjamin	1811	301		23 NJ		
Sigueras, Salvador	1805	561		20		
Sikolfield, Curtis	1851	1421		28 ME		
Silliman,						
Joseph Ashbourn	1815	193		14 PA		
Silva, Joseph	1818	36		22		
Silvera, Benito	1805	654		0		
Silvestue, Jauque	1810	356		52		
Sim, William	1810	56		21 MD		
Simkins, John	1812	77		21 MD		
Simmons, Nicholas	1805	882		55 MD		
Simmons, William	1818	9	b	28 NY		
Simms, Mearian	1814	153		28 NC		
Simms, Thomas	1809	263		32 MD		
Simo, Jose	1807	322		30		
Simon, Nicolas	1805	508		51		
Simon, Peter	1819	91		39 NY		
Simonton, George	1810	123		26 MA		
Simpson, Andrew L.	1819	108		18 NH		
Simpson, John	1815	225		30 NC		
Simpson, John	1855	178		33 RI		
Simpson, John	1807	342	y	24 SC		
Simpson, William	1814	167		19 MD		
Sinat, Paul	1809	42		26 NY		
Sinclair, Alexander	1804	316		40 SC		
Sinclair, William	1855	459		34	Ireland	
Sineo, Joseph	1809	210		40	Orleans	
Singleton, John	1804	221		36 PA		
Sinnott, Wm.	1855	236		23 NY		
Sinton, Adam	1810	210		29 MA		
Sisson, Silas S.	1815	263		14 NY		
Skidmore, Henry	1851	1340		40 VA		
Slater, James	1812	183		49 NY		
Slater, William	1812	182		12 NY		
Sleezeman, John	1805	465		24 PA		
Sloan, William	1812	76		26 PA		
Small, Elyah W.	1855	532		21 MA		
Small, Geo. W.	1855	496		37 ME		
Small, Isaac Stillman	1819	33		20 MA		
Small, Sanford P.	1855	449		27 ME		
Smith, Allen	1805	732		25 RI		
Smith, Andrew	1810	142		20 MD		
Smith, Andrew	1811	72		31 MA		
Smith, Andrew	1851	1642		16 MA		
Smith, C.	1855	310		22 RI		
Smith, Charles	1855	557		20		Germany
Smith, Charles	1807	406		24 MA		
Smith, Charles F.	1855	507		22 NY		
Smith, Edw. W.	1855	177		25 MD		
Smith, Edward	1855	566		22 NY		
Smith, Edward	1851	1498		19 PA		
Smith, Edward	1804	183		23 NY		
Smith, Elihu	1811	268		42 CT		
Smith, Frederick R.	1851	1565		24 PA		
Smith, George	1815	58		23 MD		
Smith, George	1851	1378		22 MA		
Smith, George	1804	861		29		US
Smith, George W.	1857	137		16 NY		
Smith, Henry	1818	308		29 MD		
Smith, Henry W.	1804	32		21 MA		
Smith, Isaac	1804	802		34		US
Smith, Jacob	1804	199		22 PA		
Smith, James	1806	1453		16 SC		
Smith, James	1807	396		18 DE		
Smith, James	1851	1691		21 NY		
Smith, James	1814	166		21 RI		
Smith, James	1815	183		29 MA		
Smith, John	1814	184		66 NJ		
Smith, John	1812	66		24 MD		
Smith, John	1815	134		22 MA		
Smith, John	1815	165		21 NY		
Smith, John	1815	223		31 SC		
Smith, John	1818	224		24		
Smith, John	1819	7		27		
Smith, John	1819	224		33 MD		
Smith, John	1821	67		36		
Smith, John	1851	1442		25 MD		
Smith, John	1851	1207		30 MA		
Smith, John	1851	1374		28 PA		
Smith, John	1851	1200		25 NY		
Smith, John	1810	30		24 NY		
Smith, John	1810	145		35 NY		
Smith, John	1809	234		24 VA		
Smith, John	1804	236	y	24 VA		
Smith, John A.	1855	338		22 VA		

Name	Year	No.		Age	Place	Name	Year	No.		Age	Place
Smith, Joseph	1851	1191		29 LA		Stackpole, Thos.	1818	187		30	Portugal
Smith, Josiah	1851	1393		21 MA		Stacy, William	1804	234		25 MA	
Smith, Peter W.	1819	144		24 NY		Staddard, George W.	1821	21		25 CT	
Smith, Robert	1804	206		24 PA		Stafford, David	1818	136		21 MD	
Smith, Samuel	1805	370		36 LA		Stafford, Richard A.	1806	1444		22 VA	
Smith, Samuel	1810	109		0		Stallman, William	1810	373		33	
Smith, Samuel	1810	291		20 MA		Stanfield, Thomas	1812	81		24 PA	
Smith, Samuel	1810	0		45	Madiera	Stanley, F. H.	1851	1568		25 NY	
Smith, Samuel	1815	40		26 MA		Stanley, William W.	1809	29		21 RI	
Smith, Scipio	1812	117	b	26 MD		Stannard, William F.	1855	427		22 CT	
Smith, Thomas	1851	1511		23 GA		Stanton, Christopher	1815	152		20 CT	
Smith, Thomas	1851	1496		26 PA		Stanton, William	1810	76		19 MD	
Smith, Thomas	1818	360		23 PA		Stanwood, Anasa O.	1855	280		28 ME	
Smith, Thomas	1855	340		23 PA		Staples, Thomas	1815	227		21 MA	
Smith, William	1851	1409		29 NY		Starke, Charles	1804	201		0 CT	
Smith, William	1851	1384		29 NY		Starkwether, Caleb	1815	206		28 VT	
Smith, William	1818	233		24 NY		Starr, Joseph	1810	94		35 CT	
Smith, William	1815	155		29 NY		Stawell, George	1811	20		27 PA	
Smith, William	1815	171		25 NY		Steed, Richard	1851	1525		23 NY	
Smith, William	1810	301		24		Steele, John	1815	124		21 MD	
Smith, William	1809	32		26 NY		Stemman, John	1855	209		23	Sweden
Smith, William	1810	108		21 NY		Stephens, Alexander	1811	33		29	Orleans
Smith, William H.	1855	308		31 NY		Stephens, Andrew	1805	881		26 PA	
Smith, Wm.	1855	430		21 MA		Stephens, Samuel	1806	1438		25 MA	
Snow, Henry P.	1851	1373		21 MA		Stephenson,John, Jr.	1819	60		29 CT	
Snow, William	1810	317		28 MA		Stephnsen,Ferdinand	1805	379		30 VA	
Snowden, John	1812	124		28 PA		Sterett, James	1804	318		18 KY	
Sober, John	1805	656		45		Sterrett, David H.	1821	43		19 MD	
Sobruasa,DonSt.Fago	1812	0		29 LA		Stetson, John	1811	110		18 MA	
Souly, Peter	1805	371		28 LA		Stevens, Abel	1805	749		24 MA	
Southwood, Thomas	1805	919		21		Stevens, Edward	1851	1612		31 NY	
Souty, Duroc	1810	233		25		Stevens, George	1815	198		38 PA	
Soyer, Theodore	1804	55		20	Orleans	Stevens, Jacob	1819	231	y	29 NY	
Spalding, Ralph B.	1815	151		22 MD		Stevens, John	1815	229		19 VA	
Spalter, George	1809	15		21 PA		Stevens, Peter	1811	78		25 PA	
Sparks, Robert	1819	1		0 PA		Stevens, Thomas	1818	364		23 MA	
Sparrow, James	1809	321	b	14 VA		Stevenson, Charles	1815	11	m	18 NY	
Spears, John	1805	849		27 PA		Stevenson, James	1851	1156		38 NT	
Speed, Amos	1815	91		20 MA		Stevenson, Thomas	1855	186		35 MA	
Spence, Henry	1851	1199		31		Stevenson, Thomas	1851	1478		23 NY	
Spence, John	1815	16	b	34 CT		Stewart, Charles	1851	1396		21 NY	
Spence, John	1805	671	b	45		Stewart, John	1851	1561		22 NY	
Spencer, Jesse	1819	195		18 DE		Stewart, John	1805	458		22 NY	
Spencer, John	1818	301		21 PA		Stewart, Thomas	1804	327		20 NY	
Spencer, Will.	1818	22		0 NY		Stewart, William K.	1807	346		21 NY	
Spiers, Abraham	1809	291	b	42 DE		Stickney, Peter O.	1821	72		21 NH	
Spooner, Azariah	1807	327		27 MA		Still, Charles R.	1805	805		25 MD	
Sprague, Henry	1818	100		30 MA		Stimble, Daniel	1815	270		25 PA	
Springer, Jacob	1818	156		24 MA		Stine, Shadrack	1855	458		39	
Squin, Ephriam	1818	316	y	30 MA		Stiner, Abraham	1804	144		24 PA	
Squires, Abner	1855	273		23 NY		Stitson, Sameul	1815	201		27 MA	
Squires, Charles E.	1855	272		26 NY		Stock, George	1821	57		34 NY	
St. Paul, Henry	1806	1566		0		Stockdale, Thomas	1815	218		45 MD	
Stacey, Job	1819	115		32 MA		Stoddard,EbenezerM.	1855	494		21 CT	

Name	Year	No.	Age		Origin
Stone, George	1851	1614	21 NY		
Stone, John F.	1855	226	17 ME		
Stoodley, Joseph	1819	65	52 MA		
Stoodley, Lewis, Jr.	1818	204	14 NH		
Story, Robert	1814	173	33 MA		
Stoufle, Joseph	1806	1449	30		Orleans
Stow, George	1857	140	16 MA		
Stowell, Henry	1855	503	27 NY		
Strahan, John	1805	680	22 PA		
Stratton, James	1855	450	23 MA		
Strider, Charles	1819	73	36 VA		
Strong, Oliver	1805	744	26 CT		
Strong, William	1810	103	19 MA		
Stuart, William C.	1851	1682	43 MA		
Sturges, Binio	1818	129	m 22 VA		
Sturges, John	1809	276	30 MD		
Sturges, Major	1819	74	36 MD		
Suarez, Francis	1805	564	28		
Suarez, John	1807	384	32		Orleans
Suarez, Juan	1805	785	46		
Suarez, Sidre	1805	431	23 LA		
Suissy, William	1816	64	18 LA		
Sullivan, Daniel	1816	23	30 NY		
Sullivan, John	1851	1434	24 PA		
Sullivan, Oliver	1812	157	25 DE		
Summer, Charles	1812	202	26 CT		
Sundquish, Jacob	1810	143	26 PA		
Surbey, John	1805	388	28 LA		
Sutherland, Daniel	1804	225	20 PA		
Sutherland, Peter	1811	21	28		
Sutton, Nathan	1804	162	30 NJ		
Sutton, Thomas	1855	179	25 NY		
Sutton, William	1815	69	28 VA		
Swasey, John	1819	149	25 MA		
Swift, Robert	1851	1477	24 MA		
Swinney, Michael	1804	200	27 PA		
Sylva, John	1806	1581	26		Orleans
Sylva, John	1818	26	21 MA		
Syms, James	1804	274	17 MA		
Syms, James	1804	174	17 MA		
Taber, Loring	1818	12	20 MA		
Tabler, John	1821	106	24 MD		
Taggard, George	1851	1406	27 PA		
Taguechel, Vincent	1815	135	24		
Taillard, Nicolas	1810	207	30		Orleans
Talamo, Angel	1807	389	31		
Talbot, William	1855	324	22 NY		
Talmage, Thomas	1815	127	33 NJ		
Talmager, Hezikiah	1811	299	28 CT		
Tapper, Thomas	1819	70	22 NY		
Tarbox, E. H.	1855	238	36 ME		
Tardy, Edward	1819	11	21 NY		
Targuin, Jean	1810	135	49		
Tarr, Solomon	1810	119	19 MA		
Tasge, Morice	1804	50	13		Orleans
Tauzin, Pierre	1818	274	22 LA		
Taylor, Andrew	1814	185	26 NY		
Taylor, Charles	1855	213	23 RI		
Taylor, Daniel	1809	238	26 PA		
Taylor, James	1855	442	45 NY		
Taylor, James	1851	1204	23 MA		
Taylor, James	1812	227	20 MD		
Taylor, John	1818	336	43 MA		
Taylor, John	1810	257	19 NY		
Taylor, John	1807	381	b 25 RI		
Taylor, John	1805	544	21 NJ		
Taylor, John	1806	1518	0		
Taylor, John T.	1805	519	30		
Taylor, Joseph	1804	89	29 MA		
Taylor, Joseph	1818	159	25 NY		
Taylor, Richard	1855	319	28		Gr.Britain
Taylor, William	1815	14	21 MA		
Taylor, William	1810	336	21 PA		
Taylor, Wm.	1818	160	52 NY		
Teel, David	1805	491	27 NJ		
Temer, Andrew	1815	174	24 NY		
Tenace, Antonio	1805	586	35		Orleans
Terreble, Aurely	1810	256	20		
Terrill, James M.	1821	66	20 PA		
Tessier, John S.	1810	86	46		Orleans
Tew, Joseph Davis	1851	1600	26		Ireland
Tharp, John	1810	151	28 PA		
Theibaud, Bertran	1804	648	45		
Thocay, Julian	1810	261	b 26		W.Indies
Thomas, Benjamin F.	1855	227	20 ME		
Thomas, Caleb D.	1811	187	32 MA		
Thomas, Denis	1810	232	24		
Thomas, Francis	1805	408	35 LA		
Thomas, George	1805	916	38 PA		
Thomas, George	1855	197	24 NY		
Thomas, Guilliame	1811	292	0		
Thomas, Henry	1804	86	26 NY		
Thomas, James	1805	477	b 18 NY		
Thomas, James Abel	1821	34	23 MD		
Thomas, John	1804	307	m 25 SC		
Thomas, John	1804	71	N 26 NY		
Thomas, John	1806	1529	b 29		
Thomas, John	1811	113	31		Orleans
Thomas, John	1810	50	28		
Thomas, John P.	1851	1335	21 MA		
Thomas, Peter	1804	242	0		Orleans
Thomas, Stephen	1811	85	24 DE		
Thomas, Theodore	1819	172	23 PA		
Thomas, Valetin	1806	1584	40		
Thomas, William	1810	172	33 NY		
Thomas, William	1810	332	18 NY		
Thomas, William	1805	859	18 NY		
Thomas, William	1812	129	18 MS		

Name	Year	No.		Age	Place
Thompson,Alexander	1855	570		28	England
Thompson,CharlesG.	1855	811		23	MA
Thompson, Ebenezer	1815	59		46	MA
Thompson, Henry	1818	58		20	NY
Thompson, Henry	1857	108		17	ME
Thompson, James	1857	99		21	ME
Thompson, James	1821	119		17	ME
Thompson, James	1819	20		23	MD
Thompson, James	1819	170		16	MA
Thompson, John	1818	79		33	NY
Thompson, John	1818	54		26	VA
Thompson, John	1811	264		21	SC
Thompson, John	1855	520		29	MA
Thompson, John	1855	471		22	MA
Thompson, John	1805	963		28	NY
Thompson, John	1805	353		27	LA
Thompson, John	1811	14		25	MD
Thompson, John	1810	300		41	NY
Thompson, John	1810	395		23	NY
Thompson, John	1811	25	b	23	PA
Thompson, Joseph	1809	237		27	SC
Thompson, Mark	1855	303		32	MA
Thompson, Matthew	1821	22		25	MD
Thompson, Peter	1851	1322		26	MO
Thompson, Robert	1818	180		33	
Thompson,Theodore	1818	228		34	ME
Thompson, Thomas	1815	21		26	MD
Thompson, William	1851	1636		21	ME
Thompson, William	1855	269		22	OH
Thompson, William	1855	514		25	NY
Thompson, William	1805	954		22	NY
Thompson, William	1805	682		21	MA
Thomson, John	1815	107		21	NY
Thomson, Pat H.	1855	477		24	LA
Thomson, William	1815	173		24	PA
Thomson, William	1812	52		26	
Thom, Charles	1805	796		20	CT
Thom, John	1818	335		21	NY
Thorne, John	1821	13		23	NY
Thorne, John	1851	1405		25	NY
Thorne, William	1804	84		35	NJ
Thomson, Thomas	1851	1590		36	NY
Thornton,					
Asa Frederick	1810	349		27	SC
Thornton, Martin	1815	128		29	GA
Thorp, James	1851	1666		26	NY
Threlkeld, Abner	1805	419		20	KY
Thurman, William	1851	1329		25	ME
Thursby, John	1819	80		21	NY
Thweatt, John	1809	301		39	VA
Tibbits, Giles	1809	23		26	MD
Tibie, Peter	1818	353		28	
Tilton, John	1818	2		21	MA
Timmerman,Matthew	1809	33		26	NY
Timmons, James	1814	165		22	PA
Tio, Marcos	1804	0		0	
Tisdale, Chester	1819	238		28	CT
Tissendie, John	1804	99		47	
Tissendie, John	1804	99		47	
Titcumb,JohnValentine	1804	222		29	NY
Tobin, Edward	1855	307		30	MA
Todd, Caswell T.	1814	149		30	PA
Todd, Samuel	1807	337		35	
Tognett, Able	1818	332	l	26	
Tolford, Isaac	1806	1472		21	NH
Toll, John	1821	103		36	MA
Toll, John	1819	174		35	MA
Tomasi, Pierre	1805	777		32	
Tome, Valentine	1805	775		0	
Tomlin, Patrick	1851	1538		30	CT
Tompkins, James	1811	247		25	NY
Tomsion, Vassal	1811	270		21	RI
Toner, Patrick	1851	1546		19	NY
Toomer, Henry B.	1811	282		20	NC
Toret, Manuel	1818	220		20	LA
Torren, Andrew	1819	227	b	25	Africa
Torris, William	1810	162		30	Orleans
Tosa, Juan	1805	587		16	Orleans
Toubeneau, Francis	1804	291		44	Orleans
Tough, John	1851	1513		21	MA
Toulouse, Francois	1809	262		34	Orleans
Tournier, Silvain	1815	72	m	16	LA
Towle, Jarvis	1851	1332		21	NY
Townsend, Jacob	1819	213	b	0	NY
Townsend, Jethro	1821	60		30	MA
Townsend, Willit	1851	1664		22	MA
Tracy, Andrew	1851	1621		27	ME
Tracy, N. K.	1851	1154		22	VT
Tracy, William	1818	310		28	MA
Trandberg, Francis A.	1855	536		24	Sweden
Trask, Charles	1811	67		14	MA
Trask, Stephen	1818	264		22	MA
Treat, Albert	1855	524		21	ME
Treat, Horace	1815	200		25	CT
Trelabar, Edmond	1811	87		15	NY
Trexo, Peter Joseph	1805	417		24	LA
Trial, Alexander	1851	1546		23	ME
Tribel, Francis	1810	141		0	PA
Trotter, David	1855	566		24	Scotland
Troube, Nicholas	1818	147		42	
Trow, John, Jr.	1815	207		15	MA
Trueland, William	1855	345		23	MA
Truly, Henry	1818	90	b	19	MD
Trustry, Perrey	1812	201	n	24	DE
Tueney, Thomas	1805	435		28	NY
Tufts, Samuel	1821	4		37	MA
Tulloch, James	1807	387		23	NJ
Tully, John	1821	148		21	PA

Name	Year	No.		Age/State	Origin
Tupper, Charles L. D.	1805	509		19 ME	
Turguetti, Francois	1809	254		28	Orleans
Turin, Fexix	1814	156		35	
Turner, Francis	1818	190		19 MD	
Turner, Gardner	1818	65		22 RI	
Turner, George	1818	226		24 PA	
Turner, George	1851	1159		51 ME	
Turner, Jacob	1805	455		22 MD	
Turner, John	1804	65		50 RI	
Turner, John	1815	65		23 MA	
Turner, Noah	1811	212	b	22 PA	
Turner, Robert	1815	20	b	31 MD	
Turner, Thomas	1821	70		38 NH	
Turpin, Jean Pierre	1814	212		22	
Tuthill, Charles	1811	70		21 NY	
Twiford, Pernal	1855	180		16 ME	
Twiss, Joshua	1815	222		30 MA	
Typer, William	1805	380		24 NY	
Tyson, John	1810	283		29 NJ	
Ulrich, Jacob	1810	222		21 PA	
Underwood,Ebenezer	1815	125		17 MA	
Underwood, John	1811	63		23 DE	
Vaibre, Francis	1815	4		32 LA	
Valder, Thomas	1805	887		31 DE	
Valdes, Jose	1812	0		40	
Valdes, Jose	1819	201		45	
Vallen, James	1815	273		24 PA	
Vallirae,John Baptiste	1816	68	m	19 LA	
Vallot, Pierre	1805	729		31	Orleans
Van Anden, John	1804	0		0 NY	
Vanbrunt, Franklin N.	1857	138		23 NY	
Vanderbilt, John	1811	48		32 NY	
VanKirk, Joseph	1812	82		22 VA	
Vankirk, Thomas	1805	525		40 NJ	
VanPatten, John	1805	847		21 NY	
Vas, Leonard	1819	187		25 LA	
Vaughal, Westley	1851	1673		42 MD	
Vaughan, Robert	1809	228		20 MA	
Vaury, John Peter	1805	907		18	
Vavasseur, Jean	1805	547		30	
Veangeli, Pierre	1815	55		24 LA	
Veasie, James	1855	203		22 ME	
Veazie, George	1855	225		16 ME	
Venson, Charles	1805	994	b	12	
Ventura, Antonio	1806	1429		23	
Verames, Andrew	1805	421		37	
Verdeil, Louis	1805	343		47	
Verin, Lucas	1810	85		21	
Vermeulen,					
Petrus Joannes	1851	1410		23 NY	
Vero, Francis	1809	266		23	Orleans
Verrick, Jeremiah	1804	36		19 MD	
Veselick, Joseph	1818	149		41	
Veu, Pascal	1805	978		22	
Viade, Roma	1805	398		40	
Victor, Antoine	1811	22		19	France
Vidal, Joseph	1805	515		25	
Vienne, Louis	1816	75		23 LA	
Vigier, Peter	1804	57		30	Orleans
Villacroux, Louis	1812	155		26	
Villaneuva, Nicholas	1806	1546		26	
Vincen, Peter	1805	952		43	
Vincent, Thomas S.	1815	190		23 NY	
Vincent, William	1810	329		24 NC	
Vine, William	1812	97		21 SC	
Viner, John Frederick	1804	233		31 NY	
Vinot, Philibert	1818	358		23	
Virgin, Joseph	1811	208	y	23 SC	
ViSmitt, Jacob	1855	558		25	Germany
Voshall, Daniel	1811	177		25 MD	
Voy, Thomas	1809	264		28 MD	
Vrignon, Joseph	1805	352		28	
Waddel, Thomas	1851	1333		21 NY	
Wade, John	1807	335		27 PA	
Wade, John	1811	140		32 NY	
Wade, William Henry	1855	501		30 MA	
Wagner,					
James Frederick	1851	1536		23 NY	
Waine, Benjamin	1815	239		44 MA	
Wakefield, Thomas	1855	522		33 ME	
Waldon, Daniel	1815	30	y	52 DE	
Walker, James	1851	1501		22 NY	
Walker, Peter	1811	32		25 MA	
Walker, William	1810	307		33 NY	
Walker, William	1857	67		31 NY	
Walker, William	1855	216		23 PA	
Wallace, Alexander	1815	246		14 PA	
Wallace, James	1810	310		21 MA	
Wallace, John	1814	179		25 VT	
Wallace, Robert	1851	1212		23 GA	
Wallace, William	1804	139		28 PA	
Walsh, John	1805	646		26 MA	
Walsh, Richard	1811	160		43 PA	
Walsh, William	1855	235		26 NY	
Walter, John	1806	1512		19 NY	
Wamsby, John	1812	132		20 NY	
Wansley, John	1819	206	b	35 NJ	
Ward, Ebenezer B.	1821	124		27 MA	
Ward, Henry	1804	224		22 NY	
Ward, Richard	1818	357		26 MD	
Ward, Robert	1815	144		37	
Warder, Henry	1821	73		24 MD	
Ware, Gustavis M.	1818	192		21 CT	
Warner, Daniel	1815	147		31 RI	
Warner, James	1851	1681		22 MA	
Warren, Charles	1818	97		32 MA	
Warren, Paul	1819	31	c	34 MA	
Warren, Thomas	1818	302		22 CT	

Name	Year	No.		Age	Origin
Warren, Thomas	1818	302		22 CT	
Warwick, Thomas C.	1855	432		21 PA	
Wasa, Will	1818	345		29 MD	
Waterman, Charles	1811	314		24 MA	
Waterman, William F.	1815	234		25 RI	
Waters, John	1819	28		45	
Waterson, Thomas	1855	565		27	England
Wates, Thomas	1851	1494		24 MA	
Watson, Arthur	1805	701		15 SC	
Watson, Charles	1855	464		30 NY	
Watson, David	1857	127		20 NY	
Watson, Edward	1851	1282		39 MA	
Watson, George	1816	90		24 NY	
Watson, George	1815	46		37 VA	
Watson, George	1809	20		21 NY	
Watson, Henry J.	1855	244		28 NY	
Watson, James	1855	331		27 NY	
Watson, John	1821	46		36 NH	
Watson, John	1811	111		21 PA	
Watterman, Walter	1806	1452		15 CT	
Wattis, William	1811	168		30 MA	
Watts, Wm. H.	1855	196		35 NY	
Weaver, Maxwell	1806	1496	b	20 NC	
Webb, Joseph	1818	99		17 MA	
Webber, BenjaminDe	1804	253		26 NY	
Webber, James	1818	344		28 MA	
Webber, Joseph	1804	856		19 MA	
Webster, Henry	1819	199	y	27 PA	
Webster, Owens	1821	35	b	20 NH	
Webster, Sharles	1819	229	m	20 MA	
Weedan, David	1805	412	b	27 RI	
Weedin, Warren G.	1855	530		44 RI	
Weeks, David	1819	63		24 NJ	
Weeks, Lewis	1851	1149		26 MA	
Weigh, Robert	1805	476		15 RI	
Weight, Jeremiah	1807	397		21 NY	
Welcome, Joseph	1811	81	b	28 VA	
Wella, Pablo	1805	520		30	
Wells, Francis	1805	557		19 NC	
Wells, John W.	1851	1416		21 PA	
Welsh, John	1818	231		33 NY	
Welsh, John	1809	293	y	23 VA	
Welsh, Thomas	1810	392		40 VA	
Welsh, William	1810	330		28 NY	
Welsh, William S.	1821	77		22 VA	
Wendel, Thomas	1851	1403		43 MA	
Went, Philip	1818	205		20 NY	
Wentworth,George P.	1818	177		23 NH	
West, Albert R.	1855	519		23 ME	
West, Edward	1805	961		32	
West, William	1804	247		19 PA	
West, William	1815	140		21 PA	
Western, William	1812	107		36 NJ	
Westly, Stephen	1816	54	m	26 CT	
Weston, Jacob Fox	1815	191		26 MA	
Weston, Joseph	1814	217	b	40 NY	
Westwick, William	1805	632		23 MD	
Wetzel, Henry	1809	223		23	
Wever, Albert B.	1851	1651		28 PA	
Weymouth,WilliamW.	1818	322		23 VA	
Wharf, John	1818	348		29 MD	
Wheaton,					
George Bunall	1855	502		27 RI	
Wheeler, Abel	1811	197		30 MA	
Wheeler, Charles	1851	7		27 MA	
Wheling, Conner	1815	150		24 MA	
Whipple, Joseph	1815	98		22 MA	
Whipple, Samuel	1804	130		30 NY	
White, Charles	1855	448		26 NY	
White, Charles	1819	50		28 LA	
White, Chas	1855	482		23 NJ	
White, Edward R.	1819	207		18 PA	
White, Francis	1811	157	y	21 PA	
White, George	1805	698		20 NY	
White, George	1812	167		24 MD	
White, Henry	1851	1363		26 NY	
White, James	1851	1284		22 MA	
White, James	1816	12		26 VA	
White, John	1815	236		22 NY	
White, John	1816	11		45 DE	
White, John	1810	46		25 MD	
White, Peter	1814	154		32 NJ	
White, Samuel	1809	327		23 MD	
White, Thomas	1805	890		30 MD	
White, Thomas	1821	107	y	21 PA	
White, Timothy L.	1804	188		31 MA	
White, William	1805	668		32 MD	
Whitehead, John	1805	560		23 VA	
Whitehurst, Samuel	1804	62		27 VA	
Whitewood, William	1851	1266		22 MA	
Whitey, John	1855	322		34 NY	
Whitmel, Francis	1805	807		21 NY	
Whitney, Wm.	1821	12		25	Ireland
Whittle, Charles					
Washington	1851	1641		25 MA	
Wigley, James	1818	128		21 MD	
Wilber, Rufus	1812	108		32 CT	
Wilbur, James H.	1855	493		19 CT	
Wilbur, John P.	1857	100		21 CT	
Wilby, Joseph	1811	133		10 NY	
Wilder, James	1855	535		17 IN	
Wildman, Henry	1851	1202		20 PA	
Wildy, Thomas	1811	184		19 MD	
Wilk, John	1809	239		32 PA	
Wilkins, Enoch	1811	230		22 NJ	
Wilkinson, John	1812	184		17 NY	
Wille, Lewis	1821	102		21 MA	
Willets, Reuben	1851	1512		21 NJ	

Name	Year	No.		Age/State	Extra
Willey,William Joseph	1855	241		22 ME	
William, John	1816	80		32 NY	
Williams, Charles	1819	24	n	29 PA	
Williams, David	1805	469		19 NY	
Williams, Ebenezer	1851	1399		25 CT	
Williams, Edward	1855	541		21 MA	
Williams, George	1819	78		24 MA	
Williams, James	1815	27		25 SC	
Williams, James	1816	99		21 MA	
Williams, James	1812	5		26 NY	
Williams, James	1807	405		23 MD	
Williams, James	1811	30		42 NY	
Williams, John	1811	135		24 VA	
Williams, John	1809	235		23 PA	
Williams, John	1811	176		38 PA	
Williams, John	1804	117		26 NY	
Williams, John	1806	1796		32 MD	
Williams, John	1805	870		31 NY	
Williams, John	1804	174	b	19 NC	
Williams, John	1818	239	y	28	Senegal
Williams, John	1815	56		28 MA	
Williams, John	1815	77		23 MD	
Williams, John	1818	39		20 MA	
Williams, John	1818	165		28 NY	
Williams, John	1814	216	y	27 MA	
Williams, John	1818	239	y	28	Senegal
Williams, John	1855	284		22 LA	
Williams, John	1819	89		23 MA	
Williams, John	1819	112		27 MA	
Williams, John	1855	208		17 MA	
Williams, John, 2nd	1818	359	m	39 PA	
Williams, John, Jr.	1812	169		22 MA	
Williams, Lloyd	1810	296		21 MA	
Williams, Owen	1809	24		30 MD	
Williams, Richard	1816	21		26 Ny	
Williams, Robert	1818	104		26 PA	
Williams, Robert	1810	220		21 PA	
Williams, Samuel	1812	58	y	12 NY	
Williams, Thomas	1818	276		26 MA	
Williams, Thomas	1809	299		25 VA	
Williams, Thomas	1806	1804		27	
Williams, Thomas	1805	908		22 VA	
Williams, Thomas M.	1811	253		25 VA	
Williams, Thos.	1804	267		27 MD	
Williams, Walter	1819	175		35 PA	
Williams, William	1819	57		25 MA	
Williams, William	1855	579		28 PA	
Williams, William	1819	9		22 PA	
Williams, William	1819	236		16 CT	
Williams, William	1816	81	b	18 GA	
Williams, William	1804	207	b	22 NY	
Williams, William	1804	179	m	33 SC	
Williams, William	1811	203		32 SC	
Williams, William	1809	18		46	
Williamson,Frederick	1851	1321		29	Prussia
Williamson, James	1851	1343		18 NY	
Williamson, John	1818	293		25 CT	
Williamson, John	1812	114		20 VA	
Williamson, Peter	1812	0		45	
Williamson, William	1810	75		32 VA	
Willias, William	1810	396		22 Md	
Willis, Anthony	1821	51	m	25 PA	
Willis, George B.	1821	93		14 RI	
Willis, Wright W.	1805	473		20 MD	
Willson, Bell	1811	11		22 PA	
Willson, Joseph	1804	177		31	
Willsun, John	1818	248		21 CT	
Wilson, Andrew	1851	1530		60 NJ	
Wilson, Charles	1818	252	b	22 NY	
Wilson, Charles	1809	13		21 PA	
Wilson, George	1851	1208		24 NY	
Wilson, Henry	1851	5		25 NY	
Wilson, Henry	1805	990		37 VA	
Wilson, James, Jr.	1819	138		42 MD	
Wilson, John	1851	1500		42 NY	
Wilson, John	1851	1677		30 MD	
Wilson, John	1818	55		30 NH	
Wilson, John	1805	720		25	
Wilson, John	1809	292		30 DE	
Wilson, John	1811	211		23 NJ	
Wilson, John	1810	281		20 NJ	
Wilson, John	1811	201		18 CT	
Wilson, John	1811	128		24 VA	
Wilson, John G.	1851	0		24 MD	
Wilson, John H.	1855	228		18 ME	
Wilson, Joseph	1855	233		25 MD	
Wilson, Peter	1811	83		20 PA	
Wilson, Robert	1812	140	b	17 MA	
Wilson, Thomas	1815	136		24 NY	
Wilson, Thomas	1851	1650		28 ME	
Wilson, Thomas	1819	59		21 NY	
Wilson, William	1855	412		30 ME	
Wilson, William	1855	573		32 ME	
Wilson, William	1811	154		30 PA	
Wilson, William	1809	289		59 NY	
Wilson, William	1806	1541		24 NY	
Wilton, John	1805	959		23 NY	
Wince, John	1810	104		35 PA	
Winder, John	1819	3		32 VA	
Winemore, Philip	1816	42		30 PA	
Winemore, Samuel Egleston	1804	68		23 PA	
Winship, George	1812	92		13 NY	
Winslow, Job	1812	17		24 MA	
Winslow, Samuel	1821	92		22 ME	
Winslow, Thomas	1805	980		19 MA	
Winters, Peter	1815	10	b	35 DE	
Wiser, Peter	1807	356		25 PA	

Wish, William	1851	1325		45 SC		Young, James	1811	172		21 MD
Wishart, James	1851	1180		24 MA		Young, James	1811	169		28 MD
Witham, Addison	1857	123		22 MA		Young, John	1804	0		0 MA
Witham, Thomas	1815	231		48 MA		Young, John	1819	37		28 MA
Wolfe, Jacob P.	1818	166		23 PA		Young, John W.	1855	314		23 ME
Wood, Abraham	1819	182	b	23 VA		Young, Nathaniel	1855	416		23 ME
Wood, Chalres	1805	599		28 NY		Young, Thomas	1855	185		27 NY
Wood, Charles D.	1821	96		21 MD		Young, Thomas	1804	41		33 MA
Wood, GeorgeWilliam	1855	199		21 MA		Young, William	1810	153		19 VA
Wood, James	1811	151		16 SC		Young, Zenas	1821	99		0 MA
Wood, John	1807	360		19 NY		Ysquierdo, Joseph	1809	269		34
Wood, John	1851	1146		32 NY		Ziegler, Frederick	1851	1597		21	Prussia
Wood, John	1812	211		22 MA						
Wood, Joseph	1804	187		23 DE						
Wood, Peter	1805	373		27 LA						
Wood, Quesada	1851	1581		25 NY						
Wood, Richard	1812	222		26 DE						
Wood, William	1805	665		34 PA						
Woods, Henry	1851	1313		28 OH						
Woods, Thomas	1857	141		25 PA						
Woods, William	1811	144		26 MD						
Woods, William	1811	288		20 PA						
Woodworth, George	1804	252		22 CT						
Wright, Charles	1816	18		21 NY						
Wright, Charles	1855	276		22 MA						
Wright, HoratioNelson	1819	81		20 CT						
Wright, John	1805	402		19 NH						
Wright, John	1805	403		17						
Wright, John	1810	11	y	38 VA						
Wright, John	1810	15	y	24 NY						
Wright, L.	1851	1183		37 NY						
Wright, Matthew	1804	243		17 PA						
Wright, Samuel	1804	122		35 PA						
Wright, William	1805	982		29 RI						
Wright, William	1811	307	y	23 PA						
Wustman, John C.	1812	56		35 PA						
Wyant, David	1818	286		26 NY						
Wyatt, George	1819	46		19 VA						
Wyatt, Thomas	1857	54		38 ME						
Wyatt, William	1809	19		18 MA						
Wylee, James	1851	1591		28						
Wylie, John	1804	268		20 PA						
Wyman, Joshua	1816	58		15 MA						
Yates, John J.	1821	91		23 VA						
Ybarra, Lewis	1810	131		34						
Yeaton, Benjamin, Jr.	1811	225		38 NH						
Yeaton, John	1818	285		33 NH						
Yeiser, Henry F.	1819	41		18 MD						
Yellick, Anthony	1804	102		0						
Yensen, Augustin	1816	60		28 LA						
Yglesias, Luke	1807	343		24						
Yon, Etienne	1818	171		39						
Young, Charles	1810	321		30 PA						
Young, Francis	1855	189		31 OH						

4.

Jack Avery

Age _____ 24 _

Heights _____ 5 - 4½

Complexion
Hair _____ } black
Eyes _____

Was born in New London
in the State of Connecticut
January 6 _ 1807 _

Protected before by
the Name of Avery Williams

Proof of Citizenship

Port of New Haven, Connecticut

This index of almost 4,000 names covers the period 1801 to 1843; however, there are none for 1839 or 1840, and most years are incomplete. The records are in their original order, more or less chronological by year. As in other ports, the abstracts or registers are a useful supplement to these records.

The proofs of citizenship are smaller than most applications, being about 4" wide by 6½" long. Most are not witnessed, but they do provide the basic information needed by genealogists, name, age at the time of application, and place of birth. They also give a brief description of the seaman, usually his height, and the color of his complexion, eyes, and hair.

There is an unusually large number of duplicate certificates issued for ones reported lost. A result is duplicate names on the index. Either these seamen were very careless with these important documents, or they could have been giving or selling them to others who were not entitled to them.

Black seamen account for 611 or almost 16% of the seamen indexed. There are three Indians, two of whom are identified as Mohigan Indians. As usual, one must be imaginative in reading names. "S" and "L" as in Sand or Land and Sampson or Lampson are easily confused.

Proofs of Citizenship

Port of New Haven, Connecticut

Data order: Name, Year, Age, Color, State or Country.

Name	Year	Age	Color	State
Abernethy, James	1803	25		CT
Ables, Philander	1831	20		CT
Abrams, Richardson	1838	24		ME
Addams, Samuel	1804	22		CT
Albro, Edward	1811	17		CT
Alexander, Charles	1827	41		NY
Alford, Alpheus, Jr.	1804	39		CT
Alford, Eliase	1804	42		MA
Alger, Oliver	1806	26		CT
Allen, Augustus	1805	22 b		CT
Allen, Charles	1823	19		CT
Allen, David	1804	31		CT
Allen, Henry	1843	16		CT
Allen, James	1803	16		CT
Allen, John Davis	1810	44		MA
Allen, Jonathan	1806	30		CT
Allen, Lewis	1841	40		CT
Allen, Robert	1803	23		PA
Allen, Robert	1805	24		PA
Allen, Robert	1804	23		PA
Allen, Silas	1810	15		CT
Alligood, John	1842	22 b		CT
Alling, Benjamin	1810	46		CT
Alling, Benjamin	1806	43		CT
Alling, David	1807	22		NJ
Alling, Elam	1815	26		CT
Alling, Jotham	1806	19		CT
Alling, Jotham	1805	18		CT
Alling, Lyman	1806	17		CT
Alling, Roger	1810	40		CT
Alling, Samuel	1808	20		CT
Alling, William	1809	16		CT
Allyn, Richard	1810	21		CT
Ames, Augustus	1807	23		CT
Ames, Augustus	1804	20		CT
Ames, Augustus	1803	19		CT
Ames, Cheeney	1817	25		CT
Ames, Cheney	1820	28		CT
Ames, Cheney	1821	28		CT
Ames, Cheney	1813	20		CT
Ames, Cheney	1815	23		CT
Ames, Cheney	1820	28		CT
Ames, Cheney	1808	16		CT
Ames, Isaac	1805	23		CT
Ames, Isaac	1803	22		CT
Ames, James	1816	22		MA
Ames, Uri	1803	0		CT
Anasker, John	1834	20 b		CT
Anderson, Alexander	1806	31		CT
Andrews, Benjamin	1801	15		CT
Andrews, Hercules	1813	24 b		MA
Andrews, Joseph	1805	26		CT
Andrews, Noble	1809	18		CT
Andrus, Benjamin	1804	18		CT
Angel, Peter T.	1805	33		US
Anger, Peter	1842	20		NY
Anmthony, John	1841	22 b		NY
Anthony, Abraham	1804	20 b		CT
Aplewhite, Isaac	1818	18 b		CT
Apple, Andrew	1804	28		NY
Apple, Apolus	1819	21		CT
Applewhite, Benjamin	1824	50 y		MA
Applewhite, Benjamin	1804	28		MA
Applewhite, Benjamin	1805	30 c		MA
Applewhite, Benjamin	1808	33 y		MA
Applewhite, Benjn.	1809	34 y		MA
Applewhite, Benjn.	1824	21 y		CT
Applewhite, Benjn.	1813	38 y		MA
Applewhite, Benjn.	1822	17 b		CT
Applewhite, Isaac	1819	20 y		CT
Applwhite, Benjamin	1804	29		MA
Arabas, Jack	1806	48 b		
Armitstead, James B.	1803	22		
Armstrong, Daniel	1821	24 y		NY
Armstrong, Lorenzo	1836	19		CT
Armstrong, Philander	1842	18		CT
Arnard, John	1820	21		NY
Arnold, Arittos	1818	19		CT
Arnold, Arittus	1817	18		CT
Arnold, Wait	1815	18		CT
Arnold, Whiting	1804	18		CT
Arthur, Samuel M.	1805	19		CT
Ashby, Printice	1810	15		CT
Atfard, Roswell	1803	21		CT
Atkins, Chester R.	1823	21		CT
Atkins, Hiram	1817	26		CT
Atkins, Hiram/Henry	1810	18		CT
Atkins, John	1808	30		CT
Atkins, John	1821	43		CT
Atkins, John	1804	26		CT
Atkins, William	1811	28		MA
Atting, Samuel	1806	19		CT

Attwater, Charles	1815	19		CT	Ayers, William	1815	18	CT
Attwater, Charles W.	1818	17		CT	Ayres, John	1821	35	CT
Attwater, John	1816	16		CT	Ayres, John	1805	19	CT
Attwater, John	1817	17		CT	Ayres, Josiah	1807	19	CT
Attwater, John	1816	16		CT	Babcock, Aubon	1818	14	CT
Attwater, Norman	1816	14		CT	Babcock, William	1815	14	CT
Attwater, Philips	1810	28 b		CT	Backus, John	1808	22 b	CT
Attwater, Philips	1806	25 b		CT	Backus, Marvin	1811	29	CT
Attwood, James	1831	17		NY	Backus, Mervin	1813	32	CT
Atwater, Charles W.	1821	21		CT	Bagden, Augustus	1806	28 y	CT
Atwater, Charles W.	1822	22		CT	Bagden, Benjamin	1804	24 y	CT
Atwater, Edward	1831	27		CT	Bagden, John	1836	20 y	CT
Atwater, Elnathan, II	1813	21		CT	Bagdon, James	1805	19 y	CT
Atwater, George	1813	16		CT	Bagley, Thomas C.	1843	25	ME
Atwater, Henry	1807	19		CT	Bailey, Nathl.	1807	25	CT
Atwater, Joseph	1804	34			Bailey, Thomas	1836	22 b	NY
Atwater, Joseph	1803	33		CT	Bailey, William	1834	43	RI
Atwater, Levi	1815	22		CT	Bailey, Wm.	1842	51	RI
Atwater, Levi	1810	17		CT	Baker, Elijah	1813	31	MA
Atwater, Marcus	1807	23		CT	Baker, Richard	1803	25	MA
Atwater, Marcus	1803	19		CT	Baker, Stephen	1817	26	RI
Atwater, Nath. Mix	1811	14		CT	Baker, Stephen	1833	18	CT
Atwater, Philip	1803	22		CT	Baker, Stephen	1836	22	CT
Atwater, Richd.	1817	15		CT	Bakker, Oscar	1838	19	CT
Atwater, Richd.	1824	22		CT	Baldwin, Abraham L.	1837	29	NJ
Atwater, William	1810	15		CT	Baldwin, Ammi	1804	25	CT
Atwater, Wm. A.	1833	17		CT	Baldwin, Amos	1806	27	CT
Atwell, Jesse	1805	35		CT	Baldwin, Augustus	1806	23	CT
Auger, Elihu	1803	22		CT	Baldwin, David	1806	20	CT
Auger, Isaac	1807	21		CT	Baldwin, Ebenezer	1804	22	CT
Auger, Joseph, Jr.	1803	23		CT	Baldwin, Eli	1805	23	CT
Augur, Edward B.	1809	21		CT	Baldwin, Eliphatet	1805	21	CT
Augur, Elihu	1809	27		CT	Baldwin, Enoch	1803	27	CT
Augur, Jared	1803	25		CT	Baldwin, Erastus	1803	17	CT
Augur, Joel	1811	31		CT	Baldwin, Henry	1827	17	CT
Augur, Joel	1805	25		CT	Baldwin, Jesse	1806	35	CT
Augur, Joel	1804	25		CT	Baldwin, John	1824	24	CT
Augur, Joseph, Jr.	1805	26		CT	Baldwin, Major	1809	21	CT
Augur, Peter	1806	19		CT	Baldwin, Mons	1805	17	CT
Augur, Ruben	1803	16		CT	Baldwin, Pierson	1806	23	CT
Augustus, John	1818	17 b		MD	Baldwin, Samuel	1815	23	CT
Austin, Augustus	1803	20		CT	Baldwin, Samuel	1804	27	CT
Austin, Christopher B.	1806	36		CT	Baldwin, Simon	1804	20 b	
Austin, Ezekiel	1815	25		RI	Bale, Harris	1811	18	CT
Austin, John	1816	31		CT	Balkley, Francis, Jr.	1806	18	CT
Austin, John	1817	30		RI	Ball, Harris	1811	18	CT
Austin, John	1803	18		CT	Ball, Zina	1836	36	CT
Austin, John	1805	21		CT	Banks, James	1817	22 b	MA
Averill, Chester, Jr.	1806	21		CT	Barber, Henry	1809	18	CT
Avery, Henry	1819	29		CT	Barber, Joseph	1804	31	MA
Avery, Henry	1824	29		CT	Barber, William P.	1832	30	CT
Avery, Jack	1807	24 b		CT	Barbour, Benjamin F.	1833	30	CT
Avery, Samuel	1801	16		CT	Barbour, Benjn. F.	1822	19	CT
Avosst, John	1811	0		naturalized	Bardsley, William	1843	23 b	CT

Bardsley, William	1836	15 b	CT	Basset, Josiah	1804	0		CT
Barker, Aalbert	1825	18	CT	Basseth, Abraham	1803	27		CT
Barker, Augustus	1803	20	CT	Bassett, David	1806	19		
Barker, Charles	1812	13	CT	Bassett, Edward	1807	33		CT
Barker, Charles	1811	12	CT	Bassett, Edward	1804	27		CT
Barker, David	1807	27	CT	Bassett, Freeman	1803	18		
Barker, Edward, Jr.	1805	39	CT	Bassett, Henry	1843	18		CT
Barker, Edward, Jr.	1803	33	CT	Bassett, Joseph	1807	16		CT
Barker, Foster	1811	23	CT	Bassett, Philo	1823	21		CT
Barker, Giles	1804	31	CT	Bassett, Russel	1804	29		CT
Barker, Harvey	1805	21	CT	Bassett, Russel	1803	19		CT
Barker, Harvey	1803	19	CT	Bassett, Samuel	1805	22		CT
Barker, John, Jr.	1805	15	CT	Bassett, Urial	1816	16		CT
Barker, Joseph	1811	20	CT	Bassett, Uriel	1816	16		CT
Barker, Oliver	1808	23	CT	Bassett, William	1806	19		CT
Barker, Oliver	1807	21	CT	Batchelder, L. M.	1841	17		ME
Barker, Oliver	1807	21	CT	Bates, James	1806	20		CT
Barker, Peter	1810	21	CT	Bates, Parker	1804	36		CT
Barker, Thaddeus	1804	23	CT	Batiss, Ths.	1831	14 b		CT
Barker, Wm.	1815	21	CT	Bautler, Samuel	1806	18		CT
barnes, Abraham	1837	19	CT	Beach, Almond	1804	17		CT
Barnes, Downey	1810	16	CT	Beach, Almond	1803	16		CT
Barnes, Haman T	1818	32	CT	Beach, Ammi	1810	20		CT
Barnes, Harman	1803	19	CT	Beach, Amos	1811	25 b		CT
Barnes, Henry L.	1819	19	CT	Beach, Amos	1821	35 b		CT
Barnes, Herman	1812	27	CT	Beach, Burrit	1802	22		CT
Barnes, Herman F.	1813	28	CT	Beach, Horace	1811	22		CT
Barnes, Hermon	1813	28	CT	Beach, John	1810	21		
Barnes, Johnathan	1803	18	CT	Beach, Nelson	1817	10 b		CT
Barnes, Jonathan	1803	18	CT	Beach, Squire	1805	34		CT
Barnes, Jonathan	1805	20	CT	Beach, Uriel	1807	23		CT
Barnes, Lyman	1805	20	CT	Beach, Wm.	1813	16		CT
Barnes, Noah	1803	22	CT	Beadle, John	1837	26		CT
Barnes, Pomroy	1814	16	CT	Beamont, John	1809	17		CT
Barnes, Smith	1803	29	CT	Beardslee, Talmadge	1809	23		CT
Barnes, Thomas	1805	24	CT	Beardsley, Abijah	1803	19		CT
Barnes, Thomas F.	1821	19	CT	Beardsley, Abijah	1803	19		CT
Barnes, William	1811	16	CT	Beardsley, David L.	1806	23		CT
Barnes, Zera	1817	28	CT	Beardsley, Lester	1805	24		CT
Barns, Anson	1825	18	CT	Beardsley, Lyman	1806	21		CT
Barns, Chancey	1810	39	CT	Beardsley, Obediah	1810	22		CT
Barns, Chancey	1804	33	CT	Beardsley, Philo F.	1806	20		CT
Barns, Charles Ed.	1821	19	CT	Beaument, Edmund	1804	18		CT
Barns, Curtis	1809	23	CT	Becket, William	1815	29 b		VA
Barns, Silas	1805	16	CT	Becket, William	1813	28 b		VA
Barns, William	1813	18	CT	Beckett, William	1819	33 b		VA
Barns, Zera	1810	22	CT	Beckus, John	1805	20 b		CT
Barnum, Thos.	1810	23	NY	Beebe, David	1816	18		CT
Bartholomew, Hiram	1807	18	CT	Beebe, Freeman	1820	23		CT
Bartis, Joseph	1837	20 b	CT	Beebe, Isaac	1815	22		CT
Barton, Henry	1806	24	RI	Beebe, James	1815	24		CT
Barton, Lyman W.	1837	21	MA	Beecher, John	1820	17		CT
Bartram, Joseph	1827	19 b	CT	Beecher, Joseph	1805	27		CT
Bartram, Joseph	1825	16 b	CT	Beecher, Moses	1810	19		CT

Beecher, Moses	1803	37	CT
Beecher, Thaddeus	1810	19	CT
Beecher,Thaddeus,2nd	1806	19	CT
Beecher, Thaddeus, Jr.	1805	15	CT
Beecher, William	1803	22	CT
Beecher, William P.	1815	19	CT
Beecher, WilliamParmelee	1812	15	CT
Beecher, Wilmot	1822	20	CT
Beers, Edward	1811	13	CT
Beers, John	1811	26	CT
Beers, John A.	1842	17	CT
Beers, John, Junr.	1805	15	CT
Belding, Amos	1807	19	CT
Bell, Ebenezer	1803	26	NC
Bell, James	1802	19	MD
Bell, James	1807	26	
Bell, Richard H.	1841	43	VA
Bellamy, Samuel	1816	21	CT
Bemant, Carlisle	1822	22	CT
Bement, Edmond	1803	17	CT
Bemis, Daniel	1810	23	MA
Bemont, Edmond	1809	23	CT
Bency, Amos	1815	37 b	CT
Bendley, Edwin M.	1841	23	CT
Benedict, Barnabas	1809	20	CT
Benedict, Truman	1819	22	CT
Benham, Henry	1809	16	CT
Benham, Jared	1818	25	CT
Benham, Mosses	1803	29	CT
Benham, Silas	1803	24	CT
Benham, Silas	1807	28	CT
Benham, William	1810	19	CT
Benjamin, Elias	1803	22	CT
Benjamin, George	1804	26 b	
Benjamin, John	1824	16	CT
Benjamin, Joseph R.	1828	16	CT
Benjamin, Merrit B.	1834	19	CT
Benjamin, Walter	1812	24	CT
Benjamin, Wm.	1842	21	CT
Bennet, Benj. Judson	1811	19	CT
Bennet, Philip	1805	24	CT
Bennet, Philo	1811	24	CT
Bennet, Samuel	1811	24 b	CT
Benton, Joel	1805	18	CT
Benton, Sam	1812	25 b	CT
Berry, John	1812	40 b	NY
Berry, Zachariah	1807	18	CT
Bertholomew,HiramS.	1809	19	CT
Bery, Frederick	1843	20 b	CT
Bethele, David	1806	25	MA
Betts, Solomon	1807	15	CT
Betts, William	1816	20	VT
Beuker, Harry	1809	21	CT
Bickford, James	1809	17	CT
Bickner, Ime	1841	30	NY
Bills, James	1803	13	CT
Bills, James	1807	17	CT
Bills, Thomas	1824	14	CT
Bincks, Lewis	1817	25 b	NY
Binnbury, William	1842	22	CT
Binney, Benjamin	1813	20	CT
Bird, James, Jr.	1819	21	NY
Birdsall, Samuel	1809	19	NY
Bishop, Joel	1805	20	CT
Bishop, Joel	1802	31	CT
Bishop, JustusPhelps	1831	21	CT
Bissel, Oliver	1803	21	CT
Bissell, Edward	1809	17	CT
Bissell, Lyman	1836	23	CT
Blackman,Alanson C.	1815	21	CT
Blackman, Anthony	1806	26 b	CT
Blackman, Rufus	1810	16	CT
Blake, Ebenezer	1822	21	CT
Blake, John	1824	20	CT
Blake, Jonathan	1813	40	CT
Blake, Jonathan	1804	31	CT
Blakeslee, Eneas	1803	22	CT
Blakeslee, Ruel	1804	19	CT
Blakslee, Eoreus?	1810	29	CT
Blank, Samuel	1820	33	NY
Blinn, James	1804	22	CT
Bliss, Neziah	1809	20	CT
Boardman, Isaac	1809	16	CT
Bochs, Saml. H.	1826	32	PA
Bochs, Samuel H.	1824	29	PA
Bocks, Samuel H.	1815	21	PA
Bodwell,Benj. Wyllys	1809	23	CT
Bonham, Jesse	1815	21 y	CT
Bontecou, Hamlet	1820	21	NY
Bonticon, Thos.	1805	14	CT
Bonticou, Daniel	1803	31	CT
Bonticou, William	1803	17	CT
Bonticove, Thomas	1808	17	CT
Booth, Eli	1807	36	CT
Booth, Henry D.	1826	21	CT
Booth, Victory	1807	14	
Booth, William	1815	23	CT
Boothe, Elisha	1812	19	CT
Boston, Daniel	1841	23 b	NY
Boston, Davis	1812	37 b	CT
Boston, James	1804	22	CT
Boston, James	1805	23	CT
Bostwick, Ira	1810	21 b	CT
Botchford, Alfred	1824	15	CT
Botsford, Sheldon	1815	21	CT
Bouch, Samuel H.	1825	31	PA
Boun, William	1813	31	CT

Boune, William	1807	25	CT	Bradley, Schuyler	1806	20	CT
Boune, William	1810	29	CT	Bradley, Truman	1841	18 l	CT
Bowe, Elijah	1843	24	CT	Bradley, William	1805	24	CT
Bowers, Charles	1806	20	CT	Bradley, William	1810	20	CT
Bowers, Isaac	1818	36	RI	Bradley, Wm.	1807	25	CT
Bowers, William	1836	30	NY	Bragdon, James	1805	19 yu	CT
Bracket, Alfred	1825	22	CT	Bramham,Wm.Wood.	1813	18	CT
Brackett, Lyman	1824	26	CT	Brandikin, John	1803	30	CT
Brackett, Miles	1824	19	CT	Brass, David	1823	40	MA
Brackett, William	1837	15	CT	Braughton, Orin	1818	17	CT
Bradford, Henry	1836	22	ME	Bray, William	1820	21	CT
Bradley, Abner	1806	25	CT	Breiter, Thos.	1820	26 b	NY
Bradley, Abraham	1819	25	CT	Brestol, Philander	1826	18	NY
Bradley, Abraham	1820	26	CT	Bridge, Caesar	1806	31 b	CT
Bradley, Andrew	1819	33	CT	Bridge, Nath.	1812	19	MA
Bradley, Andrew	1803	18	CT	Bridge, Nath.	1813	20	MA
Bradley, Andrew	1803	25	CT	Bridge, Prince	1824	47 b	CT
Bradley, Andrew	1805	19	CT	Bridge, Prince	1809	32 b	CT
Bradley, Andrew	1807	21	CT	Bridgham, George	1805	22	CT
Bradley, Benedict	1807	24	CT	Brigden, Daniel	1804	19	CT
Bradley, Chauncey	1810	19	CT	Brigden, Jonathan	1810	21	CT
Bradley, Chauncey	1809	17	CT	Bright, John	1838	23	NY
Bradley, Enos	1810	20	CT	Bright, Samuel	1838	21 b	MD
Bradley, Frederick	1815	15	CT	Bringden, John	1808	18	CT
Bradley, George	1819	20	CT	Brinsmaid, Joseph	1804	33 b	CT
Bradley, George W.	1820	23	CT	Brintral, Elihu M.	1823	16	CT
Bradley, George W.	1816	19	CT	Brisco, Joseph	1808	23	CT
Bradley, Herbey	1815	23	CT	Bristol, Nehemiah	1806	21	CT
Bradley, Hezekiah	1801	27	CT	Bristol, Nehemiah	1804	19	CT
Bradley, Horace	1825	16	CT	Bristol, Noble	1820	19	CT
Bradley, Horace	1809	17	CT	Bristol, Philander	1827	19	NY
Bradley, Isaac	1807	21	CT	Bristol, Stephen	1804	18	CT
Bradley, Isaac	1809	23	CT	Bristol, Vean	1810	21 y	CT
Bradley, Jairus	1805	15	CT	Bristol, Vean	1818	29 y	CT
Bradley, James	1815	35	CT	Bristol, William	1819	26 b	PA
Bradley, Jesse	1831	19	CT	Bristol, Wm.	1819	26 b	PA
Bradley, Jesse	1810	17	CT	Brocket, Abrm.	1804	22	CT
Bradley, Jno. Smith	1832	17	CT	Brocket, Benjamin	1809	40	CT
Bradley, John	1813	20	CT	Brocket, Sidney	1811	20	CT
Bradley, John	1804	19	CT	Brockett, Alfred	1823	20	CT
Bradley, John	1812	26	CT	Brockett, Charles	1843	22	CT
Bradley, John	1807	39	CT	Brockett, Lyman G.	1843	20	CT
Bradley, John	1812	26	CT	Brockett, Mraham	1803	20	CT
Bradley, Justua, Jr.	1815	15	CT	Brockett, Seymor	1815	16	CT
Bradley, Justus, Jr.	1819	19	CT	Brockett, Seymore	1841	42	CT
Bradley, Justus, Jr.	1823	22	CT	Brockett, Sidney	1813	22	CT
Bradley, Leman	1810	17	CT	Brockett, William	1811	17	CT
Bradley, Lyman	1815	25	CT	Brodie, John	1813	18	NY
Bradley, Philo	1809	18	CT	Bronson, Augustus	1809	25	CT
Bradley, Philo	1811	20	CT	Bronson, Titus	1810	21	CT
Bradley, Russell	1816	20	CT	Brook, Peter	1809	22	NY
Bradley, Saml.	1831	30	CT	Brooks, Daniel	1807	20	CT
Bradley, Saml.	1805	20	CT	Brooks, Henry	1804	27	CT
Bradley, Samuel	1804	19	CT	Brooks, William M.	1835	21 y	CT

Brooks, Wm.	1805	29		CT	Buckingham,Frederick	1815	15	CT
Brooks, Wm. M.	1843	28	y	CT
Broome, Horatio	1803	24		CT
Broughton, William	1818	18		CT
Brower, Wm.	1842	35		NY
Brown, Abijah Ellis	1807	34		VT
Brown, Benjamin	1804	21		CT
Brown, Benjamin P.	1810	16		CT
Brown, Charles	1809	20	b	NY
Brown,Christopher M.	1843	22	b	CT
Brown, Cornelius L.	1841	18	b	CT
Brown, Cornelius L.	1843	20	b	CT
Brown, Elam C.	1804	25		CT
Brown, Elam Cook	1807	28		CT
Brown, Francis H.	1815	16		CT
Brown, Gad	1822	24	b	CT
Brown, Gad	1827	29	b	CT
Brown, George	1824	26		RI
Brown, Isaac	1803	37		CT
Brown, Jabez, Jr.	1803	23		CT
Brown, James	1805	22		CT
Brown, James	1812	22		CT
Brown, Jesse	1816	28	y	NY
Brown, Jno	1832	33	b	NY
Brown, John	1837	14	b	CT
Brown, John	1841	23		ME
Brown, John	1821	19		NY
Brown, John	1820	17		CT
Brown, John	1830	30	b	NY
Brown, John	1806	17		CT
Brown, John	1807	17		RI
Brown, John	1805	26		VA
Brown, John T.	1805	17		CT
Brown, Joseph	1843	52		ME
Brown, Joseph	1802	21		NY
Brown, Joseph	1804	26	b	NY
Brown, Leverett	1825	21		CT
Brown, Saml.	1821	32	y	CT
Brown, Samuel	1810	19	y	CT
Brown, Seth	1807	18		CT
Brown, Stephen	1805	22		CT
Brown, Stephen	1822	22	b	NY
Brown, Stephen	1823	24	b	NY
Brown, Stephen	1823	25	b	NY
Brown, Thomas	1842	22		MA
Brown, Ths.	1825	34	b	NY
Brown, William	1814	25	y	NY
Brown, William	1820	26	b	NY
Brown, William	1806	26		RI
Brown, William	1806	24		CT
Brown, William	1809	22		MA
Buchanan, Wm.	1807	25		CT
Bucher, Thaddeus	1837	14		CT
Buck, Richard	1806	24		CT

Buckingham,Frederick	1815	15		CT
Buckingham, Sidney	1813	16		CT
Buckingham, Sidney	1812	15		CT
Buckland, Russel	1810	23		CT
Budington, Horace	1807	15		CT
Budington, William	1811	21		CT
Buell,Chas.Whittlesey	1811	25		NH
Buell, George	1805	25		CT
Buell, William	1809	18		VT
Buell, Wm.	1813	22		VT
Bule, James, Jr.	1819	23		CT
Bule, Philip	1811	16		CT
Bulford, Albon	1809	18		CT
Bulford, Albon	1812	21		CT
Bulford, Ira	1809	22		CT
Bulford, Ira	1806	20		CT
Bulford, Marcus	1813	17		CT
Bulkley, Hanford	1842	24	b	CT
Bulkley, Hunford	1841	24	b	CT
Bulkley, William	1806	13		CT
Bull, James	1803	32		CT
Bullard, John	1842	32		MA
Bun, Thaddeus	1808	18		CT
Bunce, Daniel	1836	23		CT
Bunce, Jason	1820	28		CT
Bunnel, Dennis D.	1835	19		CT
Bunnel, Nath.	1807	20		CT
Bunnel, Nathl.	1806	31		CT
Bunnel, Reuben	1805	19		CT
Bunnel, Warham	1803	22		CT
Bunnell, Jared P.	1817	16		CT
Bunnell, Lucins	1843	17		CT
Bunnell, Nathaniel	1805	18		CT
Bunnell, Warham	1804	23		CT
Bunnell, William	1810	19		
Bunniel, Jesse	1805	21		CT
Bunniel, Wm.	1810	18		CT
Burhnel, Shelton	1805	21		CT
Burk, William	1841	18		GA
Burnell, Nath.	1806	19		CT
Burnham, Martin	1843	26		CT
Burns, William	1804	19		PA
Burrile, Ebenezer	1806	25		CT
Burrill, Samuel	1803	28		
Burritt, Abijah W.	1816	25		CT
Burrows, Peter	1842	24	b	NJ
Burrows, William	1815	12		NY
Burt, Rodney	1803	21		MA
Burt, Samuel	1804	17		CT
Burton, John	1803	45		NY
Burwell, Leveret	1809	17		CT
Burwell, Lyman	1818	29		CT
Burwell, Robert	1811	19		CT
Bush, Gilbert	1803	19		CT

Bush, Henry	1837	22		Germany	Cannon, Lewis	1819	23	CT
Bush, William	1805	20	CT		Carr, Sienos	1832	22 b	NY
Bushnell, Sheldon	1803	20	CT		Carrier, Lucius	1836	26 b	CT
Butler, Aaron	1837	40 b	NJ		Carrier, Peter	1803	27	CT
Butler, David	1805	22	CT		Carrington,Nehemiah	1805	22	CT
Butler, George Lewis	1816	24	CT		Carrington, Robert	1832	21	CT
Butler, James	1815	23	CT		Carrington, Robert	1836	25	CT
Butler, James	1828	31 m	NJ		Carter, James	1805	26	CT
Butler, James	1807	16	NH		Carter, Jared	1824	17	CT
Butler, James	1810	18	CT		Carter, John	1810	19	CT
Butler, John	1807	31	CT		Carter, Wm.	1828	16	CT
Butler, John	1818	41	CT		Casey, Andrew J. M.	1842	16 b	CT
Butler, Merit	1810	17	CT		Casey, Roswell	1838	34 b	CT
Butler, Timothy	1806	21	CT		Cason, William	1804	18	CT
Butler, Timothy	1824	36	CT		Cass, Joseph	1810	22	NH
Butler, Timothy	1823	36	CT		Cass, Luther	1810	20	NH
Butler, William	1815	17	CT		Castle, Elisur	1807	25	CT
Butler, William	1820	22	CT		Catlin, Othaniel	1806	22	CT
Butler, William	1815	19	CT		Ceables, Ezekiel	1835	23 b	CT
Butler, William	1806	20	CT		Cermer, Henry	1809	30 b	NY
Butler, Wm.	1825	25	CT		Cezanne, James D.	1811	18	CT
Butler, Wm. H.	1826	18	CT		Chaffin, Lyman	1812	19	NH
Button, Hubbard	1819	23	CT		Chaffin, Lyman	1810	17	NH
Button, John	1843	21	CT		Chalker, William	1805	20	CT
Cadney, Henry	1836	28	CT		Chamberlin, Calvin	1815	22	CT
Cadwell, Mason	1825	19	CT		Chambers, David	1838	43 b	PA
Cady, Aaron	1804	29	MS		Champlin, Prince	1819	24 b	RI
Cain, David O.	1843	28	CT		Chandler,Chas.Henry	1812	27	CT
Calkin, Zera	1815	23	CT		Chapin, Moses	1836	17 y	NY
Calliver, Ambrose	1803	21	VA		Chapman, Chas. C.	1842	18	NY
Calliver, Ambrose	1807	25 b	VA		Chapman, Samuel	1806	34	CT
Calver, Caleb	1806	26	CT		Chapman, William	1805	23	CT
Calver, Eliakim	1806	21	CT		Chapman, William	1826	17	CT
Cam, Charles	1834	29 b	CT		Chapman, Wm.	1803	21	
Cam, Isaac	1836	34 b	CT		Chatfield, Curtis	1810	18	CT
Cambridge, Thomas	1804	21 y	CT		Chatfield, David	1810	16	CT
Came, Ambrose O.	1816	19	CT		Chatfield, Stoddard	1812	18	CT
Camp, Eli B.	1818	18	CT		Chatfield, Yarmouth	1807	40	CT
Camp, Saml.	1804	19	CT		Chatman, Jacob	1812	33	CT
Camp, Saml., Jr.	1810	27	CT		Chatman, John	1813	28 b	PA
Camp, Saml., Jun.	1806	21			Chatterton, Samuel	1804	21	CT
Camp, Samuel	1803	18	CT		Chatteston,JohnHenry	1828	17	CT
Camp, Samuel, Jr.	1822	39	CT		Chidsey, Azel	1804	23	CT
Camp, Samuel, Jr.	1811	28	CT		Chidsey, Azel	1804	23	CT
Camp, Samuel, Jun.	1815	33	CT		Chidsey, Fredk.Street	1820	16	CT
Campbell, Josiah	1812	20	NH		Chidsey, Hervey	1809	20	CT
Candce, Arnold	1805	29	CT		Chidsey, Jacob	1809	30	CT
Cande, Caleb, Jr.	1803	22	CT		Chidsey, John	1804	21	CT
Candee, Jason	1807	21	CT		Chidsey, Roswell	1806	21	CT
Candee, Timothy	1807	23	CT		Chidsey, Ruel	1803	27	
Candy, Enos C.	1804	22	CT		Chidsey, Samuel	1811	24	CT
Canfield, Jesse	1807	21	CT		Chidsey, Samuel	1809	21	CT
Canfield, Lockwood	1803	21	CT		Chidsey, William H.	1815	17	CT
Cannon, Lewis	1815	20	CT		Chiles, William	1838	18	CT

Chillendon, Augustus	1811	21		CT
Chittenden, Wm.	1805	28		CT
Church, Elisha	1811	19	b	CT
Church, Josiah	1803	34		CT
Church, Nathan B.	1822	24		CT
Church, William	1825	17	y	CT
Clark, Albert	1811	17		CT
Clark, Albert	1812	18		CT
Clark, Alfred	1809	25		CT
Clark, Ashbel	1805	25		CT
Clark, Bela	1804	19		CT
Clark, Bela	1803	17		CT
Clark, Beta	1804	18		CT
Clark, Cephas	1805	19		CT
Clark, Chester	1811	31		CT
Clark, Daniel Fitch	1819	17		CT
Clark, Daniel Phipps	1820	17		CT
Clark, Ebenezer	1804	20		CT
Clark, Enoch	1807	18		NY
Clark, Enoch	1805	17		NY
Clark, George	1815	26		NY
Clark, Harrison	1836	16		NH
Clark, Isaac	1820	25	b	NY
Clark, Isaac	1805	19		CT
Clark, James	1808	21		CT
Clark, James	1831	25		CT
Clark, James, Jr.	1815	19		CT
Clark, John	1804	16		CT
Clark, John	1813	25		NY
Clark, John M.	1843	17		CT
Clark, John W.	1803	19		MA
Clark, John, Jr.	1806	25		CT
Clark, Joseph	1807	24	b	CT
Clark, Joseph G.	1843	32		MA
Clark, Josiah	1805	19		CT
Clark, Josiah	1811	24		CT
Clark, Merit	1843	23		CT
Clark, Merit	1841	21		CT
Clark, Oliver	1805	34		CT
Clark, Othe	1806	23		CT
Clark, Reuben	1815	16		NY
Clark, Richard M.	1805	18		CT
Clark, Rufus	1807	30		CT
Clark, Samuel James	1810	16		CT
Clark, Shuman	1830	24	b	CT
Clark, Thaddius J.	1804	23		CT
Clark, William	1822	21		ME
Clark, Wm. Lewis	1807	26		CT
Clark, Wooster	1803	23		CT
Clarke, Halsey	1825	16		CT
Clarke, Mark	1807	16		CT
Clarke, Marshal	1807	19		CT
Clarke, Merit M.	1843	20		CT
Clary, Timothy	1811	22		NY
Claus, John	1805	30		CT
Claus, John	1804	29		CT
Clements, William	1827	43		CT
Clements, William	1819	35		CT
Clements, William	1810	26		CT
Clements, Wm.	1826	42		CT
Clemons, Isaac	1807	18		CT
Clinton, David H.	1824	23		CT
Clinton, Henry	1829	25		CT
Cloutman, Stephen	1807	26		MA
Coates, Samuel	1805	21		MD
Coats, Martin	1806	18	b	NY
Coborn, George	1811	22		MA
Coburn, Alexander	1802	23		VT
Coburn, Alexr. O.	1827	29		CT
Coburn, John	1824	15		CT
Coburn, John]	1825	16		CT
Coburn, Miles	1813	22		CT
Coc, Ambros	1835	20	b	CT
Coe, Chs.	1829	23	y	CT
Coe, Claudius L.	1809	24		MA
Coe, Ira	1835	22	b	CT
Coffin, Joseph	1842	25		LA
Coggerhall, Robert	1808	20		CT
Coggeshall, Charles	1811	18		CT
Coggeshall, Francis	1819	22		CT
Coggeshall, Freegift	1807	39		CT
Coggeshall, Freegift	1807	33		CT
Coggeshall, Fregift	1810	13		CT
Coggeshall, Fregift	1803	35		CT
Coggeshall, George	1803	19		CT
Coggeshall, James	1815	20		CT
Coggeshall, Robert	1803	16		CT
Coggeshall, Thomas	1818	19		CT
Coggeshall, William	1805	25		CT
Colborn, Ruben	1810	21		CT
Colbum, Erastus	1815	21		CT
Cole, Charles	1809	17		CT
Cole, George	1819	18		CT
Cole, Leander	1803	24		MA
Collier, Daniel	1805	22		CT
Collier, William, Jr.	1804	19		CT
Collins, Daniel	1808	30		MA
Collins, William	1837	27		MD
Collis, Andrew D.	1824	17		CT
Collis, Daniel	1804	16		CT
Collis, Daniel	1805	18		CT
Collis, Charles	1805	21		PA
Colson, James	1803	23		CT
Colson/Coulson, James	1805	25		CT
Colwell, William L.	1837	21		NJ
Colyer, Ezra	1843	24		CT
Colyer, Ezra	1837	21		CT
Comber, Thomas W.	1806	22		CT

Comes, Lemuel	1805	20	CT	Crawford, John	1807	25	NJ
Comstock, John	1805	21	CT	Cread, John W.	1817	18 y	CT
Conklin, Joseph	1821	21	CT	Crie, Thomas	1811	13	MA
Conkling, Bradley J.	1815	22	NY	Crocker, Daniel, Jr.	1804	17	CT
Conticou, William	1815	12	CT	Crockett, Henry	1837	28 b	MD
Cook, Abraham	1804	26	NJ	Crofton, Edward	1811	20	CT
Cook, Charles	1803	55		Crofts, Edward B.	1832	19	CT
Cook, George	1834	36	NJ	Crosby, George	1838	20 b	MA
Cook, Isaac	1804	22	CT	Crosby, Ilisha	1805	22	CT
Cook, Leveret	1811	17	CT	Crosby, John	1842	23	NH
Cook, Major	1813	19	CT	Crowel, Wm.	1812	26	
Cook, Orin	1811	27	CT	Cruttenden, Joel	1804	22	CT
Cook, Saml.	1805	21 b	NY	Culp, Nelson	1843	20	NY
Cook, Samuel	1805	0 b	NY	Culuer, Thadeus	1817	19	CT
Cook, Samuel	1805	21 b	NY	Culver, Andrew	1820	16	CT
Cook, Samuel	1803	24	NY	Culver, Caleb	1803	23	CT
Cook, Ssmuel	1803	24 b		Culver, Caleb	1808	28	CT
Cook, Thomas	1804	55		Culver, Caleb	1807	27	CT
Cook, Thomas	1805	19	PA	Culver, Caleb	1805	25	CT
Cook, William Henry	1835	18	CT	Culver, Lucius M.	1820	19	CT
Cooley, Ariel	1837	37	CT	Cumber, Thomas W.	1804	20	CT
Cooley, Ariel	1818	18	CT	Curphe, Nelson	1838	20 b	NY
Cooper, Elias	1804	18	CT	Curtis, Abner	1804	17	CT
Cooper, Jeremiah	1831	33	CT	Curtis, Abner	1805	18	CT
Cooper, Jeremiah	1820	22	CT	Curtis, Abner	1805	18	CT
Cooper, John H.	1808	27	CT	Curtis, Artemus	1811	24	NY
Cooper, Obed	1807	23	CT	Curtis, Artimas	1811	24	NY
Cooper, Peter	1806	21	CT	Curtis, Benjn.	1815	17	CT
Corbet, Dennis	1804	27	PA	Curtis, Charles	1841	14 b	CT
Corbin, Oliver	1806	18 y	CT	Curtis, Charles	1842	14 b	CT
Corbit, Dennis	1806	29	PA	Curtis, David	1803	22	CT
Cordwell, Wm.	1806	27		Curtis, David	1803	26	VT
Comer, Freeman	1825	23 b	CT	Curtis, Henry	1812	16	CT
Cory, Job	1804	28	CT	Curtis, Israel	1804	24	CT
Cory, Job	1803	27		Curtis, Jacob	1817	17	CT
Cory, Job	1809	32	CT	Curtis, James	1810	17	CT
Cory, John	1814	26	CT	Curtis, James	1809	21	CT
Coss, Rufus	1837	28 b	CT	Curtis, Joseph	1809	20	CT
Cousins, Brook	1837	19	ME	Curtis, Josiah B.	1806	16	CT
Cowles, Anson	1811	26	CT	Curtis, Levi	1812	21	CT
Cowles, Ira	1809	22	CT	Curtis, Morgan	1821	19	CT
Cox, Thomas Frederick	1838	29	RI	Curtis, Nath. Wheeler	1815	20	CT
Craft, Samuel	1805	21	CT	Curtis, Phineas	1805	40	CT
Crafts, Saml. P.	1843	19	CT	Curtis, Russel	1810	19	CT
Crafts, William	1841	21	NY	Curtis, Russell	1815	23	CT
Crampton, Jesse	1805	22	CT	Curtis, Samuel	1813	19	CT
Crampton, William	1804	25	CT	Curtis, Samuel	1811	18	CT
Crampton, Wm.	1838	19	CT	Curtis, Thomas	1836	21 b	NY
Cramton, Uriah	1806	20	CT	Curtis, Thomas P.	1843	23	CT
Crandal, Harvey	1836	28	RI	Curtis, Thos.	1803	29	SC
Crandale, John	1813	36	MA	Curtis, Wait	1807	19	CT
Crandle, John	1803	23	MA	Curtis, Wait	1805	18	CT
Crawford, Isaac	1805	16	PA	Curtiss, Rodney	1828	18	CT
Crawford, John	1805	14	DE	Cutler, Benjamin	1803	22	CT

Cutler, Benjamin	1811	29		CT	Davis, William	1804	33	CT
Cutton, Benjn.	1815	25 b	MD	Davis, Willys	1803	18	CT
Dade, Langhorne	1836	32	VA	Dawny, Hiram	1835	21 b	CT
Daggete, Elihu	1806	24	CT	Day, Horatio, Jr.	1805	23	CT
Dane, Samuel	1841	49	NY	Day, Isaac	1809	17	CT
Daniels, Bristol	1804	23 b	CT	Day, Wareham	1810	20	CT
Daniels, Brutes	1828	25 b	CT	Dayton, Spencer	1803	24	CT
Daniels, Genge E. D.	1841	14	CT	Dean, Elias	1808	18	CT
Daniels, Peter	1829	26	CT	Dean, Elias	1805	15	CT
Daniels, Peter	1805	21	NC	Dean, Henry	1811	14	NY
Daniels, Prince	1820	24 b	CT	Dean, Thomas	1819	15	NJ
Danow, Erastus	1803	22	CT	Dean, Thos.	1826	21	NJ
Darling, John	1807	18	CT	Dear, Wm. Roger	1807	16	CT
Darrow, Christopher	1805	27	CT	Deas, George	1824	37	NY
Dart, David Wm.	1821	19	CT	Death, Charles	1837	20	PA
Dart, Joseph	1807	23	CT	Deedly, Loveman	1805	25	CT
Dart, Levi	1803	17	CT	Deforest,Wm.Wheeler	1812	18	CT
Dart, William	1805	25	CT	Deforest,Wm.Wheeler	1806	12	CT
Daton, Delos W.	1842	24	NY	DeGrasse, Elias	1842	28 y	MA
Davenport, John	1811	17	CT	Degroat, William H.	1803	27	NY
Davenport, John	1813	20	CT	DeGroat, William H.	1805	30	NY
Davenport, John	1810	16	CT	DeGroat, William H.	1809	33	NY
Davenport, William	1812	16	CT	Degroat, Wm. H.	1805	30	NY
Davenport, William	1811	15	CT	DeGroat, Wm. H.	1805	29	NY
Davenport, Wm.	1815	19	CT	DeGroot, Wm. H.	1805	29	NY
Davey, Christopher	1823	33	CT	Dembar, James	1843	21 b	CT
Davidson, Abya	1803	19		Deming, Chs. T.	1834	19	CT
Davidson, Henry	1811	21	CT	Deming, Elizur	1824	18	CT
Davidson,JeremiahB.	1811	21	CT	Deming, Harry	1808	19	CT
Davidson, Treat	1809	18	CT	Deming, Henry	1812	23	CT
Davis, Benjamin	1804	17	CT	Deming, Henry	1827	36	CT
Davis, Ebnezer	1805	28	CT	Deming, Henry	1827	26	CT
Davis, Isaac	1805	18	CT	Deming, Henry	1804	15	CT
Davis, James	1809	16	CT	Deming, Henry	1804	14	CT
Davis, James L.	1821	58	CT	Deming, James	1813	26	CT
Davis,JamesSolomon	1823	60	CT	Deming, James	1805	18	CT
Davis, John	1842	17	NJ	Demming, Abner	1807	29	CT
Davis, John	1803	19	CT	Demming, Henry	1805	16	CT
Davis, John	1803	19	CT	Demming, James	1806	18	CT
Davis, John	1808	22	CT	Demming, James	1810	22	CT
Davis, John	1810	12	CT	Demon, George	1803	16	
Davis, John	1805	21	CT	Dempster, John	1842	18	NY
Davis, John W.	1820	14	CT	Denlows, James	1807	18	CT
Davis, Joseph	1811	11	CT	Dennis, Thomas	1819	27 b	VA
Davis, Russell	1807	23	CT	Denslow, James	1810	22	CT
Davis, Solomon	1806	17	CT	Deming, James	1815	29	CT
Davis, Solomon	1812	46	CT	Deryo, London	1816	26 b	NY
Davis, Solomon	1813	47	CT	Devine, John	1842	21	NY
Davis, Solomon	1820	53	CT	Dewey, Benjamin	1821	16	NY
Davis, Solomon	1804	16	CT	Dewey, Francis	1820	21	MA
Davis, Solomon, Jr.	1809	20	CT	DeWitt, John	1804	22	CT
Davis, Thomas	1803	21	CT	Dexter, George	1803	37	RI
Davis, Thomas	1824	17	CT	Dexter, Luther W.	1803	22	CT
Davis, William	1842	24 y	NY	Dexter, Sibley P.	1804	36	MA

Dickenson, William	1804	17	
Dickerman, Benj.	1806	15	CT
Dickinson, Damon	1807	18	CT
Dickinson, Harry	1807	19	CT
Dickinson, Henry	1806	17	CT
Dickinson, Henry	1805	17	CT
Dickinson, Ozias	1806	23	CT
Dickinson, Stephen	1805	18	MA
Dickman, Charles	1815	18	MA
Dickson, John	1816	16	CT
Dickson, John	1806	19	MD
Digans, Abel	1830	39 b	CT
Diggins, Stephen H.	1819	23 y	CT
Disbury, Nehemiah	1812	35 b	CT
Divine, George	1842	26	ME
Doans, John W.	1816	16	CT
Dodd, John	1803	21	CT
Dodd, Joseph	1803	16	CT
Dodd, Joseph	1805	18	CT
Dodd, Stephen	1806	18	CT
Dodd, Stephen	1807	19	CT
Dodd, Thomas	1807	20	CT
Dodd, Thomas	1804	18	CT
Dodd, Thos	1803	17	CT
Dolittle, Obed D.	1818	29	CT
Doolittle, Isaac, Jr.	1804	20	CT
Doolittle, Isaac, Jr.	1810	26	CT
Doolittle, John	1815	20	CT
Doolittle, Obed Dana	1811	22	CT
Dorman, Allen	1825	20	CT
Dorman, Allen A.	1841	36	CT
Dorman, Alling	1828	23	CT
Dorman, Amasa	1804	39	CT
Dorman, Amasa	1803	38	CT
Dorman, David	1805	11	CT
Dorman, David, Jr.	1807	13	CT
Dorman, Davis	1815	20	CT
Dorman, Henry	1818	16	CT
Dorsey, Elias	1843	26 y	MD
Dorsey, Robert	1813	15	NJ
Dossey, Robert	1815	19	NJ
Dougal, Thomas	1803	20	CT
Dougal, William	1803	23	CT
Douglass, Jeremiah	1811	19	MD
Douns, Henry	1817	19	CT
Dow, Bernah L.	1826	27	MA
Dowd, Alfred G.	1826	16	CT
Downs, Eli	1809	17	CT
Downs, Leverett	1843	27	CT
Downs, Luther	1803	24	CT
Downs, Sewell	1832	18	CT
Drake, Frank	1805	28 b	CT
Dreen, Geo.	1827	32 b	CT
Drew, Charles	1803	23	MA
Drew, John	1819	19	CT
Driver, Hervry	1819	17	CT
Duay, Thomas	1803	15	CT
Dudley, Augustus B.	1811	20	CT
Dudley, Erastus	1805	22	CT
Dudley, Russ	1805	21	CT
Dudley, William C.	1822	18	CT
Dummer, Charles	1818	23	CT
Dummit, John	1837	24 y	NY
Duncan, James	1803	22	MD
Duncan, James	1807	26	MD
Dundas, Charles	1818	26	NY
Dunn, Sirus	1837	32 b	NJ
Dunning, Joseph H.	1838	22	CT
Duplex, Mark	1822	20 y	CT
Durand, Miles	1810	27	CT
Dutcher, Wm. A.	1843	33 b	DC
Dutton, Israel	1807	23	CT
Dyer, Charles	1810	30 b	CT
Dyer, William	1805	16	CT
Dykeman, Cyrus	1815	16	CT
Earley, John	1813	23	CT
Early, John	1816	26	CT
Edeards, Wm.	1815	25 ·	CT
Edgar, William	1814	18 y	MA
Edwards, Abel	1820	23	CT
Edwards, Clark	1803	16	CT
Eggleston, John	1803	36	CT
Eld, Henry, Jr.	1830	15	CT
Elderkin, John	1805	44	CT
Eldred, Richard	1807	21	NY
Ellen, Robert	1807	26	PA
Ellis, David	1837	17	MA
Ellis, James	1817	15	CT
Ellis, William R.	1805	21	CT
Ellis, Wm. M.	1823	20	VT
Elsworth, John	1815	28 y	NY
Elwekk, Samuel	1803	24	CT
Emerson, Genge	1841	47	RI
Emery, Amaziah	1825	17	ME
Emery, David	1803	23	NJ
Emmerson, George	1841	40	RI
Emmons, Cornelius H.	1841	21	CT
Enesson, John	1819	20 b	NY
English, Harry	1820	17	CT
English, Henry B.	1836	17	CT
English, Isaac	1803	21	CT
English, James	1806	22	CT
English, Judson	1815	20	CT
English, Nathan	1805	13	CT
English, Nathan F.	1812	19	CT
English, Nathan Fred.	1810	18	CT
Ensign, Zophar	1805	19	CT
Esham, Robert	1818	25 b	MD

Estey, Joseph	1808	20		MA	Fisher, Wm. L.	1836	18		CT
Evarts, Samuel, 3	1811	21		CT	Fitch, Nathe.	1806	28		CT
Evis, Levi	1805	23		CT	Flanagan, John	1815	33		MD
Evis, Solomon	1811	17		CT	Flavel, John	1804	27		NY
Evisne, Robert	1841	20	b	CT	Fleet, Edward	1833	0		
Evison, Robert	1841	20	b	CT	Fletcher,Wm. Aug.	1822	19	y	MA
Fabens, James	1819	32		MA	Fletcher, Wm.	1825	21	y	MA
Facey, James	1811	14		MA	Flint, Elijah	1813	23		CT
Fainten, Ruben	1811	26		CT	Flint, Robert	1810	34		NC
Fairchild, George N.	1819	18		CT	Finence, William	1841	19		NY
Fairchild, Lacy	1842	22	b	CT	Flock, Jacob	1803	26		France
Fallantine, Alexander	1806	20		PA	Floyd, Washington	1841	20	y	NY
Fancher, Giles	1805	24		CT	Floyd, Washington	1842	21	y	NY
Fanen, James	1817	22		CT	Flying, Charles	1824	27	b	CT
Fanin/Farrin, John	1805	23		CT	Flying, Chs.	1825	25	b	CT
Fannin, David	1810	25		CT	Foot, David	1824	21		CT
Fanning, David	1816	36		CT	Foot, Foster	1804	17		CT
Fanning, David	1801	0		CT	Foot, Foster	1806	19		CT
Fanning, James	1819	22		CT	Foot, Hanison	1824	21		CT
Fanning, James	1809	13		CT	Foot, Jacob	1823	25		CT
Fanning, James B.	1809	13		CT	Foot, Ralph	1803	21		CT
Fanning, James B.	1810	13		CT	Foot, Saml. E	1805	17		CT
Fanning, James B.	1817	20		CT	Foot, Saml. E.	1805	18		CT
Fanning, John C.	1810	15		CT	Foote, Benjamin P.	1841	20		CT
Fanning,Thos.Hopkins	1807	20		CT	Forbes, Ichabod	1803	16		CT
Fardy, John	1842	20		MA	Forbes, James	1803	18		CT
Farmer, Jacob	1825	20	b	NY	Forbes, James	1803	18		CT
Farmer, Samuel	1841	25		ME	Forbes, James	1804	19		CT
Famham, Giles	1830	18		CT	Forbes, James	1807	23		CT
Famham, Giles	1805	18		CT	Forbes, James	1806	21		CT
Farrand, John	1801	20		CT	Forbes, Levi	1804	20		CT
Fash, John	1819	25		NY	Forbes, Levi	1816	31		CT
Faulker, Charles	1806	33		CT	Forbes,William J., Jr.	1837	16		CT
Felch, Augustus	1837	22		VT	Forbes, Wylleys	1809	16		MA
Fengurson, John	1836	25	b	NY	Ford, Benjamin	1805	21		CT
Fenn, Archibald	1805	26		CT	Ford, Benjamin	1803	19		CT
Fenn, Guy C.	1805	22		CT	Ford, Benjamin	1804	20		
Fenno, Henry	1803	16		NY	Ford, Edward	1842	21		NY
Ferran, John	1818	18		CT	Ford, John	1804	21		CT
Ferren, Major	1810	22		CT	Ford, John	1806	23		CT
Ferren, Major	1812	23		CT	Ford, Johnson	1806	24		CT
Ferrin, John	1803	21		CT	Ford, Wilas	1805	19		NY
Fesmikison,Titus, Jr.	1843	31	y	NY	Ford, William	1809	20	y	CT
Field, Bennet	1803	23		VT	Forman, John	1818	23	y	NJ
Field, George	1822	23		CT	Forshew, John	1813	29		MA
Field, Jedidiah	1805	21		CT	Forsyth, Jonn. C.	1832	35		CT
Field, Johnson	1804	25		CT	Fortune, James, Jr.	1822	19		MA
Fields, Charles	1843	20		ME	Fortune, John	1807	28	b	CT
Filley, John	1842	31		CT	Fossett, Philip	1843	22		ME
Fish, Warren	1836	19		CT	Foster, Charles	1815	15		CT
Fisher, Alexander	1841	29	l	CT	Foster, John	1810	26		MD
Fisher, Alexr.	1843	31	b	CT	Fostor, Samuel	1807	32		CT
Fisher, Ebenezer	1806	19		CT	Fowler, Abraham	1836	22		CT
Fisher, Nicholas	1804	25		CT	Fowler, Bela	1804	25		CT

Fowler, Benjamin R.	1805	26	CT
Fowler, David	1804	22	MA
Fowler, George B.	1841	9 b	NY
Fowler, Isaac	1813	15 y	CT
Fowler, James	1805	27 b	CT
Fowler, James H.	1805	19	CT
Fowler, James H.	1806	20	CT
Fowler, James H.	1815	28	CT
Fowler, Jethro	1805	33 b	CT
Fowler, Joel	1805	15	CT
Fowler, John	1804	20	CT
Fowler, Leveritt	1805	18	CT
Fowler, Luke	1805	18	CT
Fowler, Randolph C.	1834	22	CT
Fowler, Rich.	1822	33 b	CT
Fowler, Richard	1815	26 b	CT
Frances, Russell	1822	35 y	CT
Francis, John	1842	27	LA
Francis, Lewis	1836	27 b	CT
Francis, Russel	1807	19 b	CT
Francis, Russell	1824	38 y	CT
Frank, Levi	1806	28 b	CT
Frankinson, Titus	1842	28 y	NY
Franklin, Joshua	1804	29	RI
Franklin, Moses	1807	32 y	CT
Frazer, John	1813	28	VA
Frederick, George	1804	21	CT
Freeman, Aaron	1825	33 b	CT
Freeman, Cato	1820	36 b	CT
Freeman, Cato	1811	26 b	CT
Freeman, Charles	1809	19 y	CT
Freeman, Charles	1813	22 b	MA
Freeman, Charles	1821	29 b	CT
Freeman, CharlesHoma	1833	21 b	CT
Freeman, Cyrus	1833	33 b	CT
Freeman, Ebenezer	1815	19 b	CT
Freeman, Hay	1832	24 b	CT
Freeman, Isaac	1833	26 b	CT
Freeman, Jack	1809	17 b	CT
Freeman, Jack	1805	13 b	CT
Freeman, James	1815	23 b	CT
Freeman, Jason	1811	19 b	CT
Freeman, Joel	1813	21 b	CT
Freeman, Joel	1811	19 b	CT
Freeman, Levi	1804	24	CT
Freeman, Levi	1804	24 b	CT
Freeman, Mark	1812	22 y	CT
Freeman, Mark	1811	21 y	CT
Freeman, Orrin	1836	19 y	MA
Freeman, Prince	1807	22 b	CT
Freeman, Prince	1806	26 b	CT
Freeman, Prince R.	1810	19 y	CT
Freeman, Reuben	1815	13 b	CT
Freeman, Reuben	1815	33 b	CT
Freeman, Reuben	1807	26 b	CT
Freeman, Reuben	1816	14 b	CT
Freeman, Richd.	1804	24 b	RI
Freeman, Ruben	1803	20 b	CT
Freeman, Ruben	1807	23 b	CT
Freeman, Russel	1842	22 y	NY
Freeman, Russell	1842	23 y	NY
Freeman, Theodore	1809	19 b	CT
Freeman, Truman	1838	19 b	CT
Freeman, William	1816	23	MA
Freeman, Wm. W.	1842	18	NJ
Freeman, Zachariah	1819	24 b	CT
French, Chs.	1825	18	CT
French, Daniel	1809	24	CT
French, Daniel	1813	32	CT
French, Jacob	1804	21	MA
French, Joseph	1808	34	CT
Frisbee, Calvin	1806	26	CT
Frisbey, Ransom	1809	18	CT
Frisbie, Augustus	1804	20	CT
Frisbie, Charles	1809	16	CT
Frisbie, Jared	1806	16	CT
Frisbie, Major	1828	19	CT
Frisbie, Major	1826	17	CT
Frisbie, Russel	1804	23	CT
Frisbie, Russell N.	1823	21	CT
Frisbie, Stephen D.	1820	20	CT
Fuller, Aaron	1803	20	CT
Fuller, Albert	1843	21 b	MA
Fuller, Benjamin	1819	29	RI
Fuller, Lewis	1843	36 b	MA
Fuller, Michael	1815	27 b	MA
Fulsom, John	1838	19	CT
Gabrue, Henry	1809	45	CT
Gairetson, Peter	1809	29 b	NY
Galpin, Neri	1807	25	CT
Gamble, William	1805	19	DE
Gamer, Frances	1832	21 b	CT
Gardiner, James	1808	21 y	CT
Gardner, John	1837	21 b	RI
Garner, Timothy	1815	22 y	CT
Gates, William D.	1834	19	CT
Gaunt, Levi	1812	26 b	PA
Gavit, John	1812	20	RI
Gay, John	1809	35	MA
Gaylard, Linas	1807	21	CT
Gears, Benjamin	1804	25	MD
Gears, Benjamin	1803	24	MD
George, Daniel	1815	18	MA
Gibbs, Barnard	1809	20	CT
Gibbs, Berney	1812	23	CT
Giblert, Amos, Jr.	1806	27	CT
Gibson, Cyrus	1812	18 b	CT
Gibson, Isaac	1811	42 b	CT

Gibson, James	1836	27 b	DE		Grace, Ginge	1841	25	CT
Gilbert, Chester	1815	18	CT		Gracie, Sheldon	1803	26	
Gilbert, David B.	1821	18	CT		Graham, Anson	1811	17	CT
Gilbert, Edmond B.	1841	17	CT		Graham, Edward	1833	24	CT
Gilbert, Elias	1805	34	CT		Graham, Henry	1805	22	NY
Gilbert, John	1805	24	CT		Graham, James	1805	29	CT
Gilbert, Marvin H.	1837	20	CT		Graham, James	1813	36	CT
Gilbert, Thomas	1805	28	CT		Graham, James	1803	0	CT
Gilbert, Wm.	1805	24	CT		Graham, Samuel H.	1838	16	CT
Gillet, Charles	1818	19	CT		Granness,Russell, Jr.	1815	18	CT
Gillet, Merit P.	1831	28	CT		Grannis, Alvey	1813	19	CT
Gillett, Jeremiah	1805	24	CT		Grannis, Alvy	1810	16	CT
Gipson, James	1812	19	NH		Grannis, David	1808	18	CT
Glazier, John	1803	36	CT		Grannis, David	1803	19	CT
Glazier, Permenus	1803	0	CT		Grannis, Isaac	1807	18	CT
Glenney, Jonas	1815	16	CT		Grannis, Jared	1815	18	CT
Glenney, William	1807	16	CT		Granniss, Anson	1821	21	CT
Glenny, Jonas G.	1816	17	CT		Granniss, Anson	1818	18	CT
Glenny, Lacket	1809	16			Granniss, Anthl.	1809	24	CT
Glezen, James	1806	28	MA		Granniss, Palmer	1811	24	CT
Glover, Cyrus B.	1809	24	CT		Granniss, Russell	1815	17	CT
Goings, William	1841	41 y	CT		Granniss, William	1811	15	CT
Goma, Francis	1832	21 b	CT		Grannuiss,George W.	1843	18	CT
Gomen, Francis	1831	19 b	CT		Grant, Alexander	1805	37	NY
Gomer, John	1818	15 b	NJ		Grant, Alexander	1805	36	NY
Goodale, Austin	1823	23	CT		Grant, Daniel	1804	26	CT
Goodrich, Edmond	1803	18	CT		Grant, James	1804	25	CT
Goodrich, Edmund	1805	19	CT		Grant, Robert	1804	31	CT
Goodrich, Henry	1841	22	CT		Grant, Willard	1837	20	ME
Goodrich, Henry	1841	22	CT		Grass, Nicholas	1827	22	NY
Goodrich, James	1819	16	CT		Graves, Billy	1815	17	NY
Goodrich, William	1807	19	CT		Graves, Harry	1815	20	NY
Goodwin, Richd. Yale	1813	21	CT		Graves, Harry	1809	15	NY
Goodyear, James	1806	19	CT		Graves, Nicholas	1822	16	NY
Goold, Samuel	1809	21 y	CT		Graves, Richard	1812	20	CT
Gordon, Alexander	1803	23	CT		Gray, Eli	1818	21 b	CT
Gordon, William	1808	21	CT		Gray, Solomon P.	1830	26 b	CT
Gordon, William	1806	19	CT		Grayson, George	1811	21	NY
Gordon, William	1805	18	CT		Green, David	1810	15	CT
Gorham, DeForest L.	1822	18	CT		Green, David T.	1843	33	NH
Gorham, Elias	1805	38	CT		Green, George Cook	1824	26	NY
Gorham, Elisha	1805	21	CT		Green, Hiram	1843	23	NY
Gorham, Henry	1805	18	CT		Green, John	1818	14	MA
Gorham, Henry	1810	23	CT		Green, Joseph	1819	23	RI
Gorham, Henry	1804	17	CT		Green, Joseph	1801	31	
Gorham, Henry, Jr.	1803	17	CT		Green, Leveret	1810	17	CT
Gorham, William	1841	21	GA		Green, Leveret	1806	15	CT
Gould, John M.	1836	25	West Indies		Green, Leverit	1807	15	CT
Gould, John W.	1803	19			Green, Leverit	1808	15	CT
Gould, John W.	1803	20	CT		Green, Leverit	1818	25	CT
Gould, Samuel	1808	20	CT		Green, William	1815	13	NH
Gould, Samuel	1805	17 y	CT		Greene, Leverit	1803	12	CT
Goumor, Francis	1841	29 b	CT		Greggory, Titus	1805	28 b	CT
Gowens, Wm.	1827	27 y	CT		Gregory, Titus	1805	28 b	CT

Grey, Jrely	1804	16 y	CT
Griffin, DeGrass	1834	28	CT
Griffing, DeGrasse	1843	36	CT
Griffing, Henry	1805	25	CT
Griffing,HenryAugustus	1820	20 b	CT
Griffing, Hethcut	1806	21	CT
Griffing, Jared	1841	16	CT
Griffing, John	1804	20	CT
Griffing, John	1804	19	CT
Griffing, Robert	1805	32	NY
Griffing, Roger	1816	20	CT
Griffith, Joseph	1804	26	CT
Griffiths, Henry	1817	19	CT
Griswold, Giles	1804	21	CT
Griswold, Jared	1811	18	CT
Griswold, Theodore	1843	20	NY
Griswold, William L.	1843	22	CT
Griswoould,Leverit B.	1815	17	CT
Griswould, Gerard	1815	22	CT
Gross, Nicholas	1831	25	NY
Gross, Nicholas	1824	18	NY
Grun, James	1805	41 b	PA
Grun/Green, William	1805	14	CT
Guggins, John K.	1803	18	
Gurd, John	1812	19	CT
Hadley, Hervey	1802	21	CT
Hale, Ezra	1811	21	CT
Hale, Hezekiah	1810	29	CT
Hale, Moses	1825	21 y	RI
Hale, William	1843	17	CT
Hall, Amaziah	1810	19	CT
Hall, Benjamin	1809	19	CT
Hall, Cambridge	1810	26 b	CT
Hall, Cambridge	1813	26 y	CT
Hall, Cambridge	1806	22 b	CT
Hall, Frederick	1810	18	CT
Hall, Geofrey	1804	18	CT
Hall, Harry	1809	32	CT
Hall, Henry	1807	30	CT
Hall, Henry	1843	30 b	RI
Hall, Isaac	1835	25	CT
Hall, Jacob	1842	37	NY
Hall, James	1842	25	DE
Hall, James	1837	16 m	CT
Hall, Josephus	1809	23	CT
Hall, Lewis	1841	24	MA
Hall, Samuel	1823	25	CT
Hall, Samuel	1812	17	CT
Hall, Sylvester	1803	19	CT
Hall, William	1824	17 y	CT
Halladay, Walter	1805	24	CT
Halland, Henry	1832	22 b	NY
Hambleton, Bryant	1825	21 y	MA
Hamilton, Richard	1804	28	CT
Hammich, Strephon	1815	34 y	CT
Hammick, Stephen	1811	30 y	CT
Hammock, Samuel	1805	30 y	CT
Hammond, Harrison	1843	15 b	NY
Hamson, Henry	1837	33	
Hand, Leveret	1805	21	CT
Hand, Leverit	1804	0	CT
Handy, Hail	1806	22	CT
Handy, James	1804	23	CT
Haneson, Henry	1824	14	CT
Hannan, Alexander	1808	15	NY
Hanson, Frederick	1803	0	
Harde, Charles G.?	1825	21	CT
Hargill, Christopher	1810	26	
Harrington, Asahel	1815	29	CT
Harris, Charles	1816	37 b	NY
Harris, Jesse	1824	26	MA
Harris, Robert	1816	21	MD
Harrison, Charles	1803	14	CT
Harrison, David	1803	22	CT
Harrison, Horace	1806	30	CT
Harrison, Jeremiah	1809	20	CT
Harrison, Martin	1809	24	CT
Harrison, Roderick R.	1809	22	CT
Harrison, RoderickRandom	1806	18	CT
Harrison, William B.	1822	19	CT
Hart, Asa Elliott	1822	19	CT
Hart, George	1822	21	MA
Hart, George B.	1822	21	NY
Hart, Henry	1823	28 b	NY
Hart, John Eliott	1812	19	CT
Hart, Johnson	1842	22 y	PA
Hart, Levi	1805	19	CT
Hart, Lewis	1803	46	
Hart, Murray	1805	21	CT
Hart, Robert	1815	14	CT
Hart, William	1811	23	CT
Harvey, Chestrer A.	1805	18	CT
Harwood,Saml.William	1810	13	CT
Hatch, Lucius	1818	32	CT
Hatchel, David	1810	16 y	CT
Hatchet, David	1811	16 y	CT
Hathaway, Cynus	1837	34 b	MA
Hawes, Samuel	1838	37	MA
Hawkins, John	1817	21	
Hawkins, John	1805	33	MA
Hawkins, John	1810	17	MA
Hawkins, Thomas	1815	26	CT
Hawkins, Truman	1830	19	CT
Hawley, Charles E.	1838	20 b	CT
Hawley, James	1828	32 b	CT
Haycock, John	1811	19	NY
Hayden, Daniel	1807	22	CT

Hayill, Christopher	1805	21	NY		Hill, Wm. L.	1827	17	CT
Haynes, John	1813	22	MA		Hiller, Joseph	1825	17	MA
Hayward, Levi	1807	14	MA		Hills, Genyi	1843	23	CT
Hazard, Robert	1807	20	NY		Hills, Percival S.	1841	19	CT
Heath, David	1811	20	NH		Hind, Samuel	1810	23	NY
Heaton, Edward	1829	16	CT		Hinds, Sam G.	1807	21	NY
Hebbard, Daniel	1805	18	CT		Hinds,Saml.Garretson	1805	19	NY
Hebbard, Samuel	1805	17	CT		Hine, Benjamin	1809	25	CT
Hebberd, Samuel	1804	15	CT		Hine, Josiah	1810	22	CT
Hecock, William	1804	27	CT		Hine, Josiah	1806	18	CT
Hecox, George	1815	31	CT		Hine, Newton	1811	13	CT
Height, John	1818	42	NY		Hine, Wyllys	1819	16	CT
Helbury, James	1811	25	Territory of US		Hine, Wyllys	1817	15	CT
Heller, Ephraim	1803	22	PA		Hinman, Herbert	1820	19	CT
Helton, William	1841	30	NY		Hinsdale, Wolcott	1815	20	CT
Hemingway, John	1842	35	CT		Hirox, George	1804	20	CT
Hemingway, John	1841	34	CT		Hitchcock, Benjamin	1807	18	CT
Heminway, Tyler	1807	17	CT		Hitchcock, Charles	1818	22	CT
Hempsted, John, Jr.	1806	20	CT		Hitchcock, Chs.	1827	26	CT
Hemstead,Josiah, Jr.	1815	21	CT		Hitchcock, Harman	1803	18	CT
Hendickian, Enos	1824	21 b	NJ		Hitchcock, Herman	1809	24	CT
Hendrick, Hervey	1807	21	CT		Hitchcock, Herman	1815	30	CT
Hendrick, William	1804	15	CT		Hitchcock, Herman	1810	25	CT
Heninway, Thompson	1811	24	CT		Hitchcock, Horace	1818	21	CT
Henry, Verus	1808	20	CT		Hitchcock, Munson	1804	21	CT
Hepburn, David	1813	20	CT		Hitchcock, Oliver C.	1805	21	CT
Hepburn, Nathaniel	1803	36	CT		Hitchcock, Oliver C.	1806	22	CT
Hewes, Joseph	1813	22	NJ		Hitchcock,OliverCrom.	1804	20	CT
Hewins, John	1812	26	MA		Hitchcock, Sheldon	1829	25	CT
Heylegar, Colin	1815	24 b	CT		Hitchcock, Thaddeus	1807	13	CT
Hibbard, Daniel	1808	20	CT		Hitchings, Luke	1837	25 y	PA
Hibbard, James	1813	18	CT		HJenderson, Wm.	1843	24	NY
Hibbard, Sam, Jr.	1807	19	CT		Hoadley, Demings	1806	21	CT
Hibbard, Samuel	1805	42	MA		Hoadley, Dennis	1810	27	CT
Hibbard, Samuel, Jr.	1813	24	CT		Hoadley, Dennis	1803	22	CT
Hichborn, Nathaniel	1805	41	MA		Hoadley, Harvey	1803	22	CT
Hickcox, William	1806	28	CT		Hoadley, Herman	1808	24	CT
Hicks, George Wm.	1815	14	CT		Hoadley, Isaac	1808	18	CT
Hicks, Samuel, Jr.	1812	19	CT		Hoadley, John P.	1809	16	CT
Hicox, George	1807	23	CT		Hoadley, Levi	1805	24	CT
Hicox, James Henry	1807	19	CT		Hoadley, Martin	1806	26	CT
Higby, Harman	1836	29	CT		Hoadley, Martin	1803	24	CT
Hill, George	1825	29 b	CT		Hoadley, Martin	1801	22	
Hill, George	1815	19 b	CT		Hoadley, Ralph	1815	19	CT
Hill, Henry	1815	17 b	CT		Hoadley, Samuel	1810	17	CT
Hill, Henry	1813	15 b	CT		Hoadley, Samuel L.	1807	17	CT
Hill, Jacob	1843	52 b	PA		Hodge, Benjamin	1816	24	CT
Hill, James P.	1825	21	ME		Hodge, David	1805	23	CT
Hill, John	1804	23	MA		Hodge, Elias	1810	10	CT
Hill, John	1807	24	MA		Hodge, James	1838	30 b	MD
Hill, Joseph	1805	37	CT		Hoffman, Saml	1803	38	CT
Hill, Reuben	1811	21	CT		Hoffman, Saml.	1805	40	CT
Hill, Richard	1805	29	CT		Hoffman, Samuel	1805	40	CT
Hill, William	1825	21	CT		Holbook,HumphreyW.	1825	19 b	CT

Holbrook, Benjn. F.	1820	18	CT
Holbrook, David	1815	32	CT
Holbrook,HumphreyW.	1831	25 b	CT
Holbrook, Philo	1820	18	CT
Holbrook, Silas	1815	30	MA
Holdridge, Elkanah	1810	17	CT
Holland, Henry K.	1829	22	MA
Hollins, Peter	1821	25	
Holmes, Allen	1843	30 b	PA
Holmes, Jehial	1805	19	CT
Holmes, John	1803	28	CT
Holmes, Simeon	1805	49	CT
Holt, James, Jr.	1819	20	CT
Holt, Laban	1817	19	CT
Holt, William	1805	42	MA
Holt, Witlet	1818	17	CT
Holton, Thomas	1809	29	VT
Homer, Robert	1804	18	CT
Hood, James B.	1819	17	CT
Hood, John	1810	23	CT
Hood, John	1808	22	CT
Hood, John	1807	20	CT
Hooker, Alexander	1811	19 b	CT
Hooker, Alexander	1810	18 b	CT
Hooker, Ashbel	1803	23	CT
Hooker, James	1802	18	CT
Hooker, John	1803	26	CT
Hooker, Stephen	1815	25	CT
Hooper, Chauncey	1803	19	CT
Hooton, George	1832	24	MA
Hopkins, Frederick	1804	35	CT
Hopkins, William	1804	20	NH
Hopson, Ebenezer	1810	18	CT
Hopson, Ebenezer	1808	16	CT
Horton, Rufus	1837	44	MA
Horton, William	1805	36	NY
Hosmer, Erasts	1806	20	CT
Hoss, Nichols	1803	24	
Hotchkiss, Albert	1817	21	CT
Hotchkiss,AugustusE.	1837	21	CT
Hotchkiss, Benjamin	1806	22	CT
Hotchkiss, Benjamin	1807	22	CT
Hotchkiss, Calvin	1815	28	CT
Hotchkiss, Charles F.	1821	16	CT
Hotchkiss, Enos T.	1826	15	CT
Hotchkiss, Frances	1836	27	CT
Hotchkiss, Joel	1806	20	CT
Hotchkiss, Joel	1806	20	CT
Hotchkiss, John	1809	16	CT
Hotchkiss, John	1816	27	CT
Hotchkiss, Levi	1804	18	CT
Hotchkiss, Philo	1815	23	CT
Hotchkiss, Rufus	1811	20	CT
Hotchkiss, Silas, Jr.	1809	24	CT
Hotchkiss, William	1842	18	CT
Hotchkiss, William S.	1807	35	CT
Hotchkiss, Wyllys	1809	21	CT
Hoth, Jared	1803	21	CT
Houcks, William	1804	19	NJ
Hough, Allin	1810	19	CT
Hought,Ebenezer,2nd	1825	17	CT
Housten, Henry	1817	25	MA
How, John Lytvesta	1803	20	NY
Howd, Eliphalet	1804	20	CT
Howd, Ruel	1804	18	CT
Howe, Artemas	1810	19	MA
Howe, John L.	1806	22	NY
Howell, Abraham	1841	15	CT
Howell, Caleb	1826	21	NY
Howell, John	1805	16	CT
Howell, John	1810	17	CT
Howell, Leverit	1806	13	CT
Howell, Levert	1810	17	CT
Howell, Morris	1810	18	CT
Howell, Morris	1812	21	CT
Howell, William	1812	13	CT
Hoyt, Henry	1805	19	NY
Hoyt, Joseph	1805	26	NH
Hubbard, Alfred	1810	17	CT
Hubbard, Artimas	1803	28	MA
Hubbard, Dana	1810	22	CT
Hubbard, Jacob	1810	37	NY
Hubbard, John	1815	16	CT
Hubbard, John	1821	21	CT
Hubbard, Otis	1805	17	CT
Hubbard,RichardS.Jr.	1813	18	NY
Hubbard, Russell	1806	23	CT
Hubbard, Saml.	1842	27	CT
Hubbard, Seth	1807	24	CT
Hubbard, William	1806	20	CT
Hubbard, William	1809	22	CT
Hubbard, William	1817	23	MA
Hubbard, William	1822	28	MA
Hubbard, William H.	1805	22	CT
Hubbard, Wm.	1806	19	CT
Hubbell, Amon	1816	26	CT
Hubbell, Ezra	1809	24	CT
Hubbell, Genge S.	1841	20	CT
Hubbie, William	1805	16 b	CT
Hudson, Frederick	1806	20	CT
Huggins, John K.	1806	21	CT
Huggins, John K.	1803	18	CT
Hughes, Collins	1813	16	CT
Hughes, John	1816	20	RI
Hughes, Robert	1819	24	CT
Hughes, Roswell W.	1830	16	CT
Hughes, Wm.	1841	17	CT
Hule, Austin	1811	26	CT

Hulet, Alfred	1843	32 b	NY
Hull, Abiatha H.	1806	15	CT
Hull, Abiather	1806	40	CT
Hull, George W.	1841	18	CT
Hull, John G.	1841	26	CT
Hull, Leman L.	1843	15	CT
Hull, Samuel	1812	41	CT
Hull, Tony	1803	24 b	CT
Hull, Wm.	1805	32	CT
Hull, Wm. A.	1806	18	CT
Hulse, John	1805	19	CT
Hulse, John	1810	24	CT
Hulse, John	1805	19	CT
Hulse, Joseph	1806	25	CT
Hulse, William	1805	17	CT
Hulso, Joseph	1828	19	CT
Humaston, Ezra	1805	30	CT
Humaston, Ezra	1808	32	CT
Humiston, Dando	1806	22 b	CT
Humiston, Justus	1812	22	CT
Humpheys, John	1815	18	CT
Humphrey, James	1810	17	CT
Humphrey, James	1805	13	CT
Humphrey, Warren	1815	27	CT
Humphreys, James	1816	23	CT
Humphreys,JamesJr.	1813	20	CT
Humphreys,JamesJr.	1811	19	CT
Humston, Dande	1807	23 b	CT
Hunt, Charles	1809	21	CT
Hunt, Frederick, 3rd	1815	16	CT
Hunt, Henry	1805	21	CT
Hunt, Henry	1804	20	CT
Hunt, Henry	1803	19	CT
Hunt, Henry	1803	19	CT
Hunt, Hervey	1825	15	CT
Hunt, James	1803	42	MA
Hunt, James	1808	17	CT
Hunt, James C.	1828	19	CT
Hunt, John	1805	17	CT
Hunt, John	1811	23	CT
Hunt, John	1810	22	
Hunt, John, Jr.	1825	36	CT
Hunt, Samuel	1815	22	CT
Hunt, Thomas	1807	20	CT
Hunt, William	1815	18	CT
Hunt, William	1817	21	CT
Hunt, William H.	1811	26	NY
Hunter, William	1815	21	NY
Huntington, Ebenizer	1804	23	CT
Huntley, Augustus	1809	30	CT
Huntley, John	1806	25	CT
Hurbburt, Austin	1826	20	CT
Hurkles, David	1815	20 y	CT
Hurlbut, Levi	1805	19	CT
Hyde, Harry	1811	18	CT
Hyde, Henry	1810	17	CT
Hyde, Nathan	1811	16	CT
Ingersall, John	1821	23 b	NY
Ingersoll, John	1824	26 b	NY
Ingersoll, John	1822	23 b	NY
Ingraham, Edward	1815	22 y	RI
Ives, Herbey	1806	20	CT
Ives, Whiting	1809	21	CT
Jackman, Chr. B.	1832	26	MA
Jackson, Amos	1807	26 b	CT
Jackson, John	1813	33	NJ
Jackson, Riley	1820	19	CT
Jackson, Saml.	1806	19 b	CT
Jackson, Samuel	1842	24	CT
Jackson, William	1837	23 b	CT
Jackson, William	1804	36 b	CT
Jacobs, Clinton	1810	28	CT
Jacobs, Clinton	1810	27	CT
Jacobs, Harry	1811	25	CT
Jacobs, Harry	1807	21	CT
Jacobs, Harry	1806	20	CT
Jacobs, Peter	1803	22	
Jacobs, Solomon	1803	17	CT
Jacobs, Solomon	1805	19	
Jacobs, Solomon	1809	23	CT
James, Emery	1842	24	MS
James, William	1843	21 y	PA
Janes, Henry	1815	19	CT
Jearlds, Ransom	1807	17	CT
Jearlds, Thomas	1805	18	CT
Jefferies, Henry R.	1824	26	NY
Jeffery, Jesse	1819	19 y	CT
Jeffery, Marvill Edwin	1823	17 b	CT
Jeffery, Thomas	1805	26 b	NJ
Jeffery, Thomas	1812	46 b	NJ
Jeffreys, Morgan	1825	17	CT
Jenkins, Harry	1804	17 b	CT
Jeralds, Thomas	1806	19	CT
Jerould, James	1810	26	CT
Jillson, Richard	1815	19	CT
Jocelin, Abraham	1804	24	CT
Jocelin, John	1809	18	CT
Joel, Hezekiah	1803	0 I	MA
Johns, Cephas	1803	21	CT
Johnson, Agustus	1806	21	CT
Johnson, Alexis	1810	31	CT
Johnson, Amos	1809	22	CT
Johnson, Amos M.	1806	22	CT
Johnson, Arthur	1836	23	MA
Johnson, Augustus	1803	18	CT
Johnson, Augustus	1805	21	CT
Johnson, Charles A.	1835	17	CT
Johnson, Charles E.	1837	26	CT

Name	Year	Age	State
Johnson, Fowler	1803	20	CT
Johnson, Fowler	1805	21	CT
Johnson, Gershum	1811	28	NY
Johnson, Harry	1815	19 b	NY
Johnson, Harry	1816	20 b	NY
Johnson, Isaac	1819	22 b	CT
Johnson, Isaac	1819	19 b	CT
Johnson, Isaac	1821	24 b	NY
Johnson, James	1841	23 b	NY
Johnson, James	1810	28 b	CT
Johnson, Jeremiah	1810	19	CT
Johnson, Jeremiah	1806	13	CT
Johnson, John	1805	24	CT
Johnson, John	1815	19	CT
Johnson, John	1821	25 b	CT
Johnson, John	1817	21 b	CT
Johnson, Joseph	1810	19 b	MA
Johnson, Joseph	1813	21 b	NY
Johnson, Levi L.	1804	17	CT
Johnson, Levi Lewis	1807	20	CT
Johnson, Lyman	1815	21	CT
Johnson, Merit H.	1842	20	CT
Johnson, Nathan	1843	22	CT
Johnson, Nathan	1806	26	CT
Johnson, Nathan M.	1808	24	CT
Johnson, Oliver	1805	21	
Johnson, Oliver R.	1815	29	CT
Johnson, Peter	1813	22 b	VA
Johnson, Peter	1810	20 b	VA
Johnson, Peter	1808	17	
Johnson, R. A.	1842	23	NJ
Johnson, Raphael	1805	20	CT
Johnson, Robert	1837	25 b	NY
Johnson, Roswell	1806	27	CT
Johnson, Ruben	1806	27	CT
Johnson, Sheldin	1808	25	CT
Johnson, Thomas	1805	25	MA
Johnson, Thomas	1804	24	MA
Johnson, William	1804	25	NY
Johnson, Wm.	1820	30	CT
Johnson, Wm.	1817	22 b	PA
Johnson, Wm.	1809	20	CT
Johnson, Wm. C.	1807	20	CT
Jones, Henry	1837	23 b	NJ
Jones, Henry L.	1815	14	NY
Jones, James	1841	23	NY
Jones, John	1821	29 y	NY
Jones, John	1819	26 y	NY
Jones, John	1820	27 y	NY
Jones, John	1804	17	CT
Jones, John	1803	16	CT
Jones, John	1806	22	CT
Jones, Stephen	1805	24	MA
Jones, Thomas	1818	29 b	PA
Jones, William	1841	25 b	NJ
Jones, William	1805	19	CT
Jordan, Edward	1842	29 y	NJ
Josselyn, Joseph H.	1812	25	MA
Joy, Rufus	1838	29	ME
Joyce, John	1804	34	CT
Judd, Thomas	1806	28	CT
Judd, William L.	1843	17	CT
Judson, James	1841	22 b	CT
Judson, James	1837	19 b	CT
Judson, Levi	1833	24 b	CT
Judson, Lucius	1810	21	CT
Judson, Obed	1804	31 b	CT
Kaanan, Thomas	1804	24	CT
Kaanan, Thomas	1805	24	CT
Kaanan, Thomas	1808	27	CT
Kaanan, Thomas	1806	25	CT
Kaanan, Thomas	1805	25	CT
Kavugh, Lawrence	1841	36	Ireland
Keeney, Abraham	1807	16	CT
Keeney, George	1835	21	CT
Keeney, Lockwood	1822	18	CT
Keeney, Rubin	1805	26	MA
Keeney, Sheldon	1804	15	CT
Keeny, Abraham	1803	12	CT
Kelley, Dennis	1837	21 b	CT
Kellog, Rueben	1832	21	CT
Kelsch, McHenry	1828	14	CT
Kelsey, Charles	1805	21	CT
Kendrick, John	1805	21	MA
Kenley, William B.	1820	33	CT
Kennedy, Nathaniel	1841	16	CT
Kennedy, Nathmuil	1842	16	CT
Kennedy, Peter J.	1841	18	CT
Kennedy, Peter J.	1843	0	CT
Kenney, Nathaniel	1823	20	CT
Kenney, Wm.	1806	23	CT
Kenniston, Samuel	1807	31	NH
Kent, James	1842	22 b	MD
Kidder,SanforthHam.	1806	15	CT
Kimball, Jesse	1805	23	NH
Kimberley, Francis	1809	17	CT
Kimberley, George	1811	26	CT
Kimberley, Horace	1804	24	CT
Kimberley, Isaac	1811	18	CT
Kimberley, Morris	1809	22	CT
Kimberly, Charles J.	1820	15	CT
Kimberly, Eli	1811	19	CT
Kimberly, Elisha	1815	25	CT
Kimberly, Elisha	1807	17	CT
Kimberly, Elisha	1805	15	CT
Kimberly, Frances	1815	23	CT
Kimberly, George	1803	19	CT
Kimberly, Henry W.	1842	25	CT

Kimberly, Henry W.	1843	26		CT	Lanson, Isaac	1824	20 y	CT
Kimberly, Leverett	1833	30		CT	Lanson, Nelson	1829	21 y	CT
Kimberly, Leveritt	1822	19		CT	Lanson, William	1812	23 b	NJ
Kimberly, Wm.	1810	21		CT	Lanson, William N.	1824	17 y	CT
Kindal, Daniel	1803	18		CT	Larabee, David	1811	18	CT
Kindley, William	1803	16		CT	Larde, RichardGoodwin	1826	21	NY
King, George	1810	22		NY	Larkin, John B.	1807	16	CT
King, Saml. D.	1841	22		ME	Larkin, Loring	1823	15	CT
Kingsbury, Calvin	1806	20		CT	Lary, Perry	1815	25 y	PA
Kingsbury, John M.	1842	21		CT	Latimer, Elisha	1803	27	CT
Kingsbury, Sanford	1815	24		CT	Latimore, Charles	1834	39	CT
Kinley, Joseph	1811	17		CT	Latimore, Charles	1815	20	CT
Kinley, William	1809	22			Latimore, George	1819	23 y	NY
Kinley, William	1805	17		CT	Lattin, Henry	1825	26 b	NY
Kinley, William B.	1815	28		CT	Lavery, Francis	1838	19	MA
Kinley, William Brown	1810	22		CT	Law, James	1843	17 b	NY
Kinney, Geo.	1832	17		CT	Law, Wm., Jr.	1807	26	CT
Kinyon, John L	1820	23		RI	Lawney, Cato	1805	16 b	CT
Kinyon, John L.	1824	28		RI	Laws, Samuel	1841	19 b	PA
Kirkum, Bela	1810	19		CT	Lawson, John	1806	28	MA
Kirkum, Bela	1814	23		CT	Lay, Lee	1813	33	CT
Kirkum, Bela	1806	16		CT	Lcisson, Isaac	1805	21	CT
Kirkum, Caleb	1815	20		CT	Leach, Stoddard	1823	19	CT
Kirkum, Erastus R.	1825	20		CT	Leach, William	1813	22	CT
Kirtland, Ezra	1815	15		CT	Leach, William	1812	19	CT
Knapp, Ezekel	1815	44		CT	Leak, Samuel	1810	21	CT
Knapp, John	1812	26		MA	Leake, Charles	1813	21	CT
Knevels, Joseph	1805	43		Germany	Leavenworth, Ralph	1808	20	CT
Knowles, John	1808	24		VT	Lee, Benjamin	1807	30 b	DE
Knox, John	1813	21		NY	Lee, Samuel	1803	20	MA
Knox, John	1815	23		NY	Leech, William	1819	24	CT
Knox, John	1811	18		NY	Leet, Daniel B.	1803	22	CT
Knox, John	1819	28		NY	Leet, John R.	1827	18	CT
Knox, Joseph	1804	17		CT	Leet, Thomas	1816	24	NY
Kurkam, Caleb	1810	15		CT	Leffingwell, Benjamin	1805	25	CT
Kyle, Forbes	1803	17		CT	LeForge, Frea K., Jr.	1832	18	CT
Labin, John	1806	24		CT	Leforge, Henry	1806	23	NY
Laboree, Russell	1815	18		CT	Leforges, Frederick	1807	21	CT
Lake, Joel	1808	23		CT	Leforges, Frederick	1805	19	CT
Lake, Lucius	1826	18		CT	Leming, Thomas	1807	26	NY
Lake, Samuel	1820	21		CT	Lester, Richard	1842	24	CT
Lake, Samuel	1824	23		CT	Levingston, James	1804	19	NY
Lalentine, James	1829	23 b		NY	Levinston, George	1838	32 b	NY
Lamford, Thos.	1806	23		CT	Lewis, Alfred	1835	25 y	CT
Lanabee, Stephen	1841	30		MA	Lewis, Chancey	1805	22	CT
Landon, Nath.Ruggles	1805	22		CT	Lewis, Charles	1803	22 b	MA
Lane, William	1805	21		CT	Lewis, Chauncey	1803	20	CT
Lanfair, Horace	1814	20		CT	Lewis, EdwardSanford	1811	13	CT
Lanfair, Russel	1804	30		CT	Lewis, Elihu	1804	25	CT
Lanfare, Oliver, Jr.	1804	22		CT	Lewis, Geo. P.	1828	27 b	CT
Lanford, Elijah	1803	33		CT	Lewis, Jacob	1809	31 y	NY
Langdon, Edmund	1804	20		CT	Lewis, John	1813	26 b	VA
Langee, Joseph	1813	35		LA	Lewis, John	1815	26 b	VA
Lanson, Isaac	1817	13 b		CT	Lewis, John	1815	28 b	VA

Lewis, Joseph	1807	30		CT	Lord, William	1815	14		CT
Lewis, Joseph	1804	25		CT	Loring, Samuel	1811	14		MA
Lewis, Joseph	1803	25		CT	Losee, William	1804	19		CT
Lewis, Joseph	1804	25		CT	Love, William	1810	17		CT
Lewis, Ned	1815	21	b	CT	Love, William, Jr.	1821	28		CT
Lewis, William	1841	24		MD	Loveland, Trueman	1808	17		CT
Lewis, William, Jr.	1837	14		SC	Lovley, Bennet	1824	21	b	CT
Libby, John	1841	15		NY	Low, John	1806	24		MA
Lincoln, Jeremiah	1810	20		CT	Lowe, Henry	1827	27		MD
Lindley, Samuel	1805	62		CT	Lucas, Noah	1806	18		CT
Lines, Amos	1812	18		CT	Lucas, Samuel	1828	29	b	CT
Lines, David	1820	17		CT	Luddenton, Cobb	1806	16		CT
Lines, Ezra A.	1816	19		CT	Luddenton, Justin	1815	18		CT
Lines, Isaac	1810	19		CT	Luddington, Asa	1807	36		CT
Lines, John	1805	27		CT	Ludington, Caleb	1811	21		CT
Lines, Leveritt H.	1822	19		CT	Ludington, Justin	1822	24		CT
Lines, Philemon	1810	19		CT	Ludington, Justin	1833	18		CT
Lines, Shubal	1811	24		CT	Ludington, Lewis	1810	22		CT
Lines, Stephen	1805	28		CT	Ludington, William	1826	20		CT
Lines, William	1803	23		CT	Lum, Daniel	1818	19		CT
Linsby, Saml, Jr.	1803	22		CT	Lum, Daniel	1815	17		CT
Linsley, Benjamin D.	1815	22		CT	Lum, Daniel	1816	18		CT
Linsley, John	1805	19		CT	Lum, David	1803	26		CT
Linsley/Lindley,					Lum, Isaac	1805	21		CT
Hubbard Fowler	1805	30		CT	Lumes, Manning	1825	25		CT
Linzy, Ansel	1809	21		MA	Lumsdal, Stephen	1805	24		CT
Lisson, Isaac	1803	19		CT	Lumsden, Stephen	1803	22		CT
Little, Dick	1810	23	b	CT	Lumsdill, Stephen	1804	23		CT
Little, James Davis	1812	21		CT	Lusbine, John	1810	30	y	NJ
Little, James Davis	1816	25		CT	Lyman, James	1806	13		CT
Little, John	1813	22		SC	Lyman, Russel	1801	0		CT
Little, John	1813	22		SC	Lyon, Ben	1803	19		CT
Little, Richd.	1820	33	b	CT	Lyon, William H.	1823	21		CT
Little, Richd.	1830	42	b	CT	Lyons, John	1822	21		NY
Little, Richd.	1827	40	b	CT	Mack, George	1818	12		CT
Little, Samuel	1807	20	b	CT	Mack, Zadoc	1806	25		CT
Little, William	1805	20	b	CT	Mack, Zadock	1804	24		CT
Livingston, Genge	1841	34	b	NY	Mackey, James	1825	27	b	NY
Lloyd, John	1843	21		ME	Macomber, Anson	1813	20		MA
Lock, Edward	1806	23		RI	Macready, Dennis	1843	27		NY
Lock, Joshua	1825	19		ME	Macumber, Allen	1829	17		CT
Lockwood, Isaac	1803	27		VT	Macumber, Henry	1828	21		CT
Lockwood, Jack	1810	28	b	NY	Main, Wyllys	1812	21		CT
Lockwood, Samuel	1806	25		CT	Mallery, Alanson	1815	17		CT
Logan, John	1810	28		CT	Mallery, Alanson	1821	23		CT
Logan, John	1803	20		CT	Mallery, Alanson	1819	21		CT
Loomis, Alfred	1807	27		CT	Mallery, Amma	1810	29		CT
Loomis, Daniel G.	1820	22		CT	Mallery, Ezra	1825	17		CT
Loomis, Elisha	1806	27		CT	Mallery, Heman	1810	23		CT
Looney, Bennet	1820	18	b	CT	Mallery, Isaac	1810	23		CT
Looneys, Peter	1804	34	b	CT	Mallery, Jacob	1820	17		CT
Lord, Jaber	1803	30		CT	Mallery, Jesse	1815	19		CT
Lord, Nathan	1803	24		CT	Mallery, Jesse	1810	17		CT
Lord, Richard G.	1837	31		NY	Mallery, John	1820	20		CT

Mallery, Matherw	1803	21	CT	McCormick, Lewis	1808	22	PA	
Mallery, Samuel	1803	20	CT	McCormick, Lewis	1807	21	PA	
Mallery, Samuel	1805	22	CT	McCoy, Jeremiah	1806	14	NY	
Mallery, Samuel	1815	32	CT	McCredey, Wm.	1822	22	NY	
Mallery, Zina	1809	18	CT	McDonald, Joel	1804	42	CT	
Mallet, John	1803	45	CT	McDonald, Joel	1806	43	CT	
Malley, Jacob	1824	21	CT	McDonald, Joseph	1803	16	CT	
Mallory, Lyman	1810	23	CT	McDuffey, William	1841	21	ME	
Mallory, Sam.	1806	24	CT	McFarland, Daniel	1842	22		Denmark
Malone, Eli	1808	17	CT	McGinnis, Arthur	1842	26	MD	
Malone, Frederick	1802	16	CT	McGregor, Wm.	1830	25	ME	
Malone, James	1806	18	CT	McNeil, Abraham	1815	13	CT	
Malone, James	1806	17	CT	McNeil, William	1816	30	CT	
Malone, James Fred.	1827	16	CT	McNiel, Samuel	1807	21	CT	
Maltby, DeGrass	1805	23	CT	McNight (sic),Robert	1810	21	CT	
Maltby, Stephen E.	1815	19	CT	McQueen,				
Manning, William	1805	22	CT	John Still William	1805	30	CT	
Manning, William	1807	23	CT	Mead, Lucins S.	1843	22	VT	
Manser, John	1803	27	CT	Meek, Charles	1837	28	NY	
Mansfield, Alfred	1822	20	CT	Mehollin, William	1815	19	CT	
Mansfield, Archabald	1819	22 b	CT	Mehollin, Wm.	1811	15	CT	
Mansfield, Richard	1803	31 b	CT	Meigs, Frederick	1808	18	CT	
Manville, Judson	1816	39	CT	Meigs, Isaac	1806	21	CT	
Maples, Wm.	1815	24	CT	Meigs, Stephen	1804	41	CT	
Marsh, Francis B.	1805	21 y	CT	Melone, Elah	1816	25	CT	
Marsh, James	1806	23	CT	Melony, Frederick	1803	17	CT	
Marsh, James	1808	25	CT	Meloy, Edward	1805	19	CT	
Marsh, John	1811	24		Meloy, Edward	1804	42	CT	
Marshall, Robert	1841	18	ME	Meloy, Edward	1812	49	CT	
Marshall,SamuelElliott	1806	27	CT	Meloy, Edward	1808	22	CT	
Martey, Samuel J.	1822	21	NY	Meloy, Henry	1806	29	CT	
Martin, Alexander	1836	30	CT	Meloy, Merit	1818	19	CT	
Martin, John	1809	23 b	NY	Meloy, Samuel	1809	16	CT	
Martin, John	1807	22 b	NY	Mendow, Thomas	1806	16 y	CT	
Martin, John	1815	39 y	MD	Merick, Joseph	1811	19	CT	
Martin, Samuel	1812	29	MA	Merriman, Caleb	1810	26	CT	
Martin, Samuel	1841	27 b	NY	Merriman, Cato	1815	25 b	CT	
Mason, Herney	1807	24 y	NC	Merriman,Harvey Wm.	1815	19	CT	
Mason, Thomas	1842	28	ME	Merwin, Merit	1810	19	CT	
Masters, Samuel J.	1818	17	NY	Merwin, Nathan	1810	21	CT	
Mastin, William	1810	34	CT	Merwin, William	1815	22	CT	
Maston, William	1805	30	CT	Middlebrooks, Robert	1807	17	CT	
Mathews, Horace	1809	23	CT	Miles, George	1805	20	CT	
Matoon, Isaac	1815	24	CT	Miles, Samuel	1809	19	CT	
Maynard, Anson	1806	21	MA	Miles, Samuel	1813	22	CT	
McArthur, Samuel	1815	27	NH	Miles, William	1816	19	CT	
McArthur, Samuel	1817	30	NH	Mill, Joseph	1805	27	LA	
McAuthur, John	1818	27	NH	Millard, Genge	1842	31	MA	
McCabe, Felix	1805	22	PA	Millard, George	1841	30	MA	
McCann, Edward	1809	19	NY	Miller, Amos	1804	35	CT	
McCann, Edward	1806	15	NY	Miller, Darius	1804	21	CT	
McCann, John	1842	42	MA	Miller, Edward	1842	28	MA	
McClellen, Charles	1823	22	ME	Miller, George	1836	25 y	NJ	
McColly, George	1803	23	NY	Miller, Horace	1823	23	CT	

Miller, Horace	1833	32	CT
Miller, Horace	1816	16	CT
Miller, Jason	1812	21	CT
Miller, John Curtis	1804	19	CT
Miller, William	1838	21	ME
Miller, William	1842	22	NH
Mills, Joseph	1806	27	LA
Mindow, Thomas	1807	17 y	CT
Miner, Albert	1837	19	CT
Mingo, Bradford	1825	32 b	RI
Minor, Freeman	1807	18	CT
Minor, Truman	1807	18	CT
Mitchel, John	1805	15	CT
Mitchel, Wm.	1804	28	NY
Mitchell, Eawana	1842	26 y	VA
Mitchell, John	1805	14	CT
Mitchell, Lewis T.	1838	28 b	CT
Mitchell, Medad	1824	19	MA
Mix, Alfred	1812	16	CT
Mix, Alfred	1816	22	CT
Mix, Alfred	1814	20	CT
Mix, Elijah	1801	21	CT
Mix, Elisha	1810	16	CT
Mix, Elisha	1807	14	CT
Mix, Henry	1815	19	CT
Mix, Henry	1815	19	CT
Mix, Horace	1820	17	CT
Mix, James H.	1805	24	CT
Mix, James P.	1806	29	CT
Mix, Jeremiah F.	1824	18	CT
Mix, John	1805	24	CT
Mix, John	1816	12	CT
Mix, Jonathan L...	1804	15	CT
Mix, Leveret	1803	34	CT
Mix, Leveret	1809	40	CT
Mix, Leverit	1804	34	CT
Mix, Leveritt	1806	37	CT
Mix, Marvin	1804	20	CT
Mix, Marvin	1804	20	CT
Mix, Merit	1803	24	CT
Mix, Miles	1805	28	CT
Mix, Miles	1803	25	CT
Mix, Peter	1805	47 b	CT
Mix, Stephen	1807	16	CT
Mix, Timo.	1834	35	CT
Mix, Timothy, Jr.	1815	17	CT
Mix, Zina	1805	25	CT
Mnitague, Richard N.	1842	16	CT
Moffatt, Thomas	1819	24 b	NY
Moffett, Thomas	1822	27 b	NY
Moffit, James	1824	28 y	NY
Moffitt, John M.	1841	24	RI
Moger, Elijah	1810	34	CT
Molone, Downey	1814	21	CT
Molthrop, David, Jr.	1815	17	CT
Monarch,Wm.Daniel	1824	27	ME
Monroe, Hezekiah	1822	28	CT
Monroe, Jeremiah	1809	34	CT
Montcalm, Francis	1805	18	CT
Montcalm, Francis	1807	20	CT
Montcalm, Francis	1810	23	CT
Montgomery, Barney	1822	21	CT
Montgomery, Barney	1822	21	CT
Moor, Timothy	1807	18	MA
Moor, Timothy	1807	18	MA
Moore, Curtis	1808	21	CT
Moore, Elias	1835	25	MD
Moore, John	1837	22	ME
Moore, John	1813	26 y	NJ
Moore, Jonathan	1807	21	NY
Moore, Peter	1838	32 b	CT
Moore, Thomas	1841	24	RI
More, Henry	1804	22 b	NY
Morgan, Dudley, Jr.	1812	23	CT
Morgan, Elisha	1810	17	CT
Morgan, Ira	1810	18 y	CT
Morgan, Ira	1812	19 y	CT
Morgan, Isaac	1805	21	CT
Morgan, Isaac	1803	18	CT
Morgan, Reuben	1806	34	CT
Morris, Benjamin	1818	31	MA
Morris, Charles	1805	43	CT
Morris, Edmund	1816	21	CT
Morris, John	1810	20 y	CT
Morris, Joseph	1805	23	CT
Morris, Lyman	1809	16	CT
Morris, Sheldon	1815	14	CT
Morrison, Marcus	1830	22	CT
Morse, Agar T.	1816	15	CT
Morton, Samuel	1811	19	CT
Morton, Silas	1838	21	ME
Moseley, Saml. L.	1815	19 y	CT
Moses, Joseph	1804	24	CT
Moss, Joseph	1803	22	
Moss, Nehamiah	1803	19	
Moss, Nehemiah	1806	23	CT
Moss, Samuel	1816	20	CT
Moss, Samuel	1817	21	CT
Moulthrop, Chauncey	1805	17	CT
Moulthrop, Chauscey	1807	20	CT
Moulthrop, James H.	1822	18	CT
Moulthrop, Joseph	1807	15	CT
Moulthrop, Major	1804	25	CT
Moulthrop, Martin	1804	23	CT
Moulthrop, Martin	1811	30	CT
Moulthrop, Swain	1807	22	CT
Mouthrop, Joseph	1809	17	CT
Mouthrop, Levi	1807	23	CT

Mouthrop, Levi	1804	19		CT	Nichols, Charles	1813	17		CT
Mouthrop, Major	1803	24			Nichols, Edward	1837	23	b	CT
Moutthrop, John	1806	30		CT	Nichols, Harry	1811	20		CT
Moxey, Ezra	1836	21		ME	Nichols, Harry	1818	28		CT
Mulford,Barnabas, Jr.	1805	21		CT	Nichols, Isaac	1816	18		CT
Mulford, Barnabas, Jr.	1806	22			Nichols, Robert	1816	13		CT
Mullin, James	1813	31		MD	Nichols, Silas	1810	30	b	NY
Multhrop, John	1806	30		CT	Nichols, Silas	1811	31	b	NY
Munger, Ebenezer	1815	19		CT	Nichols, Silas	1811	32	b	NY
Munger, George	1806	25		CT	Nichols, Silas	1808	28	b	NY
Munroe, Philip	1811	17	b	CT	Nichols, Silas	1806	26	b	NY
Munson, Bebe	1836	17		CT	Nicholson, James	1806	17		MA
Munson, Bebe	1837	18		CT	Nickerson, Charles	1841	19		MA
Munson, Daniel Collis	1825	15		CT	Noah, Levy	1812	18	y	CT
Munson, Daniel Collis	1822	12		CT	Noble, Horace	1807	19		MA
Munson, David	1818	14		CT	Noe, William	1805	20		NY
Munson, Gorham	1810	24		CT	Norie, David, Jun.	1813	18		CT
Munson, Henry	1806	19		CT	Norman, John	1805	24		MA
Munson, Josephus	1837	16		CT	Norris, John	1818	28	b	NY
Munson, Marcus	1810	19		CT	Norris, John	1818	28	b	NY
Munson, Newman T.	1818	15		CT	Northrop, Amos	1803	37		CT
Munson, Richard H.	1808	20		CT	Northrop, Edward A.	1803	27		CT
Munson, Richard H.	1809	20		CT	Northrop, Isaac	1806	14		CT
Munson, William, Jr.	1809	22		CT	Northrop, Job	1801	14		CT
Murdock, Charles A.	1819	28		PA	Northrop, John	1809	23		CT
Murp[hy, John	1822	18		CT	Northrop, Lazarus	1803	25		CT
Murray, John	1804	22		NY	Northrop, Samuel	1803	20		CT
Murrey, Samuel	1806	23		CT	Northrop, Wm. B.	1804	23		CT
Muttoon,Chs.Northrop	1827	15		CT	Northrop, Wm. B.	1805	24		CT
Myers, Garrit	1805	16	y	NJ	Northrop, Wm. B.	1803	22		CT
Myers, Garrit	1804	15	y	NJ	Northrup, Saml. B.	1804	18		CT
Myers, Garry	1824	16	b	CT	Norton, Asa	1804	20		CT
Myers, John	1813	14	b	CT	Norton, Asa	1803	18		CT
Myrick, James	1803	33		MA	Norton, David	1803	25	b	MA
Nailes, John	1814	27		CT	Norton,Ebenezer, Jr.	1805	22		CT
Nails, John	1804	17		CT	Norton, Hiram	1820	30		CT
Nash, Simon	1806	26	b	CT	Norton, Montgomery	1803	20		CT
Nasm, Genge	1842	18		ME	Norton, Montgomery	1804	21		CT
Naylor, William	1807	23		PA	Norton, Nelson	1841	31		CT
Neal, John	1819	23		MA	Norton, Silvester	1805	21		CT
Nelson, Isaac	1809	19	y	CT	Norton,StephenPotter	1806	15		CT
Neppes, William	1807	22		PA	Noyes, Allen	1843	22		ME
Newcomb, James M.	1812	20		MA	Noyes, John	1827	17		CT
Newcomb, Robert	1841	22		MA	Noyes, Samuel	1806	24		CT
Newell, Elisha	1805	21		CT	Noyes, William A.	1816	14		CT
Newell, Wiman	1804	16		CT	Noyes, Wm.	1805	28		CT
Newman, Domengo	1836	37	b	NJ	Noyes, Wm. A.	1828	25		CT
Newton, Horace	1836	19		CT	Noyes, Wm. Allen	1826	21		CT
Newton, Lemuel	1804	20		CT	Nutter, Benjamin	1837	17		ME
Newton, Lemuel	1806	23		CT	Nuum, William	1806	21		MD
Newton, Sidney	1820	17		CT	Oaks, Henry	1806	15		CT
Newton, Sidney	1823	22		CT	Oaks, Henry	1808	17		CT
Nicholl, Isaac	1816	17		CT	Ogden, Aaron N.	1803	21		CT
Nicholls, Charles	1817	22		CT	Ogden, Thomas	1810	21		CT

Ogden, Thos	1810	20		CT	Palmer, Oren	1806	24	CT
Olmstead, David	1805	31		CT	Palmer, Peter	1810	19	CT
Olmstead, Eugene	1803	14		CT	Palmer, Peter	1815	24	CT
Olmstead, James	1803	18		CT	Palmer, Platt	1804	18	CT
Olmstead, Sheldon	1813	12		CT	Palmer, Robert	1810	21	CT
Olmsted, Ashbel	1805	22		CT	Palmer, Rodolphus	1823	19	CT
Olmsted, Eugene	1805	17		CT	Pane, Rich. R.	1804	20	NY
Olmsted, James	1803	0		CT	Pangman, Gideon	1811	18	CT
Olmsted, Lewis M.	1843	15		CT	Pangmon, Bennet	1809	24	CT
Olson/Osson, Jacob	1810	42	b	NJ	Pardee, Chester	1813	14	CT
Osborn, Amos	1804	18		CT	Pardee, Chester	1815	15	CT
Osborn, Layman	1805	14		CT	Pardee, Daniel	1808	21	CT
Osborn, Lyman	1806	15		CT	Pardee, Daniel	1806	20	CT
Osborn, Merit	1815	22		CT	Pardee, Daniel	1803	17	CT
Oson, Abraham	1810	17	b	CT	Pardee, Ebenizer	1803	14	CT
Oson, Isaac	1821	20	b	CT	Pardee, Roswell	1813	18	CT
Oson, Joseph	1824	20	b	CT	Pardee, Roswell	1812	16	CT
Oson/Olon, Joseph	1823	18	b	CT	Pardee, Samuel	1804	22	CT
Otis, Ezeliel	1806	21	b	CT	Pardee, Samuel	1803	20	CT
Oviate, Silas	1815	24		CT	Pardee, Stephen	1803	21	CT
Oviatt, John	1812	19		CT	Pardee, Stephen	1806	25	CT
Oviet, Silas	1809	19		CT	Pardu, Daniel	1807	20	CT
Ovit, William	1841	19	y	CT	Pardu, Ezekial	1806	36	CT
Ovitt, Samuel	1841	19	y	CT	Pardy, John	1842	30	Ireland
Oxford, George	1818	34	b	CT	Pardy, Moses	1803	17	CT
Page, Leonard	1805	20		CT	Parke, Leman	1816	15	CT
Page, Leonard	1803	18		CT	Parker, Benjn. F.	1821	18	NH
Page, Lucius	1815	23		CT	Parker, Edward	1822	23	CT
Page, Samuel	1803	19		CT	Parker, Edward	1819	19	CT
Paidee, Wyllys	1811	15		CT	Parker, Eliada	1804	20	CT
Pain, Ichabod	1810	24		CT	Parker, Eliada	1804	20	CT
Pain, Ichabod	1805	19		CT	Parker, John M.	1805	32	CT
Paine, Ebenizer	1803	0		CT	Parker, Noah	1812	21	NC
Paine, Ichabod	1805	19		CT	Parker, Perry	1835	15	CT
Painter, Ruben	1805	20		CT	Parker, Pierce	1805	17	CT
Palmer, Ammi	1805	23		CT	Parkis, Chandler	1806	18	CT
Palmer, Augustus	1805	20		CT	Parmale, Amos	1807	22	MA
Palmer, Edmund	1804	20		CT	Parmale, Bani, Jr.	1805	21	CT
Palmer, Edmund	1803	19		CT	Parmale, Orren	1806	20	CT
Palmer, Elias	1818	19		CT	Parmalee, John	1805	16	CT
Palmer, Erastus	1815	30		CT	Parmalee, Samuel	1804	22	CT
Palmer, Erastus	1805	20		CT	Parmele, Henry	1809	21	CT
Palmer, Erastus	1803	18		CT	Parmele, Wm.	1807	21	CT
Palmer, Henry	1812	31		CT	Parmelee, Beecher	1811	30	CT
Palmer, James	1808	27		CT	Parmelee, Jeremiah	1811	34	CT
Palmer, James	1801	0			Parmelee, Timothy	1807	16	CT
Palmer, James	1804	23		CT	Parmelee, Timothy	1806	15	CT
Palmer, James	1803	22		CT	Parmelee, Zera	1809	19	CT
Palmer, John	1811	17		CT	Parrot, Robert	1811	16	VA
Palmer, John B.	1841	19		CT	Parssons, Augustus	1809	23	CT
Palmer, Justus	1804	19		CT	Paterson, Hugh C.	1820	21	PA
Palmer, Justus	1815	23		VA	Patterson, McDonald	1811	35	b	NY
Palmer, Justus	1806	21		CT	Payne, Richard	1807	34	VA
Palmer, Justus	1807	21		CT	Payne, William	1804	21	NY

Name	Year	Age		State
Pease, Horace	1806	23		CT
Peck, Allen	1822	27		CT
Peck, Alton	1810	16		CT
Peck, Andrew	1803	20		CT
Peck, Andrew	1803	20		CT
Peck, Ansel	1812	22		CT
Peck, Charles W.	1843	16	y	CT
Peck, Dan	1822	49		CT
Peck, Dan	1803	26		CT
Peck, Dan	1805	30		CT
Peck, Dan	1812	37		CT
Peck, Ebenezer, Jr.	1811	20		CT
Peck, Ebenezer, Jr.	1810	19		CT
Peck, Elisha	1810	21		CT
Peck, Elisha	1803	14		CT
Peck, Ezbert D.	1806	16		CT
Peck, Garry	1803	19		CT
Peck, James	1803	27		CT
Peck, Jery B.	1815	27		CT
Peck, Luther	1804	19		CT
Peck, Michel, 3rd	1810	24		CT
Peck, Thos.	1803	35		MA
Peck, Vinus	1805	22		CT
Peck, Vinus	1803	21		CT
Peck, Vinus	1804	22		CT
Peden, Ahmsted?	1807	21		NC
Peek, Elisha	1805	16		CT
Peek, Luther	1805	22		CT
Peek, Wm.	1806	16		CT
Peet, Alton	1809	16		CT
Peet, Gany	1811	26		CT
Peet, Gany	1811	26		CT
Peet, Garry	1808	22		CT
Peet, Garry	1805	20		CT
Peet, John Garry	1803	19		CT
Peet, John Garry	1805	20		CT
Peirson, William	1807	20		CT
Pendleton, Edmond	1838	18		CT
Penfield, Elisha	1810	22		CT
Penfield, Richard	1812	23		NY
Penfold, Nelson	1836	19		CT
Percett, Nicholas	1804	23	b	NY
Perch, Benjamin	1816	23	b	
Perch, Benjamin]	1815	22	b	MA
Perch, Benjn.	1828	38	y	NY
Perine, James	1807	28		NY
Perkins, Abel	1807	16		CT
Perkins, Ezekiel	1804	17		CT
Perkins, Francis	1813	21		CT
Perry, David	1806	23		CT
Perry, Harry	1826	19		CT
Perry, Josiah	1806	20		CT
Peters, Thomas	1806	19	b	NC
Peters, Thomas	1804	17	b	NC
Peterson, Peter	1837	24		PA
Peterson, Thomas	1838	34	b	NY
Pettit, Edward	1841	24		NY
Phelps, Henry	1809	18		NH
Phelps, Henry	1812	21		NH
Phelps, Joseph W.	1826	16		CT
Phelps, Sewall	1807	19		MA
Phelps, William	1806	22		CT
Phelps, William	1803	19		CT
Phennox, John	1815	35		MA
Philips, Benj.Harvey	1810	24	b	CT
Philips, Edward	1825	23	b	CT
Philips, Edward	1822	19	b	CT
Philips, Fortune	1807	24	b	MA
Philips, Francis	1811	21	b	CT
Philips, John	1805	20	b	CT
Philips, John	1806	21	b	CT
Philips, Nathan	1809	22	b	CT
Philips, William E.	1806	27		RI
Phillips, Chs.	1830	43		Prussia
Phillips, Edward	1832	27	b	CT
Phillips, Leman	1830	23	b	CT
Phillips, Leverett	1842	36	b	CT
Phipps, Solomon, Jr.	1804	22		CT
Pierce, David	1805	26		CT
Pierce, Wm.	1819	17		CT
Pierpont, Evelyn	1813	22		CT
Pierson, William	1843	17		NJ
Pinkham, Benjamin	1836	25		MA
Pinto, Abraham	1805	17		CT
Pinto, John	1812	10		CT
Pinto, William	1815	21		CT
Pitcher, James	1806	22		CT
Pitcher, James	1803	17		CT
Plant, Isaac	1817	15		CT
Platt, Sidney	1804	23		CT
Platt, William	1820	22		CT
Plumb, Benoni	1805	23		CT
Plumb, David	1805	20		CT
Plumb, Isaac	1804	23		CT
Plumb, Joe	1804	25		CT
Plumb, Joel	1807	20		CT
Plumb, Trueman	1807	19		CT
Plumb, Trueman	1813	25		CT
Plumb, Truman	1809	21		
Plumb, Truman	1805	17		CT
Plumb, William	1819	22		CT
Pomeroy, Elijah	1805	20		CT
Pond, Asa	1804	22		MA
Pond, Elias	1805	18		CT
Pond, Eliphalet	1803	24		CT
Pool, Abijah	1804	22		CT
Pool, Edward	1804	28		MA
Pool, John	1815	21		MD

Pool, Wyllys	1813	20	CT
Pool, Wyllys	1810	17	CT
Porter, Benjamin	1810	20	CT
Porter, Henry	1837	19	CT
Porter, John	1807	22	NY
Porter, William	1818	32	
Potter, Allen	1823	19	CT
Potter, Allen	1824	20	CT
Potter, Bela	1806	22	CT
Potter, Brister D.	1825	29 b	CT
Potter, Walter	1806	20	CT
Potter, Wm.	1805	19	CT
Powers, Alden	1837	22	VT
Powers, Levi	1816	22	MA
Pratt, Charles S.	1841	21	ME
Pratt, Saml. M.	1805	22	CT
Prescot, Benjn. , Jr.	1813	18	CT
Price, Francis	1806	20	CT
Prime, John	1841	44 b	NY
Primus, Ham	1810	23 b	CT
Primus, Jonah	1815	25 b	CT
Primus, Nimrod	1806	45 b	CT
Primus, Peter	1807	23 b	CT
Prince, Joseph	1809	23	CT
Prindle, Joseph S.	1842	17	CT
Prindle, Joseph S.	1842	16	CT
Pye, Thomas	1804	23	NY
Queen, John	1803	28	CT
Queen, Wm.	1806	19	CT
Rae, Eben	1813	26 y	CT
Ralph, Laronzo	1843	18 y	NY
Ramsdell, Jesse H.	1842	25	CT
Randall, John	1836	46	RI
Randall, Richard	1838	24	CT
Ranney, Charles	1803	33	CT
Ranney, Saml.W., Jr.	1803	19	CT
Ransom, William J.	1811	23	CT
Ranson, Robert	1803	17	CT
Rawls, Samuel	1842	37 b	VA
Ray, James	1803	16	RI
Ray, James	1803	16	RI
Ray, Joel	1806	30	CT
Raymond, John	1803	18	MA
Rea, Philemon D.	1813	25	DE
Read, Hartwell	1806	23	CT
Read, Hartwell	1803	21	CT
Read, James	1813	33 b	MA
Read, Scipio	1819	32 b	MA
Reading, Frederick	1842	20	NY
Redfield, Griffing	1827	16	CT
Redfield, Roswell	1805	26	CT
Redfield, Wm.	1808	15	CT
Reed, Isaac W.	1843	21	CT
Reed, William	1815	19	NH
Reeve, Ephraim	1803	21	NY
Regus, Eli	1817	19	CT
Rembert, Henry	1805	21	CT
Renfield, Lewis	1837	16	CT
Reynolds, Frederick	1811	47	CT
Reynolds,FrederickJr.	1810	18	CT
Reynolds,FrederickJr.	1807	15	CT
Reynolds, James B.	1843	20	CT
Reynolds, Roswell	1822	35	CT
Reynolds, Roswell	1805	18	CT
Reynolds, Roswell	1806	19	CT
Reynolds, Roswell	1809	21	CT
Reynolds, Thomas B.	1815	27	NY
Rhodes, Peter	1818	19 b	NY
Rhodes, Remanta	1822	33	CT
Rhodes, Rhomanta	1837	47	CT
Rice, Clark	1812	22	CT
Rice, Joshua	1806	22	VT
Rice, Leverett	1813	23	CT
Rich, Francis	1837	23	ME
Rich, James	1820	18	CT
Richards, Charles	1803	17	CT
Richards, Horace	1812	15 b	CT
Richards, Jered	1810	15	CT
Richards, Stephen	1805	27	CT
Richards, William	1810	17	CT
Richardson, Amos	1837	34	ME
Richardson, John	1822	18	CT
Riggs, Hra	1827	21	
Riggs, Lyman	1807	24	CT
Riggs, Moses	1804	17	CT
Riggs, Sheldon	1804	22	CT
Riley, Andrew M.	1837	39 y	MA
Riley, James	1805	36	NY
Riley, Thos.	1810	18	NY
Rines, Samuel	1829	19	ME
Riss, James	1841	17 b	CT
Roads, Mathew	1806	17	CT
Roads, Romanta	1813	23	CT
Robbins, John	1805	27	CT
Robbins, Thomas	1842	18	ME
Roberson, Charles	1803	27	NY
Roberts, Charles	1841	22	ME
Roberts, Charles	1806	19	NY
Roberts, John	1841	25	PA
Roberts, John	1842	28	PA
Roberts,Josiah,Junr.	1805	19	CT
Robertson, Charles	1804	17	MY
Robertson, Charles	1838	21	CT
Robertson, George	1815	26	PA
Robeson, John	1829	32	NY
Robins, Saml.	1810	26 b	CT
Robins, Samuel	1806	24 b	CT
Robinson, David	1823	29	CT

Robinson, David	1829	36		CT	Rue, Henry	1836	20 y	CT
Robinson, Hobart	1824	23		CT	Rue, Lyman	1837	23 y	CT
Robinson, Ira	1803	7		CT	Rulford, Marcus	1817	21	CT
Robinson, Israil	1808	19		CT	Russee, Truman	1810	35	CT
Robinson, Jno.	1825	28 b		NY	Russel, Asael	1805	18	CT
Robinson, John	1826	25 y		CT	Russel, John Mattley	1810	21	CT
Robinson, Uriah	1805	19		CT	Russel, William	1803	16	CT
Robinson, Wm.	1812	23		NY	Russel, Wm.	1804	17	CT
Robison, Jno.	1830	33		NY	Russell, Alden	1806	19	CT
Roche, Edward	1818	13		NY	Russell, Alfred	1843	24	CT
Rockwell, George	1805	20		CT	Russell, Ansel	1842	20 b	CT
Rockwood, William	1806	17		CT	Russell, John	1822	23	CT
Rockwood, William	1805	16		MA	Russell, Royal H.	1842	19 y	CT
Roff, David	1803	23		NJ	Russell, Samuel W.	1842	16	CT
Rogers, Ammi	1824	21		CT	Russell, Sidney	1838	44 b	CT
Rogers, Caleb Smith	1813	22		VT	Ryerson, Balton	1822	26 b	NY
Rogers, Charles	1813	31 b		NY	Sabin, Daniel E.	1841	34	MA
Rogers, Henry	1819	22 y		NY	Saborie, Charles B.	1842	30	CT
Rogers, Josiah	1818	15		CT	Sackett, Horace	1843	21	CT
Rogers, Josiah	1821	19		CT	Sage, John C.	1803	35	CT
Rogers, Nathan	1815	16		CT	Sage, John C.	1809	41	CT
Rogers, Samuel	1819	21 b		CT	Sage, John Clark	1806	39	CT
Roillence, William	1805	24		MA	Sage, Lelah L.	1822	·23	CT
Rood, Amasa	1804	23		CT	Sage, Lelah Y.	1826	26	CT
Roods, Romanta	1805	16		CT	Sage, Selah Salter	1811	13	CT
Root, Loyd	1805	18		cT	Sage, William	1806	21	CT
Rose, Bela	1803	18		CT	Sage, Willis T.	1822	22	CT
Rose, Charles	1842	23		CT	Samford, Eliphatez	1807	32	CT
Rose, Erastus	1804	17		CT	Sampson, Alfonso	1838	24	CT
Rose, Hervey	1806	25		CT	Sampson, Charles	1807	19	VT
Rose, Robert	1809	21		CT	Sanderson, Charles	1819	21	MA
Rose, Robert	1811	23		CT	Sanderson, Charles	1843	45	MA
Rose, William R.	1822	21		CT	Sanderson, Charles	1821	23	MA
Ross, David A.	1805	19		LA	Sanderson, Phneas	1806	19	CT
Ross, DavidAugustus	1805	19		LA	Sanderson,William M.	1807	17	CT
Ross, George G.	1836	22		CT	Sandiford, Samuel	1807	44	NY
Ross, Lester	1843	25 b		CT	Sands, Hart	1813	23	NY
Ross, Wesley	1836	37		NJ	Sanford, Alfred M.	1835	15	CT
Roten, John T.	1813	26		MD	Sanford, David	1815	24	CT
Rowe, Austin	1809	19		CT	Sanford, David	1809	18	CT
Rowe, Austin	1808	18		CT	Sanford, Eli	1810	19	CT
Rowe, Eben	1808	21 y		CT	Sanford, Elias	1825	20	CT
Rowe, Eben	1810	23 y		CT	Sanford, Elijah	1809	37	CT
Rowe, Eben	1805	19 b		CT	Sanford, Elijah	1806	36	CT
Rowe, Ebenezer	1805	18			Sanford, Eliphalet	1803	28	CT
Rowe, Eli	1807	19		CT	Sanford, George	1836	26	ME
Rowe, Eliada	1817	19		CT	Sanford, Isaac H.	1815	19	CT
Rowe, Eliada	1825	28		CT	Sanford, James O.	1832	19 b	CT
Rowe, George	1825	18		CT	Sanford,JamesOgden	1830	17 b	CT
Rowe, George	1830	24		CT	Sanford, Joel	1813	25	CT
Rowley, Chancey L.	1804	14		CT	Sanford, Joel	1810	23	CT
Rue, Charles	1838	27 y		CT	Sanford, John	1818	44	CT
Rue, Charles	1834	24 y		CT	Sanford, Joseph	1831	16 b	CT
Rue, Francis	1837	21 y		CT	Sanford, Menemon	1811	21	CT

Sanford, Norman	1832	22 b	CT
Sanford, Norman	1830	20 b	CT
Sanford, William	1815	19	CT
Sanford, William	1811	15	CT
Sanger, Joseph W.	1810	28	CT
Sangster, Charles	1842	23	PA
Sangster, Charles	1841	23	PA
Saunders, Henry	1815	23 b	MA
Sauney, Cato	1804	15 b	CT
Sawyer, John	1818	39 b	MA
Sawyer, John Andrew	1812	21	NJ
Saxton, Linus	1810	37	CT
Saxton, William S.	1843	18	CT
Scarrit, James	1803	21	CT
Scheyler, Charles	1807	20 y	CT
Scholes, John	1810	35	naturalized
Scott, George G.	1819	16	CT
Scott, Henry	1838	28 b	NJ
Scott, James	1841	21	PA
Scott, John	1826	33	PA
Scott, Lemuel	1817	36	CT
Scott, Samuel	1809	28	CT
Scott, William	1835	20 b	NY
Scott, William	1834	19 b	NY
Scovil, Mathew	1821	20	CT
Scranton, Jonathan	1804	24	CT
Scranton, Joseph	1815	43	CT
Scull, William	1811	32	PA
Seabury, Edward	1823	28 b	NY
Seaman, John	1809	19	NY
Seamans, Lewis	1807	20	DE
Sears, Enoch	1809	29	CT
Sears, Isaac	1809	19	CT
Sears, John	1809	24	CT
Sears, John	1806	21	CT
Sears, Joseph	1809	25	CT
Sears, William	1807	14	CT
Sebrund, Edward	1841	17 b	CT
Sedam, Benjamin	1834	28 b	NY
Seeley, Holly	1805	22	CT
Selby, Robert	1804	35	CT
Selby, Thomas	1806	17	CT
Sessions, Robert R.	1813	35 b	RI
Seward, Amos	1806	20	CT
Seward, Azariah	1808	21	CT
Seward, Azariah	1806	19	CT
Seward, Azariah	1810	24	CT
Seward, Daniel W.	1805	26	CT
Seward, Daniel Wm.	1803	23	CT
Seward, Daniel Wm.	1801	22	CT
Seward, Daniel Wm.	1806	26	CT
Sexton, James O.	1842	18	CT
Seymour, Eli	1810	22 y	CT
Seymour, Richard	1805	38	CT

Shanklyn, Robert	1815	21	PA
Shannon, William C.	1811	21	NY
Sharp, David	1810	18	CT
Sharp, Ebenezer	1811	20 y	CT
Sharp, Levi	1803	21 b	CT
Sheffield, Wm. F.	1831	17	CT
Shelby, Harry	1816	20	CT
Sheldon, Anthony	1823	29	CT
Sheldon, William	1805	26	CT
Shelley, Edmond, Jr.	1806	21	CT
Shelley, Harry	1818	22	CT
Shelley, Hervey O.	1817	24	CT
Shelley, Russel	1808	22	CT
Shelly, Frederick	1829	25	CT
Shelly, Frederick	1825	21	CT
Shelly, Joel	1806	38	CT
Shelly, Joel, Jr.	1829	23	CT
Shelly, Sherman	1806	22	CT
Shelton, Lucius	1815	22	CT
Shepard, Hezekiah	1810	20	CT
Shepard, Lin	1843	31	CT
Shepard, Noah	1806	38	CT
Shepherd, Amos	1818	18	CT
Shepherd, Elias	1807	20	CT
Shepherd, Elias	1804	17	CT
Shepherd, Elihu	1806	21	CT
Shepherd, Israel	1825	20	ME
Shepherd, Jeremiah	1816	22	CT
Shepherd, John A.	1841	49	NY
Shepherd, John A.	1838	46	NY
Shepherd, Joseph	1815	18	CT
Shepherd, Merit	1828	22	CT
Shepherd, William	1803	27	CT
Shepherd, Wm.	1828	14	CT
Shepherd, Yeba	1804	26	CT
Shepherd, Zgiba	1818	41	CT
Shepherd, Ziba	1818	40	CT
Sherman, James	1811	18 y	CT
Sherman, Robert	1806	32	CT
Sherman, Robert	1804	30	CT
Sherman, Walker	1811	50	CT
Sherry, David	1806	14	CT
Sherwood, Harley	1809	19	CT
Sherwood, Willys	1807	21	CT
Shiars, Samuel	1806	19	CT
Shipman, John G.	1803	22	
Shony, Joseph	1811	17	CT
Shores, Abel Parker	1836	35	MA
Shorey, Harrison	1843	26	ME
Short, Charles	1803	26	
Short, Josiah	1805	25	CT
Short, Robert	1805	26 b	MA
Shuman, Anthony H.	1805	25	CT
Shuman, Ephraim B.	1810	22	MA

Name	Year	Age		State
Silas, Richard	1804	24	b	NY
Silby, Thomas	1807	18		CT
Silliman, Philip	1815	25	b	CT
Silliman, Philip	1811	20	b	CT
Simmons, Judah M.	1817	17		MA
Simmons, Moses	1822	35	b	NY
Simmons, Samuel	1803	38		SC
Simons, Daniel	1809	23	b	MA
Simons, Henry	1838	24		CT
Simons, John	1803	27		NJ
Simons, Moses	1813	26	b	NY
Simons, Stephen	1812	21		CT
Simons, Stephen	1810	19		CT
Simpson, Sandy	1825	27	b	NY
Sims, Alfred	1841	31	y	CT
Sims, Isaac	1835	19		MA
Sinclair, Lewis	1827	27		NY
Sisson, Charles	1816	20		NY
Sisson, Isaac	1804	21		CT
Sisson, Noah B.	1806	17		CT
Sisson, Robert	1803	21		CT
Slade, John	1836	27		VA
Small, Jacob	1836	21	b	CT
Smith, Abel	1804	23		MA
Smith, Abel G.	1805	34		CT
Smith, Abraham C.	1817	16		CT
Smith, Amos	1805	24		CT
Smith, Andrew	1810	21		CT
Smith, Anthony	1803	22	b	NY
Smith, Arron	1806	17		CT
Smith, Benajah	1811	17		CT
Smith, Benjamin	1805	29		CT
Smith, Benjamin	1805	21		CT
Smith, Benjamin	1803	19		CT
Smith, Benjamin	1804	20		CT
Smith, Benjn.	1805	29		CT
Smith, Benjn. Rose	1807	32		CT
Smith, Charles	1815	30		SC
Smith, Charles F.	1809	24		NY
Smith, Charles H.	1838	16		CT
Smith, Chauncey	1806	35		CT
Smith, Chauncy, Jr.	1821	22		CT
Smith, Chauncy, Jr.	1827	28		CT
Smith, Dan	1809	23		CT
Smith, Daniel	1807	19		CT
Smith, Danl.	1809	21		CT
Smith, David	1807	24		CT
Smith, David	1812	16		CT
Smith, David, Jr.	1807	30		CT
Smith, Ebenezer F.	1816	26		CT
Smith, Edward R.	1809	26		CT
Smith, Edwin	1838	22		CT
Smith, Elias	1810	18		CT
Smith, Elijah	1806	21		CT
Smith, Elijah	1808	22		CT
Smith, Elijah	1806	23		CT
Smith, Elijah	1816	29		CT
Smith, Elijah	1804	18		CT
Smith, Elijah	1804	18		CT
Smith, Enos	1803	20		CT
Smith, Enos	1801	0		CT
Smith, Enos	1806	31		CT
Smith, Fitch	1803	20		
Smith, George	1807	12		CT
Smith, Harry	1810	17		CT
Smith, Henry	1810	22		CT
Smith, Henry	1804	22		CT
Smith, Isaac	1805	19		CT
Smith, Isaac	1803	29		CT
Smith, Isaac	1807	21		CT
Smith, Isaac	1806	15		CT
Smith, Isaac	1811	20		CT
Smith, Isaac	1817	23		CT
Smith, Jacob	1809	27		CT
Smith, James	1809	21	y	NY
Smith, James	1810	21	y	NY
Smith, James	1815	18		CT
Smith, James	1817	20		CT
Smith, James	1815	29	y	NY
Smith, James	1803	27		
Smith, James	1837	25		ME
Smith, Jared	1803	13		CT
Smith, Jared	1805	16		CT
Smith, Jared	1804	16		CT
Smith, Jared	1806	16		CT
Smith, Jared	1806	16		CT
Smith, Jere	1803	15		CT
Smith, Jeremiah	1841	17		CT
Smith, John	1841	21		NY
Smith, John	1805	24		CT
Smith, John	1807	20		MA
Smith, John	1815	23		CT
Smith, John	1815	29	b	MA
Smith, Joseph	1809	22		CT
Smith, Joseph	1803	16		CT
Smith, Joseph	1804	18		CT
Smith, Joseph	1803	24		CT
Smith, Joseph	1803	29		CT
Smith, Josiah	1803	28		CT
Smith, Laban	1806	40		CT
Smith, Marcus	1807	17		CT
Smith, Marcus	1804	15		CT
Smith, Mark	1806	18		CT
Smith, Miles	1805	22		CT
Smith, Phineas	1803	20		CT
Smith, Richd. E.	1843	28		CT
Smith, Richd. E.	1842	27		CT
Smith, Robert	1806	24		PA

Name	Year	Age	State	Note
Smith, Roger	1801	17	CT	
Smith, Roger	1803	19		
Smith, Samuel	1805	20	MA	
Smith, Samuel	1805	22	CT	
Smith, Samuel	1821	21	CT	
Smith, Stephen	1809	32	CT	
Smith, Stephen	1806	29	CT	
Smith, Stephen	1803	26	CT	
Smith, Sylvester	1838	36	CT	
Smith, Sylvestor	1815	18	CT	
Smith, Thomas	1816	44	VA	
Smith, Thomas	1806	28	VT	
Smith, Titus	1810	24	CT	
Smith, Treat	1803	21	CT	
Smith, Vanjulius	1812	19	CT	
Smith, Warren	1815	17	CT	
Smith, William	1821	19	CT	
Smith, William	1813	28		
Smith, William	1821	32	MA	
Smith, William	1818	16	CT	
Smith, William	1809	21	CT	
Smith, William	1822	30	ME	
Smith, William A.	1812	15	NY	
Smith, William W.	1804	29	CT	
Smith, William, 2nd	1842	18	CT	
Smith, Willis	1836	21	CT	
Smith, Willis	1835	37 b	CT	
Smith, Willis	1836	38 b	CT	
Smith, Wm., 2nd	1843	19	CT	
Smith, Wm., Jr.	1842	19	CT	
Smith, Wyllis	1808	21	CT	
Smith, Wyllys	1806	20	CT	
Smithers, William	1805	25	CT	
Snyder, William	1815	32	MD	
Somers, William	1841	38 b	MA	
Soney, Timothy	1808	16 b	CT	
Sooney, Bennett	1833	30 b	CT	
Southwell, John	1806	16	CT	
Southworth,Saml.Wells	1813	26	CT	
Southworth,Saml.Wells	1805	18	CT	
Southworth,Saml.Wells	1805	17	CT	
Spairs, Samuel	1808	20	CT	
Sparks, David	1809	16	CT	
Sparnick, Henry	1815	27		naturalized
Spencer, Caleb	1811	25	CT	
Spencer, Caleb	1804	18	CT	
Spencer, Caleb	1803	17	CT	
Spencer, Christopher	1805	32	CT	
Spencer, Griswould	1806	21	CT	
Spencer, Harry	1810	27	CT	
Spencer, Harry	1803	28	CT	
Spencer, Henry D.	1837	29	CT	
Spencer, Hiram	1841	14	CT	
Spencer, James	1804	24	CT	
Spencer, John	1843	17	CT	
Spencer, John	1806	32	CT	
Spencer, Jones	1806	23	CT	
Spencer, Leonard	1806	26	CT	
Spencer, Leonard	1808	26	CT	
Spencer, Richard	1809	20		
Spencer, Richd.	1822	33	CT	
Spencer, Richd.	1824	34	CT	
Spencer, Selden	1806	20	CT	
Sperry, Eli	1804	32	CT	
Sperry, Miles	1806	27	CT	
Sperry, Moses	1804	22	CT	
Sperry, Seymour	1811	19	CT	
Sperry, Seymour]	1812	19	CT	
Sperry, William	1809	21	CT	
Spink, William	1803	17	CT	
Spink, William	1805	18	CT	
St Clair, Andrew	1818	25 b	MA	
Stacy, Joseph	1804	34	MA	
Stacy, Nymphas	1805	24	CT	
Staier, Saml.	1833	20	CT	
Stake, John	1836	47		Germany
Stake, John	1841	51		Germany
Stansbury, Samuel	1842	36	MD	
Staples, David	1803	34	CT	
Staples, Saml. W.	1819	15	CT	
Stark, Banjn. T.	1827	27	CT	
Starks, Loveland	1803	18	CT	
Starr, Benjamin	1807	29 b	CT	
Starr, Nathan	1807	23	CT	
StClair, Andrew	1819	26 b	CT	
Steadman, Sip	1809	20 y	CT	
Stebbins, Matson	1820	28	CT	
Stedman, Benjamin	1803	24	NC	
Steele, Edwin	1828	19	CT	
Stevens, Alfred	1823	16	CT	
Stevens, Daniel	1813	15	CT	
Stevens, Daniel	1815	16	CT	
Stevens, Eliphalet	1806	19	CT	
Stevens, Geo. H.	1828	16	CT	
Stevens, George	1837	27	CT	
Stevens, George	1836	25	CT	
Stevens, George M.	1813	27		
Stevens, James	1828	16	CT	
Stevens, Jesse M.	1843	18	CT	
Stevens, Jesse M.	1841	17	CT	
Stevens, John	1803	21	CT	
Stevens, John	1805	23	CT	
Stevens, John	1815	35	MA	
Stevens, Joseph, Jr.	1831	16	CT	
Stevens, Leverit, Jr.	1812	12	CT	
Stevens, Samuel	1810	21	CT	
Stevens, Sherman G.	1825	17	CT	
Stevens, Sherman G.	1827	19	CT	

Stevens, William	1825	22	CT	Sullivan, Wm.	1806	13	NY
Stevenson, Jared	1805	25 b	CT	Sutton, Isaac	1805	23	CT
Steward, John	1821	25 b	NY	Sutton, John	1841	19	ME
Stewart, Davis	1838	27	MA	Sweeten, John	1811	21	CT
Stewart, Robert	1842	29	MD	Sweeten, John	1809	19	CT
Stidmond, William	1806	22	NJ	Swett, David	1836	19	ME
Stiles, Phineas	1806	21	CT	Swezy, Andrew	1843	36 b	NY
Stiles, Phineas	1805	21	CT	Synn, William H.	1818	21	MA
Stiles, Phineas	1806	22	CT	Syphax, Henry	1818	24 y	CT
Stiles, Phineas	1805	21	CT	Tainter, Nath.	1805	22	CT
Stillman, Benj. P.	1805	16	CT	Tainter, Ruben	1805	20	CT
Stillman, Benjamin P.	1807	18	CT	Taintor, Ruben	1807	22	CT
Stillman, Pierson	1822	24	CT	Tallman, Rowde	1805	22	MA
Stine, Josiah	1808	29	CT	Talmage, Asahel	1806	22	CT
Stockdale, Thomas	1807	33	PA	Talmage, Aschel	1804	22	CT
Stocker, Burrill	1803	28	MA	Talmage, Chester	1805	26	CT
Stone, Asher	1811	20	CT	Talmage, Chester	1803	23	CT
Stone, Daniel	1811	24	CT	Talmage, James	1806	22	CT
Stone, Henry	1805	22	CT	Talmage, John R.	1824	17	CT
Stone, Herbey	1812	17	CT	Talmage, Robert	1803	20	CT
Stone, Hervey	1809	15	CT	Tarcus, Elias	1836	25 b	CT
Stone, Hubbard	1804	19	CT	Tarcus, William	1837	20 b	CT
Stone, Samuel, Jr.	1812	33	CT	Tardy, Daniel	1805	24	VA
Stone, Wm. T.	1826	23	CT	Tatem, Jonathan	1811	22	CT
Store, Henry	1804	15	CT	Tayler, James	1812	22 b	CT
Storer, Alexander	1803	16	CT	Tayler, Malachi Stent	1804	22	CT
Storer, Peter	1810	19	CT	Tayler, William	1842	27 b	MD
Storer, William	1808	20	MA	Tayler/Tyler,Stephen	1805	21	CT
Story, William	1807	20	MA	Taylor, Amos	1808	22	CT
Stow, Elisha H.	1816	18	CT	Taylor, David, Jr.	1809	24	CT
Stow, Frederick	1811	18	CT	Taylor, David, Jr.	1809	24	CT
Stow, Isaac	1807	25	CT	Taylor, Hezekiah	1836	18	CT
Stow, Isaac	1803	22	CT	Taylor, John	1823	37	CT
Stow, Lamuel	1803	18	CT	Taylor, John	1803	22	CT
Stow, Marcus	1825	26	CT	Teller, Luke	1810	28	NY
Stow, Marcus	1824	26	CT	Tenbrook, Henry	1809	23	NY
Stow, Marcus	1821	23	CT	Terrel, Abijah B.	1803	23	CT
Stow, Phineas	1803	30	CT	Terril, Abijah B.	1806	25	CT
Stow, Sam.	1804	19	CT	Terrill, Eliakim	1816	23	CT
Stowell, Alpheus	1815	30	MA	Terrill, John	1808	18	CT
Stowell, Ludovicus	1815	22	CT	Terry, John	1842	16	NY
Straton, Daniel	1803	22	CT	Thair, Sherman	1803	23	
Stratten, Daniel	1806	26	CT	Thatcher, Charles	1823	22	NH
Stratton, Daniel	1805	24	CT	Thatcher, Stephen	1804	13	CT
Streeter, Randall	1805	20	NH	Thatcher, Stephen	1809	18	CT
Striker, John	1821	17	NY	Thomas, Aaron	1803	25	CT
Strong, Erastus	1805	26	CT	Thomas, Adanijah	1803	29	CT
Strong, Erastus	1804	25	CT	Thomas, Alfred	1841	17	CT
Strong, Erastus	1831	52	CT	Thomas, Ammid	1809	37	CT
Strong, Nathan K.	1806	19	CT	Thomas, Amos	1824	19	CT
Stuart, Jacob	1841	27 b	ME	Thomas, Amos	1830	26	CT
Studson, Francis	1843	22	ME	Thomas, Amos	1803	18	CT
Stute, George	1813	21 y	CT	Thomas, Asa B.	1817	21	CT
Sules, James	1813	29 b	CT	Thomas, Asahel	1834	29	CT

Thomas, Asahel, Jr.	1815	11	CT
Thomas, Ashel	1804	21	CT
Thomas, Cato	1805	39 b	CT
Thomas, Charles	1809	19 b	NY
Thomas, Cornelius	1804	25	CT
Thomas, Cornelius	1804	28	CT
Thomas, David	1808	24	CT
Thomas, Elias	1805	23	CT
Thomas, Elias	1805	23	CT
Thomas, Elias	1803	21	
Thomas, Elisha	1807	19	CT
Thomas, Elisha	1807	20	CT
Thomas, Elizah	1805	18	CT
Thomas, Emerick	1805	19	CT
Thomas, Emerick	1806	20	CT
Thomas, Henry	1837	24 b	VA
Thomas, Isaac	1810	25	
Thomas, Isaac	1808	22	MA
Thomas, James	1804	21	CT
Thomas, James R.	1841	22	CT
Thomas, John	1804	28	CT
Thomas, John	1818	20 y	CT
Thomas, John	1821	24	LA
Thomas, Levericy	1809	24	CT
Thomas, Leverious	1804	19	CT
Thomas, Liverius	1804	19	CT
Thomas, Lovel	1804	21	MA
Thomas, Richard	1811	16	CT
Thomas, Saml. M.	1804	25	CT
Thomas, Samuel	1812	14 b	CT
Thomas, Thaddeus	1807	17	CT
Thomas, Timothy	1811	26	CT
Thomas, Timothy	1805	20	CT
Thomas, William	1812	14	CT
Thomas, Wm.	1815	23	NY
Thomas, Wm. W.	1832	21	CT
Thompson, Abel	1809	20	CT
Thompson, Augustus	1810	30	CT
Thompson, Benj.	1805	27	CT
Thompson, Birdsey	1803	17	
Thompson, Birdseye	1805	19	CT
Thompson, Curtis	1805	18	CT
Thompson, Curtis	1804	17	CT
Thompson, David	1803	15	CT
Thompson, Eben	1842	32 y	NY
Thompson, Ebenezer	1804	19	CT
Thompson, Ebin	1836	27 y	NY
Thompson, Elihu	1807	18	CT
Thompson, Elihu	1809	20	CT
Thompson, Erastus	1806	22	CT
Thompson, Harry	1803	20	CT
Thompson, Henry	1809	17	CT
Thompson, Hezekiah	1810	17	CT
Thompson, Hezekiah	1810	17	
Thompson, Isaac	1806	28	CT
Thompson, Isaac	1817	22	MA
Thompson, Isaac	1813	19	MA
Thompson, James	1817	21 b	NY
Thompson, James	1819	23 b	NY
Thompson, James	1818	22 b	NY
Thompson, James	1841	43	ME
Thompson, Jno.	1827	17	CT
Thompson, John	1842	42	ME
Thompson, John	1842	18 b	CT
Thompson, John	1836	28 b	NY
Thompson, John	1821	21	CT
Thompson, Landy	1803	18	CT
Thompson, Lemuel	1804	30	CT
Thompson, Lewis	1811	23	CT
Thompson, Lewis	1807	19	CT
Thompson, Peter	1805	23	NY
Thompson, Peter	1805	22	NY
Thompson, Robert	1818	25	NH
Thompson, Shelden	1803	18	CT
Thompson, Sheldon	1805	20	CT
Thompson, Sheldon	1803	18	CT
Thompson, Sheldon Jr	1805	21	CT
Thompson, Silas	1805	24	CT
Thompson, Stephen	1833	16	CT
Thompson, Stephen	1810	34	CT
Thompson, Sylvester	1806	23	MA
Thompson, William	1817	19	CT
Thompson, William	1818	28 b	NJ
Thompson, William	1820	18	CT
Thompson, William	1842	28	NY
Thompson, William	1803	25	CT
Thompson, Wm.	1826	26	CT
Thompson, Wm.	1831	23	NH
Thompson, Wm.	1829	29	CT
Thompson, Wm.	1813	27 b	NY
Thompson/Thomas, Henry	1832	20	CT
Thornton, Isaac	1809	21	CT
Thorp, Orrin	1807	21	CT
Throop, John Dixwell	1809	17	CT
Thurston, James	1825	19	ME
Tillden, Horatio	1803	18	MA
Tingley, Daniel	1805	38	NY
Tirrell, John	1815	26	CT
Titus, Curtis	1803	23	CT
Tobias, Calis, Jr.	1820	18 b	CT
Toby, Samuel	1807	23	MA
Todd, Wm.	1805	22	CT
Tolcutt, Asa	1810	17	MA
Tolles, Dan	1803	28	CT
Tolles, George F.	1816	31	CT
Tolles, Geo.Frederick	1811	27	CT
Tolles, Geo.Frederick	1806	22	CT

Name	Year	Age		State
Tolles, George Henry	1824	15		CT
Tolles/Potts,				
George Frederick	1812	28		CT
Tomlinson, Amon	1812	35		CT
Tomlinson, Isaac, Jr.	1815	27		CT
Tomlinson, John G.	1819	15		CT
Tomlinson, John G.	1842	21		CT
Tomlinson, Peter	1803	19		CT
Tomlinson, Ralph	1803	27		CT
Tomlinson, Ransom	1825	17		VT
Tomlinson, Runsom	1827	19		VT
Tomlinson, Silas	1817	41		CT
Tomlinson, Silas	1812	35		CT
Toumend, Jacob	1807	38		CT
Touner, Augustus	1805	18		CT
Tounsend,				
James Webster	1806	23		CT
Tounsend,Solomon,Jr	1812	26		CT
Townsend, Edward	1811	21	b	PA
Townsend, Edward	1813	23	b	PA
Townsend, George	1812	28		NY
Townsend, George	1836	22		NY
Townsend, James W.	1804	21		CT
Tracy, Peter	1841	24		MA
Treadwell, Cyrus	1820	26	y	NY
Treadwell, James	1815	24	y	NY
Treat, David	1815	22		CT
Treat, David	1810	17		CT
Treat, David	1811	10		CT
Treat, Erastua	1820	16		CT
Treat, James	1810	19		CT
Treat, Tim	1803	27		CT
Trevals, George	1841	15		CT
Trowbridge, Charles	1806	23		CT
Trowbridge, Daniel	1812	21		CT
Trowbridge, Daniel	1818	26		CT
Trowbridge, Diodeth	1803	18		CT
Trowbridge, Elias	1810	20		
Trowbridge, Elias	1808	17		CT
Trowbridge, George	1810	19		CT
Trowbridge, George	1807	16		CT
Trowbridge, George	1815	24		CT
Trowbridge, Joseph	1804	30		CT
Trowbridge,Newman,Jr	1811	29		CT
Trowbridge, Robert	1809	19		CT
Trowbridge, Roswell	1806	22		CT
Trowbridge, Roswell	1805	21		CT
Trowbridge, Stephen	1804	23		CT
Trowbridge, Timothy	1813	19		CT
Trowbridge, William	1803	30		
Trowbridge, Wililam	1809	36		CT
Trueman, Daniel H.	1829	23		CT
Truman, Martin	1834	24	b	ME
Tryon, Dennis	1804	18		
Tryon, Elijah	1804	21		CT
Tryon, Walter	1836	21		CT
Tscat?, Erastus S.	1837	33		CT
Tucker, Burton	1807	20		CT
Tucker, Gideon	1803	24		CT
Tucker, Henry	1810	23		CT
Tufts, Zachariah	1812	19		NH
Tufts, Zechariah	1811	18		NH
Turner, Alvah	1818	19		CT
Turner, Manning	1822	21		CT
Turner, Manning	1824	23		CT
Turner, Manning	1826	25		CT
Turner, Samuel	1813	19		MA
Turtihee, David T.	1806	16		CT
Tuttle, Charles	1835	19		CT
Tuttle, Daniel	1810	19		CT
Tuttle, Eli	1810	31		CT
Tuttle, Ephraim, Jr.	1804	27		CT
Tuttle, Esra	1804	17		CT
Tuttle, Jeremiah	1810	31		CT
Tuttle, John A.	1841	16		CT
Tuttle, Merriman	1804	28		CT
Tuttle, William A.	1819	23		CT
Tuttle, Wm.				
Jackson Woodhul	1813	22		NJ
Twitchell, David T.	1809	20		CT
Tyler, Edmond	1805	24		CT
Tyler, Edward	1806	23		CT
Tyler, Lemuel	1809	24		CT
Tyler, Luther	1805	40		CT
Tyler, Reuben	1803	24		
Tyler, Ruben	1806	26		CT
Tyler, William	1813	21		CT
Tynan, Joseph	1842	24		MA
Tyrell,				
Abyah Buckingham	1801	21		CT
Tyson, Thomas	1810	20		NC
Umberfield,				
Robert Albert	1809	14		CT
Upson, John	1806	23		CT
Upton, Amos	1819	18		NC
Vail, Horace	1811	15		CT
Vail, James	1815	33		CT
Vail, James	1804	18		CT
Vail, James	1804	21		CT
Vail, Leveret	1812	18		NC
Vail, Leverit	1820	27		CT
Vail, Leveritt	1821	28		CT
Vail, Leveritt	1819	26		CT
Vail, Seth	1809	22		CT
Value, Geo. W. V.	1825	14		CT
Van Dusor, David	1807	21		CT
Van Hagen, James	1819	36		NY
Van Norden, Samuel	1803	34		

Name	Year	Age		State
Van Wagner, Ralph	1818	28		CT
VanDuson, David	1805	18		CT
Veaill, Peter	1805	17		CT
Venables, James	1803	25		NY
Venry, James R.	1843	29		MA
Vensy, James R.	1843	28		MD
Ventris, William	1803	31		CT
Vincent, Stephen	1815	36		NY
Vinson, Alexander	1813	23	b	PA
Vinson, Lawrence	1801	22		NY
Vinton, Samuel	1805	24		MA
Votee, Charles	1804	18		CT
Voty, Charles	1803	17		CT
Wade, Enos	1811	29		NJ
Wade, John	1805	25		NJ
Wade, John	1804	25		NJ
Wade, John	1805	25		NJ
Wadsworth, Allen	1815	20		CT
Wadsworth, Oliver	1820	21		CT
Wagnor, Ralph Van	1806	16		CT
Wakefield, Levi	1815	23		CT
Wakeman, Levi	1821	16		CT
Walden, Edmond	1818	16		CT
Walden, George	1821	16		CT
Wales, George	1801	22		CT
Wales, Peter	1822	18	y	NY
Walker, Harry	1804	15		CT
Walker, Henry	1805	17		CT
Walker, James	1806	21		MD
Walker, James S.	1841	28		MA
Walker, Thornton	1837	38	y	PA
Walker, Thornton	1823	37	y	PA
Walker, William	1819	18		CT
Walker, William	1836	27		CT
Walkley, Roswell S.	1833	29		CT
Wallace, Edward	1824	18	y	NY
Wallace, Resden	1842	45	b	MD
Wallace, Sam. G.	1808	22		CT
Walter, Wm., Jr.	1806	21		CT
Walton, Thomas	1804	18		CT
Walton, Thomas	1803	18		CT
Ward, Bennite	1827	23		CT
Ward, Ebenezer Parmelee	1803	15		CT
Ward, Elliot	1805	16		CT
Ward, Elliott	1806	17		CT
Ward, Frederick S.	1832	19		CT
Ward, Henry	1842	15		CT
Ward, Henry	1841	14		CT
Ward, Henry	1815	18		CT
Ward, Ichabod	1805	18		CT
Ward, Jacob	1805	21		CT
Ward, James	1806	30		CT
Ward, John	1804	21	y	CT
Ward, John	1841	17		CT
Ward, Minot	1842	17		CT
Ward, Titus	1805	36		CT
Ward, Titus	1805	36		CT
Ward, William	1838	34	b	NJ
Ward, William	1823	22		CT
Ward, William	1809	17		CT
Ward, William, Jr.	1841	16		CT
Warlick, John	1842	19	y	CT
Warner, Abraham	1807	20		CT
Warner, Cato	1807	22	b	CT
Warner, George	1804	25		CT
Warner, James	1832	23		CT
Warner, John	1805	15		CT
Warner, Joseph	1803	34		CT
Warren, Anson	1815	23		MA
Waterman, John, Jr.	1811	34		CT
Waterman Joshua D.	1803	19		CT
Waters, George	1809	21		CT
Waters, George	1810	22		CT
Waters, Israel	1819	38	b	PA
Watlington, John	1803	21		CT
Watrous, Riggs	1805	25		CT
Watrous, Riggs	1803	23		CT
Watson, Jack	1807	35	b	NY
Watson, John	1817	47	b	NY
Watson, Richard	1813	23		NJ
Watsous, Riggs	1803	22		CT
Watters, John	1803	26		CT
Way, Elijah	1806	24	b	CT
Way, Elisha	1803	21		CT
Way, Elyjah	1805	24	b	CT
Way, Henry B.	1841	18		CT
Way, John	1810	18	b	CT
Way, Minzy	1820	22	y	CT
Way, Roswell	1821	21		CT
Way, Thos.	1807	18		CT
Way, Timothy	1810	41		CT
Way, William	1822	40		RI
Way, William H.	1841	17		
Way, Windsor	1813	24	b	MA
Weaver, Asa	1812	25		CT
Weaver, Asa	1813	25		CT
Weaver, Asa	1809	23		CT
Weaver, Reuben	1819	19		CT
Webber, John	1836	24		VA
Webster, David	1809	20		CT
Webster, George B.	1822	22		NY
Wedmore, Charles	1806	17		CT
Wedmore, Charles	1803	14		CT
Wedmore, Daniel	1808	16		CT
Wedmore, Daniel	1812	20		CT
Wedmore, Nath.	1807	13		CT
Wedmore, Nath., Jr.	1812	18		CT

Wedmore, Nathaniel	1806	12		CT	Wier, Samuel	1803	39		CT
Weeks, John	1810	27		NH	Wiggins, Joseph	1806	24		NY
Weir, David	1806	16		CT	Wight, Mons, Jr.	1810	19		MA
Wells, Charles A.	1836	19	y	CT	Wilcoxson, Jabez	1816	31		CT
Wells, Erastus	1803	24			Wilcoxson, Jabez	1806	22		CT
Wells, Erastus	1801	22			Wild, Richd.	1816	16		CT
Wells, George	1812	25		MA	Wilder, Daniel K.	1828	26		MA
Wells, Henry	1806	21		CT	Wilkins, Isaac	1805	25	y	NY
Wells, Isaac	1809	22		RI	Wilkins, James	1819	19		CT
Wells, Julius	1807	22		MA	Wilkinson, John	1806	28		CT
Wells, Moses	1811	40		CT	Willard, Elias	1804	46		CT
Wells, Moses, Jr.	1807	35		CT	Willard, Josiah	1805	24		CT
Wells, Nath.	1806	29		NY	Willbur, Rufus	1805	26		CT
Wells, Wheeler	1811	16		CT	Willcox, Gideon	1804	23		CT
Wells, Wheeler	1815	19		CT	Willcox, Josiah	1805	25		CT
Welman, Elias	1811	18		CT	Williams, Avery	1806	23	b	CT
Welton, Charles	1804	23		CT	Williams, Avery	1815	29	b	CT
Wert, John	1820	27	b	VA	Williams, Avery	1809	26	b	CT
West, Henry	1812	27		RI	Williams, Avery	1807	24	b	CT
West, Henry	1833	21	m	CT	Williams, Avery	1811	28	b	CT
West, Willilam	1807	12	y	PA	Williams, Avery	1811	28	b	CT
Weston, Henry	1837	24	y	CT	Williams, Charles	1807	25		CT
Weston, John	1819	29		DC	Williams, Charles	1807	25		CT
Wetton, Henry	1826	17		CT	Williams, Charles	1805	23		CT
Whatley, Samuel	1837	17			Williams, Cyrus	1824	24	y	NY
Wheadon, Amaziah	1803	23		CT	Williams, Cyrus	1822	22		NY
Whedman, Asa	1831	23		CT	Williams, David	1836	39	y	CT
Whedon, Amaziah	1805	25		CT	Williams, George	1843	22	y	NY
Whedon, Charles R.	1824	19		CT	Williams, Ginge	1843	23		RI
Wheeler, Abel	1816	35		MA	Williams, Henry	1843	15	y	CT
Wheeler, Alvin	1843	27		CT	Williams, James	1823	26	b	NY
Wheeler, Chauncy	1819	19		CT	Williams, James	1809	26	b	NY
Wheeler, Daniel	1815	24		CT	Williams, Jehu	1841	26		PA
Wheeler, Erastus	1807	20		CT	Williams, John	1838	33		CT
Wheeler, Erastus	1806	20		CT	Williams, John	1841	24		MD
Wheeler, Thomas	1838	26		PA	Williams, Joseph	1827	29	b	SC
Wheeler, William	1819	20		CT	Williams, Peter	1821	30	y	CT
Wheeler, Wm.	1832	22		MA	Williams, Peter	1823	32	b	CT
Wheeler,Wm.Munson	1829	14		NY	Williams, Richard W.	1809	24		CT
White, Aaron	1803	19			Williams, Rob	1827	24		NY
White, Aaron	1804	20		CT	Williams, Robert	1829	25		NY
White, Aaron Clark	1805	21		CT	Williams, Rufus	1815	21	b	CT
White, Aaron Clark	1806	23		CT	Williams, Samuel	1818	19	y	CT
White, Elisha	1803	24		CT	Williams, Samuel	1822	17	b	RI
White, John	1804	26		MA	Williams, Samuel N.	1805	29		PA
White, Ruben	1803	22		NC	Williams, Thomas	1843	21	y	NY
White, Timothy	1805	16		CT	Williams, Thomas	1841	20	y	NY
White, Timothy	1805	17		CT	Williams, Thomas	1837	18	y	NY
Whiting, Ralph	1836	21		CT	Williams, Thomas	1818	18		MD
Whitlock, Thadeus	1815	26		CT	Williams, William	1841	24	b	NY
Whitmore, Joseph	1805	35		CT	Williams, William	1836	21	b	NY
Whittlesey, Azaziah	1805	24		CT	Williamson, William	1815	19	b	MA
Whittlesey, Chauney	1801	16		CT	Willimson, James	1838	31		NY
Widmere, Nelson	1827	18		CT	Willis, Richard	1824	27		MA

Willmott, Philo	1803	18	CT
Willoughby,Augustus	1812	19	CT
Willoughby,Augustus	1810	17	CT
Willoughby, Charles	1816	26	CT
Willoughby, Charles	1813	24	CT
Willoughby, Charles	1806	18	CT
Willoughby, Charles	1803	14	CT
Willoughby, John	1805	27	CT
Willoughby, John	1808	28	CT
Willoughby, John	1809	29	CT
Willson, Peter	1804	32	CT
Wilmot, Philo	1805	21	CT
Wilmot, Philo	1803	0	CT
Wilmote, Amos, Jr.	1803	25	CT
Wilson, Alexander	1842	23	NY
Wilson, Charles	1815	26 b	LA
Wilson, Charles	1814	26 y	LA
Wilson, James	1811	30	DE
Wilson, James	1841	38 b	PA
Wilson, James	1843	38	NY
Wilson, James, Jr.	1807	21	MA
Wilson, John	1841	28 b	CT
Wilson, John	1806	19	NY
Wilson, John	1805	18	NY
Wilson, Lewis	1809	25 b	CT
Wilson, Ths.	1822	28	NY
Winslow, Benjamin F.	1841	22	ME
Wire, Joseph	1811	13	CT
Witson, Stephen	1824	44 y	NY
Wittum, James	1811	21	VT
Wolcot, Alfred	1815	21	CT
Wolcot, Elijah	1806	14	CT
Wolcott, Alexander	1817	17	CT
Wolcott, Alfred	1813	19	CT
Wolcott, Alfred	1818	23	CT
Wolcott, Alfred	1811	16	CT
Wolcott, Elijah	1812	21	CT
Wolcott, Harry	1805	17	CT
Wolcott, Henry	1813	25	CT
Wolcott, Lyman	1807	18	CT
Wolcott, Lyman	1807	17	CT
Wolcott, Rodolphus	1818	19	CT
Wollcot, Rodolphus	1815	17	CT
Woodbeck, Samuel	1810	28 b	NY
Woodbuk, Samuel	1809	29 b	NY
Woodford, Grove	1804	19	CT
Woodhouse, Sylvester		1815	21 CT
Woodruff, Daniel	1805	24	CT
Woodruff, Danl.	1806	25	CT
Woodruff, Moses	1807	33	CT
Woodruff, Ozem	1804	16	CT
Woods, Elisha Lewis	1810	26	CT
Woods, John	1841	31 y	MD
Woods, John	1842	32 y	MD
Woodward, John	1805	23	CT
Woodward, John	1806	24	CT
Woodward, John	1807	25	CT
Woolcot, Alfred	1807	13	CT
Woolcot, Elijah	1809	17	CT
Woolcot, Elijah	1808	16	CT
Woolcot, Elijah	1807	15	CT
Woolcot, Henry	1810	23 y	CT
Woolcot, Henry	1809	22	CT
Woolcot, Henry	1807	21	CT
Woolcott, Elijah	1815	23	CT
Woolcott, Henry	1812	24	CT
Woolcott, Henry	1809	23	CT
Woolcott, Lyman	1809	20	CT
Woolsey, Charles W.	1834	36 b	CT
Wooster, Charles	1837	16	CT
Wooster, Henry	1824	23	CT
Wotcott, Lyman	1813	24	CT
Wotton, John	1806	24	MA
Wright, Daniel	1811	23	MA
Wright, David	1810	22	MA
Wright, David, Jr	1841	18	CT
Wright, Elizur	1803	23	CT
Wright, James B.	1806	28	CT
Wright, Josiah	1811	24	NH
Wright, Samuel, Jr.	1806	16	RI
Wright, William	1805	18	CT
Wyer, John Allen	1810	31	
Wylie, Samuel H.	1831	13	CT
Wylley, Samuel	1843	22	ME
Yale, Anson	1801	26	CT
Yale, Anson	1801	26	CT
Yale, Nathaniel	1809	37	CT
Yepon, Joseph	1820	22 y	CT
Yeppon, Joseph	1826	28 y	CT
Yeppon, Joseph	1834	34 y	CT
Yetman, Asa B.	1816	27 y	CT
Yorke, John	1804	21	CT
Young, David	1813	38	MA
Young, Ezekiel	1812	17	MA
Young, Thomas	1818	26 y	NJ
Zacus, Elias	1832	20 b	CT
Zadoes, Isaac	1812	21 b	CT
Zarcus, Samuel	1823	20 b	CT

Bath 88

No. 159

I
County of ____ of ____ and State of ____ in the ____
do testify and declare, that *Christian H. Cruse* now present,
and applying for a Certificate of Protection, was born in *Copenhagen*
Kingdom of Denmark & Naturalized at
Puritan State of Maine

Lincoln ss—PORT OF BATH

Sworn to this ____ day of *December* 184__

BEFORE ME   COLLECTOR.

No. 113

I
County of ____ of ____ and State of ____ in the ____
do testify and declare, that *John Gustaf Graumberg* now present,
and applying for a Certificate of Protection, was born in *Finland*
Empire of Russia

Sworn to this *28th* day of *October* 184__ ss—PORT OF BATH

BEFORE ME   *J. Malley* & COLLECTOR.

Seamen's Protection Certificate Applications

Port of Bath, Maine

This is an index to 3,449 applications filed between 1833 and 1868. Registers, the quarterly reports made by Collectors of Customs, exist to fill some of the many gaps.

In using this index it is essential to note the number as well as the year the application was filed. The original chronological order of these records is preserved. They are not alphabetical. An advantage to this arrangement is that researchers can see who the other seamen were who applied about the same time .

Seamen applying for Protections in Bath were born in 22 states and the District of Columbia, and in 12 foreign countries. Nonetheless, these records are more parochial than those of other ports: 76% of the men applying in Bath were born in Maine.

Unlike applications filed in Philadelphia and New Orleans, the applications are not large, ornate documents. They are about 3 1/2" x 8". They appear to have been printed three to a page and the Collector, using a ruler, tore them apart. You may need to look at applications filed about the same time if a part of the application you are researching is missing. In most other ports the applications are notarized by a public official. In Bath there is no notary; the application is completed by the Collector of Customs.

Seamen's Protection Certificate Applications

Port of Bath, Maine

Data order: Name, Year, Number, Color, Age, State or Country

Name	Year	Number	Color	Age	State/Country	Name	Year	Number	Color	Age	State/Country
Abbott, Charles L.	1861	70		23 ME		Alley, Alden A.	1856	24		21 ME	
Acorn, George S.	1836	38		31 ME		Alley, Osborne T.	1856	25		22 ME	
Acuorth, Charles F.	1847	65		30 MD		Alley, Stanley	1860	56		24 ME	
Adams, Edward L.	1854	157		19 ME		Alley, William H.	1845	117		22 ME	
Adams, George H. F.	1854	160		17 MA		Alley, William S.	1856	59		14 NY	
Adams, Joseph C.	1836	60		21 ME		Ames, Franklin J.	1864	62		32 ME	
Adams, Samuel J.	1857	164		22 ME		Ames, Henry	1842	71		21 NY	
Adkins, William H.	1850	30		0 ME		Ames, Isaac L.	1853	126		17 NH	
Agry, William	1848	117		38 ME		Ames, Phineas K.	1853	220		24 ME	
Ahlers, Thomas H.	1861	60		24 NY		Anderson, George	1855	223		22 ME	
Aitchison, George C.	1861	54		52	Prussia	Anderson, James	1855	164		20 NY	
Albee, Wilmot	1861	68		39 ME		Anderson, Job	1847	125		50 ME	
Albro, George	1850	69		38 RI		Anderson, Michael	1857	128		21 ME	
Alden, Joseph B.	1856	88		30 MA		Anderson, Sewall	1857	159		19 ME	
Alexander, Albert H.	1865	44		18 ME		Anderson, William	1848	192		23 ME	
Alexander, Albion D.	1841	188		19 ME		Andrews, Eben	1857	101		16 ME	
Alexander, Charles	1842	130		22 ME		Andrews, John	1854	93		35 ME	
Alexander,Charles M.	1862	23		16 ME		Antonia, Francis	1854	80	m	25 NY	
Alexander, Francis	1854	62	b	45		Apease, William B.	1848	200	b	25 CT	
Alexander,FrederickW	1862	48		15 ME		Arnold, Edwin G.	1849	431		21 ME	
Alexander, George L.	1867	6		14 ME		Arnold, Julias C.	1853	168		19 CT	
Alexander,Leonard B.	1856	167		19 ME		Arras, Thomas P.	1845	1		26 ME	
Alexander, Martin	1836	115		19 ME		Atkins, James	1845	19		24 ME	
Alexander, Oscar M.	1864	28		18 ME		Atkins, Lemuel	1859	91		20 ME	
Alexander, Samuel B.	1849	337		25 ME		Atwood, Elmon P.	1848	41		20 ME	
Alexander, Thomas L.	1849	338		19 ME		Atwood, George B.	1845	1		20 ME	
Alexander, Wm. H.	1859	34		17 ME		Aune, George W.	1856	156		18 ME	
Alfford, Amasa A>	1855	108		21 MA		Austin, Charles F.	1860	14		21 ME	
Allard, Joseph	1860	28		18 ME		Austin, James	1855	24	b	33 NJ	
Allen, Albert	1836	110		23 ME		Austin, Jessie B.	1855	71		19 ME	
Allen, Alden B.	1849	139		26 ME		Austin, Oliver O.	1836	100		21 ME	
Allen, Augustus N.	1847	50		18 MA		Austin, Prince Lucien	1856	120		15 ME	
Allen, Edmund	1848	32		46 ME		Avenill, Frank	1855	159		21 ME	
Allen, Francis	1839	25		21 ME		Averill, Thomas	1848	208		21 ME	
Allen, Henry	1842	82		20 MA		Avery, John M.	1847	141		15 ME	
Allen, James	1848	218		24 ME		Avery, John W.	1849	373		41 ME	
Allen, James	1856	178		25 ME		Avery, Joshua L.	1855	89		23 ME	
Allen, John	1854	196		34 NY		Avey, Richard R.	1854	145		27 ME	
Allen, John	1849	409		24 PA		Ayer, Gilbert H.	1854	6		19 ME	
Allen, Joseph W.	1842	46		18 PA		Ayre, George S.	1847	23		17 ME	
Allen, Peter	1854	195		33 NC		Babb, Robert	1849	27		51 ME	
Allen, Thomas I.	1850	59		18 ME		Babcock, John C.	1848	99		25 ME	
Allen, Thomas S.	1858	26		49 MA		Bachelder, Silas T.?	1854	57		21 ME	
Allen, Warren L.	1849	270		21 ME		Bailey, Christopher F.	1839	157	b	40 MA	
Allen, William	1848	140		24 ME		Bailey, Franklin	1845	11		30 MA	
Allen, William	1848	26		46 ME		Bailey, Jesse	1845	112		22 ME	
Allen, William G.	1847	44		28	Germany	Bailey, Lyman	1848	3		21 NY	
Allen, William H.	1845	163		16 ME		Bailey, Paul C.	1849	138		27 ME	

Baily, George W.	1845	129	19 ME
Baker, Charles W.	1849	225	23 ME
Baker, Edward J.	1857	114	25 ME
Baker, James	1854	244	23 NY
Baker, John V.	1864	70	22 RI
Baker, Marcus A.	1859	60	37 ME
Baker, Samuel	1859	11	39 ME
Baker, Thomas	1863	33	23 ME
Baker, Thomas E.	1853	211	17 MA
Baker, William A.	1842	74	23 ME
Balden, Joseph	1854	79	28 MA
Baldwin, William	1850	48	18 MA
Ballard, Ephraim L.	1849	429	18 ME
Ballon, William H.	1856	53	16 MA
Baristo, George	1857	27	38 ME
Bark, Saren	1836	105	16 ME
Barker, Charles W.	1857	163	20 MA
Barker, Edw. H.	1854	271	17 ME
Barker, George M.	1853	122	18 ME
Barker, Henry F.	1859	15	20 ME
Barker, Joseph	1848	229	24 MA
Barker, Samuel	1848	60	30 ME
Barnard, Joseph	1847	81	31 MA
Barney, Thomas	1842	65 b	24 MA
Barney, William	1855	149	21 NY
Barnstorf, Henry	1853	153	24 NY
Barr, Duncan	1856	4	28 PA
Barr, George	1847	49	17 VA
Barr, William H.	1845	78	23 NC
Barratt, William	1850	14	17 ME
Barron, Charles	1839	101	18 ME
Barstow, David	1836	129	21 ME
Barstow, Nathl.	1849	267	24 ME
Barstow, Peleg N.	1849	269	22 ME
Barstow, Samuel F.	1863	42	19 ME
Barstow, William	1863	47	21 ME
Barstow, William H.	1842	4	18 ME
Barter, Andrew	1848	119	22 ME
Barter, Andrew	1854	274	27 ME
Barter, Marstin	1862	52	21 ME
Barter, Martin	1848	190	21 ME
Barter, Stephen M.	1856	71	26 ME
Bartlett, Andrew	1854	175	23 ME
Bartlett, David G.	1849	183	17 ME
Bartlett, Erastus	1848	223 I	45 MA
Bartlett, George W.	1849	268	22 ME
Bartlett, John C.	1849	274	33 ME
Bartlett, Richard H.	1849	164	23 ME
Basford, William	1836	76	19 ME
Bassett, Ruel H.	1836	95	21 ME
Baster, Stephen G.	1864	60	19 ME
Batchelder, Elijah	1845	108	16 ME
Batchelder, Emerson C.	1863	39	18 ME
Batchelder, Samuel E.	1860	45	44 ME
Bateman, Nathan	1853	81	30 VA
Bates, A. Judson	1849	120	22 ME
Bates, Orrin	1849	151	20 ME
Baxter, Charles G.	1849	212	21 ME
Baxter, Jordan	1853	84	20 ME
Bayant, Joseph W.	1849	16	21 ME
Bayly, Robert	1853	154	24 ME
Beal, Albion	1839	107	16 ME
Beal, Bradford P.	1850	37	20 ME
Beal, Isaac	1847	155	21 ME
Beale, Edward K.	1853	99	15 ME
Beale, Jeremiah	1847	182	31 ME
Beals, George	1853	139	18 ME
Beals, James	1850	3	47 ME
Beals, John R.	1849	87	28 ME
Bean, William	1855	182	20 NH
Bearce, Horace W.	1860	59	16 ME
Beaton, John	1836	132	22 MD
Beck, Joseph L.	1836	121	22 ME
Bedford, Henry	1848	146	25 ME
Beedle, Van R.	1855	175	15 ME
Beedler, Leroy W.	1865	41	19 ME
Bell, Jeremiah	1849	287 b	28 DC
Bells, George	1848	230	24 MA
Bengon, Henry S.	1856	78	16 MA
Bennett, Henry	1854	273	23 MA
Bennett, John	1847	58	41 ME
Bennett, Sidney A.	1868	17	22 ME
Bennett, Silas L.	1849	24	25 ME
Benson, Amasa	1842	101	20 ME
Berns, Samuel	1850	117	27 NY
Berries, Alexander	1845	50	27 NY
Berry, Alfred L.	1842	167	23 ME
Berry, Arthur	1850	120	19 ME
Berry, Henry R.	1843	63	22 ME
Berry, Horatio	1848	8	19 ME
Berry, John	1848	42	18 MA
Berry, Sabin J.	1850	153	22 ME
Berry, Samuel	1849	149	41 ME
Berry, Samuel H.	1845	45	24 NJ
Berry, Thomas B.	1856	106	18 ME
Berry, Wililiam C.	1847	191	18 ME
Betson, James L.	1848	127	26 ME
Bibber, Randall D.	1864	33	19 ??
Bibber, Randall D.	1861	57	16 ME
Bible, John	1861	42	32 ME
Bickford, Chauncy A.	1859	77	37 ME
Bickford, George W.	1847	140	18 ME
Bickford, Isaac	1853	115	24 ME
Bickford, Jonathan L.	1836	64	17 ME
Bickford, Joseph W.	1858	3	24 ME
Bickmore, Samuel	1857	145	21 ME
Bickmore, William H.	1857	147	19 ME
Bigelow, Charles E.	1855	202	20 ME
Billington, Daniel C.	1849	29	39 ME
Bird, Franklin	1859	88	29 ME
Bird, John	1848	75	22 MA
Bisbee, Henry	1847	70	18 ME

Name	Year	No.	Age	Place
Bishop, Frederic	1865	51	31 ME	
Bishop, P...	1839	170	19 CT	
Bl;air, Daniel	1839	141	24 ME	
Black, Alexander	1858	42	19 ME	
Black, Daniel	1855	27	28 ME	
Blackington, Henry	1854	221	16 MA	
Blackledge, Freeman	1855	29	30 ME	
Blackman, Eliphilalet	1853	30	27 ME	
Blackman, William O.	1865	12	20 ME	
Blagden, James	1864	74	15 ME	
Blagden, James W.	1848	212	25 ME	
Blagdon, James W.	1842	128	20 ME	
Blair, David	1849	396	19 ME	
Blair, Ephraim	1839	130	20 ME	
Blair, Leander	1849	301	24 ME	
Blair, Samuel	1849	69	25 ME	
Blair, Warren	1860	19	17 ME	
Blair, William	1857	154	28 ME	
Blair, Wm. H.	1847	130	18 ME	
Blake, John S.	1849	407	25 NY	
Blake, Thomas	1846	167	20 ME	
Blanchard, Albert P.	1859	33	30 ME	
Blanchard, George	1849	74	18 ME	
Blanchard, Henry C.	1863	35	18 ME	
Blanchard, James A.	1849	339	28 ME	
Blanchard, James B.	1849	210	42 ME	
Blanchard, James M.	1863	24	17 ME	
Blanchard, Levi M.	1836	86	18 ME	
Blanchard, Lewis	1856	148	20 NY	
Blanchard, Marcellus	1848	238	18 ME	
Blanchard, Raymond	1854	167	21 ME	
Blanchard, Samuel L.	1848	245	24 ME	
Blanchard,Samuel M.	1848	17	18 ME	
Blanchard, William	1839	33	17 ME	
Blanchard, William	1857	94	33 ME	
Blasdell, Samuel	1849	312	18 ME	
Blasedell, Robert	1848	14	14 ME	
Blasland, FrederickR.	1855	30	19 ME	
Blasland, Hiram A.	1857	118	20 ME	
Blen,Edmund F. or T.	1849	57	30 ME	
Blin, Marshall	1849	329	22 ME	
Blin, Samuel P.	1849	333	24 ME	
Blins, Benjamin	1839	106	18 ME	
Bliss, Edmund W.	1854	270	46 MA	
Blockford, Henry	1854	11	19 MA	
Blodgett, Edwin R.	1857	104	18 ME	
Blodgett, Henry	1855	205	18 ME	
Blodgett, John	1848	172	21 VT	
Blunt, Benjamin	1849	35	19 ME	
Bodfish, Albert G.	1849	139	33 ME	
Bolton, James	1849	258	28 NY	
Bond, John	1848	189 b	22 MD	
Bond, John	1853	132	22 LA	
Bond, William	1853	21	23 MD	
Boodly, Robert	1847	110 b	23 NJ	
Booker, Algernon L.	1842	129	17 ME	
Booker, Arvin	1853	56	17 ME	
Booker, James B.	1849	277	29 ME	
Boon, Andrew	1850	10 b	20 DC	
Borchers, Thomas	1848	237	24	Denmark
Borchers, William	1849	345	21 ME	
Borten, James D.	1855	161	24 OH	
Bosworth, Charles E.	1849	176	20 ME	
Bosworth, John H.	1860	16	16 ME	
Bosworth, Robert	1858	74	16 ME	
Boulin, Thomas	1848	51	24 NY	
Bourke, William	1848	244	38 ME	
Bourne, Alexander	1849	18 b	23 MA	
Bourne, William L.	1848	159	30 MA	
Bovey, William L.	1855	45	18 ME	
Bow, Egbert	1849	249	42 MA	
Bowen, John	1858	54	31 RI	
Bowers, Benjamin E.	1855	39 m	20 ME	
Bowker, Henry M.	1849	236	28 ME	
Bowker, Isaac N.	1861	15	18 ME	
Bowker, John M.	1849	237	34 ME	
Bowker, Lettsome	1836	26	16 MA	
Boyd, Jackson	1857	160	28 ME	
Boyd, Loring N.	1842	110	22 MA	
Boyle, William G.	1855	207	23 LA	
Boyntin, Walter	1854	127	14 ME	
Boynton, Isaac C.	1850	33	25 ME	
Boynton, James C.	1853	77	21 ME	
Boynton, Joseph	1854	185	17 ME	
Bradbury, Henry	1836	70	16 NY	
Bradley, George A.	1864	7	16 ME	
Brady, James	1864	12	24 NY	
Brady, John	1848	159	31 PA	
Bragdon, Lyman	1855	109	15 ME	
Bragdon, Samuel N.	1839	118	21 ME	
Brainard, John C.	1849	37	23 ME	
Bran, John E.	1854	156	19 ME	
Brandes, Richard	1847	51	27 ME	
Branson, Samuel	1849	380 b	29 NJ	
Brew, Robert C.	1854	200	41 NY	
Brick, George H.	1855	98	16 ME	
Briggs, Albion D.	1859	78	18 ME	
Briggs, Ephraim B.	1845	2	22 MA	
Briggs, George D.	1836	6	14 ME	
Briggs, Gilman	1853	54	23 ME	
Briggs, Peter	1842	1	19 ME	
Brighton, Charles	1849	290	26 MA	
Brimigion, William	1836	106	29 ME	
Brislin, Dennis	1853	217	21 NY	
Britt, Jacob	1836	122	27 ME	
Brooks, George W.	1847	179	23 ME	
Brooks, John	1854	218	20 RI	
Brooks, William	1836	37	22 ME	
Broomfield, Berry	1849	71 b	58 NY	
Brown, Abner	1839	53	31 PA	
Brown, Albert	1854	243	18 ME	
Brown, Ambrose W.	1849	216	18 ME	

Brown, Augustus D.	1849	140		29 ME	Burke, Thomas	1858	6	31 NY
Brown, Charles	1848	77		23 PA	Burleigh, Henry O.	1849	128	23 NH
Brown, Charles	1848	199		25 MA	Burleigh, Walter A.	1849	129	29 ME
Brown, Charles	1853	206		21 ME	Burnes, James	1858	55	20 NY
Brown, Charles	1856	30		32 ME	Burnham, Allen M.	1857	29	28 ME
Brown, Charles B.	1850	132		29 ME	Burnham, Edward L.	1868	18	22 ME
Brown, Charles L.	1839	152		19 ME	Burnham, James	1848	11	15 ME
Brown, Charles R.	1855	179		26 NY	Burnham, James O.	1860	10	27 ME
Brown, Charles W.	1847	156		22 ME	Burns, Charles	1857	40	21 MA
Brown, Daniel	1847	76		21 ME	Burns, John W.	1856	97	38 ME
Brown, Edwin F.	1858	71		21 ME	Burns, William	1848	246	20 ME
Brown, Eli	1855	177	b	38 MD	Burns, William	1850	114	22 NY
Brown, Elijah	1864	25	b	29 MA	Burnside, Robert	1856	183	25 ME
Brown, Frank H.	1855	116		15 MA	Burr, David	1842	72	25 NJ
Brown, George	1861	80		22 ME	Burrows,FrancisAdams	1853	4	21 NY
Brown, George W.	1859	75		24 ME	Burt, A. H.	1857	79	23 ME
Brown, Hartley	1854	272		17 ME	Burt, David	1845	89	27 NY
Brown, Henry	1856	128		28 NY	Bush, Samuel, Jr.	1850	65	21 ME
Brown, James	1848	70		23 NY	Bushe, Simon	1854	7	36 ME
Brown, Joel P.	1836	90		16 ME	Butler, Charles H.	1858	8	17 ME
Brown, John	1849	290		23 ME	Butler, Flavel	1855	49	28 ME
Brown, John	1849	35	b	23 MA	Butler, Henry M.	1847	100	0 ME
Brown, John	1848	182		32 RI	Butler, James	1849	353	21 ME
Brown, John	1847	59		27 ME	Butler, John	1848	180	21 MA
Brown, Joseph F.	1856	44		21 ME	Butler, Parker P.	1842	44	18 ME
Brown, Melville	1849	185		19 ME	Butler, Rufus G.	1856	158	23 ME
Brown, Oliver, Jr.	1848	120		18 ME	Butler, Shepherd N.	1841	119	32 ME
Brown, Samuel	1849	307		15 ME	Butler, Spencer D.	1858	7	20 ME
Brown, Silas M.	1863	45		22 ME	Butler, Spencer G.	1856	56	18 ME
Brown, Stillman	1845	48		25 ME	Butler, Sumner P.	1839	132	17 ME
Brown, William	1856	29		25 ME	Butman, Wilfred S.	1860	20	14 ME
Brown, William	1853	32		17 ME	Butt, Benjamin	1853	12	24 PA
Brown, William F.	1861	48		32 RI	Butt, Henry	1853	13	21 PA
Brown, William F.	1850	43		18 MA	Butterfield, Andrew	1853	74	23 ME
Brown, William L.	1836	12		21 ME	Butterfield, Eligah D.	1847	42	20 NY
Bruce, Alfred L.	1867	12		18 ME	Cahill, Michael	1862	35	15 MA
Bruce, Charles W.	1857	115		17 ME	Cain, John	1868	20	21 PA
Bruns, James	1856	82		19 ME	Cain, Stillman	1842	25	21 ME
Bryant, Daniel P.	1855	129		19 ME	Call, Bordin A.	1864	65	18 ME
Bryant, George	1853	148		26 ME	Call, David	1844	130	19 ME
Bryant, Orlando	1849	31		47 MA	Call, Edward	1847	54	20 ME
Buck, Morris	1848	109		30 PA	Call, Elnathan	1842	75	21 ME
Bucknam, Henry	1853	71		22 ME	Call, George	1849	299	18 ME
Budd, Charles H.	1836	16	b	24 NY	Call, George	1847	82	16 ME
Buie, John	1854	170		23 WI	Call, James, Jr.	1842	76	19 ME
Bumhaw, Joseph	1856	23		23 ME	Call, Jarvis L.	1860	22	22 ME
Bunker, George	1849	117		20 NY	Call, Leander W.	1859	36	15 ME
Bunker, James T.	1848	81		19 ME	Call, William G.	1848	27	19 ME
Bureau, Albert	1864	39		22 MA	Callear, Archibald	1864	69	26 NY
Burgess, Joseph	1854	250		20 ME	Callender, John	1842	170	22 MD
Burgess, William	1848	97		28 MA	Camble, Samuel	1848	87	29 MD
Burgess, William	1850	37		27 ME	Cameron, William	1836	117	17 ME
Burk, Mark L. H.	1849	92		27 ME	Campbell, A.	1861	63	36 NY
Burk, Michael	1855	107		29 MA	Campbell, Arthur	1848	226	23 MA
Burk, Richard	1853	14		27 MA	Campbell, David	1853	92	39 CT
Burke, Joseph W.	1848	43		17 ME	Campbell, Dergald	1849	112	21 GA

Name	Year	No.	Age/State
Campbell, John	1849	358	28 ME
Campbell, John	1836	58	25 ME
Campbell, John	1859	55	18 ME
Campbell, John W.	1857	83	32 NY
Campbell, Robert E.	1857	36	16 ME
Campbell, Stephen	1855	4	22 ME
Campbell, Warren	1853	205	21 ME
Canby, George	1845	94	22 MD
Cand, Columbus	1842	166	22 ME
Cannon, Caesar	1855	196 b	24 DE
Cappers, Daniel H.	1853	166	22 ME
Card, James	1848	142	24 ME
Card, John C.	1849	415	21 ME
Card, John W. L.	1842	12	20 ME
Card, Simeon	1853	173	18 ME
Cardwell, William P.	1853	128	21 ME
Carew, Francis	1855	229	25 NY
Carey, Frank	1857	52	27 NY
Carle, Howard	1857	38	20 ME
Carleton, Ephraim R.	1858	73	21 ME
Carlisle, John D.	1847	12	26 ME
Carlton, George	1839	92	18 ME
Carlton, Lemuel J.	1857	112	19 ME
Carney,EdwardW. W.	1853	16	21 ME
Carney, James	1850	98	26 NY
Carney,JohnD. Oscar	1847	142	17 ME
Carr, Henry	1847	109	22 MA
Carr, James	1858	57	21 NY
Carr, Robert	1849	23	23 NY
Carr, Winchester	1836	72	16 ME
Carroll, Charles J.	1856	162	20 ME
Carroll, Charles T.	1854	209 m	52 LA
Carroll, Dennis	1849	316	25 MA
Carroll, Thomas	1847	87	43 LA
Carter, Charles J.	1864	17	19 ME
Carter, Charles J.	1867	15	22 ME
Carter, David S.	1863	36	20 ME
Carter, Frederick	1864	53	18 ME
Carter, John	1847	20	41 ME
Carter, John	1839	151	17 NH
Carter, Josiah	1850	4	39 ME
Carter, Lewis D.	1867	14	23 ME
Cartook, George F.	1864	23	28 MA
Carvile, John	1842	147	17 ME
Cary, Michael	1848	236	22 ME
Cash, John	1853	95	28 ME
Cass, Timothy	1857	7	21 ME
Castner, George W.	1854	126	24 ME
Cate, Daniel	1854	268	37 ME
Cate, James S.	1857	140	44 ME
Caulfield, Thomas	1854	28	20 ME
Cavan, William T.	1847	193	22 NY
Cawbell, George C.	1858	27	30 LA
Center, Samuel	1836	114	27 ME
Center, William	1849	232	46 MA
Center, William Alfred	1849	234	17 ME
Chadbourn, Charles	1845	57	15 ME
Chadbourne,WilliamS.	1864	1	36 ME
Chadburn, Josiah	1842	108	22 ME
Chamberlain,CharlesH	1849	44	29 ME
Chambers, Archibald	1850	16	21 ME
Chambers, Jeremiah	1848	93	21 NJ
Chancy, Alden B.	1836	3	20 ME
Chancy, Cyrus	1847	105	23 ME
Chandler, Jesse	1849	173	27 ME
Chapman, John	1850	85	25 NY
Chapman, John	1845	37	21 NY
Chase, Alfred	1849	136	18 ME
Chase, Amos L.	1839	169	29 ME
Chase, Artemus C.	1849	393	25 ME
Chase, Charles H.	1849	215	19 ME
Chase, David	1857	3	22 ME
Chase, Edward	1855	236	21 ME
Chase, George	1859	26	29 MA
Chase, George F.	1865	19	17 ME
Chase, John	1855	145	51 ME
Chase, John G.	1855	12	51 MA
Chase, Stephen P.	1854	176	24 ME
Chickering, Alpheus	1857	124	32 NH
Child, William	1847	165	20 ME
Church, Daniel	1856	107	38 PA
Church, John C.	1856	87	23 ME
Clancey, John H.	1867	5	15 ME
Clancy, Edward	1855	18	24 ME
Clancy, James T.	1862	36	20 ME
Clane, Peter	1842	66 b	35 NY
Clapp, Bartlet	1845	124 b	14 NY
Clark, Andrew	1845	136	24 NY
Clark, Charles H.	1854	65	19 ME
Clark, Cyrus M.	1864	64	20 ME
Clark, David	1848	103 b	19 NJ
Clark, Emerson	1849	246	39 MA
Clark, Frederic A.	1863	26	24 ME
Clark, George A.	1855	126	21 SC
Clark, George D.	1856	3	20 ME
Clark, Henry C.	1849	248	26 RI
Clark, James	1849	224	24 ME
Clark, John	1845	98	25 NY
Clark, John	1855	117	42 MA
Clark, Joseph	1848	100	19 ME
Clark, Joseph	1848	206	26 ME
Clark, Melville C.	1855	156	18 ME
Clark, Rufus	1856	147	28 ME
Clary, Frederick	1849	150	20 NY
Clary, William	1848	24	24 NY
Clayton, Lewis	1850	156	21 MA
Cleason, Franklin	1853	221	18
Cleaveland, George	1847	98	21 ME
Cleaves, Robert	1854	259	26 ME
Clements, James	1853	175	23 MA
Cleveland, Benjamin	1862	60	15 NY
Cliff, Thomas	1854	132	25 ME

Clifford, Charles	1839	126		17 ME	Cornish, George	1839	55	33 MD
Clike, James	1855	138	b	21 MD	Costello, John H.	1857	92	18	Ireland
Closson, James P.	1839	112		19 ME	Costellow, David E.	1845	75	22 ME
Closson, Reuben	1854	8		20 ME	Costigan, John	1864	73	22	Ireland
Cobb, Rufus S.	1860	27		40 ME	Cota, Alexander	1842	92	18 ME
Cobb, Samuel G.	1845	28 .		21 ME	Cotter, Charles H.	1863	14	20 ME
Coburn, Albion	1856	14		20 ME	Cottle, Jackson	1853	140	17 ME
Coburn, Justus	1845	135		30 ME	Cottle, Winthrop	1848	63	18 ME
Colborn, George	1848	5		21 ME	Couillard, Charles W.	1855	135	16 ME
Colburn, Charles	1854	71		30 PA	Courson, Charles H.	1853	97	19 ME
Colburn, Joseph F.	1848	150		25 ME	Cousins, Henry	1867	1	20 NY
Colby, Joseph W.	1855	82		20 ME	Cox, Charles W.	1855	22	21 ME
Colby, Josiah	1854	10		19 ME	Cox, George H.	1858	61	17 ME
Colby, Samuel	1845	79		18 ME	Cox, James H.	1839	37	b	21 CT
Colby, William W.	1853	170		22 ME	Coyle, John	1845	46	24 PA
Cole, Edwin A.	1855	242		30 ME	Crahan, William	1856	26	18 ME
Cole, Isaac	1845	123 I		32 RI	Craig, James, Jr.	1847	176	20 ME
Coleman, George	1847	169		34 MA	Crandall, Wm. H.	1858	98	25 RI
Coleman, John	1850	74		27 NY	Cranus, William	1847	78	21 PA
Coleman, Philip B., Jr.	1855	50		19 ME	Crawford, John S.	1858	67	16 ME
Coll, Ezekiel	1849	50		18 ME	Crawford, Lorenzo M.	1860	34	20 ME
Collins, Abijah	1839	103		56 MA	Crawford, William	1855	208	21 ME
Collins, Dennis	1856	100		18 MA	Cresey, David E.	1860	3	16 ME
Collins, George B.	1858	53		18 MA	Cresey, William J.	1848	115	19 ME
Collins, Nicholas	1847	45		27 NY	Crips, Moses	1853	66	36 ME
Collins, Thomas	1848	217		22 ME	Crocker, Benjamin H.	1854	129	18 ME
Colson, David	1854	165		15 ME	Crocker, Jefferson	1848	98	46 ME
Colson, Eben, Jr.	1862	16		19 ME	Crocker, William B.	1854	49	48 ME
Colson, Joseph C.	1845	122		16 ME	Crocker, Wm. L.	1847	129	16 ME
Conant, Charles H.	1861	32		19 ME	Crockett, Horace	1856	39	25 ME
Conant, Frederic L.	1854	163		18 MA	Crockett, Richard	1850	99	23 ME
Conant, J. T.	1859	17		20 ME	Cromwell, Alden	1854	237	17 ME
Conant, Sumner	1859	16		18 ME	Cromwell, Simon, Jr.	1855	228	34 ME
Conden, Edmund	1847	75		22 MA	Cromwell, William	1842	132	21 ME
Conley, Elisha	1863	46		31 ME	Crooker, Charles S.	1860	64	18 ME
Conley, Martin	1857	88		22 ME	Crooker, Isaac, Jr.	1849	327	23 ME
Connell, Charles	1850	97		26 NY	Crooker, James L.	1854	238	17 ME
Connor, Charles John	1849	298		23 NY	Crooker, John F.	1858	65	16 MA
Considine, Daniel	1850	124		23 ME	Crosby, Charles C.	1862	42	18 ME
Cook, Benjamin	1836	111		25 MA	Crosby, John, Jr.	1849	133	21 ME
Cook, George H., Jr.	1850	64		21 ME	Crosby, Nelson	1859	72	26 ME
Cook, Samuel	1839	129		23 ME	Crosby, Theofles	1855	166	28 ME
Cook, William	1854	84		26 MA	Crowell, Edmund A.	1854	122	26 ME
Coombs, Albert	1855	19		26 ME	Crowell, Joseph	1839	113	19 ME
Coombs, Albion M.	1848	228		17 ME	Crowell, William	1850	54	18 ??
Coombs, Asher G.	1865	6		19 ME	Crowell, William	1848	216	27 NY
Coombs, Edwin	1848	161		18 ME	Crowley, John	1859	45	18 ME
Coombs, Elisha	1839	26		19 ME	Crozier, George	1848	104	b	26 DE
Coombs, George A.	1863	10		16 ME	Cruse, Christian F.	1845	159	31	Denmark
Coombs, Samuel	1861	2		34 ME	Crwker?, Zacheus	1839	146	21 ME
Cooney, John	1850	63		22 ME	Cudworth, Andrew	1856	13	20 ME
Cooper, Calvin	1848	114		24 MA	Cumming, Hugh	1847	128	18 FL
Cooper, Thomas	1842	150		18 ME	Cummings, Charles	1854	217	22 ME
Copeland, Wm. M.	1849	386		25 ME	Cummings, George	1849	127	25 ME
Corbin, Jerome	1856	160		28 ME	Cummings, James H.	1864	68	18 NY
Cornish, Elijah	1857	54		17 ME	Cunningham, Hutchings	1856	146	23 ME

Name	Year	No.	Age
Cunningham, Warren	1854	229	20 ME
Curlsile, Franklin	1856	1	21 ME
Currier, Albert P.	1861	1	27 ME
Currier, Albinia	1856	21	16 ME
Currier, Phineas	1865	55	25 ME
Curry, Jacob	1845	86	25 DC
Curry, William	1850	39	24 ME
Curtes, Charles	1847	30	42 ME
Curtis, Andrew	1854	206	22 NY
Curtis, Charles	1845	61	22 ME
Curtis, Daniel S.	1839	129	19 ME
Curtis, David	1855	112	50 CT
Curtis, Elijah L.	1849	132	30 MA
Curtis, George	1856	165	21 ME
Curtis, George H.	1861	76	19 ME
Curtis, Henry S.	1854	144	17 ME
Curtis, Hezekiah A.	1863	29	22 ME
Curtis, John B.	1850	112	28 ME
Curtis, John W.	1845	72	21 ME
Curtis, Lorenzo	1847	177	20 ME
Curtis, Martin M.	1855	16	21 ME
Curtis, Parker C.	1861	25	16 ME
Curtis, Thomas K.	1839	124	19 ME
Curtis, William H. H.	1864	21	23 ME
Curtis, William K.	1849	305	17 ME
Curtis, Wm. H. H.	1856	72	15 ME
Cury/Carney, Howard	1845	160	23 ME
Curzon, Edward H.	1855	78	17 ME
Cushing, James L.	1857	45	17 ME
Cushing, Royal J.	1859	86	23 ME
Cushing, Thomas, Jr.	1836	82	18 ME
Cushing, William L.	1848	47	15 ME
Cushman, Wales H.	1859	4	23 ME
Cushman,WilliamA.L.	1848	169	15 ME
Cutter, Dwight	1856	58	20 ME
Dacket, Rodolph	1853	89	23 NY
Dalton, William A.R.	1855	171	19 ME
Daly, Zebedee L.	1854	103	40 ME
Damah, Daniel B.	1856	63	18 ME
Dane, Solomon S.	1839	89	19 ME
Danow, Gilbert R.	1842	50	28 CT
Darling, Samuel R.	1855	180 b	22 ME
Darrah, John	1849	251	24 ME
Dashington, Roger C.	1849	410	26 PA
Date, William R.	1856	131	20 NY
Davenport, James L.	1854	58	23 ME
Davidson, George	1842	78	25 PA
Davis, Augustus P.	1849	90	14 ME
Davis, Byron	1849	144	17 ME
Davis, Charles H.	1849	434	24 ME
Davis, Daniel	1856	70	14 ME
Davis, Francis	1849	145	20 ME
Davis, George	1849	296	24 NY
Davis, Hiram B. S.	1854	72	20 ME
Davis, James L.	1836	120	23 ME
Davis, Joel E.	1854	90	17 ME
Davis, Joel E.	1855	198	18 ME
Davis, John	1849	64	21 MA
Davis, John	1848	101	20 MA
Davis, John	1847	113	18 ME
Davis, John, 2nd	1849	135	32 ME
Davis, Lewis	1854	60 m	40 ME
Davis, Nicholas H.	1857	153	17 ME
Davis, Raymond	1849	143	13 ME
Davis, Sam W.	1836	119	18 ME
Davis, Samuel A.	1849	433	20 ME
Davis, Scott C.	1861	35	21 ME
Davis, Shepard	1850	5	43 ME
Davis, Simon	1862	31	19 ME
Davis, Thomas B.	1845	84	20 ME
Davis, Thomas E.	1849	43	17 NY
Davis, William B.	1842	35	27 ME
Davis, William H.	1859	103	27 ME
Day, Alexander J.	1847	187	18 ME
Day, Campbell W.	1854	262	22 ME
Day, Daniel	1856	102 b	32 NJ
Day, Eben	1847	7	30 ME
Day, George H.	1849	285	16 ME
Day, Nathl.	1849	327	17 ME
Day, Samuel	1856	184	20 ME
Day, Stephen	1845	144	19 ME
Day, Thomas	1839	115	21 ME
Day, William A.	1849	73	19 ME
Day, William T.	1861	75	20 ME
Dean, George	1850	66	17 ME
Dean, Henry A.	1856	10	20 ME
Dearborn, David	1854	15	22 ME
Dearborn, Henry	1853	193	17
Dearborn, Rufus	1853	194	19
Dearborn, Rufus G.	1856	153	22 ME
DeBois, Robert E.	1836	46 b	17 NY
Decker, Christopher	1849	286	35 ME
Decost, Benjamin	1856	20	18 ME
DeCost, Benjamin	1855	24	17 ME
Decrow, William B.	1858	96	21 ME
Deering, Gardinor	1857	18	22 ME
Deighan, Peter	1849	56	21 ME
Delano, Aaron E.	1848	136	21 ME
Delano, Calvin	1842	40	26 ME
Delano, George H.	1858	79	21 ME
Delano, George S.	1839	146	20 ME
Delano, Henry A.	1854	105	16 ME
Delany, Peter	1848	191	23 MA
Dellow, John	1849	14	18 ME
Deloyne, Jacob	1847	16 b	37 NY
DeMott, Job	1839	142	17 ME
Denham, Robert C.	1853	78	16 ME
Denham, Thomas	1864	36	21 ME
Denham, Wm. R.	1859	38	20 ME
Dennett, Alfred W.	1857	64	17 ME
Dennison, James	1849	15	35 NY
Densmore, Florence	1862	37	18 ME

Name	Year	No.	Age/State
Desprez, Fitz Wm.	1845	62	21 PA
Devereau, Nicholas	1849	6	22 MA
Devereux, John	1850	148	51 ME
Deymore, Henry	1855	5	21
Dickerson, George	1857	129	24 ME
Dickinson, Hallowell	1854	278	17 ME
Dickinson, James	1847	116	28 CT
Dickinson, Wiley	1865	59	19 ME
Dickson, James D.	1865	13	28 NY
Dill, James C.	1857	116	16 ME
Dillon, James E.	1864	79	17 ME
Dinsmore, John O.	1849	374	33 ME
Dinsmore, Samuel B.	1839	90	17 ME
Dixon, Samuel	1850	89	31 VA
Doane, Charles	1839	57	16 MA
Dodge, Asa	1850	5	37 ME
Dodge, Daniel J.	1849	168	25 ME
Dodge, Isaac M.	1847	10	26 NH
Dodge, James H.	1845	31	21 ME
Dodge, Joseph L.	1839	150	19 ME
Dodge, Stephen A.	1857	138	21 ME
Dolan, James	1854	40	26 ME
Dole, Jefferson M.	1836	101	16 ME
Dolliff, John	1849	265	44 ME
Dolliver, William	1856	165	27 ME
Donnell, Henry C.	1862	22	16 ME
Donnell, Nathaniel J.	1861	64	22 ME
Donovan, Cornelius	1848	151	22 ME
Donylap, Chan	1847	89	23 NY
Doran, John	1845	87	18 MA
Dort, John	1855	92	25 ME
Doughty, Charles A.	1858	21	23 ME
Doughty, David	1849	323	17 ME
Doughty, George L.	1839	133	27 ME
Doughty, Issacha	1849	324	19 ME
Doughty, James	1841	222	22 ME
Doughty, James	1847	40	18 ME
Doughty, John	1836	67	20 ME
Doughty, Stephen, Jr.	1849	322	21 ME
Doughty, William H.	1857	24	14 ME
Douglas, Gilman L.	1848	107	19 ME
Douglass, Asa A.	1850	78	16 ME
Douglass, Asa A.	1856	28	21 ME
Douglass, Isaac M.	1857	63	13 ME
Douglass, John	1836	113	22 ME
Douglass, Roderick A.	1862	56	20 ME
Douglass, Thomas	1849	231	19
Dow, Charles H.	1849	61	20 MA
Dow, George R.	1865	56	19 ME
Dow, James, Jr.	1845	58	32 ME
Dow, Peter C.	1856	36	18 ME
Dow, Thomas H.	1849	423	20 ME
Dowling, Samuel B.	1849	214	32 ME
Downay, Joseph	1854	126	22 NY
Downey, William	1849	82	0 ME
Doyen, Eben C.	1854	123	20 ME
Doyle, Henry G.	1865	39	14 MA
Drake, Theodore H.	1839	93	22 CT
Dresser, Tobias P.	1847	79	16 ME
Drew, Clark	1842	112	29 ME
Drew, George E.	1849	244	26 ME
Drew, George W.	1854	63	25 MA
Drew, John H.	1850	126	16 ME
Drew, Sydney L.	1863	13	19 ME
Drew, Thomas	1850	50	22 NY
Driscoll, John	1842	30	21 NY
Driskil, Daniel	1849	97	20 MA
Drummon, George L.	1848	158	22 ME
Drummond, Alfred L.	1849	348	19 ME
Drummond, Ezekiel B.	1839	160	18 ME
Drummond, William	1850	94	22 NY
Drummond, William H.C	1849	89	17 MD
Dryden, Charles	1856	19	21 LA
Dryhurst, William	1842	19	21 PA
Ducett, Charles M.	1859	80	16 ME
Ducett, Francis H.	1853	134	16 ME
Dudley, Lewis H.	1854	128	18 ME
Duffey, John	1854	187 b	35 MD
Duggan, Christopher	1853	223	20 ME
Dumak, James	1856	91	28 MA
Duncan, Fred C.	1863	31	17 ME
Duncin, Frederick C.	1847	48	27 NH
Dungan, James O.	1853	82	18 ME
Dunham, Andrew E.	1842	121	16 ME
Dunham, Charles R.	1860	7	19 ME
Dunham, William	1856	117	17 ME
Dunlevey, James	1850	123	19 ME
Dunlevy, John	1856	62	29 ME
Dunning, Elijah	1842	119	22 ME
Dunning, George A.	1862	7	18 ME
Dunning, Robert	1857	49	15 ME
Dunning, Robert	1842	143	25 ME
Dunsmoor, John	1849	172	32 ME
Dunston, James F.	1848	203	24 ME
Dunton, Abner T.	1855	124	17 ME
Dunton, Daniel H.	1849	240	22 ME
Dunton, George W.	1848	162	23 ME
Dunton, James L.	1865	47	23 ME
Dunton, Manson D.	1856	22	37 ME
Durgen, Augustus	1847	203	16 ME
Durham, John	1836	42 b	29 PA
Durham, Thomas	1853	167	19 ME
Dwyer, George	1854	231	21 MA
Dwyer, Matthew	1853	46	40 MA
Dyer, Daniel	1845	154	24 ME
Dyer, David E.	1860	30	17 ME
Dyer, Edwin	1854	199	40 ME
Eagle, John	1858	50	15 ME
Eagle, John	1860	2	17 ME
Eames, Francis F.	1842	95	14 ME
Eames, Henry	1849	318	16 ME
Eames, Lewis L.	1849	364	17 ME

Name	Year	No.	Age	State
Eason, Peter	1836	19	22	ME
Eastman, Edwin G.	1850	125	17	ME
Eastman, Parker	1857	139	19	ME
Eastman, Reuben	1842	151	28	ME
Eastman, William	1836	96	20	ME
Eaton, Alfred	1854	107	18	ME
Eaton, Alpheus	1856	27	17	ME
Eaton, Alpheus	1857	57	18	ME
Eaton, Francis E.	1854	42	18	ME
Eaton, Isaac O.	1857	67	17	ME
Edes, Charles	1848	202	25	MA
Edgcomb, CharlesW.	1855	83	18	ME
Edgecomb, John	1850	26	24	ME
Edson, Alvin R.	1848	130	21	VT
Edwards, B. A.	1853	144	23	ME
Edwards, James	1847	36	27	NJ
Egecomb, Melville D.	1854	56	15	
Eisan, James	1862	34	40	ME
Eisan, James	1849	422	29	ME
Ekins, West E.	1842	37	17	OH
Elden, Henry J.	1845	54	19	ME
Elder, Isaiah	1845	63	25	ME
Eldridge, George	1842	64	26	CT
Ellers, Charles	1848	133	32	NY
Elliot, Charles C.	1842	31	20	ME
Elliot, Henry O.	1862	9	16	ME
Elliot, Henry P.	1863	16	18	ME
Elliot, James	1849	239	64	ME
Elliot, John	1850	57	25	ME
Elliot, John	1845	13	18	ME
Elliot, Stephen F.	1839	123	17	ME
Elliott, Charles	1850	58	16	ME
Elliott, Thomas	1856	125	31	MA
Ellis, Ivory, Jr.	1847	172	20	ME
Ellis, John	1850	68	26	SC
Ellis, William	1850	73	20	MA
Ellsworth, George H.	1845	65	17	ME
Elrick, David	1849	295	22	NY
Elwell, Alvah W.	1863	20	19	ME
Emerson, John L.	1854	203	18	ME
Emerson, Joseph E.	1845	5	25	NH
Emery, Alba	1849	275	23	ME
Emery, Benj. Fifield	1849	156	28	ME
Emery, Charles D.	1860	39	17	ME
Emery, Enos	1849	276	21	ME
Emery, Israel M.	1855	227	19	ME
Emmons, John M.	1858	34	21	ME
Emmons, Joseph	1849	81	18	ME
Emmons, William H.	1849	155	22	ME
English, Robert	1845	161	31	ME
Errington, Thomas	1855	68	27	PA
Erskin, William	1842	113	21	ME
Erskine, Cyrus	1849	334	23	ME
Erskine, John K.	1849	184	26	ME
Erskine, Wesley C.	1860	57	26	ME
Evans, Charles	1858	70	19	ME
Evans, Henry	1864	26 b	30	MA
Evans, John	1860	54	24	NY
Eve, John M.	1856	92	20	NY
Ewen, Henry	1855	17	31	MA
Fair, John	1853	23	28	ME
Fairfowl, Charles B.	1849	313	18	PA
Fairley, Hugh	1842	111	17	MA
Faras, Adolphus	1849	77	26	LA
Fargo, Thomas L.	1854	189	0	ME
Farnham, Allen F.	1849	271	26	ME
Farnham, George	1848	210	22	ME
Farnham, Jacob T.	1857	43	18	ME
Farnham, Joshua	1847	104	0	ME
Farnham, Thomas, Jr.	1845	120	19	ME
Farnsworth, James	1862	45	18	ME
Farquharson, William	1847	38	18	MA
Farr, Dennis G.	1849	359	17	ME
Farrell, John	1860	4	25	ME
Farrin, George	1848	164	20	ME
Farrin, William J.	1848	112	22	ME
Farrin, Winthrop	1839	98	17	ME
Farrington, Charles	1853	141	16	ME
Farris, Allen C.	1850	95	28	ME
Faught, Frederick, Jr	1849	279	29	ME
Fawal, William	1853	218	20	NY
Felker, William	1849	369	25	ME
Fenlason, Charles	1845	127	23	ME
Fenley, Benjamin W.	1849	104	24	ME
Ferguson, James	1856	85	23	ME
Ferguson, Robert A.	1849	336	22	ME
Field, Stephen S.	1858	24	18	ME
Fields, William	1853	206	17	MA
Finney, Nathl.	1856	133	38	ME
Fisher, Andrew	1847	3	28	PA
Fisher, Frederick R.	1862	17	18	ME
Fisher, Henry	1862	19	19	ME
Fisher, Horace	1842	41	25	NH
Fisher, Lincoln P.	1853	138	21	ME
Fisher, William	1855	157	21	ME
Fitch, Albert	1862	51	25	ME
Fitz, Ephraim	1849	113	19	ME
Fitzgerald, George	1847	37	24	MA
Flaherty, John	1861	20	23	MA
Flanders, Frank	1864	29	24	ME
Flannigain, AndrewM.C	1850	7	21	MD
Fletcher, Elijah M.	1855	184	31	ME
Fletcher, Ozias	1855	185	21	ME
Fletcher, Thomas	1836	89	30	ME
Fling, Albert A.	1861	74	19	ME
Flint, Edward W.	1863	43	23	ME
Flowers, John	1859	65	35	NY
Floyd, James A.	1856	7	18	ME
Fobes, Andrew	1853	100	18	ME
Fogg, Edward H. P.	1853	34	19	ME
Fogg, Jeremiah	1842	47	40	ME
Fogg, William H.	1853	33	16	ME

Foley, John	1856	98		22 NY			
Foley, Mark S.	1859	82		17 ME			
Follansbee, Benjamin A.	1847	144		31 ME			
Follansbee, Charles	1847	138		32 ME			
Folsom, Artemas L.	1847	2		22 ME			
Foot, Constant	1854	230		24 ME			
Forbes, Nehemiah	1847	127		18 MA			
Ford, Ebenezer B.	1847	147		18 ME			
Forman, Washington	1855	178	b	31 MA			
Forsaith, John	1850	38		20 ME			
Foster, George	1848	92		24 ME			
Foster, George F.	1854	179		18 NH			
Foster, John	1849	109		23 ME			
Foster, John	1847	152		26 MA			
Foster, Jones	1857	56		17 ME			
Foster, Rudolph	1856	140		28 PA			
Foster, William	1848	222		28 NY			
Foster, William M.	1849	79		30 ME			
Fowl, Warren	1839	82		21 ME			
Fowle, Franklin	1856	177		21 ME			
Fowler, Crosby	1849	125		21 ME			
Fowler, Joseph	1842	96		23 MA			
Fowler, William	1849	326		24 ME			
Fox, Charles A.	1854	254		16 ME			
Fox, William	1854	16		18 ME			
Francis, Samuel	1857	84		35 MA			
Frank, Isaac F.	1854	47		24 ME			
Frank, Peter	1858	28		38 LA			
Franklin, Charles	1854	264		18 ME			
Franklin, Thomas	1855	26		17 AL			
Fraser, John	1853	222		24 ME			
Frazer, Charles	1857	39		23 MA			
Frazer, William	1849	67		17 ME			
Frazier, William O.	1865	7		18 ME			
Freeman, Charles	1845	30		21 MA			
Freeman, George	1857	110	b	22 ME			
Freeman, George H.	1865	45		21 ME			
Freeman, James	1857	99	m	19 ME			
Freeman, John	1849	162		30 ME			
Freeman, John B.	1842	161		19 ME			
Freeman, Osius F.	1849	22	b	24 ME			
Freeman, Telemachus	1854	252	b	25 VA			
French, Bela	1845	139		23 ME			
French, John C.	1849	179		39 ME			
French, Joseph N.	1853	28		23 ME			
Frisbee, John	1842	107		17 ME			
Frost, Alden B.	1839	31		20 ME			
Frost, Charles W.	1861	28		21 ME			
Frost, Fairfield	1857	91		19 ME			
Frost, Hiram	1861	30		17 ME			
Fry, John	1857	55		20 ME			
Frye, John	1853	142		16 ME			
Frye, John R.	1845	23		21 MA			
Frye, Levi	1849	28		35 VT			
Fuller, Alonzo	1861	26		22 ME			
Fuller, George G.	1855	199		16 ME			
Fuller, Lenall	1842	146		20 ME			
Fulton, Alexander P.	1847	83		15 ME			
Funbish, Benjamin	1847	53		24 ME			
Gage, Henry W.	1850	119		18 ME			
Gahan, Anthony	1857	22		18 ME			
Gale, George A.	1863	23		21 ME			
Gallagher, Philip	1845	47		38 ME			
Galloway, William	1853	147		26 ME			
Gamble, George A.	1848	94		20 VA			
Gannett, George O.	1861	14		18 ME			
Gannon, John	1848	38	b	29 MD			
Gardin, Silas A.	1856	69		20 ME			
Gardiner, Albert	1859	35		16 ME			
Gardiner, George	1853	62		18 ME			
Gardiner, Henry M.	1859	40		21 ME			
Gardiner, John	1859	42		19 ME			
Gardiner, Parkman	1854	185	b	18 ME			
Gardiner, Samuel	1850	113	b	29 NJ			
Gardiner, William F.	1853	8		15 PA			
Gardner, Charles	1857	133		20 ME			
Gardner, James	1842	49		22 NJ			
Gardner, John	1845	77		20 PA			
Gardner, John A.	1847	90		45 MA			
Garland, Charles B.	1836	51		21 NH			
Garner, Robert	1839	83		29 MA			
Gatchell, Calvin W.	1855	154		22 ME			
Gatchell, Charles L.	1853	40		20 ME			
Gatchell, Jere E.	1868	22		26 ME			
Gatchell, Mark C.	1857	96		22 ME			
Gates, Andrew	1847	15		18 ME			
Gates, Henry	1848	102		22 NY			
Gaubert, Charles H.	1864	80		19 ME			
Gay, David, Jr.	1842	126		17 ME			
Gay, James M.	1847	95		0 ME			
Gaylord, Henry R.	1853	125		19 MA			
Gaynor, William	1854	234		21 ME			
Getchell, Abiel L.	1849	201		43 ME			
Getchell, Frederick A.	1856	115		16 ME			
Getchell, George T.	1856	93		17 ME			
Getchell, John Q.	1857	51		21 ME			
Getchill, George T.	1861	33		21 ME			
Geyer, Scott	1863	44		21 ME			
Gibbons, Thomas P.	1856	15		18 ME			
Gibson, Selden	1849	45		34 ME			
Gifford, Thomas	1853	27		22 ME			
Gilchrist, Albion	1849	80		14 ME			
Giles, George J	1848	125		26 ME			
Giles, John, Jr.	1836	50		42 ME			
Giles, Joseph	1858	103		47 ME			
Giles, Samuel	1857	30		27 ME			
Gillam, George	1849	325		25 ME			
Gillis, Daniel	1855	63		22 ME			
Gillis, John	1854	202		21 NY			
Gillis, Michael	1855	114		28 NY			
Gillispie, John	1849	53		20 ME			

Name	Year	No.	Age/State		Name	Year	No.	Age/State
Gilmore, James	1848	134	22 NY		Green, David	1836	40	23 NY
Gilmore, John	1854	227	15 ME		Green, Henry W.	1839	155	16 ME
Given, Freeman L.	1854	102	23 ME		Green, James	1855	72	20 ME
Given, John	1859	39	17 ME		Green, John G.	1836	17	24 ME
Given, John O.	1836	24	17 ME		Green, Joseph T.	1853	110	19 ME
Given, Samuel S.	1859	63	18 ME		Green, Stephen	1849	270	22 ME
Given, William	1836	29	19 ME		Greenleaf, Daniel D.	1864	85	29 ME
Glazier, George A. M.	1848	220	27 ME		Greenleaf, Eben. M.	1856	35	19 ME
Glenn, John	1847	158	33 GA		Greenleaf, Nathaniel	1848	211	24 ME
Goddard, Henry	1849	317	27 ME		Greenleaf, Orenthail	1862	50	21 ME
Goddard, John L.	1847	31	30 ME		Greenleaf, Samuel A.	1855	58	22 ME
Godfrey, Frederick E.	1867	9	19 ME		Greenleaf, William	1847	150	20 ME
Golder, Jordan, Jr.	1857	48	17 ME		Greenlow, Abel M.	1865	37	18 ME
Golding, Thomas	1855	219	25 PA		Grew, William G.	1853	190	17 NY
Goodspeed, Isaac J.	1847	209	17 MA		Gridley, James W. L.	1849	264	25 MA
Goodspeed,					Griffin, Benjamin	1848	116 b	22 VA
James M. H	1858	60	0 ME		Griffin, Charles H.	1853	105	17 ME
Goodspeed, Theodore	1849	327	21 ME		Griffis, Edward	1836	53	37 ME
Goodwin, Abraham F.	1836	93	22 ME		Groesbeck, Garret S.	1857	6	18 NY
Goodwin, James F.	1847	183	22 ME		Groton, Isaac M.	1853	165	21 ME
Goodwin, James O.	1854	143	35 ME		Grover, Harrison	1845	40	17 ME
Goodwin, Joseph H.	1856	149	17 ME		Groves, Shepherd	1847	195	21 ME
Goodwin, Robert	1855	217	25 PA		Grows, Charles C.	1836	24	30 ME
Goodwin, William	1849	208	47 ME		Gunnulson, John	1856	121	35 ME
Gordon, James	1848	52	40 MA		Guptill, Alfred	1854	226	26 ME
Gordon, William	1854	92	23 PA		Guthrie, David	1858	63	25 Scotland
Gore, Abdon	1849	119	21 ME		Gwyther, John	1850	71	23 NY
Gore, John	1849	54	57 ME		Hacker, John A.	1847	166	17 ME
Gorham, Eli	1848	18	21 ME		Hacker, William	1849	362	21 ME
Gormin, James	1853	24	26 MA		Haddon, Charles W.	1847	137	35 PA
Goslin, John	1847	47	30 MA		Hadley, Benjamin	1850	155	22 ME
Goss, Chester	1848	54	38 VT		Hagan, Charles C.	1862	25	17 ME
Gould, Charles H.	1865	4	21 ME		Hagan, Thomas E.	1861	51	50 ME
Gould, Isaiah H.	1858	75	19 ME		Haggerty, Timothy	1856	145	28 NY
Gould, Melvin	1854	159	15 ME		Haines, Winfield L.	1864	15	17 ME
Gould, Peter	1859	100	17 ME		Hale, Clarkson P.	1849	332	38 NH
Gove, Eben.	1848	166	22 ME		Hale, Edward	1854	174	20 MA
Gove, Hartley W.	1854	213	21 ME		Haley, Horatio N.	1857	68	25 ME
Gowell, John D.	1860	29	17 ME		Haley, James	1850	20	20 ME
Gowell, Leonard	1853	76	24 ME		Haley, James A.	1856	45	16 ME
Gowell, Robert	1848	151	20 ME		Haley, James A.	1856	41	16 ME
Gramberg,					Haley, John E.	1859	87	24 ME
John Gustaf	1845	113	29 Russia		Hall, Alfred	1857	85	21 PA
Grant, Adelaide A.	1856	169	21 ME		Hall, Charles A.	1855	158	19 ME
Grant, George W.	1859	102	21 ME		Hall, Charles B.	1859	84	19 ME
Grant, Lewis	1857	142	32 NY		Hall, George E.	1860	21	24 PA
Grassy, Joseph W.	1848	58	16 MA		Hall, Isaac B.	1849	257	26 ME
Graves, Convers L	1848	214	15 MD		Hall, Isaac R.	1849	283	30 PA
Gray, Charles	1839	80	18 ME		Hall, Jacob	1845	93	34 NY
Gray, Charles	1854	104	30 AL		Hall, James E.	1861	10 b	30 PA
Gray, Gardner	1845	107	22 ME		Hall, James R.	1865	23	16 ME
Gray, George	1845	152	19 ME		Hall, John B.	1856	150	22 ME
Gray, John	1849	47	23 ME		Hall, John C.	1847	63	0 ME
Gray, Lemuel C.	1856	174	18 ME		Hall, John L.	1849	197	22 MA
Gray, Nathaniel	1847	89	21 ME		Hall, Paul P.	1849	282	34 ME
Green, Alfred	1836	65 b	18 PA		Hall, Samuel M.	1857	105	19 ME

Name	Year	No.	Age/State	Extra
Hall, Thomas S.	1855	2	19 ME	
Hall, Wallace	1836	97	18 ME	
Hall, Watterman	1856	84	24 ME	
Hall, William D.	1839	164	19 ME	
Hall, Woodbury	1859	83	27 ME	
Ham, Edmund H.	1842	124	26 ME	
Hamington, Ephraim	1849	228	18 ME	
Hamlin, Alfred	1855	206	19 ME	
Hamlin, Edmund M.	1864	89	16 ME	
Hammond, Charles W.	1849	59	24 MA	
Hammond, John	1848	138	23 NY	
Hancock, James	1836	14	48 MA	
Hancock, James E.	1855	23	20 RI	
Haney, Charles	1853	127	16 ME	
Hanks, Robert V.	1849	416	18 ME	
Hanlon, John	1855	102	24 PA	
Hanscom, Sumner	1849	209	26 ME	
Hanson, Charles H.	1850	138	22 ME	
Hanson, George T.	1857	127	18 ME	
Hanson, Hans	1850	157	28	Denmark
Hanson, James T.	1857	125	23 ME	
Hanson, William P.	1856	134	16 ME	
Harding, Nathaniel	1842	114	23 ME	
Harding, Nelson	1854	228	28 ME	
Harding, Silas	1856	34	18 MA	
Hardlette, Warren R.	1847	33	34 ME	
Hardy, Ezra T.	1849	193	26 ME	
Harkins, John	1853	212	18 MA	
Harkins, Roger	1853	210	16 MA	
Harkstrom, Constantine	1849	192	28 ME	
Harman, John	1839	96	18 RI	
Harman, William J.	1849	245	23 ME	
Harmanson, Christian	1855	121	22 NJ	
Harmon, Albert	1853	87	17 ME	
Harmon, John C.	1847	91	19 ME	
Harmon, Leonard	1849	273	39 ME	
Harmon, William	1849	272	45 ME	
Harmond, Henry	1859	52	27 NY	
Harnish, Charles	1857	143	21 MA	
Harra, John	1849	367	26 NH	
Harriman, Calvin	1865	1	18 ME	
Harrington, Alexander	1845	68	21 ME	
Harrington, Henry	1855	192	20 ME	
Harrington, James S.	1859	3	38 ME	
Harris, Amos	1860	23	40 ME	
Harris, Benjamin R.	1856	75 b	53 VA	
Harris, Charles P.	1860	51	25 ME	
Harris, Edward O.	1849	163	22 ME	
Harris, James	1848	187	22 ME	
Harris, Thomas G.	1854	38	18 ME	
Harrison, George W.	1849	361	20 ME	
Harrison, Samuel	1854	50	26 DC	
Harrison, Wm.	1836	69	38 PA	
Hartwell, John N.	1839	163	22 ME	
Hartwell, William	1859	99	17 ME	
Harvell, George D.	1847	18	15 ME	
Harvey, Edward C.	1847	5	21 MA	
Harvey, James	1855	150	29 MA	
Harvey, John	1855	240	18 ME	
Harward, Thomas P.	1859	67	19 ME	
Harwood, Joseph	1839	110	22 ME	
Haseltine, James E.	1848	178	22 ME	
Haskell, Edwin	1857	65	20 ME	
Haskell, James L.	1849	249	30 ME	
Haskell, Joseph H.	1847	6	15 ME	
Haskill, Frederick A.	1849	175	21 ME	
Haskins, Hale M.	1836	55	29 ME	
Haskins, Samuel	1845	7	39 MA	
Hasten, James	1855	221	22 NY	
Hatch, Fraancis	1855	37	19 ME	
Hatch, Jesse L.	1853	101	19 ME	
Hatch, Lorring W.	1854	30	20 ME	
Hatch, Wesley W.	1857	4	19 ME	
Hathorn, Joesph J.	1856	172	19 ME	
Hathorne, Barzillai W.	1861	81	22 ME	
Havener, Isaac W.	1865	54	23 ME	
Hawes, Nathl.	1855	174	20 ME	
Hawes, Zebedee T.	1855	137	21 ME	
Hawks, Joseph	1849	86	20 NY	
Hayes, Francis	1853	56	22 MA	
Hayne, John	1848	239	31 MA	
Haynes, Hollis M.	1856	46	17 ME	
Hayward, John	1847	148	19 ME	
Hazard, George	1842	8	20 NY	
Hazlip, John J.	1847	151	17 ME	
Heald, Allen	1850	108	28 ME	
Heald, Odiorne	1845	116	20 ME	
Healley, Thereen A.	1863	41	19 MA	
Healy, Abraham, Jr.	1859	46	22 MA	
Hearnson, John H.	1854	150 b	18 ME	
Heath, Henry M.	1865	58	21 ME	
Heath, John	1856	82	25 ME	
Heath, John J.	1854	39	21 ME	
Hebberd, Leemon	1849	255	37 ME	
Hector, Charles	1849	10 b	19 PA	
Heiggins, William H.	1842	141	16 ME	
Henderson, Peter	1847	80	21 MA	
Henderson, William	1864	13	39 LA	
Henke, Henry C. A.	1856	137	29 NY	
Hennessey, Daniel	1868	21	24 ME	
Hennesy, Andrew	1860	6	26 ME	
Henry, George	1836	79	18 ME	
Henry, Robert B.	1849	124	25 ME	
Herbert, Edw. P.	1854	118	16 ME	
Herbert, James	1856	11	19 MA	
Herran, Michael	1853	177	19 NY	
Herrick, Isaac	1862	46	18 ME	
Herrick, John W.	1839	95	19 ME	
Herriman, Ephraim G.	1847	161	18 ME	
Hersey, Augustus M.	1855	21	0 ME	
Hersey, George R.	1853	162	24 ME	

Name	Year	No.	Age/State
Hersey, Levi E.	1855	119	18 ME
Hesse, Julius M.	1863	34	27 MA
Hesseltine, harles H.	1859	90	28 ME
Heuston, Ezekiel R.	1850	28	25 ME
Hickey, Charles E.	1847	9	27 NH
Hickey, Edward	1848	91	21 ME
Hickey, William	1845	119	25 ME
Hicks, Augustus	1848	59 b	20 NY
Hicks, James	1854	131	27 ME
Higgins,Bradstreet R.	1849	372	17 ME
Higgins, David L.	1850	62	31 ME
Higgins, Edward	1836	127	18 ME
Higgins, James M.	1849	390	19 ME
Higgins, John E.	1848	227	19 ME
Higgins, Jordan J.	1839	108	17 ME
Higgins, Joseph	1849	280	24 ME
Higgins, Martin	1862	54	26 ME
Higgins, Melvin B.	1845	150	17 ME
Higgins, Miles	1850	75	19 PA
Higgins, Solomon F.	1848	163	23 ME
Higgins, Solomon F.	1855	165	30 ME
Higgins, Thomas	1854	149	22 PA
Higgins, William T.	1848	32	18 ME
Hildreth, Edwin P.	1853	109	16 ME
Hill, Charles H.	1855	28	25 ME
Hill, Daniel	1854	48	22 ME
Hill, Francis H.	1848	23	24 ME
Hill, George E.	1848	39	24 NY
Hill, Huldah	1855	190 m	33 ME
Hill, James F.	1848	7 b	24 ME
Hill, Reuben	1855	10	24 ME
Hill, Stephen	1850	9 b	25 MD
Hill, Tobias, Jr.	1850	76 b	17 ME
Hillard, George	1845	126	20 ME
Hiller, Matthew	1864	22	24 MA
Hilling, Frederick	1860	65	18 ME
Hilling, John	1847	122	29 England
Hillman, Albion H.	1867	8	25 ME
Hilton, Edwin	1859	101	22 ME
Hilton, Joseph W.	1856	173	15 ME
Hilton, Osgood	1849	349	21 ME
Hinckley, Joseph E.	1836	88	20 ME
Hinds, John	1853	42	33 MA
Hinds, John F.	1848	61	24 ME
Hinkley, David W.	1842	139	22 ME
Hinkley, Ephraim	1839	148	21 ME
Hinkley, Hamsin	1854	99	17 ME
Hinkley, Harding L.	1853	53	20 ME
Hinkley, James L.	1862	39	16 ME
Hinkley, Lemuel	1842	80	18 ME
Hinkley, Thomas	1848	123	16 ME
Hinkley, William B.	1858	64	17 ME
Hinkly, Orin	1848	177	19 ME
Hitchcock, Hartley D.	1859	79	18 ME
Hitchcock, Samuel P.	1856	168	22 ME
Hnowles, Joseph W.	1867	5	33 MA
Hoak, Newman E.	1853	113	19 ME
Hodgdon, George W.	1864	54	24 ME
Hodgdon, Hiram	1849	75	35 ME
Hodgdon, Payson	1853	202	22 ME
Hodgdon, Stephen G.	1836	15	15 ME
Hodgdon, Westbrook	1855	104	18 ME
Hodgkins, Charles E.	1849	111	19 ME
Hodgkins, Francis W.	1836	85	15 ME
Hoffman, John D.	1861	49	16 ME
Hogan, Collins M.	1842	45	19 ME
Hogan, James L.	1846	118	23 ME
Hogan, William H.	1849	358	36 ME
Holbrook, John	1855	36	18 ME
Holbrook, John Q. A.	1849	235	26 ME
Holcomb, James	1856	77	24 NJ
Holder, Robert W.	1857	25	25 ME
Hollis, Thomas J.	1842	36	28 ME
Holman, Charles	1853	47	24 NY
Holmes, Charles	1847	57	14 MA
Holmes, Charles Edward	1859	76	17 ME
Holt, Charles S.	1865	2	26 ME
Holway, Rodney J.	1849	376	22 ME
Hood, Edwin H.	1854	190	21 NY
Hooper, Isaac	1855	243	23 ME
Hooper, William B.	1855	152	18 MD
Hopkins, Nelson	1863	7	42 ME
Hopkins, Robert F.	1856	139	24 PA
Hopkins, William	1856	9	50 ME
Hopkssic, Andrew S.	1862	49	23 ME
Horn, Daniel A.	1855	81	21 ME
Horn, William C.	1863	3	19 ME
Horsey, James	1849	38 b	22 MD
Horton, Leonard W.	1847	66	22 RI
Hoskin, Chas.	1855	115	16 MA
Houghton,Constantine	1848	37	19 ME
Houghton,Silas Avry?	1839	127	18 ME
Houston, Robert E.	1856	151	23 NY
Houston, William H.	1865	35	23 ME
Howard, Benjamin	1839	104	51 ME
Howard, Franklin C.	1849	335	17 ME
Howard, West	1849	341	40 ME
Howe, George	1849	20	18 ME
Howland, Henry	1856	60	20 MA
Hoyt, Ebenesen	1849	212	20 ME
Hoyt, Nathaniel	1836	20	31 ME
Hoyte, Edwin F.	1847	32	24 ME
Hubbard, Charles	1845	103	16 ME
Hubbard, Jeremiah	1842	9	47 ME
Huey, Robert	1861	4	19 ME
Huey, William	1849	306	23 ME
Hughes, Michael	1849	271	21 ME
Huisman, John	1867	2	37 MA
Humphrey, Henry	1836	11	45 ME
Hunt, David	1849	363	16 ME
Hunt, George M.	1867	13	25 ME

Hunt, James S.	1845	104		18 ME	Jenkins, George	1856	109	17 ME
Hunt, Richard	1839	158	b	38 RI	Jenkins, John	1848	73	31 MD
Hunt, Thomas H.	1854	133		31 ME	Jenkins, William	1839	56	26 MD
Hunt, Wm. B.	1854	146		18 ME	Jenks, John H.	1855	82	16 ME
Hunter, Wildes	1856	50		15 ME	Jennings, Thomas H.	1849	100	22 ME
Hunter, William	1855	146		27 MA	Jessop, Samuel	1853	149	25
Huntriss, James	1845	36		22 ME	Jewell, Charles	1857	21	20 ME
Huskins, Joseph D.	1863	40		20 ME	Jewell, Charles H.	1849	110	19 ME
Hussey, Edward B.	1849	222		27 ME	Jewell, Octavius M.	1857	46	17 ME
Hussey, Francis A.	1849	409		18 ME	Jewett, Clark B.	1855	233	20 ME
Hussey, Llewellyn	1848	224		21 ME	Jewett, Edwin H.	1860	38	16 MN
Huston, Henry C.	1847	189	b	26 ME	Jewett, Francis E.	1859	94	17 ME
Hutchings, Langdon	1841	75		16 ME	Jewett, George F.	1856	155	18 ME
Hutchings, William	1839	122		23 ME	Jewett, George W.	1854	182	22 ME
Hutchins, Albion P.	1849	242		25 ME	Jewett, John B.	1849	7	38 ME
Hutchins, John A.	1842	51		29 ME	Jewett, William	1846	166	29 ME
Hutchins, Reuben F.	1865	3		26 ME	Jewett, Wm. H.	1854	164	18 NH
Hutchins, William	1858	5		18 ME	Jipson, David	1848	124	21 ME
Hutchins, William	1855	70		18 ME	Johns, Samuel	1848	96	25 NY
Hutchison, Wm. St.	1845	92		41 ME	Johnson, Albion	1849	188	20 ME
Hyde, James L.	1849	161		19 ME	Johnson, Alexander	1842	67	32 PA
Hyer, Robert	1855	106		22 TX	Johnson, Andrew	1845	134	28 PA
Hynes, James	1849	220		31 ME	Johnson, Anson	1847	186	22 ME
Ince, Richard	1854	245		35 MA	Johnson, Charles	1854	181	m 24 PA
Ingall, Emory G.	1854	52		18 ME	Johnson, Charles	1854	134	18 ME
Ingraham, Martin	1856	188		21 ME	Johnson, Charles	1854	130	25 NY
Ingraham,TheodoreL.	1849	174		38 ME	Johnson, Charles	1855	122	24 MA
Ives, Barynett	1853	179		25 NY	Johnson, Charles W.	1853	57	20 ME
Ives, Bennett	1854	136		26 NY	Johnson, Coleman	1856	32	m 34 ME
Jack, Charles	1853	52		19 ME	Johnson, Ebenezer C.	1849	406	16 ME
Jack, George H.	1845	17		19 ME	Johnson, Freeman	1850	129	18 ME
Jack, George W.	1859	37		16 ME	Johnson, Gorham S.	1856	119	18 ME
Jack, Robert	1850	135		21 ME	Johnson, Henry	1854	180	32 Germany
Jackson, Charles	1861	58		24 NY	Johnson, Henry	1848	110 b	29 NY
Jackson, Darius W.	1865	49	b	22 ME	Johnson, James	1849	152	22 MA
Jackson, Edwend	1842	84		22 ME	Johnson, Jonathan	1848	185	45 ME
Jackson, George W.	1858	23		27 ME	Johnson, Joseph	1857	103	22 ME
Jackson, James	1850	131	b	28 ME	Johnson, Joseph A.	1848	86	18 ME
Jackson, James M.	1863	27		24 ME	Johnson, Josiah	1854	232	32 ME
Jackson, John	1845	51		30 NY	Johnson, Levi D.	1856	141	18 ME
Jackson, William	1855	139	b	22 NY	Johnson, Levi D.	1864	40	26 ME
Jackson, Wm. H.	1839	156		34 NY	Johnson, Rhoda	1853	111 b	22 ME
Jacobs, Lewis	1850	142		18 VT	Johnson, Richard M.	1847	207 b	47 MD
James, Edward	1848	150		20 ME	Johnson, Robert	1845	32	20 MA
James, Henry	1855	105		26 PA	Johnson, Senall H.	1854	257	20 ME
James, Joseph	1850	134		39 ME	Johnson, Thomas	1847	52	19 ME
Jameson, Alvah	1849	243		40 ME	Johnson, Thomas	1849	55	39 PA
Jameson, Charles	1847	204		20 CT	Johnson, Thomas J.	1850	53	23 ME
Jameson, George W.	1849	304	b	27 MA	Johnson, William	1859	19	39 PA
Jameson, Rufus	1836	99		16 ME	Johnson, William	1854	202	25 NY
Jamison, Charles P.	1849	159		25 ME	Johnson, William F.	1865	16	31 VT
Janson, Carl August	1862	14		19 NY	Johnson, William H.	1849	321	18 ME
Januson, George	1845	132		21 ME	Johnson, William H.	1842	104	32 PA
Jefferson, Alva	1839	119		20 ME	Johnston, John H.	1853	6	18 ME
Jefferson, Anthony	1854	51	b	22 NY	Johnston, Thomas	1853	9	47 ME
Jemison, John A.	1842	39		27 CT	Jones, Charles W.	1855	181	19 ME

Name	Year	No.	Age/State	Note
Jones, David W.	1854	255	21 PA	
Jones, Edmund	1845	16	21 NC	
Jones, Edward	1858	12	19 ME	
Jones, Emery	1847	157	20 ME	
Jones, Francis	1849	83	23 PA	
Jones, George M.	1854	220	24 ME	
Jones, Henry F.	1854	158	16 ME	
Jones, Jerome P.	1850	109	26 ME	
Jones, John	1859	18	20 RI	
Jones, John C.	1848	1	20 NJ	
Jones, John L.	1853	189	28 MD	
Jones, John S.	1857	78	25 MA	
Jones, Josiah S.	1836	31	20 MA	
Jones, Perez B.	1849	101	24 ME	
Jones, Thomas	1854	83	24 PA	
Jones, Thomas C.	1850	111	43 MA	
Jonston, Richard	1848	167	18 MA	
Jordan, Andrew J.	1848	143	20 ME	
Jordan, Barton R.	1854	111	26 ME	
Jordan, Charles P.	1847	206	24 ME	
Jordan, Daniel	1836	108	23 ME	
Jordan, Eben	1854	31	21 ME	
Jordan, Francis	1836	57	16 ME	
Jordan, Francis C.	1853	100	33 ME	
Jordan, Francis E.	1853	101	19 ME	
Jordan, John	1853	102	21 ME	
Jordan, John	1856	37	27 MD	
Jordan, Joseph B.	1854	33	23 ME	
Jordan, Ward	1845	140	19 ME	
Jordan, Wm. B.	1854	260	16 ME	
Joseph, Peter	1865	53	31 AL	
Joy, Daniel	1850	36	49 ME	
Kahrs, Theodore	1865	21	20 ME	
Kalden, Henry E.	1855	15 m	22 MA	
Kaler, Gardner	1853	18	20 ME	
Kallock, Amariah	1849	202	41 ME	
Keeffe, John	1856	122	26 ME	
Keeley, George	1857	61	25	Ireland
Keely, George	1848	121	17 NY	
Keen, William	1855	204	33	N. F.
Keene, Charles William	1842	133	15 ME	
Keene, Henry C.	1849	413	19 ME	
Kehail, Alexander	1850	144	23 ME	
Kelley, Arthur	1839	81	22 ME	
Kelley, Edward	1861	55	28 NY	
Kelley, George	1860	13	26 MA	
Kelley, George M.	1858	4	26 ME	
Kelley, James	1845	56	22 MA	
Kelley, James H.	1848	198	22 MA	
Kelley, John	1855	55	23	Ireland
Kelley, William	1836	5	14 ME	
Kellogg, Frederick H.	1848	54	23 ME	
Kelly, Samuel E.	1848	243	17 MA	
Kelly, Samuel W.	1836	66	25	England
Kelsey, Albert	1845	128	21 VT	
Kelsey, John F.	1847	17	15 ME	
Kelsey, Wentworth S.	1845	143	22 ME	
Kemp, Thaddeus P.	1860	1	30 ME	
Kendall, Charles S.	1862	10	14 ME	
Kendall, George H.	1855	66	18 ME	
Kendall, Thomas	1847	190	33 ME	
Kennedy, Thomas	1855	163	20 MA	
Kenney, James M.	1849	428	22 NY	
Kenney, Joseph A.	1848	15	17 ME	
Kennison, Wm. W.	1857	72	28 MA	
Keyed, A. J.	1857	14	28 NY	
Kidder, Hamilton C.	1864	32	17 ME	
Kief, John	1854	81	21 ME	
Kilby, Howard	1854	204	26 ME	
Kiley, John	1856	136	15 ME	
Kilton, Alanson K.	1854	17	23 ME	
Kimball, Artemas L.	1849	198	24 ME	
Kimball, Charles	1839	54 b	25 PA	
Kimball, George L.	1855	173	22 ME	
Kimball, Sylvester R.	1847	133	22 MA	
Kincaid, Abraham	1845	85	20 ME	
Kincaid, John	1849	189	19 ME	
King, Charles	1857	35	21 MA	
King, George	1853	163	13 ME	
King, George B.	1859	25	37 MA	
King, Harry	1855	242	18 ME	
King, John	1857	155	40 MA	
King, John	1854	1	16 ME	
King, John W.	1847	171 b	36 TN	
King, Marcus	1836	107	26 PA	
King, Mark	1849	403	21 ME	
King, Robert	1853	137	19 ME	
King, Stillman W.	1850	154	16 ME	
King, William	1847	139	22 ME	
King, William	1857	108	14 MA	
King, Zenus, Jr.	1847	114	25 ME	
Kingsbury, Asah	1855	209	22 ME	
Kingsbury, William H.	1859	6	17 ME	
Kingston, John	1845	33	21 ME	
Kintamy, Joachim	1845	101	26 NY	
Kirkpatrick, Robert	1857	9	19 SC	
Kittredge, Benjamin H.	1849	392	19 ME	
Knight, Charles P.	1859	62	15 ME	
Knight, Edward T.	1861	61	16 ME	
Knight, Elbridge W.	1863	15	21 ME	
Knight, Ford	1865	11	23 ME	
Knight, Frederick P.	1862	18	16 ME	
Knight, George L.	1862	33	17 MA	
Knight, James L.	1839	105	21 ME	
Knight, Nicholas T.	1853	96	54 ME	
Knight, Sidney B.	1864	72	17 ME	
Knight, Zacheus T.	1865	14	23 ME	
Knowles, Henry	1850	60	16 MA	
Lagriff, Joseph	1848	57	20 MA	
Laine, Orlando A.	1839	94	28 CT	
Lakin, John	1854	112	33 NY	
Lakin, Thomas	1849	180	19 NY	

Lalley, James S.	1855	100	19 ME	
Lally, James	1849	300	18 ME	
Lally, James	1850	100	18 ME	
Lamb, George	1861	9	36 NY	
Lambard, David C.	1853	172	18 ME	
Lambert, Charles	1848	234	33 ME	
Lampson, John M.	1854	101	18 ME	
Lampson, Moses T.	1855	35	20 ME	
Lancaster, Carlton	1855	38	18 ME	
Lancaster, Jacob A.	1855	193	22 ME	
Lancaster, Wellington	1847	1	18 ME	
Lancaster, William	1845	14	19 ME	
Lander, George A.	1858	14	48 ME	
Lander, George W.	1849	153	28 ME	
Landerkin, Llewellyn	1847	28	18 ME	
Lang, William	1842	70	26 ME	
Langill, Andrew	1855	20	20 MA	
Larkin, Joseph	1853	106	22 ME	
Larrabee, Alfred P.	1848	139	16 ME	
Larrabee, Amos A.	1858	33	19 ME	
Larrabee, Charles W.	1836	21	13 ME	
Larrabee, Frank A.	1863	11	14 ME	
Larrabee, Horace	1864	90	14 ME	
Larrabee, John P.	1857	98	18 ME	
Larrabee, Jotham C.	1848	16	28 ME	
Laskey, Thomas S.	1836	10	36 MA	
Latchford, Richard A.	1848	135	25 VA	
Laurence, Charles W.	1857	41	23 ME	
Laurence, Frederick D.	1859	92	19 ME	
LaVauge, Jeremiah	1849	62	23 MA	
Lavoy, Rodolph	1861	77	30 ME	
Lawin, Benjamin M.	1850	39	26 MA	
Lawrence, Benjamin, Jr	1858	30	16 ME	
Lawrence, David	1842	171	21 ME	
Lawrence, Washington	1836	104	24 ME	
Lawrence, William	1857	17	41 ME	
Lawrence, William	1865	9	45 ME	
Lawyer, Charles E.	1855	32	21 ME	
Leach, James W.	1856	142	18 ME	
Leach, Thomas J.	1853	7	20 ME	
Learned, Augustus	1847	27	17 MS	
Leary, William	1848	194	22 MA	
Leavett, George W.	1847	180	18 ME	
Leavitt, Abizer	1863	38	22 ME	
Leavitt, Charles P.	1859	69	18 ME	
Leavitt, Israiel	1845	27	19 ME	
Ledgley, Charles P.	1850	130	19 ME	
Ledgley, Nathaniel	1842	156	18 ME	
Ledgley, Otis	1849	181	18 ME	
Lee, Alfred	1860	11	21 RI	
Lee, Benjamin	1856	76	26 NY	
Lee, Emery	1855	151	40 MA	
Lee, John G.	1850	72 b	35 RI	
Leeman, Alexander P.	1847	181	20 ME	
Leeman, John E.	1847	180	22 ME	
Leeman, Joseph	1845	10	22 ME	
Lees, Alexander David	1859	97	31	England
LeFever, Robert	1853	152	23 PA	
Legget, Thomas	1853	158	26 NY	
Leighton, Albert F.	1849	121	23 ME	
Leighton, David H.	1853	63	16 ME	
Leighton, James	1855	201	18 ME	
Leitch, William C.	1860	52	36 PA	
Leland, Ezra	1842	20	18 ME	
Lemont, John S.	1859	68	17 ME	
Lemont, Thomas M.	1860	61	21 ME	
Lennan, George	1865	60	18 ME	
Lenox, Walter	1855	130	32 ME	
Leonard, George W.	1864	19	20 ME	
Leonard, James	1855	57	0 MA	
Leonard, Jerome	1854	205	23 ME	
Leslie, Samuel	1859	13	29 NY	
Levy, John	1842	62 b	22 MA	
Lewall, Hiram T.	1853	5 m	18 ME	
Lewall, Hiram T.	1854	169 m	19 ME	
Lewis, Albion	1864	87	22 ME	
Lewis, Charles	1856	110 b	25 VA	
Lewis, Charles	1853	91	26 PA	
Lewis, Daniel W.	1863	32	22 ME	
Lewis, Edward	1842	61	27 NY	
Lewis, Euclid H.	1859	61 m	13 ME	
Lewis, Isaac	1839	125	22 ME	
Lewis, James	1842	27 b	17 ME	
Lewis, John	1854	95	25 NY	
Lewis, John	1855	140 m	20 LA	
Lewis, Merritt E.	1864	43	24 ME	
Lewis, Richard	1858	31	24 NY	
Lewis, Robert	1855	90	21 ME	
Lewis, William	1836	91	22 ME	
Lewis, William P.	1850	115	21 ME	
Lewis, Zena H.	1856	159	38 ME	
Lewis, Zina H.	1857	95 b	40 ME	
Lewis, Zina H.	1836	98	17 ME	
Leyffert, George	1853	150	26 NY	
Libby, Arthur	1836	32	21 ME	
Libby, Benjamin	1849	131	31 ME	
Libby, Benjamin F.	1849	154	23 ME	
Lillan, Charles W.	1853	75	20 ME	
Lille, James	1848	13 b	30 NY	
Lilly, Jude	1848	118	20 ME	
Lilsby, John A.	1850	32	30 ME	
Limmons, George H.	1847	67	24 MA	
Lincoln, Ebed	1857	122	52 ME	
Lincoln, Francis	1861	16	45	Belgium
Lincoln, Francis	1856	118	34 ME	
Lincoln, John	1867	6	28 ME	
Lincoln, Richard	1853	136	22 MD	
Lincoln, Wakefield G.	1859	12	21 ME	
Linekin, Orrington	1854	188	20 ME	
Linquist, Charles	1858	56	25 PA	
Linscott, William H.	1853	103	15 ME	
Lint, Robert	1856	116	24 ME	

Name	Year	No.	Age/State		Name	Year	No.	Age/State	
Linuth, Richard	1849	247	52 RI		Lucas, James H.	1854	242	17 ME	
Lisson, Charles L.	1850	136	24 ME		Lundrigan, William	1855	75	19 ME	
Litchfield, Elijah	1842	120	17 MA		Lwett, Winfield L.	1865	18	21 ME	
Litchfield, Henry	1850	152	18 ME		Lynch, James	1856	30	28 NY	
Litchfield, Horace	1842	140	18 ME		Lynch, Thomas	1854	154	23 NY	
Littlefield, Alonzo M.	1856	187	21 ME		Lynch, William	1839	36	17 MA	
Littlefield, Henry	1848	62	17 ME		Lynn, Frederick F.	1848	33	23 ME	
Littlefield, Isaac A.	1839	27	22 ME		Lynott, Edward A.	1854	117	16 ME	
Littlefield, Moses	1845	32	38 ME		Mack, James	1849	170	22 ME	
Livingston, John H.	1855	167	35 NY		Mackee, John	1854	222	24 NY	
Loach, Isaac	1850	13	22 ME		Mackey, James	1849	302	18 ME	
Lockman, John W.	1842	55 b	30 MD		Macking, John E.	1857	151	21 ME	
Logan, Alexander B.	1861	19	36 MD		Macwell, William	1849	5	25 ME	
Loiett, Josephia	1854	109	16 ME		Macy, George A.	1849	195	20 ME	
Long, Albert D.	1858	76	17 MA		Mahagan, James	1854	67	22 NY	
Long, John	1848	72	25 NJ		Mahoney, William	1853	135	23 NY	
Long, Owen	1839	34	22 ME		Maines, Robert	1836	75	21 ME	
Long, William	1853	208	21 MA		Maines, Warren	1836	74	23 ME	
Longapu, Thomas	1854	108	42 LA		Mainland, James	1857	28	33	Scotland
Longfellow, JohnB. H.	1859	64	20 ME		Mains, Alfred M. C.	1850	118	21 ME	
Loomer, Frederic	1848	83	27 MA		Makay, John	1849	65	26 ME	
Looyd, Chares	1855	134	34 RI		Malcolm, James T.	1854	267	18 ME	
Lord, Alexander	1847	192	50 ME		Malcolm, John	1847	160	22 NY	
Lord, Charles D.	1858	102	16 ME		Malcom, Frank P.	1860	33	20 ME	
Lord, George	1847	118	13 ME		Malony, Isaac	1854	22	21 LA	
Lord, George H.	1849	36	21 ME		Maloon, Samuel	1856	113	18 ME	
Lord, James	1862	57	18 MA		Maloon, Solon H.	1849	158	17 ME	
Lord, John	1853	196	16		Mandans, John	1854	88	19 NY	
Lord, Philip	1853	213	31 MA		Mann, Charles	1854	81	18 MA	
Lorwell, Joshua, Jr.	1854	140	26 ME		Mann, Hugh	1856	143	25 ME	
Lothrop, Alson A.	1856	101	17 ME		Manning, Edward	1854	138	27 MA	
Loud, Charles L.	1848	22	23 ME		Manning, James	1853	214	24 MA	
Loud, Elihu	1839	32	18 ME		Mannuel, Michael	1842	152 b	27 ME	
Loud, William M.	1857	137	32 ME		Manson, Alpheus	1850	42	19 ME	
Loughton, Charles W.	1855	162	22 PA		Manson, Cleveland B.	1836	103	15 ME	
Loule, Nathan	1853	17	18 ME		Manson, Homer	1861	40	21 ME	
Love, John G.	1849	261	27 LA		March, Jonas	1855	148	30 ME	
Lovejoy, Kimball	1849	169	25 ME		Marcus, Charles	1849	400	27 VA	
Lovejoy, William	1849	203	58 ME		Marin, Joseph F.	1848	76	37 MD	
Lovett, George	1858	46	23 OH		Marr, Albion	1859	27	24 ME	
Low, Warren	1836	52	15 MA		Marr, Dennis J.	1854	75	18 ME	
Low, William, Jr.	1849	115	21 ME		Marr, Josiah L.	1854	98	17 ME	
Lowell, Abner I.	1858	36	18 ME		Marr, Lemuel	1853	69	21 ME	
Lowell, Averil L.	1856	111	21 ME		Marr, Rufus H.	1858	20	21 ME	
Lowell, David B.	1847	196	27 ME		Marr, Thomas R.	1858	103	20 ME	
Lowell, George	1864	81	14 ME		Mars, Aamasa	1849	360	16 ME	
Lowell, Henry B	1858	25	17 ME		Mars, John W.	1849	105	24 VA	
Lowell, James	1849	4	30 ME		Mars, Thomas H.	1849	266	21 VA	
Lowell, John C.	1839	131	17 ME		Marsh, Albert	1849	204	27 ME	
Lowell, John S.	1854	91	23 ME		Marsh, James	1861	41	31 CT	
Lowell, Samuel S.	1849	253	26 ME		Marshall, Edward	1855	73	30 ME	
Lowell,WilliamR., 2nd	1860	46	18 ME		Marshall, Farnsworth	1859	47	21 ME	
Lowry, Charles	1854	225	22 ME		Marshall, Joseph	1847	45	20 NY	
Loyd, Alexander	1847	86	29	Scotland	Marshall, Othniel C.	1848	207	22 ME	
Lubec, Joseph	1856	182	33 ME		Marshall, Seth	1845	130	22 ME	
Lucas, Henry	1848	188	26 NY		Marson, George	1858	83	17 ME	

Marson, James	1849	70	16 ME		McDermot, Thomas	1839	35	18 MA
Marson, Joseph	1855	8	27 ME		McDonald, Angus	1854	36	47 ME
Marstin, William P.	1854	18	13 NY		McDonald, Angus	1857	12	49 ME
Marston, Charles M.	1853	19	22 ME		McDonald, Charles	1849	357	24 ME
Marston, Edward M.	1848	36	18 ME		McDonald, Charles	1845	41	26 NY
Marston, William H.	1854	249	19 ME		McDonald, James	1853	3	21 ME
Martin, John	1857	86	37 PA		McDonald, James N.	1854	4	24 ME
Martin, Thomas H.	1859	85 b	30 MA		McDonald, John	1857	31	38 ME
Martin, William	1847	123	25 ME		McDonald, William	1853	219	36 ME
Mason, Alonzo	1854	208	17 ME		McDonald, William	1848	71	22 SC
Mason, George	1845	91	17 ME		McDonald, William M.	1848	157 b	18 ME
Massick, Joseph	1842	42	32 naturalized		McDonnell, James	1847	121	21 ME
Masters, William	1850	6	35 NY		McDonnell, Joseph	1856	123	28 MA
Mather, Thomas	1845	95	22 ME		McDougall, John	1854	216	29 ME
Mathes, Henry	1850	149	24 PA		McFadden, Reuben	1849	49	28 ME
Mathew, Thomas J.	1857	15	33 ME		McFadden, Thomas	1857	81	32 ME
Mathews, Joseph	1848	196	19 ME		McFarlaine, Robert	1848	35	25 PA
Matson, John, Jr.	1842	48	19 ME		McFarland, Malcom	1848	56	29 NY
Matteasby, Rufas	1853	169	25 ME		McGillivray, James	1854	82	41 ME
Mattheus, James C.	1853	103	18 ME		McGlede, Peter	1854	233	21 MA
Matthews, Edmund	1836	4	27 ME		McGrath, Thomas	1858	86	34 ME
Maverick, Charles	1862	2	25 NY		McGunnagel, William	1848	215	42 MA
Maxcy, Ira	1848	40	23 ME		McHugh, Charles	1848	106	25 NY
Maxwell, Charles	1850	104	20 ME		McIntire, Jeremiah	1847	69	18 ME
May, David	1855	230	20 NY		McIntire, Tallman	1858	94	18 ME
May, Moses	1848	48	18 ME		McIntosh, Edward	1853	133	28 ME
May, Samuel E.	1847	74	14 ME		McIntyre, Hugh	1854	212	29 ME
Mayers, Charles O.	1862	32	15 ME		McKay, John	1857	100	21	N. B.
Mayers, W. T.	1857	74	24 ME		McKee, James	1848	55	21 SC
Mayo, Stephen G.	1855	125	25 ME		McKeney, George	1850	44	19 ME
Mayo, William E.	1853	184	25 ME		McKenn, James	1848	233	23 MA
McAllister, William	1855	235	19 RI		McKenney, Francis	1849	401	25 MA
McArdle, Henry	1859	56	26 ME		McKenney, John L.	1836	47	17 ME
McAvoy, John	1857	149	22 NY		McKenney, Thomas	1836	36	22 ME
McCabe, Arthur	1848	79	54 MD		McKenzie, Henry	1849	96	30 NY
McCarthy, William	1854	148	22 MA		McKin, Francis	1856	171	22 ME
McCarty, Benj. F.	1849	218	21 ME		McKinney,			
McCarty, John	1861	44	36 ME		Charles F. or H.	1839	143	18 ME
McCarty, John	1857	8	19 ME		McKinney, Joseph, Jr.	1845	69	15 ME
McCawley, Frederic	1854	106	27 MA		McKinney, Joseph, Jr.	1853	36	21 ME
McClein, John	1857	82	23 ME		McKinney, Ozias	1854	192	19 ME
McClintock, John S.	1860	12	23 ME		McKown, Horatio S.	1856	96	44 ME
McClure, Alfred	1842	43	29 MA		McKown, John	1854	41	20 ME
McCollam, Thomas	1853	151	28 MA		McKown, Joseph R.	1853	203	18 ME
McCollister, Daniel W.	1855	127	16 RI		McLane, Lamuel	1856	129	31 MA
McConnell, Anthony	1845	96	29 PA		McLane, Samuel	1854	5	28 MA
McConnell, Peter	1848	50	21 NY		McLaughlin, Thomas	1865	46	20 NY
McCorest, Hugh	1855	220	19 NC		McLaughlin, William	1853	58	20 NY
McCorison, James	1842	97	19 ME		McLean, Allan	1861	79	21 MA
McCorles, Henry	1842	63	23 NY		McLean, David	1847	55	28 NY
McCoy, Thomas	1836	81	18 NY		McLean, George W.	1849	319	21 ME
MCCray, William	1845	153	15 ME		McLean, James	1848	225	22 NY
McCube, William	1849	21	24 TX		McLean, Murdock	1855	40	18 ME
McCullane, Andrew	1848	147	19 ME		McLellan, Archibald	1853	200	22 ME
McCutchen, Samuel	1857	156	18 ME		McLellan,			
McDaniel, Thomas	1847	85	21 ME		Bevier Depuey	1858	68	15 LA

McLellan, Charles	1849	1	32 ME
McLellan, Edgar	1854	86	28 ME
McLellan, George O.	1857	16	19 ME
McLellan, James	1853	209	22 MA
McLoon, Charles H.	1863	18	21 ME
McLoon, Frank	1865	36	19 ME
McMann, Edward	1854	64	22 OH
McManus, Asa	1836	116	20 ME
McMitchell, Wilder	1855	133	26 ME
McMullen, Alexander	1849	19	28 ME
McNeil, Archibald	1847	64	25 CT
McNeill, Daniel	1854	19	19 MA
McNeill, John	1853	43	20 ME
McPharson, Hugh	1847	173	18 ME
McPhee, Daniel	1856	130	26 VA
McPhee, Donald	1855	9	21 ME
McPherson, John	1853	44	24 ME
McPherson, Mathew	1855	79	18 ME
McQuamie, Lauchlin	1854	207	19 ME
McQuarine, Daniel	1850	77	22 ME
McQuarrie,Charles H.	1859	74	21 ME
McQuarrie, Daniel	1860	42	23 ME
McQuarrie, Lawrence	1860	43	25 ME
Meaden, Thos H.	1855	69	22 ME
Meady, Daniel F.	1847	170	21 MA
Meady, Frederick	1849	331	26 ME
Meady, Stephen B.	1858	90	30 ME
Meady, Thomas	1855	169	35 ME
Means, Joseph	1848	145	26 ME
Mejury, John	1855	61	20 MA
Melcher, George M.	1836	49	19 ME
Melonson, Augustine	1855	76	25 ME
Meloy, Charles	1856	99	21 ME
Menithew, William	1849	233	38 RI
Mereen, Elbridge T.	1861	7	18 ME
Mereen, Samuel	1857	121	17 ME
Merithew, Thomas R.	1846	164	25 ME
Merrell, Henry	1839	100	16 ME
Merrell, James T.	1847	145	16 ME
Merrill, Enos A.	1842	118	18 ME
Merrill, Francis B.	1847	143	17 ME
Merrill, George W.	1856	161	20 ME
Merrill, Henry	1839	100	16 ME
Merrill, James T.	1849	330	19 ME
Merrill, James W.	1858	22	18 ME
Merrill, Lewis	1849	310	19 ME
Merrill, Richmand L.	1854	253	20 ME
Merriman,BenjaminA.	1849	419	20 ME
Merriman, Enos	1861	36	21 ME
Merritt, Charles	1853	85	19 ME
Merritt, Frederick A.	1865	5	20 ME
Merritt, Joshua	1856	189	45 ME
Merrow, Lewis T.	1842	99	18 ME
Merry, John A.	1842	52	17 ME
Merry, Samuel, Jr.	1848	165	22 ME
Merryman, Franklin	1850	105	19 ME
Merryman,NehemiahC.	1849	395	18 ME
Merryman, Thomas	1865	40	29 ME
Merryman, William C.	1854	211	16 ME
Merson, Stephen I.	1845	147	22 ME
Meservey, George L.	1853	188	17 ME
Meservey, Gideon	1847	112	27 ME
Meservey, Joseph	1857	144	26 ME
Meyer, Augustus	1848	195	18 RI
Miller, Alexander	1847	71	23 NY
Miller, George W.	1850	40	30 NY
Miller, James M.	1845	29	22 ME
Miller, John	1856	6	29 MA
Miller, John	1856	16	0 ME
Miller, John W.	1847	35	21 MA
Miller, Thomas	1847	14	45 ME
Miller, William G.	1850	116	22 ME
Millet, Andrew	1854	87	43 MA
Milligan, Abraham	1848	201 b	24 ME
Milliken, Otis	1858	29	24 ME
Mills, Henry	1842	136	19 ME
Mills, William	1854	68	24 MD
Minnick, William	1854	2	16 ME
Minot, Edward A.	1857	60	26 ME
Minot, James F.	1848	154	20 ME
Minot, Juber D.	1848	122	19 ME
Minot, Rufus R.	1848	155	18 ME
Minott, John C.	1857	109	21 ME
Mitchell, Benjamin L.	1839	145	26 ME
Mitchell, Charles H.	1857	70	26 ME
Mitchell, Edward	1855	103	31 NH
Mitchell, Edward H.	1839	121	19 ME
Mitchell, James F.	1857	97	16 ME
Mitchell, John	1854	89	25 MA
Mitchell, John B.	1842	149	18 ME
Mitchell, John P.	1855	160	19 ME
Mitchell, John, Jr.	1845	80	24 NC
Mitchell, Joseph	1854	251	21 ME
Mitchell, Robt. P.	1850	21	26 ME
Mitchell, William	1856	126	17 ME
Mitchell, Wm. T.	1855	128	16 NY
Molau, William C.	1845	38	24 NY
Molony, George	1861	43	25 ME
Monroe, Charles F.	1855	200	21 ME
Monroe, James	1856	43	36 ME
Monson, John B.	1854	13	45 ME
Monteith, William	1861	56	19 NY
Montgomery,EdwardL.	1849	146	20 ME
Montgomery, Frederick	1853	11	29 ME
Montgomery, William	1849	142	34 ME
Moody, Palmer L.	1849	241	24 ME
Mooers, Benjamin	1848	68	19 ME
Mooney, Nicholas, Jr	1849	58	16 ME
Moore, Bradford H.	1862	1	23 ME
Moore, Charles D.	1861	67	16 ME
Moore, David A.	1849	262	24 NH
Moore, Ebenezer	1842	165	25 ME

Name	Year	No.	Age/State	Notes		Name	Year	No.	Age/State	Notes
Moore, George E.	1855	203	16 ME			Morton, Daniel H.	1864	56	23 ME	
Moore, Henry	1849	33	20 PA			Morton, Enos	1845	8	22 ME	
Moore, John	1845	55	21 ME			Morton, George H.	1856	68	28 ME	
Moore, Simon	1853	94 b	43 NC			Moserve, Henry	1836	87	20 ME	
Moore, Thomas	1862	20	20 MA			Moses, Albert	1849	405	18 ME	
Moore, William T.	1856	79	26 ME			Moses, Charles E.	1860	63	19 ME	
Moran, James	1853	215	20 MA			Moses, Charles O.	1860	62	19 ME	
Morang, Robert	1865	20	23 ME			Moses, Henry W.	1858	16	18 ME	
Morey, Smith	1848	29	22 RI			Mosher, William	1856	54	31 ME	
Morgan, George L.	1854	124	29 NY			Moulton, Charles D.	1858	78	16 ME	
Morgan, George W.	1847	119	19 ME			Mountfort, Robert	1855	111	17 ME	
Morgan, James	1845	52	25 MA			Mow, William	1848	69	43 NY	
Morgan, William	1836	34	22 ME			Mullen, George	1840	131 b	26 PA	
Morison, John B.	1836	54	28 ME			Mullen, John	1849	98	22 NH	
Morrill, Ebenezer	1849	342	41 ME			Mullens, James	1864	5	28 ME	
Morris, John	1850	41	23 NY			Mullens, James	1861	82	26 ME	
Morrison, Augustus G.	1856	61	18 ME			Mullens, John	1864	4	25 ME	
Morrison, James	1854	265 m	20 VA			Mulligan, James	1857	59	22 ME	
Morrison, John M.	1848	19	20 ME			Munay, Charles	1855	25	21 ME	
Morrison, Luther	1849	293	19 MA			Munroe, Alexander	1848	193	24 MA	
Morrison, Mark L.	1849	432	15 ME			Munsey, Jonathan	1856	125	24 ME	
Morrison, Parker H.	1854	277	17 ME			Munson, John W.	1847	88	0 ME	
Morrison, Parker P.	1850	35	20 ME			Murphy, Charles W.	1847	72	18	Cape Briton
Morrison, Samuel	1853	45	18 MA			Murphy, Frederick	1848	66	15 ME	
Morrison, Samuel H.	1847	24	17 ME			Murphy, James	1842	131	18	naturalized
Morrison, Thomas	1847	185	22 ME			Murphy, John	1849	311	21 ME	
Morrison, Timothy B.	1863	37	21 ME			Murphy, John	1853	124	15 ME	
Morrison, William	1850	46	34	England		Murphy, Owen G.	1858	35	19 ME	
Morrow, Richard H.	1853	121	20 ME			Murray, Osborn D.	1863	1	20 ME	
Morse, Albion H.	1849	431	16 ME			Murray, William D.	1862	62	38 ME	
Morse, Augustus N.	1847	163	19 ME			Murray, Wm.	1849	385	27 ME	
Morse, Charles A.	1864	75	24 ME			Murry, Thomas	1855	222	35 NY	
Morse, Charles C.	1860	47	17 ME			Myers, George	1847	39	24 MA	
Morse, Charles H.	1849	102	23 ME			Mynick, Edward E.	1854	142	17 ME	
Morse, David	1849	356	42 ME			Nagle, Michael	1857	62	16 ME	
Morse, David L.	1847	162	24 ME			Nash, James H.	1854	186	14 ME	
Morse, George E.	1856	127	17 ME			Nason, Charles	1850	61	17 ME	
Morse, George S.	1836	123	24 PA			Nason, Joseph D.	1836	68	17 ME	
Morse, George W. or H.	1850	139	18 ME			Nason, Moses	1865	48	41 NH	
Morse, Jacob G.	1863	36	20 ME			Nason, Samuel	1853	195	16	
Morse, James	1842	155	20 ME			Neal, Albert	1845	83	20 ME	
Morse, James A.	1849	256	18 ME			Neal, Alfred G.	1857	111	23 ME	
Morse, John G.	1842	154	21 ME			Neal, Edward H.	1858	80	26 ME	
Morse, Llewellyn A.	1859	95	17 ME			Neal, George H.	1858	39	19 ME	
Morse, Lucius K.	1863	21	26 ME			Nealey, Horace W.	1850	25	18 ME	
Morse, Martin	1853	143	16 ME			Neill, Reubin S.	1854	53	17 ME	
Morse, Robert	1845	133	20 ME			Nelson, Eli H.	1853	199	23 ME	
Morse, Thomas	1849	30	42 ME			Nelson, John	1848	74	32 PA	
Morse, William H.	1850	87	37 NY			Nelson, John L.	1848	183	22 NY	
Morse, William H.	1864	44	22 ME			Nelson, William	1862	13	23 NY	
Morse, Winfield L.	1856	94	16 ME			Nevens, William	1849	92	0 ME	
Morten, Thomas	1848	3	25 ME			Newby, William W.	1849	3	22 NY	
Mortin, Daniel	1868	19	49 ME			Newcomb, Samuel G.	1845	106	22 ME	
Morton, Albert	1847	77	15 ME			Newell, Frederick	1849	147	19 MA	
Morton, Alfred	1845	9	21 ME			Newell, Joseph	1849	186	50 MA	
Morton, Cornelius B.	1849	199	42 MA			Newell, Joseph A.	1847	149	18 ME	

Name	Year	No.	Age/State		Name	Year	No.	Age/State
Newell, William H.	1853	73	18 ME		Oliver, Arthur	1839	23	22 ME
Newhall, John L.	1858	81	34 MA		Oliver, Benjamin L.	1850	36	21 ME
Newman, George	1853	59	22 MD		Oliver, Cyrus W.	1862	29	22 ME
Newton, James	1849	378	26 PA		Oliver, David E.	1853	70	17 ME
Newton, Thomas	1849	377	28 PA		Oliver, Ebenezer	1847	159	20 ME
Nichols, Charles K.	1848	137	15 ME		Oliver, Edwin M.	1855	84	17 ME
Nichols, Charles P.	1850	47	15 ME		Oliver, Elbridge H.	1857	80	23 ME
Nichols, Cyrus B.	1855	31	16 ME		Oliver, Henry	1853	60	21 NY
Nichols, David F.	1856	181	20 ME		Oliver, James	1839	22	0 ME
Nichols, George L.	1850	23	19 ME		Oliver, John H.	1836	78	20 ME
Nichols, James Wm.	1848	153	15 ME		Oliver, John H. Jr.	1867	16	17 ME
Nichols, Jasper N.	1848	25	16 ME		Oliver, Lendale B.	1856	105	26 ME
Nichols, Joseph	1847	19	18 ME		Oliver, Llewellyn	1858	95	23 ME
Nichols, Joseph	1864	9	27 ME		Oliver, Llewellyn	1848	170	17 ME
Nichols, Melville C.	1839	159	18 ME		Oliver, Loring C.	1847	134	21 ME
Nichols, William F.	1861	37	21 ME		Oliver, Moses O.	1839	117	22 ME
Nicholson, Kenneth	1855	7	26 MA		Oliver, Philip D.	1862	26	19
Nickels, Henry M.	1847	146	19 ME		Oliver, Samuel L.	1855	46	20 ME
Nickerson, Allen R.	1861	85	19 ME		Oliver, Stearns W.	1858	92	18 ME
Nickerson,CorneliusG.	1848	90	17 ME		Oliver, Thomas	1845	121	23 ME
Nickerson, David	1850	45	21 ME		Oliver, William A.	1847	153	20 ME
Nickerson, Ingraham	1845	138	22 ME		Oliver, William O.	1847	135	22 ME
Nickerson, Thomas F.	1861	84	35 ME		Olsen, Swen	1855	132	32 Norway
Nicles, William	1863	25	28 PA		Ome, William	1849	118	23 ME
Niles, Francis	1836	126	34 ME		Orr, Charles Henry	1842	29	18 ME
Noble, Charles E.	1853	68	15 ME		Orr, Reed	1848	34	26 ME
Noble, Eleazer R.	1849	130	31 ME		Orr, Thaddeus J.	1847	202	25 ME
Noble, Franklin	1854	78	16 ME		Osborne, John	1842	5	31 ME
Noble, John	1839	84	26 ME		Osborne, William	1847	93	24 ME
Noble, William	1849	157	28 ME		Osgood, Francis E.	1858	91	15 ME
Noble, William H.	1853	108	16 ME		Osgood, Reuben	1842	115	26 MA
Nockton, John	1845	158	27 ME		Osgood, William M.	1865	17	42 NH
Nolan, William	1849	17	24 NY		Otis, Harvey L.	1845	105	26 ME
Noonan, Wm.	1854	279	18 ME		Otis, James S.	1836	84	18 ME
Norman, William	1853	156	35 MD		Otis, Samuel	1845	44	50 ME
Norris, Benjamin W.	1849	165	30 ME		Owen, Charles W.	1858	15	17 ME
Norris, George W.	1847	120	17 ME		Owen, Isaac W.	1849	346	35 ME
Norris, Reuel W.	1845	146	21 ME		Owen, James	1849	351	18 MA
Northrup, James H.	1864	83	13 ME		Owen, Jeremiah, Jr	1850	137	21 ME
Norton, Albion	1854	20	23 ME		Owen, John	1860	5	23 MA
Norton, Banjas R.	1849	421	20 ME		Oxnard, Edward P.	1856	55	18 ME
Norton, Henry	1849	296	33 ME		Oyer, Thomas	1853	2	19 NY
Norwood, William	1842	79	24 NY		Packard, Theodore H.	1856	81	18 ME
Nowell, Rufus	1849	238	27 ME		Page, James H.	1836	27	17 ME
Noyes, Allen	1842	21	20 ME		Page, Joel R.	1855	238	19 ME
Nutter, George Albert	1848	184	17 ME		Page, Thomas B.	1849	141	24 ME
Nutter, George F.	1839	78	0 ME		Page, Thomas H.	1854	139	24 MA
Nutting, William	1836	2	17 ME		Paine, Theodore H.	1858	85	23 ME
O'Neel, Daniel	1847	92	26 MA		Paishley, Albert	1836	73	17 ME
Oakes, Eben P.	1856	180	25 ME		Palmer, Augustus	1847	201	24 ME
OBrien, James	1859	54	30 ME		Panott, William	1849	418	22 MA
Ogilvie, Archibald	1848	152	25 ME		Parker, Alfred	1845	70	20 ME
Ogle, Isaac	1849	63	23 MA		Parker, Arthur H.	1863	22	20 ME
Oliver, Albion	1865	15	25 ME		Parker, Elias F.	1849	103	26 ME
Oliver, Alfred L.	1850	92	19 ME		Parker, Henry	1864	57	32 N. S.
Oliver, Alvin	1861	39	21 ME		Parker, James	1854	201	38 NY

Parker, Nathaniel	1836	125	20 MA
Parker, William	1853	55	35 MA
Parker, William F.	1855	80	24 NY
Parks, David	1839	109	19 ME
Parks, David N.	1864	71	16 ME
Parmeter, Orville B.	1839	38	18 ME
Parsens, George	1848	232	27 ME
Parsons, Ozias	1854	248	23 ME
Partridge, Charles E.	1864	51	19 ME
Partridge, Reubin	1854	14	26 ME
Patridge, Charles E.	1860	40	15 ME
Patridge, Charles O.	1864	48	20 ME
Pattee, Charles H.	1849	32	16 ME
Pattee, George G.	1862	30	26 ME
Patten, Abel M.	1855	218	19 ME
Patten, Alfred	1856	163	18 ME
Patten, Andrew M.	1867	3	19 ME
Patten, Bardwell	1842	10	21 MA
Patten, Charles E.	1850	79	16 ME
Patten, D. Albert	1857	119	18 ME
Patten, David S.	1855	51	17 ME
Patten, Gilbert E. R.	1839	113	16 MA
Patten, Jarvis	1845	76	18 ME
Patten, Octavius H.	1864	27	26 ME
Patten, Oscar	1857	66	17 ME
Patten, Rogers G.	1853	61	17 ME
Patterson,Corydon T.	1860	55	24 ME
Patterson, Jacob	1858	88	21 NY
Patterson, John W.	1857	1	47 PA
Patterson, Martin	1849	120	34 MA
Patterson, William	1849	85	21 NY
Patterson, William	1854	171	28 MA
Patterson, Wm. M.	1855	232	21 ME
Pattie, Hiram E.	1845	162	17 ME
Paul, James	1848	80	24 MA
Paul, Liberty	1847	108	22 CT
Paul, Nelson F.	1849	427	26 ME
Payne, Castanos	1848	241	18 ME
Payson, Mobeck M.	1859	53	27 ME
Peach, George W.	1859	22	17 ME
Peaks, Farwell B.	1842	38	39 ME
Pearson,			
Edmund Dwight	1857	106	16 ME
Peaslee, James	1836	128	35 ME
Peck, Ralph C.	1857	71	16 CT
Peirce, George W.	1861	83	37 ME
Peirce, John W.	1847	136	17 ME
Pembrook, John	1859	89	16 ME
Pendleton, Andrew	1864	3	29 ME
Pendleton, Andrew L.	1854	166	21 ME
Pendleton, Isaac N.	1862	5	16 ME
Penfield, Charles	1860	8	45 ME
Pennell, Robert	1849	226	35 ME
Pepper, George	1861	6	21 ME
Pepper, George	1859	14	19 ME
Percey, John B.	1861	11	22 ME

Percy, Abraham C.	1845	82		18 ME
Percy, David G.	1857	19		22 ME
Percy, David G.	1856	108		21 ME
Percy, James B.	1857	73		22 ME
Percy, James G.	1842	164		23 ME
Percy, Samuel R.	1847	11		19 ME
Perkins, Abraham	1850	86	m	18 ME
Perkins, Amos J.	1859	21		23 ME
Perkins, Benjamin	1849	379		19 ME
Perkins, Charles J.	1854	121		18 ME
Perkins, Charles J.	1842	122		21 ME
Perkins, Charles J.	1859	66		23 ME
Perkins, Daniel W.	1860	58		24 ME
Perkins, Joseph A.	1849	171		34 MA
Perkins, Samuel	1849	342		26 ME
Perkins, Stephen	1848	141		24 CT
Perkins, Thomas M.	1847	200		19 ME
Perkins, William	1856	80		19 ME
Perkins, William H.	1848	2		21 ME
Perow, John	1858	2		19 ME
Perry, John, Jr.	1845	109		19 ME
Perry, Joseph B.	1853	83		16 ME
Perry, Joseph B.	1854	63		17 ME
Peters, Daniel	1842	89		21 ME
Peters, George	1855	6	m	22 ME
Peters, James	1848	111	b	40 VA
Peters, James C.	1849	414		17 ME
Peters, Washington	1850	101	b	24 ME
Peterson, Charles W.	1848	30		24 MA
Peterson, Christian	1850	81		21 LA
Peterson, John	1842	81		21 MA
Peterson, John A.	1854	276		18 ME
Peterson, John P.	1855	113		23 ME
Pettigrew, Joseph G.	1855	224		29 ME
Pettingill, Charles F.	1864	59		17 ME
Pettingill, George	1854	97		18 ME
Pettingill, Ubert L.	1849	200		36 ME
Peva, George	1856	138		19 ME
Phelan, Patrick	1854	239		23 NY
Phelan, William	1854	240		19 NY
Phelps, John M.	1854	59		18 ME
Philbrick, George	1849	178		19 ME
Philbrick, Samuel	1845	4		28 NH
Philbrook, Artemas	1850	110		19 ME
Philbrook, James M.	1855	48		14 ME
Philbrook, Thomas	1855	136		18 ME
Phillips, David	1853	25		22 NY
Phillips, Samuel	1849	297		22 RI
Pickins, Isaac H.	1836	33		19 ME
Pierce, Franklin	1864	37		26 MD
Pierce, Hiram	1849	142		22 MA
Pierce, John T.	1849	72		31 MA
Pierce, Jonathan	1854	110		22 ME
Pierce, Lorenzo	1848	173		27 MA
Piercy, George	1845	60		39 DC
Pigot, Edward E.	1842	125		17 MA

Name	Year	No.	Age/State
Pike, Thomas	1850	158	21 MA
Pillsbury, George W.	1853	123	17 ME
Pinkham, George	1845	115	21 ME
Pinkham, George W.	1848	209	19 ME
Pinkham, Hiram	1854	224	34 ME
Pinkham, Lorenzo	1847	192	21 ME
Pinkham, Warren	1836	92	29 ME
Piper, Benjamin	1836	44	20 NH
Pitchell, Allen G.	1854	26	49 RI
Pitcher, Samuel	1849	78	28 MA
Pitts, Anthony P.	1857	165	56 NY
Plant, Anthony	1855	93	45 ME
Plaskett, John C.	1839	147	30 MD
Plaster, Henry	1853	65	21 NY
Platt, George	1841	2	22 NY
Plumer, Alden	1842	3	21 ME
Plummer, Cyrus	1850	128	24 ME
Plympton, William	1849	137	27 MA
Pomroy, Lewis	1856	8	34 ME
Pomroy, William	1853	145	22 ME
Pool, James	1847	184	16 ME
Poole, Charles	1842	83	20 MA
Poole, Warren	1854	35	42 MA
Poor, Isaac	1842	16	19 ME
Poor, John	1850	17	19 ME
Porter, Frederick S.	1853	29	0 ME
Porter, James	1859	7	26 NH
Porter, Timothy	1864	61	21 ME
Potter, Charles W.	1850	31	0 ME
Potter, George N.	1855	99	21 ME
Potter, Henry	1854	21	19 ME
Potter, Jeremiah P.	1845	53	22 ME
Potter, John G.	1863	5	18 ME
Potter, Roland E.	1849	207	18 ME
Potter, Thomas L.	1856	95	24 ME
Potter, William L.	1856	170	19 ME
Potter, Woodbury A.	1864	76	19 ME
Potts, John	1849	402	19 NY
Power, Reed W.	1847	168	20 ME
Powers, Charles	1859	73	27 ME
Powers, Gilbert P.	1855	42	18 ME
Powers, Israel	1839	86	22 ME
Powers, Joseph	1854	155	26 LA
Powers, Joseph M.	1865	43	17 ME
Powers, Miles H.	1859	96	23 ME
Powers, Patrick	1855	43	19 ME
Powers, William F.	1845	148	25 ME
Pratt, Asa	1849	134	29 ME
Pratt, James B.	1848	148	21 ME
Pratt, Lorenzo	1847	106	17 ME
Preble, Ebenezer	1860	9	38 ME
Preble, George H.	1848	168	18 ME
Preble, Harvey	1864	91	17 ME
Preble, James	1859	5	23 ME
Preble, James P.	1853	171	20
Preble, John	1850	122	21 ME
Preble, Lemuel H.	1850	140	18 ME
Preble, Noble	1853	64	19 ME
Preble, Stephen	1850	121	18 ME
Preble, Willington	1861	23	21 ME
Preble, Wm. J.	1842	13	28 ME
Prenty, Henry	1847	94	21 GA
Prescot, Levi	1842	138	22 ME
Prescott, Danforth	1849	206	25 ME
Prescott, W. H. A. C.	1847	96	17 ME
Preston, Philip	1850	84	17 MA
Prible, Gordon L.	1853	164	20 ME
Price, Charles	1853	146	25 NY
Prindale, William	1854	73	20 ME
Provost, Henry	1849	116	22 NY
Puchard, Joseph	1854	197	26 ME
Pugh, John	1855	244	16 ME
Pugsley, James	1858	69	19 MA
Pullet, Christopher	1856	186	41 ME
Purington, John Louville	1850	102	17 ME
Purington, Levi	1839	97	36 ME
Purington, Nathaniel	1839	29	19 ME
Purington, William W.	1863	12	19 ME
Purinton, George	1848	22	17 ME
Purrington, George	1856	48	20 ME
Purrington, Thomas S.	1855	110	17 ME
Purrington, Wm. H.	1856	179	21 ME
Pushard, Frederick G.	1864	52	22 ME
Quick, Robert B.	1856	57	16 DE
Quimby, Oliver H.	1859	28	17 ME
Quincy, Henry	1855	210	19 ME
Race, Stephen H.	1847	46	23 NY
Rackleff, Stephen T.	1849	126	42 ME
Rackliff, Alexander E.	1849	108	31 ME
Ragan, Henry M.	1855	44	16 ME
Ragan, Stephen	1854	241	17 ME
Ragon, George	1861	18	19 ME
Ragon, John	1862	28	18 ME
Rairden, Samuel L.	1849	162	22 ME
Ramsay, Joseph W.H.	1853	181	17 ME
Randale, Lincoln	1839	88	17 ME
Randall, George	1842	102	35 ME
Randall, George L.	1849	391	49 NH
Randall, Humphrey A.	1856	42	16 ME
Randall, Isaac	1836	77	23 ME
Randall, Sylvanus	1854	100	20 ME
Randall, William	1849	84	0 NY
Randall, William A.	1853	197	20 ME
Ranks, Thomas R.	1854	275	15 ME
Raubin, Antis Joseph	1865	50	21 LA
Rawdon, Richard	1849	2	23 MA
Rawley, James	1855	216	16 ME
Raymond, Benjamin	1842	32	20 ME
Raymond, James	1842	157	19 ME
Raymond, Thomas	1845	73	27 PA
Reccord, William	1853	102	16 ME
Redmond, Robert	1854	172	24 NY

Reed, Calvin N.	1850	1	22 ME	
Reed, Cephas	1846	168	19 ME	
Reed, Charles	1856	112	18 ME	
Reed, Charles H.	1864	18	18 ME	
Reed, David	1856	31	21 ME	
Reed, Enoch M.	1856	90	22 ME	
Reed, Frederick A.	1861	45	14 ME	
Reed, George L.	1857	33	18 ME	
Reed, Isaac	1857	75	17 ME	
Reed, Jacob T.	1862	41	18 ME	
Reed, James T.	1862	40	20 ME	
Reed, James T.	1842	22	16 ME	
Reed, John	1857	2	27 ME	
Reed, John A.	1864	55	24 ME	
Reed, John R.	1854	123	18 ME	
Reed, Joseph	1848	31	20 MA	
Reed, Jotham	1847	102	23 ME	
Reed, Levi	1849	221	46 ME	
Reed, Mandley	1854	236	21 ME	
Reed, Matthew P.	1836	48	19 ME	
Reed, Noah	1849	122	22 ME	
Reed, Robert	1857	90 m	17	N. B.
Reed, Samuel D.	1855	176	55 MD	
Reed, Thomas L.	1865	10	35 ME	
Reed, Thomas L.	1850	2	19 ME	
Reed, Timothy B.	1857	47	18 ME	
Reed, Timothy B.	1859	29	20 ME	
Reed, William H.	1848	85	38 ME	
Reed, William J.	1862	21	19 ME	
Reed, Wm.	1845	141	24 MA	
Reed, Worrall	1842	98	17 ME	
Reeves, Wm. G.	1836	30	34 CT	
Reid, Thomas B.	1855	65	38 ME	
Remick, Benjamin	1857	34	29 ME	
Remick, George	1861	5	28 ME	
Remick, Joseph	1849	404	46 ME	
Reynolds, Elisha W.	1855	172	28 ME	
Rhoades, Saml. G.	1864	82	20 ME	
Rich, Charles E.	1854	214	20 ME	
Rich, Franklin	1846	165	37 MA	
Rich, George W.	1864	11	23 ME	
Rich, John L.	1854	94	16 ME	
Richardson,CharlesJ.	1850	11	34	England
Richardson,GeorgeT.	1854	120	21 ME	
Richardson, James	1849	250	25 ME	
Richardson, James	1859	23	25 ME	
Richardson, Lewis C.	1854	223	16 ME	
Richardson, Nicholas	1859	24	27 ME	
Richardson, Putnam	1858	101	20 ME	
Richardson, Thomas	1847	60	23 NY	
Richdson, George T.	1855	33	20 ME	
Ricker, Charles B.	1856	18	22 ME	
Ricker, Lorenzo	1847	164	18 ME	
Ricker, Rufus	1849	252	44 ME	
Rideout, Converse	1836	28	19 ME	
Rideout, David	1845	59	19 ME	
Rideout, Hujhey	1855	215	21 ME	
Rideout, Martin V. B.	1855	41	18 ME	
Rideout, Rodman D.	1845	151	17 ME	
Rideout, Silas E.	1850	150	19 ME	
Rideoutt, Charles T.	1862	43	20 ME	
Rider, Alden	1861	71	20 ME	
Rider, Henry	1842	145	22 ME	
Ridley, Isaac M.	1849	425	0 ME	
Ridont, Jona..	1856	65	20 ME	
Riley, George	1842	93	18 NJ	
Riley, George	1847	68	39 NH	
Riley, William	1855	94	21 GA	
Riley, William H. S.	1861	38	47 ME	
Rily, Edward	1854	193	22 NY	
Rines, Erastus	1849	292	20 ME	
Ring, John E.	1857	26	18 ME	
Rinqat, Charles	1847	73	21 MA	
Rittal, Philip H.	1857	141	30 ME	
Rittal, William L	1856	50	19 ME	
Rivers, Peter	1848	131	20 RI	
Roach, Edward	1858	17	15 ME	
Roach, Franklin	1836	7	18 ME	
Roach, Hiram	1845	145	20 ME	
Roach, John A., Jr.	1849	389	18 ME	
Roach, Joseph A.	1857	135	17 ME	
Roach, Samuel J.	1845	114	23 ME	
Robbins, Benjamin	1850	93	21 ME	
Robbins, David D.	1847	126	23 VT	
Robens, Edwin	1854	29	21 ME	
Roberson, Charles	1847	194	27 ME	
Roberts, Charles	1854	147	23 RI	
Roberts, John	1853	107 b	56 ME	
Roberts, John F.	1842	135	20 ME	
Roberts, John T.	1863	28	31 ME	
Roberts, William	1848	126	24 PA	
Robertson, James	1842	23	39 VA	
Robins, John	1848	4	19 ME	
Robins, William	1854	27	24 ME	
Robinson, Alexander	1854	215	22 ME	
Robinson, Alfred T	1839	136	18 ME	
Robinson,AlpheusS.O.	1842	88	21 ME	
Robinson, Dennis	1848	213	20 ME	
Robinson, George	1845	74	22 PA	
Robinson, Henry B.	1859	71	19 ME	
Robinson, Hiram	1848	67	17 ME	
Robinson, James	1854	235	18 ME	
Robinson, James	1856	52	24 PA	
Robinson, Orville A.	1860	15	17 ME	
Robinson, Samuel	1842	160	25 ME	
Robinson, Thomas	1845	125	21 ME	
Robinson, Thomas	1842	28	23 ME	
Robinson, Thomas B.	1859	70	17 MA	
Roderick, Thomas	1855	191	20 ME	
Roff, Levi	1864	2	29 ME	
Rogen, John	1854	151	21 NY	
Rogers, Ephraim	1854	261	16 ME	

Bath 114

Name	Year	No.	Age/State		Name	Year	No.	Age/State	
Rogers, Henry	1854	45	19 ME		Sampson,Thomas,Jr.	1836	71	20 ME	
Rogers, John	1836	22	27 ME		Sanborn, Albert	1850	19	28 NY	
Rogers, John	1845	26	26 NY		Sanborn, James	1864	34	27 ME	
Rogers, John	1858	38	19 ME		Sandborn, Daniel	1836	18	40 ME	
Rogers, Joseph	1839	28	18 ME		Sanford, Victory	1859	44	31 NY	
Rogers, Nathl. L.	1856	17	19 ME		Santander, Manuel	1854	247	21 LA	
Rogers, Robert	1853	185	39 ME		Sarbell, James T.	1864	67	25	Norway
Rogers, William	1855	211	19 ME		Savage, Albert G.	1849	430	18 ME	
Rolley, Andrew J.	1854	9	27 ME		Savage, Charles B.	1862	12	20 ME	
Rollin, Edward	1842	69	26 VT		Savage, John	1856	124	32 NY	
Rollins, Abel	1836	8	25 ME		Savage, Leonard	1847	13	22 ME	
Rollins, Convers	1849	411	24 ME		Savage, William J.	1848	128	18 ME	
Rollins, Elbany	1845	111	19 ME		Savels, John	1848	240	21 ME	
Rollins, George W.	1855	53	16 MA		Sawyer, Charles	1853	116	15 ME	
Rollins, Lemuel L.	1833	1	19 ME		Sawyer, Henry	1857	158	22 ME	
Rook, George W.	1847	188	21 ME		Sawyer, Isaac, Jr.	1849	187	36 ME	
Ross, Herman F.	1849	344	26 PA		Sawyer, James	1849	259	33 ME	
Ross, James	1850	51	47 MA		Sawyer, John	1845	34	39 ME	
Ross, John	1849	408	30 NY		Sawyer, Oliver	1857	89	39 ME	
Ross, Leander H.	1856	2	25 ME		Sawyer, Zenas	1849	68	23 ME	
Ross, Loami	1849	350	19 ME		Scanulan, Michael	1848	231	25 ME	
Ross, Noah A.	1853	117	18 CT		Schell, Charles F.	1854	161	20 NJ	
Ross, Peter	1861	21	22 PA		Schoonbeck, John H.	1849	46	28	Holland
Ross, Robert B.	1859	59	28 ME		Scollay, William	1849	25	19 ME	
Ross, Thomas	1850	133	22 ME		Scott, George E.	1847	124	19 ME	
Rothelle, Henry	1849	12	24 NY		Scott, William	1847	41	18 NY	
Rowe, Alexander	1857	77	23 ME		Scully, Alvin P. B.	1849	40	15 ME	
Rowe, Andrew J.	1856	104	16 ME		Sears, Moses	1864	47	22 ME	
Rowe, John	1859	32	24 ??		Sedgley, Fuller D.	1848	149	19 ME	
Royal, Thomas	1855	225	29 ME		Sedgley, John	1856	49	21 ME	
Rudolph, William E.	1848	204	20 ME		Sedgley, Noble M.	1857	113	21 ME	
Ruffell, William H.	1848	174	25 NY		Segeberg,ValentineV.	1863	17	18 ME	
Runnels, Elisha W.	1847	4	21 ME		Seiders, Charles A.	1858	87	54 ME	
Rush, Geo. W.	1856	190	20 ME		Seiders, Merrill	1861	3	20 ME	
Rush, Henry C.	1864	30	24 ME		Sewall, Arthur	1857	130	22 ME	
Rush, William B.	1857	152	26 ME		Sewall, Darius	1836	13 b	21 ME	
Russell, Arthur T.	1855	13	18 ME		Sewall, Frank	1858	62	21 ME	
Russell, Benjamin T.	1861	46	15 ME		Sewall, William H.	1862	27	20 ME	
Russell, Benjamin T.	1864	77	18 ME		Sewall, William M.	1850	141 b	23 ME	
Russell, Chalres A.	1842	103	17 ME		Shaw, Frank B.	1864	92	22 ME	
Russell, David	1853	174	21 ME		Shaw, George H.	1853	182	16 ME	
Russell, James	1864	24 b	30 MA		Shaw, John O.	1855	153	16 ME	
Russell, Nelson R.	1849	426	24 ME		Shaw, John S.	1842	100	19 ME	
Russell, William	1856	89	23 NY		Shaw, Joseph	1853	37	17 ME	
Russell, William	1864	38	25 MA		Shaw, Parmenio C.	1849	225	33 MA	
Ryan, James H.	1867	10	17 ME		Shaw, Thomas	1853	129	20 ME	
Ryan, Michael	1849	307	24 NH		Shea, Benjamin F.	1860	37	27 ME	
Ryan, Thomas	1855	118	33 ME		Shea, John	1849	289	29 LA	
Rynes, Thomas	1848	236	23 MA		Shea, Peter	1856	73	23 ME	
Salley, Thomas S.	1858	19	18 ME		Shea, Thomas	1857	157	17 ME	
Sallie, Dexter	1861	34	17 ME		Shea, William H.	1859	3	36 ME	
Sallie, Warren W.	1860	50	18 ME		Shehan, John	1854	37	28 ME	
Salsbury, Henry	1849	34	24 RI		Shelw, George W.	1849	382	21 ME	
Sampson, George F.	1861	29	18 ME		Shepard, Benjamin	1849	318	22 ME	
Sampson, James, Jr.	1855	141	22 ME		Shepard, Caleb H.	1859	58	18 ME	
Sampson, Randall	1861	31	20 ME		Shepard, William C.	1854	191	22 MD	

Sherlock, Joseph	1854	211	18 ME
Sherman, John D.W.	1854	141	16 ME
Sherman, Robert	1848	132	19 RI
Shirley, John	1848	53	16 ME
Shoobert, James	1861	52	29 NY
Shortliff, William	1850	127	28 MA
Shurtleff, Charles F.	1856	38	14 PA
Shurtliff, Edward	1854	43	17 NY
Sidd, Alanson L.	1855	144	28 PA
Silsby, Charles B.	1836	35	16 ME
Silsby, Joseph B.	1849	41	24 ME
Silsby, Oliver E.	1862	59	19 ME
Simmons, Albert	1857	146	20 ME
Simmons, Alonzo R.	1854	256	21 ME
Simmons, George	1847	175	28 ME
Simmons, Thomas	1850	96 b	23 PA
Simpson, Andrew	1855	1	36
Simpson, Asa M.	1849	254	24 ME
Simpson, Isaiah H.	1849	260	22 ME
Simpson, John H.	1848	144	22 ME
Simpson, Louis P.	1849	263	27 ME
Simpson, William	1850	107	28 ME
Sinclair, John	1847	56	24 MD
Sitler, Albert	1855	67	23 ME
Skelten, John J.	1863	30	18 ME
Skelton, Johnson J.	1864	14	19 ME
Skofield, Matthew	1857	37	51 ME
Skolfield, John T.	1859	93	21 ME
Skolfield, Thomas H.	1849	223	21 ME
Skolfield, William	1849	309	18 ME
Skolfield, Winthrop F.	1848	156	19 ME
Slade, George	1853	112	27 RI
Small, Alfred S.	1848	179	19 ME
Small, Artemas	1842	34	18 ME
Small, Ebenezer	1847	44	20 ME
Small, George B.	1839	153	20 ME
Small, George H.	1847	107	21 ME
Small, George H.	1839	154	20 ME
Small, George T.	1861	59	21 ME
Small, George W.	1855	34	20 ME
Small, Isaac	1853	86	19 ME
Small, James W.	1857	148	21 ME
Small, Joseph	1836	59	19 ME
Small, Lemuel	1839	162	25 ME
Small, Loring B.	1850	22	15 ME
Small, Nahum P.	1850	103	16 ME
Small, Nathaniel	1847	26	19 ME
Small, Sewall	1847	154	20 ME
Small, Simeon F.	1858	10	22 ME
Small, Solomon	1842	158	24 ME
Small, Thomas	1849	398	18 ME
Small, William H.	1855	77	18 ME
Small, William H.	1847	197	16 ME
Smith, Abraham	1845	43 b	36 NY
Smith, Charles	1847	62	35 PA
Smith, Charles	1855	226	23 ME
Smith, Charles B.	1861	50	27 ME
Smith, Charles W.	1842	68	26 CT
Smith, Eben R.	1836	131	23 MD
Smith, Frederick Wm.	1861	22	30 PA
Smith, George	1854	198	33 DE
Smith, George	1849	213	29 LA
Smith, George	1853	64	24 RI
Smith, George A.	1849	148	30 ME
Smith, George, Jr.	1836	39	23 MA
Smith, Henry	1863	35	46 ME
Smith, Henry S.	1839	30	23 ME
Smith, James	1842	116	22 ME
Smith, James	1855	143	20 ME
Smith, James	1855	212	28 ME
Smith, James	1855	131	22 LA
Smith, James A.	1854	119	16 ME
Smith, James A.	1864	41	26 ME
Smith, James A.	1861	78	23 ME
Smith, James L.	1857	11	20 ME
Smith, James L.	1854	66	35 MA
Smith, James P.	1847	25	21 ME
Smith, John	1845	49	30 NY
Smith, John	1845	71	23 PA
Smith, John	1848	46	17 ME
Smith, John	1854	125	19 NY
Smith, John	1853	88	16 ME
Smith, John	1855	120	25 MA
Smith, John	1856	184	22 ME
Smith, John G.	1847	117	22 NH
Smith, John P.	1842	94	26 ME
Smith, John T.	1855	47 b	25 ME
Smith, Joseph O.	1854	246	15 ME
Smith, Otis	1848	44	18 ME
Smith, Peter	1855	56	0 MA
Smith, Richard R., Jr.	1847	131	16 ME
Smith, Sydney	1839	135	21 MA
Smith, Thomas	1845	81	45 ME
Smith, Thomas	1855	237	22 MA
Smith, William	1855	62	22 ME
Smith, William	1855	52	17 ME
Smith, William	1842	24	33 VA
Smith, William	1858	41	27 NY
Smith, William B.	1849	103	45 ME
Smith, William H.	1860	17	18 ME
Smith, William M.	1853	93	20 ME
Snell, Charles F.	1860	52	17 MA
Snipe, Charles H.	1855	195	27 ME
Snow, Gilbert	1853	183	19 ME
Snow, Henry P.	1849	388	21 MA
Snow, Henry R.	1849	314	19 NY
Snow, John S.	1854	54	15 ME
Snow, Merritt	1849	308	18 ME
Snow, Nathl. G.	1855	170	19 ME
Snow, Rodney	1853	179	16
Snow, Stephen	1863	8	20 ME
Snowman, Alexander	1862	3	24 ME

Name	Year	No.	Age/State	Name	Year	No.	Age/State
Soule, Lemuel H.	1853	114	19 ME	Stanwood, Frank L.	1859	30	15 ME
Soule, Lewis J.	1854	116	25 ME	Staples, George	1848	181	23 LA
Southard, Alexander	1842	127	18 ME	Staples, John	1847	111	18 ME
Southard, Henry	1858	13	24 ME	Stebbins, Silas	1849	399	29 MA
Southard, Sewall	1847	101	24 ME	Stein, George	1849	288	34 NY
Southard, William	1847	97	0 ME	Stetson, Benjamin F.	1858	32	34 ME
Sparks, David C.	1850	24	17 ME	Stetson, Stephen C.	1853	51	21 ME
Sparks, John H.	1845	42	17 ME	Stevens, Albert Henry	1864	46	17 ME
Sparks, Joseph L.	1853	207	12 ME	Stevens, Barzillai	1855	3	19 ME
Spaulding, Daniel	1849	94	26 ME	Stevens, Daniel	1853	204	16
Spaulding, William	1842	11	38 ME	Stevens, Daniel	1857	44	48 ME
Spear, Charles	1848	78	31 ME	Stevens, George W.	1845	3	25 MA
Spear, James	1849	48	42 MA	Stevens, James T. R.	1865	61	15 ME
Spear, James H.	1850	15	22 ME	Stevens, John	1847	84	18 CT
Spear, Robert	1839	167	18 ME	Stevens, John F.	1849	40	21 ME
Spear, Robert L.	1854	173	16 ME	Stevens, Joseph E.	1864	35	21 ME
Spencer, John	1849	407	27 NC	Stevens,Nehemiah L.	1857	150	20 ME
Spencer, Joseph W.	1849	194	25 ME	Stevens, Theodore A.	1863	9	19 ME
Spencer, Levi	1860	24	18 ME	Stevens, Washington	1836	56	21 ME
Spencer, Samuel	1836	109	23 ME	Stevens, Wm. H.	1856	175	18 ME
Spencer, William	1847	29	40 NY	Steward, Hiram L.	1849	166	22 ME
Spenney, James	1836	122	21 ME	Steward, James	1850	82	18 CT
Spinney, Ezra	1836	130	22 ME	Stewart, Alexander	1849	387	17 MA
Spinney, Milton	1867	4	21 ME	Stewart, Jacob	1836	41	22 ME
Spinney, Nelson	1836	112	26 ME	Stewart, William	1849	294	28 ME
Spinney, Palmer O.	1858	93	19 ME	Stickler, John H.	1839	79	28 NY
Spinney, Thomas	1853	160	25	Stilkey, Andrew J.	1861	69	23 ME
Sprague, Edwin E.	1865	31	19 ME	Stilkey, William	1853	41	20 ME
Sprague, Gilmore P.	1853	198	19 ME	Stilphen, Leonard D.	1864	58	22 ME
Sprague, James A.	1861	12	18 ME	Stilphin, Orison, Jr.	1860	18	20 ME
Sprague, John	1864	20	14 ME	Stilphin, Thomas	1864	45	35 ME
Sprague, John L.	1862	44	19 ME	Stinchfield, Amasa P.	1842	17	24 ME
Sprague, John N.	1864	6	23 ME	Stinsin, John A.	1853	72	20 ME
Sprague, Mitchell D.	1854	266	22 ME	Stinson,CharlesG.M.	1842	15	23 ME
Sprague, Samuel E.	1848	186	16 ME	Stinson, Ephraim E.	1839	138	21 ME
Sprague, William P.	1857	32	22 ME	Stinson, Frederick M.	1860	60	19 ME
Spratt, Stephen	1849	303	21 ME	Stinson, John F.	1855	194	25 ME
Sprayer, Watson	1839	116	18 ME	Stinson, Samuel P.	1845	131	27 ME
Spring, John C.	1856	5	24 NY	Stitler, Richard	1849	99	24 NY
Springer, John W.	1849	371	30 ME	Stocks, Wm.	1836	43	39 NY
Springer, Parlin	1842	142	33 ME	Stone, Solomon	1849	227	58 ME
Springer, Stephen	1856	67	18 ME	Storer, David W.	1836	25	15 ME
Sproul, Henry	1856	103 b	25 MD	Stover, Enoch	1862	55	19 ME
Sproule, Rufus C.	1842	33	21 ME	Stover, John A.	1849	281	23 ME
St. Clir, Gilbert M.	1863	4	24 ME	Stow/Storn, William	1839	128	22 NJ
St.Clair, Louis	1848	88	25 MA	Stowell, Joseph N.	1867	7	28 RI
Stacey, Charles A.	1861	53	21 ME	Straker, Thomas	1854	127	23 LA
Stacey, Samuel W.	1861	65	19 ME	Stratton, James	1847	205	23 NY
Stacy, John H.	1854	66	17 ME	Streeter, Henry B.	1849	366	25 VT
Stacy, Oliver W.	1854	64	18 ME	Strickley, John	1849	343	28 ME
Standish, Charles L.	1855	231	21 ME	Strout, Obed	1854	32	21 ME
Standish, Miles	1853	50	0 ME	Strout, William	1858	49	51 ME
Stanhoke, George W.	1847	179	20 ME	Stuard, John	1848	219	21 ME
Stanley, Alexander	1855	74	41 ME	Stuart, James	1845	20	20 ME
Stanley, James F.	1858	59	18 ME	Stuart, William H.	1848	235 b	26 ME
Stanwood, Edwin	1853	99	16 ME	Sturdivant, John Q.A.	1854	168	25 MA

Sturgis, Charles M.	1860	25	19 ME	
Suas, Peter	1859	1	m 22 ME	
Sullivan, Thomas	1849	95	21 MA	
Sutton, William H.	1847	34	28 ME	
Swaim, Otis R.	1859	51	32 ME	
Swan, Fenno B.	1858	89	35 ME	
Swan, Oliver F.	1848	126	53 ME	
Swan, William	1850	52	b 22 NY	
Swan, Wm. Alonzo	1850	91	20 ME	
Swanton, George W.	1862	38	17 ME	
Swanton, Henry A.	1854	96	21 ME	
Swanton, William	1857	162	27 ME	
Swasey, Zina H.	1842	153	15 ME	
Sweetland, Edward	1845	90	20 ME	
Swett, Elvin C.	1862	4	20 ME	
Swett, Harvey	1854	210	44 ME	
Swett, Robert P.	1856	47	21 ME	
Swett, William S.	1842	90	20 ME	
Sylva, John	1865	52	40 AL	
Sylvester, Frank L.	1867	11	18 ME	
Sylvester, Henchman	1856	152	26 ME	
Sylvester, Isaac	1842	6	39 ME	
Sylvester, James	1856	176	18 ME	
Sylvester, Mark L.	1865	24	17 ME	
Sylvester, William	1857	102	25 ME	
Syms, William	1855	54	23 ME	
Synnott, Daniel	1862	53	25 ME	
Talbot, Charles W.	1855	101	16 ME	
Talbot, William	1854	115	38	England
Talbot, William	1865	62	54	England
Tallman, Charles C.	1857	69	15 ME	
Talpey, John H.	1855	142	20 ME	
Tappan, Thomas P.	1849	219	28 MA	
Tarbell, Charles W.	1856	154	15 ME	
Tarbox, Cornelius	1836	102	27 ME	
Tarbox, Orrington L.	1855	86	21 ME	
Tarbox, Zachariah	1842	117	24 ME	
Tayler, Josiah B.	1836	45	27 ME	
Taylor, Clement	1861	47	17 ME	
Taylor, Clemment	1860	35	56	Sweden
Taylor, Daniel	1848	160	23 ME	
Taylor, James C.	1850	38	28 ME	
Taylor, Marshal	1847	174	21 ME	
Taylor, Nathl. C	1864	78	20 ME	
Taylor, Samuel	1855	147	36 ME	
Taylor, Simeon	1859	49	20 ME	
Taylor, William	1853	49	26 ME	
Taylor, William	1845	25	40 MD	
Tebbets, John R.	1842	144	17 ME	
Tempest, Henry	1849	365	25 MA	
Templeton, John	1850	55	17 MA	
Tenney, Albert F.	1858	66	18 ME	
Tewell, Louson	1845	164	35 VT	
Thomas, Consider, Jr	1839	140	16 ME	
Thomas, Henry	1836	23	29 MA	
Thomas, Henry Al.	1848	12	44 ME	

Thomas, Isaac N.	1849	340	44 MA	
Thomas, James	1865	42	16 ME	
Thomas, John	1845	155	17 ME	
Thomas, John S.	1853	118	13 ME	
Thomas, Joseph A.	1858	45	27 ME	
Thomas, William Laws	1860	53	25 MA	
Thompson, Andrew J.	1854	74	20 ME	
Thompson, Charles W.	1858	44	34 ME	
Thompson, Christopher Jr.	1849	355	25 ME	
Thompson, Dixey W.	1858	43	18 ME	
Thompson, Edwin	1856	33	17 ME	
Thompson, Furber A.	1855	97	20 ME	
Thompson, George	1855	14	19 ME	
Thompson, George	1842	148	18 ME	
Thompson, Haty	1847	21	31 ME	
Thompson, Jacob	1848	108	22 PA	
Thompson, James L.	1861	62	18 ME	
Thompson, John	1861	17	45	Denmark
Thompson, John	1847	99	17 ME	
Thompson, John	1853	159	31 NY	
Thompson, John	1855	96	35 PA	
Thompson, John	1854	137	25 MA	
Thompson, John T.	1845	157	17 ME	
Thompson, Osborn	1854	77	16 ME	
Thompson, Richard E.	1849	205	21 ME	
Thompson, Willard	1858	18	20 ME	
Thompson, William	1864	66	21 ME	
Thompson, William	1862	61	25 NY	
Thompson, William	1854	152	23 MD	
Thork, Eliphalet	1856	83	20 ME	
Thorndike, Lewis H.	1865	8	18 ME	
Tibbete, Emerson	1842	163	18 ME	
Tibbets, Francis P.	1849	397	22 ME	
Tibbets, George M.	1856	40	18 ME	
Tibbets, Hartley L.	1864	88	21 ME	
Tibbets, Hugh S.	1855	64	20 ME	
Tibbets, James F.	1853	201	18 ME	
Tibbets, James M.	1861	8	21 ME	
Tibbets, James M.	1857	123	18 ME	
Tibbets, Thomas	1847	8	20 ME	
Tibbets, Thomas	1845	102	15 ME	
Tibbets, Timothy	1849	88	28 ME	
Tibbits, Ephraim	1842	53	24 ME	
Tibbits, Thomas	1836	83	22 ME	
Tiele, Nicholas G.	1860	32	26 ME	
Tilton, Charles	1853	39	26 ME	
Tobey, Enos M.	1859	48	20 ME	
Tobin, James	1847	43	19 PA	
Toby, William	1849	354	29 ME	
Todd, John P., Jr.	1858	58	17 ME	
Toothaker, George	1849	412	18 ME	
Toothaker, Jesse E.	1857	13	18 ME	
Toothaker, Samuel H.	1849	368	24 ME	
Toothaker, Seth	1850	35	18 ME	
Topman, George	1848	64	24 NY	

Totman, Elisha L.	1839	39	40 ME	
Totman, William H.	1855	155	21 ME	
Tow, David A.	1854	219	29 ME	
Tower, John K.	1849	420	17 ME	
Townsend, George	1861	27	22 ME	
Townsend, James H.	1855	60	23 NH	
Townsend, William	1842	18	28 NH	
Trask, George W.	1836	118	18 ME	
Trask, Joseph R.	1842	134	18 ME	
Travers, William	1836	9	18 ME	
Tribon, Frederic C.	1858	97	16 ME	
Trote, Job H.	1865	22	23 ME	
Trott, Frazier B.	1855	85	16 ME	
Trott, Joseph C.	1864	16	15 ME	
True, William L.	1855	95	18 ME	
Trufant, Ayers	1853	35	16 ME	
Trufant, John H.	1845	91	16 ME	
Trull, George F.	1858	100	18 ME	
Trull, John G.	1858	99	21 ME	
Trundy, Josiah T.	1864	63	19 ME	
Tucker, Charles	1857	87	24 MA	
Tucker, Charles E.	1864	31	15 ME	
Tucker, George W.	1859	81	15 ME	
Tunno, WilliamDellany	1842	87	27 SC	
Turner, Austin	1848	242	18 ME	
Turner, James	1849	9 b	25 MD	
Turner, Moses T.	1849	105	22 ME	
Turner, Owen	1842	162	15 ME	
Turner, Stephen W.	1848	50	22 ME	
Tuttle, Benj. F.	1849	177	23 ME	
Tuttle, John W.	1845	156	24 MA	
Tuttle, William H.	1849	167	30 ME	
Twining, Joseph	1850	49	27 MA	
Twombly, Charles W.	1853	191	32 ME	
Twombly, Daniel	1842	106	27 MA	
Varnam, Ralph	1857	93	19 ME	
Varney, Hix	1839	111	21 ME	
Varney, Robert	1848	21	26 ME	
Varnum, Chafin	1849	11	52 ME	
Varnum, Nathan	1836	62	18 ME	
Varnum, Ralph	1856	114	20 ME	
Verney, James W.	1858	9	24 ME	
Verney, Joseph S.	1857	76	19 ME	
Viannah, Francis J.	1850	88	39 NY	
Vickery, Parker N.	1855	59	19 ME	
Wade, A. D. S.	1863	6	30 MA	
Wade, Cleveland B.	1849	123	23 ME	
Wadley, George D.	1849	383	32 ME	
Wadsworth, William P.	1854	67	20 ME	
Waffle, James	1848	113	23 NY	
Waitt, John A.	1845	110	19 ME	
Wakefield, Charles E.	1862	58	23 ME	
Wakefield, James F.	1859	57	15 ME	
Wakefield, John	1855	168	29 MA	
Wakefield, John C.	1856	166	30 MA	
Walbridge, Porter	1850	80	21 CT	
Walde, Turner	1839	99	24 ME	
Walde, WinthropTurner	1839	99	24 ME	
Walker, Albion W.	1849	51	25 ME	
Walker, Benjamin	1858	84	21 ME	
Walker, George	1849	93	29 PA	
Walker, James E.	1853	104	22 ME	
Walker, John	1849	52	23 ME	
Walker, William	1849	107	22 ME	
Wallace, Absalom	1850	8	22 ME	
Wallace, Almon	1847	22	17 ME	
Wallace, Bradbury P.	1849	362	16 ME	
Wallace, William	1839	24	17 ME	
Wallace, William B.	1849	160	25 ME	
Wallander, Charles	1854	46	45	Sweden
Ward, Albion	1853	98	17 ME	
Ward, Francis	1855	88	24 MA	
Ward, George R.	1864	49	21 ME	
Ward, Joel	1853	176	19 ME	
Ward, Martin E.	1855	11	19 ME	
Ward, Thomas	1861	66	20 ME	
Ward, William H.	1857	120	22 ME	
Ware, James	1853	130	20 NY	
Ware, James H.	1857	5	18 ME	
Warner, William	1850	70	30 CT	
Warren, Edwin R.	1858	77	19 ME	
Warren, James	1855	239	23 MA	
Warren, James P.	1857	10	18 ME	
Warren, John	1849	321	24 ME	
Warring, B. L.	1849	361	29 ma	
Washburn, Allen H.	1854	263	19 ME	
Washburn, John	1848	84	27 MD	
Waterhouse, Frank K.	1855	197	25 ME	
Waters, Hiram	1854	258	22 CT	
Waters, Luke	1853	22	19 NY	
Waters, Mountsier	1842	85	30 MA	
Waters, Samuel L.	1842	137	18 ME	
Watson, George	1845	39	37 ME	
Watson, Sanford	1856	66	17 ME	
Watt, James O.	1848	205	25 ME	
Watts, Edward	1845	99	26 NY	
Watts, Samuel, Jr.	1839	165	15 ME	
Wave, Hiram	1848	129	24 ME	
Weaver, John	1854	194	36 RI	
Webb, Frank J.	1857	58	20 ME	
Webb, Henry, Jr. B.	1839	137	17 ME	
Webb, Robert	1848	105	22 MA	
Webb, Rufus	1855	186	24 ME	
Webber, Amasa	1860	49	20 ME	
Webber, Charles	1850	67	31 MO	
Webber, Dexter	1845	22	22 ME	
Webber, Ira H.	1847	132	22 ME	
Webber, Rufus	1861	24	45 ME	
Webber, Stephen J.	1845	21	17 ME	
Webster, Francis E.	1849	114	22 ME	
Webster, Hiram	1842	159	26 ME	
Weeden, William A.	1845	6	31 NY	

Weeks, Albert	1849	76	16 ME		White, Lawson W.	1853	38	16 ME
Weeks, Francis	1854	76	23 ME		White, Mark	1855	91	23 ME
Weeks, George S.	1862	11	24 ME		White, Samuel	1855	87	19 ME
Weeks, Rufus B.	1862	24	19 ME		White, Thomas	1850	12	21 VA
Welch, Edward	1853	224	24 ME		White, Wm. H.	1857	50	22 ME
Welch, George W. M.	1845	88	16 ME		Whitehouse,E. Melvin	1858	11	20 ME
Welch, James	1853	20	22 ME		Whitehouse, William	1848	28	39 ME
Welch, John	1854	65	26 PA		Whitman, Parker M.	1839	79	16 ME
Welch, Pattrick	1854	113	25 ME		Whitmore, Franklin D.	1861	72	22 ME
Welch, Samuel B.	1853	192	25 ME		Whitmore, Jacob D.	1842	86	17 ME
Welch, William	1853	10	18 ME		Whitmore, Nathl. M.	1849	394	16 ME
Weld, William L.	1842	77	17 ME		Whitmore, Patrick D.	1849	347	17 ME
Weldon, James	1859	8	19 NH		Whitmore,StephenW.	1848	49	20 ME
Wellman, Eben	1853	79	17 ME		Whitney, Alpheus	1864	84	24 ME
Wells, Fedenc L.	1853	80	18 ME		Whitney, Hiram	1853	131	22 ME
Wells, George G.	1854	61	30 ME		Whitney, Samuel M.	1847	103	16 ME
Wells, John P.	1854	55	21 ME		Whitney, William H.	1856	64	18 ME
Wentworth, Albert P.	1849	229	19 ME		Whittaker, William	1859	50	26 MA
Wentworth,George R.	1845	126	23 ME		Whittam, James P.	1864	50	21 ME
Wentworth, James	1854	3	21 ME		Whitten, William S.	1857	42	20 ME
Wentworth,William M.	1849	381	23 ME		Whittley, James	1849	284	24 NH
West, George N.	1865	38	19 ME		Wiggin, Samuel	1849	410	18 ME
Westin, John	1849	182	25 ME		Wight, Timothy V.	1857	126	25 ME
Westman, Andrew	1839	87	19 ME		Wilcox, Charles L.	1858	72	16 ME
Westman, Peter	1855	214	31 ME		Wilcox, Joseph	1847	208 b	22 RI
Weston, Rufus B.	1849	375	26 ME		Wilcox, Rufus E. B.	1850	56	22 NY
Weston, Samuel T.	1850	90	29 ME		Wilcox, Thomas R.	1848	221	22 ME
Weston, William H.	1848	171	39 RI		Wilde, Isaiah N.	1848	197	17 ME
Wetherbee, Alfred H.	1860	26	18 ME		Wildes, Alonzo P.	1857	23	18 ME
Weymouth,George M.	1859	41	34 ME		Wildes, Asa E.	1849	158	20 ME
Weymouth, Orrin	1849	328	17 ME		Wildes, Daniel B.	1847	167	20 ME
Whalen, Daniel	1842	168	25 ME		Wildes, Philip H.	1839	40	19 ME
Wheeler,AlexanderR.	1853	48	27 ME		Wildes, Silas C.	1849	352	21 ME
Wheeler, Benjn. F.	1848	82	27 ME		Wildes, William H.	1855	189	21 ME
Wheeler, Charles	1848	95	25 MA		Wildes, Zina H.	1845	15	20 ME
Wheeler, Charles K.	1856	157	16 ME		Wilkinson,CharlesM.L.	1858	104	36 ME
Wheeler, Charles T.	1857	134	17 ME		Willett, Charles E.	1856	185	25 ME
Wheeler, George W.	1854	25	39 NY		Willey, Charles	1859	9	17 ME
Wheeler, John	1857	161	48 ME		Williams, Almon H.	1863	2	15 ME
Whelpley, George N.	1856	144	22 MA		Williams, Andrew	1858	52	22 CT
Whilimons,Charles A.	1854	135	17 xx		Williams, Benjamin	1853	119	30 MA
White, Bradford	1836	63	20 ME		Williams, Charles	1845	67	16 ME
White, Calvin G.	1839	161	15 ME		Williams, Charles H.	1862	6	22 ME
White, Edward J.	1839	166	20 ME		Williams, Daniel	1849	190	16 MD
White, Franklin	1860	41	25 ME		Williams, David P.	1842	109	21 ME
White, Frederick W.	1850	151	19 ME		Williams, Drummond	1842	14	24 ME
White, George H.	1854	184	18 ME		Williams, Gilman L.	1849	320	20 ME
White, Gustavus A.	1849	218	20 ME		Williams, James	1836	124	21 MA
White, Henry	1853	1	20 OH		Williams, James	1842	54 b	25 PA
White, Henry L.	1845	149	23 ME		Williams, James	1855	183	24 ME
White, James	1847	61	21 NY		Williams, John	1856	132	40 ME
White, James	1856	87	22 MA		Williams, John	1853	31	20 ME
White, James H.	1864	8	21 MD		Williams, John	1850	83	44 NY
White, James W.	1849	384	24 ME		Williams, John	1849	8	20 ME
White, John	1848	10	27 ME		Williams, John	1845	137	16 MA
White, John	1857	53	24 ME		Williams, John	1849	230	30 NY

Williams, John	1836	61	27 MA	
Williams, John	1858	40	25 ME	
Williams, John H.	1845	35	b	26 PA
Williams, John, Jr.	1853	186	22 ME	
Williams, Joseph D.	1860	31	17 ME	
Williams, Loring	1845	118	18 ME	
Williams, Peter	1853	157	28 NY	
Williams, Samuel J.	1853	187	18 ME	
Williams, Stephen A.	1862	44	22 ME	
Williams, William	1849	39	42 NH	
Williams, William H.	1845	97	21 ME	
Williams, William L.	1853	120	17 ME	
Williams, Wm.	1836	80	20 NY	
Williamson, Richard	1853	26	65 PA	
Williamson, William	1849	26	30 ME	
Willis, Frederick A.	1862	8	17 ME	
Willis, James H.	1855	123	20 ME	
Wilson, Banjamin B.	1849	251	26 ME	
Wilson, Charles	1839	91	21 MA	
Wilson, Charles	1853	90	28 PA	
Wilson, George	1854	153	25 MA	
Wilson, George	1850	18	19 NY	
Wilson, Henry A.	1853	180	16 ME	
Wilson, Horace E.	1860	36	17 ME	
Wilson, James	1849	91	24 FL	
Wilson, John	1842	91	20 RI	
Wilson, John	1845	100	25 PA	
Wilson, John	1854	70	22 NY	
Wilson, John	1853	15	28 MA	
Wilson, John	1854	34	24 ME	
Wilson, John	1850	106	22 ME	
Wilson, John	1858	37	26	France
Wilson, John	1864	86	28 ME	
Wilson, John	1859	43	24 MA	
Wilson, John D.	1857	117	16 ME	
Wilson, John H.	1845	18	23 PA	
Wilson, Rufus	1839	149	21 ME	
Wilson, Samuel	1856	51	28 ME	
Wilson, Thomas	1850	143	m	24 MD
Wilson, Thomas	1864	10	29 NY	
Wilson, Washington D.	1849	291	16 ME	
Wilson, William	1854	69	23 MA	
Wilson, William H.	1839	134	b	21 MD
Winchenback, Banj.	1859	20	34 ME	
Wing, Isaac H.	1847	178	15 ME	
Winslow, Jesse	1839	120	16 ME	
Winslow, Job	1839	139	24 ME	
Winslow, John	1854	12	19 ME	
Winslow, Lorenzo D.	1845	142	17 ME	
Winter, Francis A.	1839	102	19 ME	
Winter, James M.	1836	94	19 ME	
Winter, William P.	1849	191	27 ME	
Winters, William	1845	12	38 ME	
Witchell, William	1849	429	30 PA	
Withington, Samuel J.	1854	24	39 VT	
Wolcott, Lorenzo	1839	168	19 ME	
Wolston, Charles H.	1861	13	16 ME	
Wood, George	1855	213	32 PA	
Wood, Jacob	1858	47	36 MA	
Wood, James	1854	23	26 MA	
Woodbury, James	1856	90	18 ME	
Woodman, Nathaniel	1842	73	35 NH	
Woods, Nicholas	1860	44	35 ME	
Woodside, Adam	1842	105	20 ME	
Woodside, Charles P.	1859	98	18 ME	
Woodside, George A.	1859	31	19 ME	
Woodside, James	1849	42	24 ME	
Woodward, Beriah L.	1862	47	19 ME	
Woodward, John	1842	123	30 ME	
Woodward, Newell	1849	196	26 ME	
Woodward, William C.	1839	85	19 ME	
Wooster, David	1859	10	44 ME	
Work, Abel E.	1854	44	19 ME	
Work, Asaph	1849	278	29 ME	
Work, Oscar	1857	20	15 ME	
Work, Thomas L.	1842	154	18 ME	
Wormwood, T. G.	1849	412	20 ME	
Worthley, Emory	1849	315	19 ME	
Woton, Joseph	1853	67	17 ME	
Wotton, Moses	1855	241	22 ME	
Wotton, William	1849	66	21 ME	
Wright, Jackson L.	1849	108	21 ME	
Wright, John	1858	48	22 NY	
Wright, John	1864	68	31 ME	
Wright, Joseph E.	1849	60	26 ME	
Wright, Lemuel	1853	161	38 NY	
Wright, Llewellyn A.	1857	107	22 ME	
Wright, Llewellyn A.	1863	19	27 ME	
Wright, Silas	1848	65	23 ME	
Wright, Thomas E.	1858	51	23 NY	
Wright, William	1854	85	25 MA	
Wylie, David R.	1857	131	28	N. S.
Wylie, Robert E.	1855	188	21	NovaScotia
Wylie, Robert E.	1856	74	22	Nova Scotia
Wyman, Charles	1850	27	24 ME	
Wyman, Charles W.	1854	162	17 MA	
Wyman, Francis A.	1842	169	19 ME	
Wyman, Henry T.	1860	48	19 ME	
Wyman, James G.	1857	136	19 ME	
Wyman, Llewellyn S.	1848	9	16 ME	
Wyman, Sumner	1849	370	26 ME	
Yates, Robert	1856	12	25 ME	
Yeaton, Seth H.	1854	269	17 ME	
York, Edward	1845	66	21 ME	
York, Isaac	1842	26	21 ME	
York, Samuel F.	1849	13	22 ME	
Young, Andrew	1854	114	20 NY	
Young, Charles	1850	34	20 NY	
Young, Ellis H.	1856	135	26 ME	
Young, John	1861	73	37 ME	
Young, Nehemiah N.	1861	86	17 ME	
Young, Robert	1857	132	24 ME	

The State of Alabama, } ss.
City and County of Mobile.

Be it Known, *That on this* 28 *day of* May in *the year of our Lord, one thousand eight hundred and* Forty five *Before me,* Joshua S. Secor, *a* **Notary Public,** *duly commissioned and sworn, in and for said County, and dwelling in the* City *of* Mobile, *personally came* George Hawes *who made oath that he is* A CITIZEN OF THE UNITED STATES, *and that he was born in* Barnstable *in the State of* Massachusetts, *that he is* twenty one *years of age; and, that he is* five *feet* eleven *inches in height, has* brown *hair,* light *complexion, and that he has* blue *eyes.*

And, also, at the same time, personally appeared before me the said Notary, F. W Backstrom *who, also, made oath that he is well acquainted with the above named* George Hawes *and that he verily believes that he is a native of* Barnstable *in the State of* Massachusetts

F. W Backstrom   George Hawes

Given *under my hand and Seal Notarial, at Mobile, this* 28 *day of* May *A. D. 184* 5

J. S. Secor
Notary Public

Proofs of Citizenship

Port of Mobile, Alabama

This is an index to the 865 proofs of citizenship submitted by seamen applying for a Seaman's Protection Certificate between 1819 to 1859. Abstracts are available for 1837 to 1860. These proofs, as well as the abstracts, contain many gaps.

The records are in chronological order, more or less, by year so it is necessary for the researcher to look through all the records in the appropriate year.

Special care must be taken in using these records. The handwriting of one official who wrote about half the documents is almost illegible so researcher will find many oddly spelled names in the index. Others are much easier to read. You will find discrepancies between the name of the seaman on the face of the document compared to the one on the back, for example, William on the front and Thos. on the back. The former is more likely to be accurate.

Mobile was a cosmopolitan port and there are 32 naturalized seamen, and seamen from most of the eastern seaboard states. While the forms often fail to provide the nationality of foreign born seamen, they usually give the date and place of naturalization.

As one would expect in the deep South in this period, there are almost no men of color — there is one seaman with colored complexion and two Indians. Most proofs do not indicate color.

Proofs of Citizenship

Port of Mobile, Alabama

Data order: Name, Year, Age, Color, State or Country

Name	Year	Age	Color	State or Country
Abbot, Thomas	1826	19	NY	
Abbott, Martin L.	1838	30	VA	
Adams, Alpheus	1838	26	ME	
Adams, Samuel B.	1837	21	MA	
Albro, William	1829	18	RI	
Alexander, George	1837	16	RI	
Alexander, Joseph	1833	28	MA	
Allen,Andrew Jackson	1837	18	NJ	
Allen, James	1852	21	NY	
Allen, William	1838	23	NY	
Ames, Charles	1838	19	ME	
Ames, Granville	1857	22	MA	
Ames, James	1826	22	ME	
Anderson, Cone N.	1838	20	NY	
Anderson, John	1838	22		
Anderson, Nathaniel	1824	28	VA	
Anderson, Peter	1826	44	PA	
Anderson, Peter	1827	24	MA	
Anderson, William	1825	26	MD	
Andrews, John	1833	28	PA	
Annis, Thomas	1850	27	MA	
Arnold, Swn H.	1840	17	RI	
Asworth, Charles	1844	35	MD	
Attwater, John K.	1827	25	CT	
Austin, Valentine	1838	21	NY	
Awkward, Anthony	1827	23	DC	
Babcock, Elisha	1826	23	RI	
Babcock, George W.	1857	25	NJ	
Babcock,Nathaniel C.	1857	23	NJ	
Baker, Benjamin	1843	25	NY	
Baker, Erastus	1838	25	CT	
Baldwin, Peter	1857	17	CT	
Balek, Wm.	1851	40		naturalized
Ballard, Daniel B.	1829	24	ME	
Barnard, Alexander	1851	19	MA	
Barrett, John D.	1827	18	MA	
Barss, David	1856	40	MA	
Barstow, Caleb	1855	20	NY	
Bartels, Frederick	1845	0	NY	
Bartlett, Frederick	1840	24	NH	
Barton, Benjamin	1826	27	LA	
Bassett, Sylvester W.	1853	0		
Bastin, John	1826	0		
Batchelder,William F.	1828	29	MA	
Bathnick, Josiah	1838	25	MA	
Battle, Nathan W.	1820	22	NC	
Beasleay, Charles	1827	36	MD	
Beile, Francis	1844	33		naturalized
Berry, Ebenezer	1837	20	RI	
Bexter, Ebenezer	1855	26	MA	
Biddle, George W.	1826	17	PA	
Blackford, John	1821	32	MA	
Blanchard, Elbridge G.	1838	23	ME	
Blethen, Nathaniel	1827	41	ME	
Boay, William	1856	25	NY	
Boeger, Henry	1845	25	MD	
Bona, Emanuel	1855	24	PA	
Bosburgh, Nelson	1845	27	NY	
Bostic, William	1833	24	PA	
Botsford, Isreal	1855	18	CT	
Bowdish, Peter	1826	32	NC	
Bowlin, Francis	1838	0		
Bowman, John	1826	40	NJ	
Boyd, Thomas	1826	28	NY	
Boyington, John	1827	17	ME	
Braagdon, George	1829	41	ME	
Brackway, Geo	1820	0		
Bradbury, James P.	1844	36	VT	
Bradley, Justus, Jr.	1828	27	CT	
Brainard, James M.	1833	17	CT	
Brierly, John	1821	36	SC	
briggs, Geo.	1851	17	MA	
Brighton?, John	1851	6	MA	
Broadfield, Benjh.	1858	22		naturalized
Brodley, John S.	1858	27	ME	
Brooks, Martin S.	1833	17	CT	
Brown, Charles	1855	25	MO	
Brown, Charles	1851	28		naturalized?
Brown, Elisha	1833	38	RI	
Brown, Elisha	1833	23	NH	
Brown, John	1827	38	NY	
Brown, John	1837	0	PA	
Brown, John W.	1829	25	MA	
Brown, Loyel	1821	20	NH	
Brown, William	1824	29	NY	
Brown, William	1821	30	NY	
Brown, William	1829	49	MA	
Brown, William	1825	29	NY	
Bryer, Jeremiah	1833	27	ME	
Bugger, Nicholas	1850	28	NY	
Burger, George H.	1827	33	MD	
Burns, John S.	1840	16	MA	

Name	Year	Age	State	Note
Burns, William	1827	28	MD	
Burrill, Ebenezer	1829	23	MA	
Burrows, Charles H.	1857	29	CT	
Burrows, James	1840	27	ME	
Burrus, James	1845	41	NY	
Burton, Jacob Charles	1840	30	NY	
Buxton, John H.	1851	30	MA	
Cahaor/Calson, Joshua	1857	43		
Caldwell, Tristra B.	1838	19	MA	
Calhoun, James	1825	27	SC	
Call, George	1825	31	ME	
Callaghan, Jeremiah	1855	24	NY	
Callaghan, William	1851	24	ME	
Callett, Herbert	1856	20	RI	
Cambridge, Indenib A.	1857	50	DE	
Cameron, Allen	1850	17	ME	
Campbell, James	1821	20	NY	
Campion, Edward	1855	22	NY	
Canr/Carr, James	1827	28	NY	
Caravan, James	1842	25	MA	
Carr, Richard	1845	22	NY	
Carrell, Thomas	1845	29		Great Britain
Carrington, John	1854	14	MS	
Carroll, Martin	1856	17		
Carson, Abraham	1837	28	NY	
Carson, Baker	1837	22	NJ	
Cartiss, Harrison	1843	22	CT	
Caswell, Joseph	1822	18		
Cedar, Andrew	1854	30	PA	
Center, Enoch	1827	27		
Chandler, Henry	1842	19	MA	
Chaples, Samuel	1845	19	ME	
Charles, David	1845	0	NY	
Chilcott, George W.	1857	28	ME	
Chipman, Stephen S.	1855	22	MA	
Christian, John	1826	44	MD	
Church, Thomas	1826	25	CT	
Clark, Ebenezer	1824	24	NY	
Clark, Ebenezer	1824	24	NY	
Clark, Henry	1827	26	NY	
Clark, Henry	1856	25	VA	
Clark, John	1822	19	ME	
Clark, Thomas	1824	20	RI	
Cleman, Hugh M.	1820	0	PA	
Clough, William	1833	20	NH	
Coats, H. Wyatt	1845	21	NY	
Cobb, Isaac M.	1829	27	ME	
Cochran, William	1857	23	NY	
Cogswell, Charle Henry	1851	15	NY	
Colby, Nathan	1824	0	MA	
Coleman, Wm.	1855	39	MA	
Colins, Daniel	1838	27	ME	
Collie, John	1856	25		naturalized
Collins, Edward	1855	21	NY	
Colton, Peter	1838	20	NY	
Connor, Charles	1824	24	MA	
Cooper, Peter	1851	24	MA	
Corley, Edward	1829	17	NY	
Cornwell, John W.	1827	23	NY	
Corte, Francis	1821	21	LA	
Cota, Alexander	1843	20	ME	
Cowing, Charles	1828	28	ME	
Cowles, Freedom H.	1845	20	NY	
Crandle, William	1824	25	ME	
Crannell, Robert	1828	29	CT	
Crawford, Stephen H.	1857	27		
Creighton, William	1838	25	MA	
Crocker, George	1820	0	MA	
Crocker, William H.	1855	20	NY	
Cummings, Charles	1851	18	ME	
Curtis, Leno	1843	57		naturalized
Cushman, Charles	1845	22	NH	
Daily, John	1845	30		naturalized
Dale, John	1821	39		
Davidson, Calvin	1845	21	LA	
Davis, John	1838	22		
Davis, John M. B.	1840	23	MA	
Davis, Samuel R.	1833	18	NY	
Dawson, Brooks	1820	15	VA	
Dean, Charles	1820	34	ME	
Dean, John	1838	28	NY	
Dearing, James C.	1838	31	MA	
Deary, John	1854	27		Ireland
Delano, Ephraim	1833	28	ME	
Demaris, James	1855	18	NJ	
Devarzey, Charles	1824	30	MD	
Dexter, John	1821	30	PA	
DeYampert, Thomas J.L	1853	19	AL	
Dinslow, Abner	1827	16	ME	
Dixon, John W.	1838	24	ME	
Dixon, Thomas	1826	34	NY	
Doan, William H.	1827	15	CT	
Doane, Freeman	1826	24	MA	
Dockendorff, James	1826	0	ME	
Dockham, Henry	1844	19	ME	
Docton, George	1855	25	NY	
Dodge, Samuel	1827	23	RI	
Dominick, John	1820	45	LA	
Donell, Samuel W.	1853	0		
Donnally, Michael	1840	20	PA	
Dougherty, Charles	1824	32	PA	
Dow, Levi	1837	42	MA	
Down, George	1826	25	MD	
Downe, Benjamin B.	1837	34	ME	
Dubois, Lewis	1826	15	NY	
Dulin, Gerand	1829	33	DC	
Dumie, Edwd. S.	1853	18	AL	
Duncan, John	1845	23	NY	

Dunlap, Alexander	1826	23	NH		French, George Roul.	1828	19	MA
Dunn, Mordicai	1829	0	NJ		French, Mathew	1844	42	Ireland
Dunn, William	1855	16	NY		French, William	1855	25	PA
Dunton, Daniel	1842	27	MA		Frost, Nathaniel	1828	23	MD
Dwelly, James L.	1851	23	ME		Fullerton, John	1851	18	ME
Egan, Charles	1827	38	PA		Fulls, Samuel	1859	18	ME
Eichner, William	1828	27	OH		Gage, Robert	1851	30	NY
Eldrige, James	1840	27	MA		Gallagher, Robert	1854	18	NY
Elliott, Thomas N.	1833	44	ME		Gammans, Earl	1838	30	MA
Ellison, John	1827	21	MA		Gardiner, Benjamin F.	1828	23	CT
Ellneas?, Samuel	1853	0	MD		Garity, Charles	1851	29	PA
Emerson, John	1826	0	ME		Garrison, Wm.	1855	17	NJ
Emery, Hugh W.	1828	24	ME		Garvin, John	1837	35	NY
Emery, Thomas	1829	25	NC		Gates, Warren	1820	21	MA
Enderson, William	1857	24	ME		Geers, Thomas	1828	18	MA
Engelnan, John	1855	0	naturalized		George,James homas	1845	14	AL
Eslava, Thomas	1845	16	AL		Georgeies, John	1844	26	NJ
Everett, David B.	1845	19	ME		Gerishen, Charles	1822	20	NY
Fairall, James	1845	21	MA		Gibbs, Joshua E.	1855	17	MA
Falcon, Francis	1845	55	naturalized		Gilbanles, Benjamin	1850	0	NY
Fales?, William H.	1829	22	ME		Giles, Arthur	1838	16	ME
Farris, Augustus	1854	24	MA		Gillespie, Robert	1838	28	MA
Feekill, Jacob	1833	18	MA		Godfrey, Amos	1838	27	NJ
Feely, Peter	1838	25	NY		Goodspeed,Benjamin	1820	18	MA
Fellows, Moses	1827	26	NH		Googins, W. B.	1854	19	MA
Ferguson, William	1845	31	NY		Gordon, Banjn.	1844	27	MD
Finley, Charles	1851	23	PA		Gould, Joseph	1829	23	ME
Finney, Thomas H.	1828	23	VA		Gower, John H.	1827	24	ME
Fish, Andrew Lovell	1840	20	MA		Graff, Joseph	1851	26	Italy
Fisher, John	1854	25	naturalized		Granniss, Horatio	1824	36	CT
Fisher, Wm.	1852	22	MA		Green, Albert	1840	17	RI
Flaherty,ThomasHenry	1855	30	NY		Green, Daniel	1854	21	NY
Fletcher, James	1840	26	ME		Green, Ebenezer G.	1843	30	MA
Flinn, Morris	1845	25	NY		Green, Herman H.	1825	23	NH
Fobes, Andrew J.	1845	19	MA		Green, William	1820	0	NY
Foley, Samuel	1851	20	CT		Grover, Thomas D.	1827	15	PA
Folsom, William	1840	25	ME		Groverman, Frederic	1826	30	VA
Fontelieous, Jean	1837	0	MS		Grusk, Nathaniel	1824	25	MA
Forbes, Charles	1844	18	CT		Hackett, Richard	1827	30	ME
Foreman, John	1833	35	MA		Hadley, John A.	1837	36	ME
Foreman, Robert	1826	33	VA		Hadwin, JamesWash.	1840	48	RI
Forsman, Wm.	1853	0	CT		Haford, Obediah	1837	20	ME
Forster, Wesley	1855	23	MD		Hagget, George	1827	21	MA
Forsyth, William	1827	16	CT		Haines, John	1826	20	PA
Fort, Charles	1856	19	NJ		Haines, Robert O.	1833	23	NJ
Fosdick, Philip	1827	25	MA		Hale, George Rhodes	1833	13	RI
Foster, James W.	1857	23	MA		Hall, Elijah	1838	14	ME
Foster, John	1822	22	NY		Hall, James	1820	16	MA
Foster, John	1833	0	Ireland		Hall, James H.	1851	20	ME
Foster, Solomon	1838	23	ME		Hall, John	1851	22	ME
Fountaine, Frances	1829	34	LA		Hall/Hull, William	1827	36	NH
Fox, James W.	1825	27	ME		Hamilton, Joseph	1824	24	NY
Frazier, John	1838	18	MD		Hampton, Nathan	1851	39	ME
Fredericks, Charles	1845	30	MA		Hannah, Samuel M.	1820	36	PA

Harding, Wm. L.	1838	19	MD		Howes, Charles S. F.	1853	21	MA
Hardy, Joseph	1842	17	ME		Howes, Joel	1837	13	MA
Harker, John C.	1838	34	NC		Hubbard, Benjamin	1829	30	ME
Harris, Jabez	1827	24	MD		Hubbard, Isaac	1827	28	ME
Harris, Jesse	1825	27	ME		Huldon, Parker N.	1856	17	
Harris, John	1840	28	NY		Hume, Nicholas	1827	40	MA
Harris, William R.	1845	24	CT		Huns, Albert	1855	21	NY
Harrison, William	1845	23	MA		Hyland, William	1825	23	ME
Hart, James	1838	35	DC		Ingalls, Benjamin	1827	25	ME
Hartshorn, Nathaniel	1838	18	ME		Jack, Thomas B.	1824	26 I	NY
Harvey, John	1825	24			Jackson, James M.	1845	25	PA
Harvey, William	1829	17	ME		Jackson, Thomas	1826	25	VA
Harvie, William H.	1827	15	PA		Jackson, Thomas	1825	21	VA
Haskel, Aaron	1821	16	MA		Jacobs, Antonio	1855	26	naturalized
Haskell, John	1828	28	MA		Jacquelin, H. E.	1855	17	LA
Haskin, John J.	1833	28	MA		Jacquelin, H. Victor	1855	19	LA
Hasper, Edward	1842	18	MA		Jaycox, Samuel H.	1828	22	NY
Hatch, Daniel	1833	29	ME		Jenett, Nathaniel	1820	0	NC
Hatson, James	1854	27	NY		Jennings, Freeman	1827	26	CT
Hawes, George	1845	21	MA		Jewell, Ebenezer	1833	23	ME
Hawkins, Curlies	1840	27	NH		Johnsen, Thomas	1856	22	MD
Hayden, William J.	1856	22	ME		Johnson, Frederick	1855	19	MD
Haynes, Newton	1840	18	CT		Johnson, Harry	1845	27	naturalized
Hayward, Charles J.	1838	28	NY		Johnson, John S. S.	1826	30	VA
Heard, Robert H.	1844	22	ME		Johnson, Peter	1844	30	NJ
Hedgecock, Oliver	1826	34	NY		Johnson, Thomas	1825	28	NY
Hendrick, William	1845	28	MD		Johnson, Thomas	1826	21	MD
Henley, Joseph	1824	40	PA		Johnston, George	1829	34	MA
Henry, Calop	1838	21	RI		Johnston, Israel	1826	26	ME
Henry, John	1824	16	VA		Jones, Edwin T.	1854	20	NH
Hewlett, Octavus	1820	18	VA		Jones, Evan	1845	22	MA
Hickey, Andrew	1825	20	MA		Jones, John	1826	22	CT
Hicks, Zephaniah	1828	23	ME		Jones, John	1845	17	LA
Higgin, Lewis	1826	17	ME		Jones, Wm. O.	1826	20	MD
Higgins, Asa	1828	20	ME		Jordan, Dominicus	1820	0	ME
Higgins, Benjamin	1826	13	ME		Jordan, Israel	1845	44	ME
Hill, Henry	1828	23	DE		Journeay, William	1838	22	NY
Hill, Irving S.	1857	24	DE		Judkins, Moses H.	1843	32	ME
Hiller, George	1826	32	ME		Judson, Henry	1838	19	AL
Hilt, John	1851	29	NY		Kavanagh, Joseph	1852	24	NY
Hodges, Lenon	1828	21	VA		Keating, William H.	1833	25	ME
Hodgkins, Benj. P.	1854	21	MA		Keen, George N.	1852	22	MA
Hodgkins,NathanielN.	1854	23	MA		Keith, Joseph	1829	23	ME
Holden?, Peter	1852	32	NJ		Kelham, Charles	1829	21	VA
Holmes, Benjamin	1853	24	MA		Kellogg, Enas	1824	48	MA
Holmes, John	1822	25			Kelly, James	1854	25	MA
Holmes, John James	1838	20	NY		Kendrick, Hiram	1856	21	MA
Holmes, Lemar	1853	0			Kenny, Edward	1851	37	RI
Hosmer, Jesse	1837	22	ME		Kent, Thomas	1826	29	NY
Hosses, Leonard	1829	22	ME		Kidder, Albert	1829	24	ME
How, Franklin	1844	22	MA		Kilburn, Charles H.	1852	20	MA
Howard, Charles	1858	28	NY		King, Oscar	1844	22	AL
Howard, Thomas F.	1827	25	MA		Knight, Henry	1838	23	LA
Howard, William	1853	20	ME		Knight, James	1845	26	PA

Knight, William	1824	23	ME		Marr, Dennis	1856	20	MA
Knox, Kingsbury	1829	17	ME		Marsen, Joseph	1854	25	ME
Knox, Kingsbury	1833	22	ME		Marshall, Joseph, Jr.	1856	20	ME
Kustsman, L. B.	1856	25	NY		Marson, Alfred	1827	18	ME
Laboytean, William	1825	28	NY		Martin, Charles	1851	36	NY
Lackhand, William	1855	22	MA		Martin, Francis	1859	20	MA
Lagley, Thomas	1852	24	MD		Martin, Meub	1856	19	NJ
Lambert, John P.	1828	25	NY		Martinez, Rafael	1828	30	LA
Lane, Timothy	1828	22	ME		Mather, Ezra S.	1844	21	CT
Langley, Samuel A.	1833	20	RI		Mather, Robert M.	1820	0	
Langley, Smith	1845	20	NH		Mathison, Henry	1826	27	NY
Langphier, William	1840	20	CT		McCalla, Andrew	1838	47	PA
Lano, Joseph C.	1837	23	MD		McCarthey, James	1854	26	WI
Laurence, Robert	1825	54	DE		McCarthy, Henry	1854	26	naturalized
Lavoe/Leslong,Augustus	1845	24	LA		McCartney, Peter	1844	19	VT
Lawrence, Charles	1851	34	NY		McClintock, Jason	1838	26	ME
Layman, Charles	1845	45	MA		McConnell, Anthony	1855	42	PA
Lee, Joseph	1824	29	PA		McCurdy, Richard L.	1821	19	CT
Lee, Thomas	1826	23	MD		McDonald, Daniel	1855	25	ME
Leeds, Edward T.	1840	0	ME		McGrady, Edward	1845	27	NY
LeGallais, Godfrey	1840	24	MA		McGuin, John	1837	21	ME
Leith, George	1838	21	NY		McGuire, John	1838	25	PA
Leland, Augustus L.	1852	15	ME		McIndre, Saml	1850	22	ME
Leland, Ezra	1852	17	ME		McIntyer, Thomas	1837	27	ME
Leland, Orien H.	1852	24	ME		McIntyre, Richard	1845	27	NY
Leroy/Leaory, Charles	1827	21	NY		McIntyre, Rufus	1829	23	ME
Lester, Henry	1838	23	CT		McKinnon, Daniel	1845	31	naturalized
Levensaler, Orris	1837	19	ME		McLane, Charles A.	1837	19	RI
Lewis, Francis W.	1845	30	NY		McNulty, James	1827	38	PA
Lewis, James	1838	19	DE		McPherson, Daniel	1845	27	ME
Libby, James M.	1855	21	ME		McVay, John	1855	22	NY
Libby, William J.	1840	18	ME		Meekings, Benjamin	1840	26	MD
Lindsey, Thomas	1829	17	ME		Meles, Charles	1827	22	LA
Linnell, Shuble	1854	38	MA		Merchant, William	1844	22	MA
Littlefield, Alvah	1833	23	ME		Merrill, John	1824	23	ME
Littlefield, William	1829	23	ME		Mervill, Alexander	1829	31	ME
Lome, Joseph Wm.	1853	25	Gr. Br.		Middleton, John	1838	22	CT
Lourey, William	1843	48	RI		Miller, Charles	1828	18	CT
Love, John	1827	20	ME		Miller,CharlesFrederick	1838	16	LA
Lyon, Henry	1827	0	ME		Miller, George	1826	0	
Mack, Andrew	1852	31	ME		Miller, John	1838	19	LA
Mack, Thomas	1845	21	NY		Miller, William	1828	27	MD
Mackey/Meky, James	1828	19	ME		Miller, William	1828	0	MD
Macomber, Josiah F.	1852	23	ME		Millikin, Alexander	1827	28	ME
Macon, Thomas H.	1856	14	AL		Miner, Joseph	1833	24	CT
Macumber, James	1824	21	ME		Mitchell, James	1840	0	ME
Madkins, Zebedee	1840	20	MD		Montgomery, Robert	1845	30	ME
Magee, Charles	1851	30	NY		Moore, Charles	1826	40	PA
Mains, John	1838	35	NH		Moore, Isaac R.	1845	22	ME
Malin, Thomas	1826	45			Moore, James	1827	21	NH
Mangen, Francis	1837	0	naturalized		Moore, William	1845	30	NY
Mansfield, James	1820	21	TN		Morgan, Evean	1838	22	PA
Maprey, Robert	1844	25	ME		Morgan, John	1828	21	MA
March, Enoch	1824	24	MA		Morgan, Taleford	1822	27	

Morgan, William	1821	21	NH		Perkins, John	1828	19	NY
Morris, John Benedict	1827	23			Perkins, Thomas H.	1840	16	ME
Morrison, John	1845	21	MA		Perry, Otis	1837	26	ME
Morton, William	1854	30	MA		Perry, Rufus A.	1828	19	MA
Mowlam, John	1819	24	MA		Peters, Andrew	1828	24	ME
Moxcey, Arthur D.	1838	24	ME		Petty, Minor B.	1833	17	NY
Muhollann, John	1844	28	VA		Petty, Smith	1843	21	NY
Mull, Eli	1840	30	MD		Philips, William	1828	20	MA
Mullany, James	1858	31	NY		Phillips, Elisha	1828	24	ME
Mullikin, William	1828	32	MD		Pierce, James H.	1838	22	MA
Murch, Leonard	1829	25	OH		Pillado, Peter	1828	38	LA
Murrey, Henry	1821	25	CT		Pinkham, Noah	1821	19	ME
Myers, Abm. S.	1845	24	AL		Pino, John	1833	33	LA
Nash, John	1828	34	RI		Pinson, Willilam H.	1836	0	NY
Neal, Robert	1824	34	VA		Popple, Francis	1843	34	RI
Needham, Josiah	1829	24	MD		Porter, Andrew	1827	25	MA
Nelson, Elias	1828	28	NY		Porter, John	1833	18	ME
Nelson, John	1843	27	ME		Post, Collin	1827	17	CT
Nelson, Magnus	1821	26	NY		Post, Russel D.?	1820	0	
Nelson, Oliver	1851	23	NY		Potter, James	1827	21	MA
Nevans, Charles	1824	20	MA		Potter, William	1851	21	MA
Nichols, Owen	1829	29	MA		Prate, Thomas	1829	40	VA
Nicol, George	1826	17	PA		Pratt, Jabez	1827	18	CT
Norman, William	1843	23	NY		Prosser, Frederick	1833	22	PA
Norris, Joseph	1856	21	ME		Prowden, Charles	1840	30	SC
Norris, Robert S.	1845	35	MD		Pyecraft, William	1856	24	MD
Norton, Francis A.	1855	26	ME		Quincy, Hebon	1838	22	ME
Oberg, L. J.	1826	17	LA		Quinn, James	1845	27	NY
Oldner, Joshua Smith	1824	26	VA		Quinn, Michael	1854	28	ME
Oliver, Charles	1828	29	ME		Ramsdell, Henry W.	1828	22	MA
Oliver, Charles	1833	32	ME		Raymond, Richard	1838	25	MA
Oliver, John	1829	37	NY		Read, Charles S.	1829	23	RI
Orreus, Edward	1852	32	ME		Read, James	1826	22	NY
Osband, Jonathan	1827	25	NY		Reagh, George	1825	34	
Osborne, James L.	1856	25	NY		Reeves, Philip	1826	27	NY
Otis, Robert	1828	18	RI		Reid, John	1850	20	MA
Park, James	1833	32	OH		Rennes, Edwin H.	1838	17	MA
Park, James	1840	30	NJ		Reynolds, Charles	1844	30	NY
Park, William R.	1845	23	OH		Reynolds, Jesse	1828	53	PA
Parker, Ferdinand A.	1857	18			Reynolds, Robert M.	1837	25	NJ
Parks, George	1833	25	MD		Rhoads, Jonas	1844	14	PA
Parle, Joseph	1838	31	NY		Rhodes, Daniel	1857	32	MA
Parrott, John S.	1844	24	MD		Rice, David W.	1845	32	MA
Parshall, Levi	1838	21	NY		Richards, William	1845	25	PA
Parsons, James	1827	27	NY		Richardson, Arthur	1826	31	
Parsons, William	1821	25	DC		Richardson, Oran	1826	18	ME
Peabody, Nicholas	1822	27			Rivers, William	1838	24	ME
Pearson, Daniel C.	1828	30	RI		Roberts, James	1829	30	NH
Pease, Jonathan	1828	29	MA		Roberts, Robert	1856	20	NY
Peaslee, Calvin	1845	39	NH		Roberts, Thomas	1820	0	MA
Peate, Thomas	1845	45	NY		Roberts, Thomas W.	1838	25	CT
Peck, George	1827	18	RI		Robertson, Robert	1829	31	ME
Peck, John	1838	24	ME		Robinson, Charles	1855	22	MA
Pendleton, Richard	1838	20	ME		Robinson, Clark	1824	16	ME

Robinson, James	1855	19	PA		Smith, Andrew	1826	39	NY
Robinson, John W.	1827	28			Smith, Anson	1820	25	CT
Robinson, Silas	1838	38	CT		Smith, Axal	1855	28	naturalized
Robirtson, John	1828	33	MA		Smith, Charles	1838	38	NY
Roderigo, Baptiste	1821	0	LA		Smith, Charles	1822	0	MA
Rodrigues, Raphael	1828	24	LA		Smith, Daniel	1851	38	PA
Rogers, Spencer	1826	0	NC		Smith, David	1845	24	MA
Rollins, Alexander	1840	39	ME		Smith, Edward	1824	27	NY
Ronan, Jasu	1857	25	naturalized		Smith, Edward H.	1844	36	PA
Ropes, William A.	1827	22	MA		Smith, Francis	1829	28	CT
Rosco, William	1838	30	ME		Smith, George	1828	27	NY
Rosins?, George	1852	24	MA		Smith, George W.	1845	19	MA
Ross, Edwin	1844	31	RI		Smith, Henry	1819	20 c	PA
Round, John M.	1820	29	PA		Smith, Hugh	1851	31	NY
Rudolph, William S.	1834	34	PA		Smith, Isaac	1851	21	MA
Ryan, John	1840	21	NY		Smith, James	1828	25	ME
Salsbury, John	1826	23	ME		Smith, James	1837	21	MD
Salvary, John	1845	24	LA		Smith, James P.	1829	25	ME
Samson, Isaiah	1856	19	NJ		Smith, Jefferson	1828	22	ME
Sanbom, Charles A.	1845	23	ME		Smith, John	1822	0	
Sartele, William A	1844	25	ME		Smith, John	1828	42	MA
Saunders, George	1844	21	NY		Smith, John	1845	25	MA
Sayre, John, Jr.	1824	24	NJ		Smith, John	1855	39	naturalized
Sayres, John, Jr.	1824	24	NJ		Smith, John	1845	31	NJ
Schoonmaker, Francis	1829	14	NY		Smith, John	1824	40	ME
Scofield, Clement	1820	0	ME		Smith, John William	1855	44	NY
Scollick, William	1850	18	NY		Smith, Meriwether W.	1828	22	VA
Scott, John W.	1838	28	NY		Smith, Samuel	1826	36	NY
Seaman, Gideon	1842	35	NY		Smith, William	1828	0	PA
Seargent, James	1824	21	NY		Smith, William	1838	27	PA
Seaver, William	1845	21	MA		Smith, William	1838	19	MA
Sentes, Michael	1828	32	LA		Smith, William	1826	20	ME
Shade, Samuel	1840	18	DE		Smith, William	1829	23	PA
Sharp, Robert	1826	28	NY		Smuk?, James	1854	25	MA
Sheppard, William	1840	25	MA		Smyth/Smith, Charles	1824	19	NY
Sherburne, Samuel	1843	27	NH		Snell, George	1827	24	PA
Sheridan, Richard	1833	28	MA		Snow, Moses	1844	28	ME
Sherman, Ichabod, Jr.	1824	18	MA		Snowbale, James	1851	18	ME
Sherman, Robert	1856	26	RI		Southwick, John Tyler	1828	14	MA
Sherry, David	1844	29	NY		Spencer, Frederick W.	1833	23	CT
Shipley, Walter	1855	24	NY		Spink, Charles	1827	26	RI
Shippard, William	1850	19	NY		Spring, Jacob	1824	18	ME
Shuky, Edward	1833	23	LA		Spywood, Orrin	1838	22 l	RI
Siddons, William M.	1855	26	NY		Starbuck, Edward F.	1827	21	MA
Simington, George	1842	14	ME		Starkey, Niles P.	1838	18	CT
Simmans, James	1850	28	MA		Steams, Samuel S. Jr.	1833	23	MA
Skolfield, Joseph	1851	35	ME		Stemer, John	1829	22	ME
Sky, Wm.	1856	19	ME		Stephens, David	1854	14	NY
Slight, Samuel	1845	21	NY		Stephens, William	1828	22	NY
Small, George	1838	21	ME		Steuart, Archibald Chas.	1858	25	naturalized
Small, Henry C.	1844	18	ME		Stevens, Pardon W.	1833	19	RI
Smith, Abraham	1851	22	ME		Stewart, Alford	1827	20	NY
Smith, Allen	1827	25	NY		Stewart, William C.	1828	25	PA
Smith, Amos	1838	20	NH		Stewart, William R.	1827	20	NY

Name	Year	Age	State/Country
Stilwell, Charles	1827	23	NJ
Stockton, Robert	1852	30	TN
Stonman, Charles D.	1844	29	MA
Stott, James	1845	22	DC
Stratten, John	1838	32	MD
Stuart, William	1837	24	MD
Sturges, Burr	1851	38	CT
Styron, Benjamin	1833	22	NC
Summers, Thomas	1826	37	NY
Sutherland, Alexander	1842	26	ME
Suydam, Daniel R.	1826	16	NY
Sweeny, Roderick A.	1826	20	NY
Swift, Henry W.	1838	23	NY
Sychle, Cheton	1855	32	Italy?
Taitim, Robert	1824	31	NY
Tapley, Henry	1845	38	MA
Tayler, Wm.	1853	29	PA
Taylor, Benjamin	1825	44	NJ
Taylor, John	1854	25	MA
Taylor, Lewis	1852	20	ME
Taylor, Prince H.	1854	19	MA
Tebbets, James	1822	20	
Teel, Charles	1843	37	RI
Thomas, Bloomfield	1853	33	ME
Thompson, Charles	1845	28	MA
Thompson, Edward K.	1840	23	ME
Thompson, John	1843	32	NY
Thompson, John	1827	20	
Thompson, Joseph	1827	32	ME
Thompson, Thomas	1828	25	ME
Thompson, Thomas	1853	20	MA
Thompson, Wm.	1854	34	Sweden
Tighe, Owen	1854	25	Great Britain
Tilford, John E.	1838	23	NY
Tilson, Edward C.	1829	22	ME
Tilton, Charles	1827	26	MA
Tilton, Lewis S.	1856	25	NJ
Toby, Albert	1840	20	ME
Tompkins, Henry	1840	25	NY
Townsend, Charles W.	1857	18	NJ
Townsend, David	1837	23	NJ
Townsent, Moses	1827	29	MA
Tracy, Francis	1826	33	PA
Travers, William	1837	19	ME
Triggs, James	1844	23	MA
Triggs, John	1829	30	MA
True, Joseph	1825	38	NY
True, Joseph	1824	37	Sweden
Truet, William	1840	21	NJ
Trusell, Horatio	1828	18	ME
Tucker, Samuel	1826	30	NY
Tuell, John	1821	15	RI
Turner, Joseph Edw.	1845	19	ME
Turney, Thomas S.	1834	23	CT
Ulmer, Philip	1829	50	VA
Urie, William	1838	23	MD
Urquhart, John	1820	0	
Vandewater, William	1829	17	NY
Vangilder, Levi	1838	26	NJ
Vleeser, Edwin M.	1853	0	PA
Vurtice, Nicholas	1828	46	FL
Walker, George W.	1845	21	DC
Walker, Samuel	1826	19	MA
Wall, Aaron S.	1828	20	ME
Wall, Joseph	1843	19	ME
Wallace, Joseph	1845	15	NH
Walling, James	1820	39	NJ
Ward, Henry	1856	25	ME
Water, CoventonBroad	1824	23	MD
Waters, Luke	1857	24	NY
Watson, James M.	1824	24	ME
Webb, Thomas	1853	25	naturalized
Webb, William J.	1827	22	PA
Webber, William	1838	32	ME
Weeks, Charles	1840	19	ME
Welch, George	1828	24	VA
Welford, H.	1855	25	MA
Wellmonton, Samuel	1829	21	MA
Welsh, David	1826	22	VT
Wescot, Moses	1833	34	England
West, Charles	1851	25	PA
West, Robert	1852	25	MA
West, Wilder W.	1855	22	MD
Weyman, John F	1852	31	naturalized
Wheaton, William E.	1851	51	PA
Whipple, James	1852	27	MA
White, Benjamin	1826	21	NY
Whitfield, Thomas	1829	15	NY
Wier, Robert G.	1850	15	AL
Wilkinson, William	1855	22	NY
Willcutt, Joseph W.	1852	20	MA
Willette, Nicholas B.	1845	17	PA
Williams, George	1826	31	ME
Williams, George	1838	38	PA
Williams, James	1829	23	PA
Williams, James B.	1827	23	MA
Williams, John	1856	23	MD
Williams, John	1824	38	NY
Williams, John	1853	0	NY
Williams, Ransford	1857	18	CT
Williams, Samuel	1833	33	CT
Williams, Walter	1845	23	NY
Williams, William E.	1838	22	CT
Williams, William H.	1829	20	CT
Willmott, David P.	1824	29	SC
Wilson, Andrew	1829	0	NJ
Wilson, David	1851	25	NY
Wilson, Edward A.	1829	25	MA

Wilson, John	1825	24	NY
Wilson, John	1843	27	MD
Wilson, Joseph	1833	32	ME
Wilson, Samuel	1822	0	PA
Winsor, Zenas	1824	40	MA
Winters, Eber C.	1827	24	NY
Winthrop, Willard	1857	19	MA
Witherington, DavidH.I.	1837	0	ME
Woods, Moses	1828	29	MA
Woodward, Isaac	1826	20	ME
Woodworth, George H.	1843	29	CT
Wright, Abel	1837	0	NY
Wright, George P.	1840	31	VA
Wymes, James	1826	20	RI
Yerger, Josiah	1854	30	PA
Young, Charles T.	1844	27	ME

These may Certify all whom it may concern that
Daniel Morman was Born in the Town of
Stafford in the Town of Wethersfield County of
Hartford & State of Connecticut where his truth
please Lord and now hath is now Serving
In testimony whereof I have hereunto Set my
hand this 31st day of March AD 1797

Joseph Bushby

Proofs of Citizenship

Port of Middletown, Connecticut

This is an index to 851 proofs of citizenship submitted to obtain a Seaman's Protection Certificate for the periods 1796-1801 and 1805 to 1861. Obviously, many applications are missing. This lacuna is filled in part by the abstracts or registers the National Archives holds for this port.

Printed forms were not utilized and the handwriting is often difficult to read. However, these proofs sometimes give significant genealogical information, such as the names of the seaman's parents, or interesting information such as the name of the ship the seaman served on, or his position in the crew such as cook.

Many seamen reported that they had lost their protection and were issued new ones, so their names appear twice in the index.

These records are in their original order. In other words, they have not been reorganized alphabetically, so it is necessary to search through all the proofs filed for a given year. Researchers should note that some documents contain the name of more than one seaman.

Seamen's Protection Certificate Applications

Port of Middletown, Connecticut

Data order: Name, Year, Age, Color, State or Country.

Name	Year	Age	Color	State
, David, Capt.	1801	0		CT
, Eleahim	1806	19 N		CT
, Andrine	1807	28		
Abbey, Russel	1796	0		
Abbey, David	1796	0		
Adams, Saml.	1799	0		
Adamson, Francis	1801	0		NY
Alford, Daniel	1804	0		
Alford, Nathaniel	1802	0		CT
Ames, Daniel	1800	0		NY
Anderson, Alex	1803	0		CT
Arnold, Welman	1805	19		CT
Arnold, Ebenezer	1805	13		CT
Arnold, Asahel	1809	18		CT
Attwood, Whiting	1809	0		CT
Attwood, Whiting	1805	18		CT
Attwood, Whiting	1805	18		CT
Augaid?, Joseph	1799	0		CT
Bachus, Peter	1813	43		
Backwood, Luther E.	1804	0		NH
Bagley, Ambron	1800	16		CT
Bailey, Thomas	1799	20		CT
Bailey, Abijah	1800	0		
Bailey, Elias	1804	18		CT
Bailey, Samuel	1796	0		CT
Bailey, Meiggs	1796	0		CT
Bailey, Soldon	1800	0		
Bailey, Daniel	1801	0		CT
Bailey, Russel	1801	21		CT
Baisden, James	1803	0		CT
Baker, Bailey	1805	0		
Barber, Elisha	1802	0		CT
Barkus, Marvin	1796	15		
Barney, James	1798	16		CT
Barns, Nathaniel	1801	0		CT
Barrett, William	1800	0		
Bates, Lewis	1796	0		CT
Baxter, Samuel	1804	0		
Baxter, Samuel	1803	0		
Beadl.., Manning	1804	0		
Beasman, Joseph	1796	0		CT
Bedle, John	1800	0		
Beebe, David	1797	19		CT
Beebe, Orson	1818	0		CT
Belden, Harry	1809	0		CT
Belden, John	1798	0		CT
Beldin, Luther	1801	21		CT
Belfast, Drek	1809	0 b		CT
Bell, Thomas	1803	31		NJ
Benton, John	1804	24		
Benton, John	1803	0		
Benton, Tyler	1796	0		CT
Benton, William	1806	21		CT
Berme, William	1800	0		
Bidwell, Benjamin	1800	0		
Bidwell, Wareham	1801	0		
Bigelov, John	1803	0		CT
Bildin, Allen	1806	0		CT
Billings, Eleakim	1807	20		CT
Bishop, Samuel Harry	1801	0		
Bishop, Reuben	1804	20		
Black, Albert	1800	0		
Blackston, John	1799	0		
Blakeley, Wm. Henry	1806	0		CT
Blatchley, Oliver	1797	0		CT
Blin, Joseph	1802	0		CT
Blin, Levi	1798	18		CT
Bliss, Calvin	1801	0		
Bliss, Francis	1815	0		MA
Bliss, Moses	1807	19		
Blyn, William	1796	0		CT
Blyn, Shingleton	1796	0		
Blyn, Daniel	1796	0		
Boam, Job	1806	0 N		CT
Boardman, George	1796	34		
Bolden, Samuel	1800	0		
Boley, Daniel	1797	0		CT
Bonfoey, David	1799	20		CT
Boon, Ichabod S.	1813	23		CT
Borce, John	1809	0		
Bordman, Daniel	1797	0		CT
Bordman, Daniel	1798	0		CT
Bordmann, Fradrik	1798	0		CT
Bordmun, Fand..ck	1797	0		CT
Boston, Dick	1798	0		CT
Bottley, William	1798	0		CT
Bow, Isaac	1799	0		
Bowen, Benaish	1797	0		
Brainard, Enos	1798	0		CT
Brainard, Joseph	1798	0		CT
Brainard, Hely	1798	0		CT
Brainard, David	1809	0		CT

Name	Year	Age	State
Brainary, Heli	1803	0	
Brainerd, Heli	1796	0	CT
Brainerd, Rily	1801	0	CT
Brainerd, Seth	1798	0	CT
Brainerd, Ely	1800	26	CT
Brewer, Reuben	1800	0	CT
Brewer, Reuben	1798	20	CT
Brewster, John	1797	0	CT
Brewster, John	1800	17	
Brigden, Thomas, Jr.	1796	27	CT
Brigden, Michael	1796	22	
Briggs, Jonathan	1803	35	
Brines, John	1797	26	CT
Broad, Joseph	1803	0	
Brockway, Rodney	1807	22	CT
Brooks, Sylvan..	1807	20	
Brooks, William	1801	18	
Brooks, Russel	1800	20	CT
Brooks, Calvin	1800	0	
Brooks, William	1799	0	CT
Brooks, Stephen	1800	0	
Brooks, Joseph	1800	0	
Broughton,Thadeous	1805	26	MA
Brown, Timothy	1801	0	
Brown, George	1806	0	NY
Brown, James	1801	0	
Brown, Seth	1800	16	CT
Brucker, William	1801	0	
Brucker, William	1805	0	MA
Buck, Samuel	1797	29	CT
Bulkley, James	1798	0	CT
Bulkley, Gushom	1809	0	CT
Bunce, Perez	1798	0	CT
Bunee, Charles	1799	0	
Bunnll, Frank	1800	0	
Bunu, William	1796	0	
Burk, Charles	1800	0	
Burke, John	1800	0	CT
Burnham, Hizikiah	1800	0	
Burnham, Hezekiah	1800	20	
Burnham, James	1798	0	CT
Burnham, Hiel	1807	0	VT
Burtorham, James	1800	0	
Bush, William	1801	0	CT
Bush, Joseph	1800	0	
Bush, Joseph	1803	17	
Butler, James	1797	30	CT
Butler, Leonard	1803	18	
Butler, William	1796	16	CT
Butler, Demas	1797	0	CT
Butler, Ebenezer	1798	0	CT
Butler, David	1799	0	
Butler, Joseph	1796	0	CT
Butler, Leonard	1800	0	CT
Butler, David	1818	32	CT
Butler, Matthew	1808	48	MA
Buy, Nath., Jr.	1800	24	CT
Cadwell, Timothy, Jr.	1803	20	MA
Caldwell, Saml	1801	0	
Calles, Nath'	1800	0	
Cam, Truman Ira	1860	29 y	CT
Camp, Hezekiah	1796	29	CT
Canda, John, Jun.	1801	23	CT
Cannon, Charles	1804	0	CT
Carey, Joseph	1800	0	
Carrison, John	1818	0 b	
Carter, Aron	1811	14 m	CT
Cary, Joseph	1801	0	CT
Casse, Isaac	1800	0	
Catlin, Truman	1801	0	CT
Catton, Hunt	1800	0	CT
Chadwick, John	1796	21	MA
Chamberlain,Leonard	1804	0	
Chapel, George	1806	0	NY
Chapman, Niel	1800	0	
Chapman, Henry	1801	0	
Chapman, Benjamin	1809	0	CT
Church, Timothy	1805	0	CT
Clapp, John	1801	19	
Clark, Lemuel	1798	21	CT
Clark, Daniel	1797	14	CT
Clark, John, 2nd	1798	21	CT
Clark, Daniel	1801	19	
Clark, Robert	1800	19	CT
Clark, Samuel	1808	0	
Clark, Asa	1805	22	CT
Clark, Hezekiah	1805	0	CT
Clark, Saml. Foster	1796	35	
Clark, Henry	1807	19	CT
Clark, Stephen	1807	20	CT
Clark, Michael	1796	19	
Clark, Samuel, III	1797	18	CT
Clark, Zelotes	1800	15	CT
Clark, Christopher,Jr.	1800	18	CT
Clark, Danl.	1807	17	
Clark, Daniel	1801	19	CT
Clark, Asa	1800	18	CT
Clark, Nathaniel	1819	24	CT
Clark, Darius	1819	0	CT
Clark, Sterling	1809	0	
Clark, William	1811	0	CT
Cobb, Martin	1800	0	
Cobum, Amariah	1804	0	MA
Coffin, Charles	1806	0	MA
Cole, Elijah L.	1798	0	
Collier, William	1806	0	
Colliers, John Joseph	1823	21 b	CT
Collins, John	1797	20	CT

Collins, Levi	1796	0	CT	Denison,Jedediah, Jr.	1803	15	CT
Colson, Boswell	1800	19	CT	Denison,Jedediah, Jr.	1804	15	
Colton, Elijah	1800	0		Denison, Jeremiah	1796	0	CT
Colton, Ashley	1801	0	MA	Dibbell, Richard	1801	0	CT
Combs, Andrew	1798	0	CT	Dimock, Henry	1801	0	CT
Comstock, William	1800	19	CT	Dodd, Edward	1803	0	CT
Comstock, Saml., Jr.	1800	0	CT	Dorrell, William	1815	25	NJ
Comstock, Griswould	1800	18	CT	Dudd, James	1801	0	
Comstock, Curtis	1796	30		Dumbar, Bennet	1801	0	MA
Comstock, Josiah	1800	29	CT	Dunham, John	1797	0	CT
Comstock, Samuel	1799	29	CT	Dunham, Philemon	1801	0	MA
Comwell, Joseph	1797	30	CT	Durrell, John	1804	0	DE
Cone, Elisha	1801	0	CT	Durry, George	1798	0	NY
Cone, Robert	1802	0	CT	Dutton, Thomas	1807	0	CT
Conklin, Cornelius	1813	21	NY	Edwards, Elishu	1799	18	CT
Connell, John	1804	0		Edwards, Elisha	1801	0	CT
Cook, William T.	1807	0	CT	Elderkin, Elisha	1802	0	CT
Cook, George	1801	0	CT	Elderkin, Henry	1800	0	
Cooper, Israel	1803	0	VT	Eldukin, John	1805	0	
Cornell, Joseph	1800	32		Eliott, Saml.	1799	30	CT
Corning, Ephraim	1799	15	CT	Elliott, Ewled	1815	15	CT
Coterill, Richard	1796	0		Ellis, Ebenezer	1818	0	MA
Cotton, Timothy	1796	34	CT	Ells, Edward	1796	29	
Cotton, Timothy	1807	18	CT	Ely, Ira	1807	0	CT
Crane, Curtiss	1804	27		Ely, Horatio Gates	1797	21	CT
Crane, Abner	1807	25	CT	Endicott, James	1800	0	
Creamor, Michael	1797	37	CT	Evans, Isham	1804	0	
Crompton, William	1805	0		Fairbanks, David	1805	33	CT
Crooke, Jonathan	1799	0	CT	Fairbanks, David	1797	23	CT
Crosbey, Saml.	1799	0		Fairbanks, Barakiah	1796	28	
Crosbey, Elisha	1801	0		Fairbanks, Barachiah	1800	0	CT
Crouch, Joseph	1808	0		Farman, Nathaniel	1800	24	CT
Cruttendon, Gilbert	1799	20	CT	Farman, James	1800	20	CT
Cummings,AndrewW.	1800	0		Farnam, Nathanal	1798	0	CT
Cunningham,Archibald	1801	0		Farnam, Elias	1805	27	CT
Curtie, George	1798	0	CT	Fcethsay, Daniel	1799	0	CT
Curtis, James	1811	25	CT	Feaknes, Edward	1815	0	MA
Curtis, Cyrus	1796	0	CT	Field, Wickam	1799	23	CT
Curtiss, Nathaniel	1796	0	CT	Fish, Allen	1803	0	
Cyke, James Ten	1804	0		Flagg, Benjamin	1797	27	CT
Daniels, Joseph	1797	19	CT	Foote, Saml Edw	1805	0	
Daniels, Isaac	1806	16	CT	Forest, Elizer	1800	0	CT
Daniels, Joseph	1859	38	CT	Forest, John	1800	0	CT
Daniels, Aaron	1861	19 c		Fosdick, Clement	1813	25	CT
Danils, Joseph	1801	15	CT	Foseneor, Vanioh	1798	38	CT
Darling, Henry	1804	44		Fowler, John, Jun.	1801	22	MA
Dart, Chauncey	1809	0	CT	Fox, Vaniak	1797	0	CT
Davis, Elijah	1796	27	CT	Fox, Joel	1806	25	CT
Dealing, Jabez	1796	0		Fox, Horace	1804	0	
DeAngelis, Lewis	1804	44	CT	Fox, George	1804	0	
Deling, Elijah	1803	0		Fox, Frederic	1806	0	CT
Deming, Iraad	1800	0		Fox, Harvey	1809	20	CT
Deming, Simeon	1802	0		Fox, Simeon	1806	0	
Deming, Allyn	1802	40	CT	Franklin, Warren	1799	20	CT

Franklin, Ishi	1801	20	CT
Franklin, Moses	1806	0	CT
Freeman, Sawny	1806	38 b	CT
Freeman, Caesar	1796	0	CT
Freeman, James	1809	0	DC
French, James	1796	23	CT
Frise, George	1801	18	
Frise, George	1801	18	SC
Gardiner, James	1799	0	
Gasomer, Abel	1800	0	
Gay, Calvin	1796	0	CT
Gaylord, Samuel	1804	21	
Gaylord, Vester	1801	15	CT
Gaylord, William	1800	0	
Gaylord, Stewart	1805	21	
Glading, William	1798	0	CT
Glading, Joshua	1804	0	CT
Goff, Silas	1796	0	
Golpin, Jesse	1801	0	
Gomer, Francis	1807	0 N	
Goodrich, Joshua	1799	23	CT
Goodrich, John	1799	0	CT
Goodrich, Israel	1796	0	CT
Goodrich, Levi	1797	21	CT
Goodrich, Hirvey	1806	0	CT
Goodrich, Allen	1800	0	
Goodrich, Wart	1800	0	CT
Goodrich, Silas	1798	0	
Goodrich, Nathaniel	1800	0	CT
Goodwin, Thomas	1798	16	CT
Gorton, Thomas	1799	0	
Grawell, Jewiel	1800	17	CT
Green, Wilson	1799	19	CT
Green, Jared	1803	16	CT
Greenfield, Thomas	1797	0	
Greenfield,ArchibaldW	1803	0	CT
Greenwood, George	1801	0	CT
Grimes, Richard	1809	0	CT
Grimes, Harry	1801	0	
Grimes, Harry	1801	17	CT
Grinold, Jared	1805	17	
Griswold, Daniel	1796	0	
Griswold, Moses	1797	22	
Grossman, William	1801	0	MA
Grumnsy, Thomas	1806	17	CT
Grunwold, Sylvester	1803	0	
Halberrt, Seth	1800	26	CT
Hale, Sineea?	1798	0	
Hale, Wm.	1801	0	
Hall, Ephraim	1806	20	CT
Hamilton, John	1798	21	CT
Hammedieu,Josep L.	1806	25	CT
Hammock, George	1803	0	CT
Harper, Benjamin	1804	0	MA

Harrington, Jeremiah	1799	30		RI
Harris, James	1796	0		
Harris, Stephen	1805	0		CT
Hart, Charles	1809	12		
Hartlund, Bushnell	1805	23		CT
Haskall, Stephen	1804	20		
Haskel, Barnabas	1801	20		
Haslicutt, David	1798	0		CT
Hatch, Levi	1807	37		
Hatch, Daniel	1804	26		
Hatch, John	1807	16		
Hatch, Lansus	1803	12		MA
Hawley, Linus	1815	0		CT
Hayden, Feler	1803	20		CT
Hayden, Uriah	1803	20		CT
Hayden, Richard	1805	18		CT
Heady, Aaron	1805	19		
Heft, John	1804	0		
Heith, John	1797	22		CT
Hellyer, Philo	1796	15		
Hemt, Harry	1801	0		
Henly, Henry	1799	0		
Herrington, Lyman	1796	21		
Hich, David	1798	0		CT
Higgins, Winslow	1809	0		CT
Hill, Elijah	1804	0		
Hill, Joseph	1803	0		CT
Hills, Epaphras, Jr.	1800	0		CT
Hindley, Henry	1807	0		MA
Hnalbut, James	1796	21		
Hocasr?, Isaac	1801	0		
Hodgkins, Robert	1796	23		
Holden, Johnathan	1796	30		
Hollister, William	1809	0		
Hollister, George	1800	0		CT
Holloway, John	1803	0		MA
Hollowback, Ned	1803	0	b	CT
Holmes, Ralph	1809	0		CT
Holmes, Thomas	1798	0		CT
Hording, Eleazer	1803	0		MA
Hormer, Horatio	1800	0		
Hormon, George	1800	0		
Hosmer, George	1804	25		CT
Hubbard, Jacob	1807	36		CT
Hubbard, Daniel	1796	0		CT
Hubbard, Reuben	1799	18		CT
Hubbard, Enoch	1800	0		
Hubbard, George,2nd	1803	23		
Hubbard, Enoch	1797	20		CT
Hudson, Joseph	1806	0		CT
Hulet, Joseph	1801	0		
Hull, Ebbe	1799	30		CT
Hunham, Jacob	1802	0		NY
Hunt, Washington	1807	0		CT

Huntley, Philo	1804	0			Lewis, Jonah	1797	0	CT	
Huntley, Christopher	1796	0	CT		Liffinguard, Henry	1807	0	CT	
Huntley, Augustus	1801	0			Linn, William	1803	0	CT	
Huntly, Charles	1804	0			Little, Lymas	1806	25 N	CT	
Hurd, Benjamin	1807	18	CT		Lockwood, Samuel	1800	19		
Hurlbut, William	1809	19	CT		Lockwood, Samuel	1800	0		
Hurlbut, Pericles	1799	23	CT		Lolder, Elijah	1800	0	MA	
Husoon, Francis	1804	0 b	DE		Lombard, Thomas	1818	0	MA	
Ingersoll, Rowland	1800	0			Lomis, Alfred	1796	0	CT	
Jackson, Abraham	1798	0 b		U. S.	Loomis, Ralph	1797	21		
Jackson, Abraham	1801	0 b	NY		Lord, Hezekiah	1798	31	CT	
Jadwin, Robert	1804	0			Lord, Hezekiah	1797	30	CT	
Jepson, William	1796	0	CT		Loveland, John	1802	0	CT	
Jepson, James B.	1801	0	CT		Lydr, Hezekiah	1808	0	DC	
Johnson, Alvat	1803	0			Mabee, Henry	1809	27	NY	
Johnson, Comfort	1796	0			Magans, Uziel	1804	0	CT	
Johnson, Timothy L.	1807	20	CT		Marrik, Charles	1801	0		
Johnson, Comfort	1797	24	CT		Marsh, Christopoher	1800	21	CT	
Johnson,Ebenezer,Jr	1800	0	CT		Marshall, Thomas, Jr.	1808	0		
Johnson, Thomas	1807	0			Marshall, Benjamin	1798	0	CT	
Johnson, Zenus	1800	19	NY		Martin, Ephraim	1808	20	CT	
Johnson, Alen	1796	0	CT		Mason, Thomas	1800	17	CT	
Jones, Seth	1796	0	CT		Mather, Cotton	1797	0	CT	
Jones, Jeremiah	1796	17	CT		Mather, Elsworth	1800	0		
Jones, Daniel	1806	20	CT		Mayne, Joseph	1805	0		
Junior, John	1815	19 m	CT		McCall, James	1806	0	CT	
Keeny, Aaron	1801	0			McCollum, Duncan	1803	22	CT	
Keeny, Allen	1801	0	CT		McDermand, James	1805	26		
Keith, William	1800	16	CT		McKam, James	1809	0	CT	
Keith, William	1800	16			McKinstry, John	1801	27		
Kelley, Elijah	1797	24	CT		McNelly, John	1803	21	CT	
Kellogg, Samuel	1807	0			Meggs/Meigs, Elihu	1800	21	CT	
Kellogg, Samuel, Jr.	1811	23	CT		Mershall, Benjamin	1806	27	CT	
Kelly, John	1803	20	SC		Merwin, Daniel	1796	0	CT	
Kelsey, Ebor	1800	20	CT		Metcaff, Calvin	1799	0		
Kelsey, Calvin	1801	0	CT		Mildrim, Luther	1801	17		
Kelsey, Tom...	1802	0	CT		Mildrum, Owen	1801	17		
Kessey, Asa	1799	0	CT		Miller, Collins Saml.	1796	18		
Kilborn, Thomas	1800	0			Miller, George R.	1811	10	MA	
Kilborn, Ashbel	1801	18			Moniken, Aaron Smith	1796	0	CT	
Kilbourn, Wm.	1800	0	CT		Montague, William	1804	0		
Kiney, John	1804	0			Moon, William	1807	0	CT	
Kirtland, John	1800	0			Morely, Wm.	1798	0		
Knowles, Ruel	1796	0	CT		Morgan, Prince	1800	27 N	CT	
Knowles, Ruell	1796	0			Morgan, Prince	1803	22	CT	
Lag/Sag, Giles	1806	21	CT		Morrelly, John	1809	0	NY	
Lage?, Justus	1801	0	CT		Morril, Hezekiah	1800	0		
Lago?, George	1801	0	CT		Moseley, Senica	1809	0	CT	
Lanphur, James	1809	0	CT		Moseley, William	1804	0		
Lawrence, Philotas	1806	20	MA		Mott, Elihu	1801	0	CT	
Lawrence, Russell	1801	0			Mulford, Jonathan	1805	0	NY	
Lee, Heze	1801	0	MA		Munroe, George	1804	0	RI	
Lee, Robert	1806	0	CT		Naskett, John	1800	0		
Lewis, Nathan	1799	0	CT		Norton, Joseph S.	1818	0	CT	

Norton, Jeremiah	1796	0	CT		Price, John	1804	19	
Norton, Samuel	1799	0	CT		Prior, Gidson	1803	0	
Nott, Isaac	1805	16	CT		Prott, Allen	1803	22	
Nott, Isaac	1805	15	CT		Puket, James	1797	25	CT
O'Daniels, James	1798	16	CT		Ramsay, Alexander	1802	0	CT
O'Daniels, John	1796	16	CT		Ranney, Rhodocei?	1800	0	
O'Daniels, John	1796	16			Ranney, Moses	1800	0	
Olivee, Frederic	1800	0	c?		Ranney, Comfort	1801	0	CT
Otis, Stephen	1800	0			Ranney, Simeon	1805	0	CT
Paddock, Richard	1804	16			Ray, David	1807	17	
Palmer, Urban	1809	0			Ray, Wzra	1807	0	CT
Palmer, Nhemiah	1800	0			Redfield, Poley	1800	0	CT
Parmela, Jered	1800	18			Redfield, Ebenezer	1802	0	CT
Parmelee, Garner	1799	22	CT		Rich, Eleazer Gilbert	1797	20	CT
Parsons, David	1807	17			Rider, Obed	1801	29	NY
Parti, Thorn	1800	0			Rigbey, William	1800	0	CT
Pasco, Jonathan	1803	0	CT		Riley, Nath.	1803	18	CT
Payne, Moses	1801	0			Risley, Noah	1801	0	CT
Pearl, Erastus	1809	25			Risley, Elihu	1798	0	CT
Peaster, John	1807	0	SC		Risley, Isaac	1796	19	
Peck, Joseph	1797	0	CT		Robbins, Joshua	1800	19	
Peck, David H.	1809	21	CT		Robbins, Warner	1797	27	CT
Peck, James	1796	0	CT		Robbins, Joshua	1804	17	
Pelton, Mosses	1806	44	CT		Robbins, Roger	1799	20	CT
Pelton, Charles	1801	0	CT		Roberts, James	1807	16	CT
Pembteton, Thomas	1800	19	CT		Roberts, Joel	1804	18	CT
Pennoyer, John G.	1801	0			Roberts, Willm.	1797	24	CT
Perone, Domingo	1803	22			Roberts, James Ozias	1804	0	
Perone, Domingo	1803	27			Robin, Joshua	1800	0	
Perry, Joseph	1806	18	VT		Robinson, Shadrack	1803	0	CT
Petton, John	1804	0	NY		Rockwell, Benjamin	1804	21	
Phelps, Benjamin	1796	0			Rogers, George	1860	20	DE
Pierce, John	1818	0	CT		Rogers, John	1796	38	CT
Pierce, Stephen	1801	0	CT		Rose, Amos	1800	0	
Pierce, Thomas L	1803	0	CT		Rowland, Uriah	1804	0	
Pierce, Daniel	1796	21	CT		Russel, Samuel	1800	16	CT
Pitkin, Henry	1803	0			Russell, Robert	1807	14 N	
Pitt, Charles	1804	18			Russell, Jonathan	1800	0	
Porter, Asahel	1800	22	CT		S..nnard, William	1807	19	CT
Porter, Joel	1804	0			Sag, George	1796	22	
Porter, William	1802	0	CT		Sag/Lag, Justnd	1804	28	CT
Porter, William	1815	0	MA		Sag/Lag, Russel?	1805	24	CT
Potter, Joshua	1800	15	CT		Sage, Christoher	1797	26	CT
Powers, Lewis	1861	24	CT		Sage, Willet Mathew	1798	18	CT
Powers, James, Jr.	1809	42	CT		Sage, Francis	1804	26	
Prat, Alfred	1804	16	CT		Sanders, Joseph	1803	17	CT
Pratt, Amzi	1805	0			Sanders, Samuel	1807	41	CT
Pratt, Allen	1798	22	CT		Sanford, Chas.	1801	0	
Pratt, Walter	1800	15	CT		Sanford, Elijah	1796	21	CT
Pratt, Wolten	1806	20	CT		Saunders, Samuel	1815	47	CT
Pratt, Oliver	1796	0	CT		Saunders, Martin D.	1801	0	CT
Pratt, Amosa	1805	20	CT		Savag, Absalom	1798	17	CT
Pratt, Walter	1803	0	CT		Savage, Danl. Stow	1803	16	CT
Pressey, John	1815	0	MA		Savage, Simon	1801	0	CT

Name	Year	Num	State
Savage, Simeon	1800	18	CT
Sawyer, George A.	1797	19	CT
Saye, Silvester	1798	17	CT
Schovel, Lewis	1800	0	
Scovil, Wells	1806	17	CT
Scovil, Henry	1805	19	
Scovil, Smith	1804	0	
Scranton, Israel	1804	0	
Seans, Mathew	1797	0	CT
Sears, Aaron ?	1796	0	CT
Sears, Charles	1801	0	CT
Setten, Thomas	1815	0	NY
Seymes, Robert	1801	0	
Shaddock, Stephen	1797	0	CT
Sharp, Lamson	1800	0 N	
Shaw, Abner L.	1806	0	MA
Shepard, Luther	1801	0	CT
Shepard, Charles	1800	0	CT
Shepard, Richd.	1801	20	CT
Shepard, Bartlet	1797	0	
Shepard, William	1806	26	CT
Sherman, Leal	1815	30	CT
Shipman, Samuel	1805	23	CT
Shipman, John	1804	20	
Shipman,	1800	0	
Shipman, Seth	1804	0	
Shipmas, Samuel L.	1806	23	CT
Shniler, Jeremiah	1796	26	CT
Shuyler, Charles	1809	0	
Simmons, Peter	1797	0	
Simons, John	1798	25	CT
Skinner, John	1800	0	
Sloughton, Augustus	1801	0	
Smith, Reuben	1799	18	CT
Smith, Horace	1809	0	CT
Smith, Chalenge	1797	24	CT
Smith, Levi	1798	28	CT
Smith, Hazeal	1800	0	
Smith, Charles	1800	22	CT
Smith, Seth	1801	21	
Smith, Caleb	1803	0	VT
Smith, Seth	1798	0	CT
Smith, Stephen	1804	31	
Smith, Cpophras?	1800	0	
Smith, Parcy	1797	0	CT
Smith, Charles L.	1800	22	CT
Smith, Hamlet	1800	0	
Smith, Levi	1798	28	CT
Smith, John, Junr.	1800	25	CT
Smith, Jeremy	1800	0	CT
Smith, Enos	1797	22	CT
Smith, Jonathan	1803	34	
Smith, Hazael	1796	0	CT
Smith, Jonathan	1800	0	
Smith, Seth	1801	19	CT
Smith, Hezakiah	1805	37	CT
Smith, Chas. L.	1860	19	NY
Smith, James	1797	23	NY
Sooter, William	1804	12	
Southworth, Ezra	1800	20	CT
Spencer, Stephen	1799	21	CT
Spencer, John	1807	19	CT
Spencer, James	1796	25	CT
Spencer, John	1804	16	
Spencer, Hollistio	1801	0	CT
Spencer, Cole..	1801	0	
Spencer, Horace	1800	0	
Spencer, George	1800	0	
Spencer?, Lee	1801	0	
Stebbins, Joseph	1805	19	CT
Steel, Harry	1798	0	CT
Stewart, James	1796	0	CT
Stewart, Pomp	1800	0	
Stillman, Frances	1800	0	
Stillman, Samuel	1801	0	CT
Stillwell, Darius	1807	15	CT
Stilwell, Jeremiah	1797	0	PA
Stocking, John	1801	0	
Stocking, Nathaniel	1800	18	CT
Storking, Nathaniel	1805	23	CT
Stow, Amos	1796	36	
Stow, William	1797	21	CT
Stratten,Samuel, 2nd	1796	0	CT
Strong, David	1796	27	CT
Strong, Reuben	1800	0	
Strong, Walter	1800	20	CT
Strong, Daniel	1796	20	CT
Stan, Daniel, Jr.	1797	21	CT
Swears, John L. H.	1860	28 y	OK
Swoill, Martha	1796	0	CT
Syfax, Livi	1806	0 b	
Talbot, Southmaid S.	1801	0	
Talcott, Anson	1804	0	
Taylor, Roswell	1809	0	CT
Taylor, Abil?	1803	0	CT
Taylor, Abiel	1797	21	CT
Taylor, Henry	1804	18	
Thanney, Harvey	1812	18	CT
Thayer, Seth	1801	0	
Thomas, Herman	1797	0	CT
Thomas, David	1809	0	CT
Thomas, Arnold	1815	0	RI
Thomas, Eliphalet	1796	0	
Thomas, Prince	1800	24	CT
Thomas, Eliphalet	1800	0	CT
Thomas, Herman	1800	0	
Thompson, Lyman	1811	17 b	MA
Thumgood, Walace	1859	35 b	DE

Thuney, Aaron	1803	0	CT
Tibbals, Seth	1804	0	
Tinker, George	1796	26	
Tisdel, William	1809	32	CT
Towner, Reuben, 2nd	1799	18	CT
Tracy, James	1799	29	CT
Travise, John	1815	0	NY
Treadwell, James	1801	17	CT
Treat, Horace	1809	0	CT
Treat, John	1800	0	
Treat, Joseph	1804	18	
Tribble, Joseph	1807	24	
Truman, Dennis	1804	15 m	
Tryon, Samuel	1807	18	CT
Tryon, Stgephen	1796	15	
Turner, William H.	1804	0	
Turner, Reubin	1806	15	CT
Turner, Harrison	1806	24	CT
Tybbels, Demmon	1809	0	CT
Tyler, Samuel	1799	0	CT
Tyler, Selden	1807	0	CT
Tyler, David	1807	0	
VanHorn, Harvey	1815	23	MA
Vibbert, William	1799	0	CT
Wadsworth, Hezekiah	1801	0	CT
Wadsworth, James	1796	21	
Wadsworth, David	1796	0	
Wadsworth, Samuel	1804	0	
Wadsworth, Amon	1803	0	CT
Wadsworth, Samuel	1804	0	
Wagner, Jacob	1804	13	
Wait, Francis D.	1811	25	NH
Walker, Abial	1801	0	
Walker, Ashley	1801	0	
Walker, John	1805	0 N	CT
Ward, John	1796	0	CT
Ward, Asher	1800	18	
Ward, Abner	1809	0 b	CT
Ward, Ira	1798	0	CT
Warner, George	1800	0	
Warner, Orin	1809	18	CT
Warner, Coros?	1804	30	
Warner, John	1796	24	
Warner, Theodore S.	1809	18	VT
Warner, Theodore S.	1809	17	VT
Warner, Theodore S.	1808	17	VT
Warner, James	1803	0	MA
Warner, Joseph	1815	22	CT
Warner, Cnos?	1800	0	
Warren, John	1809	27	CT
Warren, Thomas	1800	0	
Watenous, Ephariam	1807	17	CT
Waterbury, Simeon	1803	0	
Waterbury, Simeon	1804	0	

Waterbury, Joseph	1805	0	
Waterhouse, Russel	1805	20	CT
Waterman, John O.?	1799	30	CT
Watson, Rodesic	1805	22	CT
Watson, William	1801	0	
Watson, Aaron	1807	19	CT
Watson, William	1801	0	CT
Weaver, Jonth.	1796	0	
Webb, Samuel	1804	16	CT
Weble, Arza	1806	21	CT
Welch, Thos	1799	27	CT
Weller, Hezekiah, Jr.	1799	0	
Weller, Hezekiah, Jr.	1799	0	
Welles, Chester	1799	0	
Wells, Donald	1818	0	CT
Wells, Elisha Robbins	1800	16	
Wells, Jonathan	1796	43	CT
Wells, Henry Knox	1800	15	
West, Ebenezer	1803	0	
West, George	1811	0	NY
Wetmon, Elisha	1803	0	
Wetmore, Joseph	1796	26	CT
Wetmore, Stephen, Jun.		1800	0
Whitbey, Benjamin	1796	0	NC
White, Justus	1809	12	
White, James	1823	0	MA
White, Thomas	1797	23	CT
White, Isaac	1798	18	CT
White, Samuel	1799	19	CT
White, Alexander	1801	0	CT
White, Wm.	1801	13	CT
White, Charles	1800	0	
White, Asa	1804	17	
White, John	1797	28	CT
White, Asa	1800	0	
Whittelsey, Samuel Williams	1800	33	
Whittelsey, none given	1800	0	
Whittlesey, Henry	1805	22	CT
Willard, John	1799	22	CT
Wilcox, Samuel	1800	21	CT
Willes, Jonathan	1803	29	
William, Prince	1806	0 b	
Williams, George	1805	18	CT
Williams, Charles, Jr.	1804	0	CT
Wing, Hezekiah	1804	0	
Wood, Richard	1806	19	CT
Woodhou.., Titen	1800	0	
Woodhouse, James	1805	15	
Woodhouse, Joseph	1804	19	
Woods, Alexander	1803	0	
Wright, Jedediah	1807	18	CT
Wright, Jedediah	1806	17	CT
Wright, Elijah	1796	26	

Wright, Doty Lord	1818	22	CT
Wright, David	1811	20	MA
Wrisle, George	1796	0	CT
Yeamans, David	1800	0	CT
Yeer, Elihu, Jr.	1799	0	

UNITED STATES OF AMERICA.

DISTRICT OF COLUMBIA,
ALEXANDRIA COUNTY—TO WIT:

ON this day the _Eleventh_ ——— of _April_ ———
in the year of our Lord one thousand eight hundred and _Eleven_ ———
before me, CLEON MOORE, Notary public, for the Town and County of
Alexandria, in the District of Columbia, residing therein, and by law admit-
ted and sworn, personally appeared. _Richard M. Lobre_ and made oath according
to Law that he is a native Citizen of the United States of America born in the Town of Portsmouth
State of New hampshire & has been with respect to make the travels of of Richard M. Lobre is about
six years old in the Town of Lancaster in the State of Pennsylvania which he always used & will
he is about born and has known him ever since, having said is ____ being years old here to form
forts, to the truth of which the said Richard M. Lobre about which I will and swift he
him to protection from the Collector of United States, which he last will of forty and got one
given Richard M. Lobre by Legal at of the United States there — Witness my hand Sealof
Office this 11th day of April 1811.

Cleon Moore
Notary Pub

Seamen's Protection Certificate Applications

Port of Alexandria, District of Columbia

It is interesting to note that at this time Alexandria was still in the District of Columbia. It and all the District lying south of the Potomac River were retroceded to Virginia in 1846.

There are 684 records in this index of applications filed in Alexandria between 1803 and 1838. The records are incomplete. Some years have only a token number of applications; some years have none.

Notaries in Alexandria did not use printed forms, so each notary's format is different, making the information difficult to read quickly. Normally the notary's name is given first, then the name and place of birth of the witness, then the name of the seaman and his place of birth. Look for the seaman's name following "bearer."

Most notaries failed to give the age of the seaman, but many did give information about the seaman's family. They might note the name and trade of the father, or perhaps tell where the seaman's parents were currently living or if they were deceased. They may tell where the seaman grew up.

Seamen's Protection Certificate Applications

Port of Alexandria, Virginia

Data order. Name, Year, Age, Color, State or Country.

Name	Year	Age	Color/State
Adams, Robert	1811	0	MD
Adams, William	1811	0	MD
Addison, John	1822	0	MD
Addison, John	1819	0	MD
Aiworth, Charles	1838	0	
Akin, Job	1807	0	MA
Aldridge, Richard	1811	0	PA
Aldridge, Richard	1811	21	
Alexander, Jos. L.	1817	18	VA
Allen, Michael	1821	0	VA
Alverson, Jeremiah	1805	18	VA
Alverson, John	1805	0	VA
Anderson, James	1805	0	NC
Anderson, John	1807	0	MD
Anderson, Joseph	1807	0	NJ
Andrews, Wm.	1811	0	MA
Armstrong, James	1809	0	VA
Armstrong, John	1807	0	VA
Austin, Orivel	1807	0	VA
Bagget, John	1811	0	VA
Barber, John	1817	0	MA
Barker, Joshua	1809	21	VA
Barnes, John	1807	0	VA
Barr, John	1820	0	PA
Barrett, John	1822	0	SC
Barry, George	1807	0	VA
Barry, John	1805	0	MD
Bartell, Joseph H.	1822	0	MA
Bartlet, Saml	1805	21	PA
Batton, James	1805	0	VA
Bayley, Joe	1805	0	MA
Bayne, John	1809	0	VA
Beachum, Isaac	1805	18	MD
Beal, Richard	1809	0	VA
Beall, William	1805	0	VA
Beek, David	1807	0	MA
Beesley, Henry	1805	0	VA
Bele, Joseph	1809	0	DE
Benchell, Warren	1805	0	MD
Bennett, John	1838	0	VA
Benson, Charles	1805	0	VA
Berry, John	1809	18	VA
Bevan, Thomas	1838	26	SC
Beyea,			
Charles Benjamin	1817	0	MA
Bignal, William	1807	0	DE
Blackstone, Edward	1811	0	MA
Blackstone, Nathaniel	1817	0	MD
Bladen, John D.	1811	0	VA
Blair, John K.	1805	0	NY
Bland, Peter	1811	0	NY
Blincoe, John	1808	0	VA
Blunt, Joseph B.	1807	0	
Boarman, Gerard S.	1808	0	MD
Boasman,			
Bennett Hoskins	1807	0	MD
Bogard, Abraham	1811	0	NY
Boice, Clermont	1822	0	MD
Booth, George	1811	0	MD
Booth, Sam	1817	0	MD
Boss, Philip T.	1807	0	RI
Bowie, James	1805	0	MD
Bowler, John	1822	0	VA
Bowling, Jerard	1807	0	VA
Bozwell, Nehemiah	1809	0	MD
Bramble, Assa	1817	0	MD
Brancome, James	1805	0	
Brannell, Thomas	1811	0	VA
Brant, Soloman	1805	16	NY
Brightman, Joseph	1805	0	MA
Brinnon, John	1805	0	VA
Brnh?, PhilipAugustus	1809	0	VA
Brook, Thomas	1809	0	MD
Brooke, Benjamin M.	1809	0	VA
Brown, Adam	1811	0	SC
Brown, George	1838	23	MA
Brown, Joseph	1811	0	MA
Brown, Nathe	1820	0	
Brown, Thomas	1820	0	MD
Brown, Watson	1805	0	VA
Bruce,			
Benjamin Franklin	1817	0	VA
Brunner, George	1809	0	DC
Budd, Elijah	1805	0	VA
Bullman, John	1811	0	MD
Bullock, James	1807	0	MD
Bullock, Jeremiah	1811	0	MD
Burch, Francis	1822	0	
Burges, Wm.	1805	0	VA
Burn, Jacob Campell	1807	0	RI
Burnele, Joseph	1811	0	MD
Burnes, Jesse	1805	0	VA

Burnham, David	1809	0	MA	
Buttler, Cornelious	1809	0	MA	
Butts, John	1820	0	DC	
Campbell, James	1805	0	PA	
Carroll, Thomas	1805	0	MD	
Carter, Richard	1809	0	VA	
Carter, Theophilus	1805	0	ME	
Carter, Thomas	1822	0	ME	
Cartwright, Thos.	1811	15	DC	
Carver, Daniel	1807	0	MA	
Carver, James	1807	0	MA	
Cary, Joseph	1811	0	CT	
Casey, Nicholas	1809	0	NJ	
Cave, John	1805	0	VA	
Cecil, Thomas	1807	0	MD	
Chase, Barzillae	1821	0	MA	
Christie, Gordon	1807	19	CT	
Churchill, Henry	1822	0	MA	
Churchill, Mandal	1822	0	MA	
Clark, Mark	1805	0	NC	
Clark, William Morten	1807	0	VA	
Clawson, Edward	1809	0	PA	
Clement, Robert	1805	0	MD	
Clements, Gerrard	1811	0	MD	
Cliff, Burwell	1811	0	VA	
Clift, Evul	1809	0	VA	
Cob, Warren	1822	0	MA	
Cockerile, John	1807	21	VA	
Coffin, John	1822	0	NY	
Cole, John	1817	0	CT	
Cole, John, Jr.	1817	0	MA	
Cole, Nehemiah	1805	0	MA	
Coleby, Daniel	1820	0		
Coleman, Thomas	1805	0	DE	
Colley, Even	1838	22	ME	
Collins, Learge	1822	0	VA	
Collins, Samuel	1805	0	PA	
Connor, Owen	1811	0	MD	
Conrad, John	1809	0	PA	
Cook, Edward	1817	0	MD	
Cook, John, Jr.	1807	0	PA	
Cook, Lewis	1809	0	VA	
Correca, Anthonio	1805	0		Portugal
Covert, John	1807	0		
Covert, John	1807	0	MD	
Cowdan, John	1809	0		Ireland
Cox, William	1807	0	MD	
Crandall, Philip	1822	0		
Crandle, Philip	1821	0	VA	
Crawford, David	1822	0	ME	
Crawford, James	1809	0	NY	
Crivele, John	1807	0	MA	
Crivell, John	1807	23		
Crocker, Samuel	1838	18	ME	
Crosswell, Hanson	1811	0	MD	
Cruse, Thomas H.	1811	0		
Davies, Andrew D.	1809	0	NY	
Davies, Benjamin	1811	21		England
Davis, Edward	1811	0	VA	
Davis, John	1805	0		S. Wales
Davis, John	1821	0	MA	
Davis, Jonathan	1807	0	RI	
Davis, Wm.	1817	0		
Dawsen,				
Miles Hutchison	1809	0	VA	
Dawson, Mathias	1811	22	NJ	
Day, Samuel	1807	0	MA	
Deakins, William	1805	0	VA	
Decasnap, William	1811	0	MD	
Delastatius, Severn	1809	0	VA	
Denty, Thomas	1809	0	MD	
Dexter, Abner	1822	0		
Dial, William	1811	0	MA	
Doe, Andrew	1807	0	NH	
Dolph, Joseph	1811	0	MA	
Dooley, James	1805	0	MD	
Douglas, Archibald A.	1809	0	VA	
Douglas, Heatly Arch.	1809	0	VA	
Dowell, Isaac	1807	0	VA	
Dowell, Thomas	1809	0	VA	
Doyle, Arthur	1811	0	NY	
Drew, Charles	1805	0	MA	
Duffy, Allen	1807	0	VA	
Dulin, Gerard	1811	0	VA	
Dunham, Clifford	1820	26	MA	
Duples, RobertWharton	1809	0	MA	
Dyer, Charles	1809	0	MA	
Dyer, Francis	1807	0	MD	
Dyer, Robert W.	1811	0	MD	
Dykes, Robert	1805	0	VA	
Eldridge, Warren	1809	0	MA	
Eldrige, Levi	1807	0		
Ellens, John	1805	0	MA	
Ellison, William	1838	19	NY	
Ennis, Barton	1805	0	MD	
Evans, Charles	1817	24		
Evans, Francis	1805	0	MD	
Evans, Joseph	1822	0	PA	
Evans, Robert	1809	0	VA	
Eveson, Warren N.	1838	18	MA	
Ewark, Horatio	1805	0		
Fairbrothy, John	1805	31	MD	
Falburt, Bennet	1817	0	DC	
Fales, Timothy	1811	0	RI	
Farnham, Joshua	1805	0	ME	
Ferrier, John	1811	21		
Fisher, Frederick	1809	18	PA	
Fisher, Tiakle	1822	0	VA	

Fitzgerald, John	1809	0		MD
Flannigan, Brian	1820	0		MD
Fleatherly, Thomas	1807	0		MD
Fleming, James	1811	0		SC
Fleming, John	1805	0		PA
Fleming, Thomas	1805	0		PA
Flemming, James	1809	0		VA
Fletcher, George	1805	0		PA
Fletcher, Henry	1809	0		VA
Fletcher, John	1811	0		MA
Fletcher, William	1811	16		MD
Fletcher, Wm.	1811	0		MD
Fogg, Beniah	1817	0		MA
Fogg, Benjamin	1822	0		
Ford, William B.	1807	0		PA
Forrke, Richard	1809	0		MD
Fountain, Charles	1817	0		VA
Fowler, William	1811	17		MD
Fox, David	1822	0	c	VA
Foxwell, Charles	1809	0		MD
Foyles, Aron	1805	0		MD
Franklin, Nehemiah	1811	0		MD
Frazier, John	1808	0		MD
Freeman, Benjamin	1807	0		MD
Friend, Edmond	1821	0		RI
Fry, Peter	1809	0		VA
Fry, William	1811	0		MA
Fuller, Alexr.	1822	0		MA
Fulton, Jacob C.	1838	17		DC
Fulton, Joseph	1807	0		
Gage, Seth	1809	0		MA
Gaither, Walter	1807	0		NC
Gallon, James	1805	0		NY
Gambrill, John	1805	0		MD
Garland, William	1807	0		NY
Garrett, George	1805	0		NJ
Garrison, Boswell	1809	0		DC
Gibbons, John	1805	0		MD
Gibbs, Varsick	1805	0		MD
Gilpen, John	1807	0		VA
Gird, Joseph C.	1809	0		GreatBritain
Godfrey, Knowles	1811	0		MA
Goff, William	1817	0		CT
Going, John	1805	0		VA
Gordon, James	1820	0		PA
Gould, Charles	1838	28		MA
Graham, George	1817	0		DC
Graham, Henry	1838	23		NY
Graves, Caleb	1811	16		VA
Gray, John	1811	0		Ct
Grayson, Spence	1805	0		VA
Green, Bennett, Jr.	1805	0		MD
Green, Thomas	1805	0		MA
Greenough, Robert	1822	0		MA

Greenwood, David	1838	20	ME
Gretter, George G.	1811	0	
Griffiths, John	1822	0	ME
Grinalds, Henry	1811	15	VA
Grinnal, Wilford	1822	0	MD
Grinsted, Wm.	1807	0	NC
Groverman, Frederick	1809	0	VA
Groverman, William, Jr.	1811	0	VA
Gwatkins, John	1805	0	VA
Haight, William	1822	0	
Hainey, John	1807	21	VA
Haley, Thos	1805	23	VA
Hammersly, Thomas	1809	0	MD
Hammond, David	1838	18	MA
Hammond, William	1805	0	VA
Haney, Daniel	1811	0	VA
Haney, Elias	1809	0	VA
Harden, Joseph	1807	0	PA
Hardy,			
Charles Overton	1809	0	MD
Hardy, Thomas Lebert	1809	0	MD
Harkum, Cyrus	1807	0	VA
Harlan, James H.	1805	0	PA
Harper, Robert	1821	17	DC
Harris, Henry	1805	0	ME
Harris, John	1805	0	MD
Harriss, John	1805	0	NY
Harsewell, Charles	1807	0	MA
Hart, Charles	1838	31	MA
Hartzbergar, Joseph	1811	0	LA
Harvey, Edward	1822	0	MA
Harvey, Henry	1811	0	DE
Hatch, Woodbery	1817	0	MA
Hathaway, John	1805	0	MA
Hatton, Peter	1809	17	MD
Henderson, James	1805	0	PA
Hewes, John, Jr.	1805	0	VA
Hill, Godardus	1805	0	PA
Hill, Thornton	1809	0	VA
Hilton, William	1807	0	VA
Hinckley, Ebenezer N.	1817	21	MA
Hinkley, Spencer	1805	0	MA
Hinton, Richard Brint	1807	0	PA
Hipkins, Samuel	1811	0	VA
Hisler, Martin	1822	0	ME
Hogan, Thomas	1805	0	VA
Hower, Samuel Hall	1811	0	MA
Howland, Thomas	1805	0	MA
Howsen,			
Ewell Fitzgerald	1807	0	VA
Howsen, Vincent	1807	0	VA
Hoyt, William	1805	0	NY
Huart, William	1817	0	VA
Hubbard, James	1822	0	ME

Hubert, Thomas	1807	0	VA
Huddell, John	1808	0	PA
Huddey, William	1805	0	PA
Hudnall, Loroy T.	1807	0	VA
Hughes, Andrew	1811	0	DC
Hughes, Andrew F.	1820	0	
Hughes, Elihu	1811	0	VA
Hughes, John, Jr.	1809	0	VA
Hull, Joseph	1821	0	NY
Hunt, John	1805	0	MD
Hunter, John, Jr.	1809	0	VA
Hunter, Nathaniel	1811	0	VA
Hunter, William	1821	22	DE
Hurd, Samuel	1817	0	CT
Hurley, William	1805	0	MD
Hutchings, Joseph	1805	0	MA
Hutchinson, James	1822	0	VA
illegible, Caleb	1811	17	
Insley, Zachariah	1805	0	MD
Irish, Banjamin	1817	0	MA
Irish, Isaac	1811	0	RI
Irvine, William	1811	0	GA
Jackson, James	1805	0	VA
Jackson, Lewis	1805	0	VA
Jacob, Edward W.	1809	0	MD
Jacobs, Bartholomew	1805	0	MD
James, Alfred	1820	17	VA
James, Noble	1805	0	DE
James, Sackker	1807	0	VA
Janey, John	1817	0	
Jenkins, John	1805	0	MD
Jenkins, Obed B.	1838	17	DC
Jenkins, Richard	1805	0	VA
Jewett, Wm.	1807	0	VA
Johnson, James	1811	22	RI
Johnson, John C.	1822	0	MD
Johnson, Jonathan	1817	0	MA
Johnson, William	1811	0	DC
Johnson, William	1807	0	VA
Johnston,			
Charles Pearson	1821	0	VA
Johnston, James	1817	0	VA
Johnston, James	1817	0	MD
Johnston, Lewis	1808	0	CT
Johnston, Samuel	1805	0	MA
Johnston, William	1807	0	
Jones, Nickolas	1838	19	NY
Jones, William	1807	0	MD
Kelly, Joseph Miss	1838	0	MD
Kelly, Richard	1807	0	VA
Kemp, James	1807	34	MD
Kening, James	1821	0	CT
Kennedy, Henry	1807	0	MA
Kent, William	1807	0	NY
Kent, Wm.	1811	0	VA
Keys, Thomas	1805	0	VA
Kilbraith, James	1807	0	MD
King, Edward	1805	0	MD
King, George	1807	0	NY
King, Thos.	1822	0	DC
Kinney, Joseph	1838	0	ME
Knott, Charles	1805	24	MD
Korn, Charles	1807	0	PA
Lacock, Daniel	1807	0	VA
Landres,HednryWhite	1807	0	CT
Lane, Timothy	1820	0	NY
Lanham, Asa	1809	22	MD
Lanham, Elias, Jr.	1809	0	MD
Laurence, George	1809	0	MA
Lawrason, James, Jr	1811	0	VA
Lee, James	1807	0	MD
Lewis, David	1811	35	NJ
Lewis, David	1807	23	
Lewis, David	1807	0	MA
Lewis, David	1807	0	MA
Lewis, Isaac	1809	0	MD
Lewis, James	1822	0	CT
Lindsay, Anthony	1822	0	MD
Linnin, William	1807	0	PA
Linton, George	1809	0	MD
Lnchett, Fielder	1809	0	
Lockerman, William	1807	0	MD
Lockwood, Benoire	1822	0	RI
Long, Solomon	1821	0	
Longdon,GeorgeCraig	1811	0	VA
Lyle, William	1822	0	DC
Lymburn, John	1807	0	VA
Lynch, Thomas	1805	45	MD
Lyon, James S.	1811	0	NJ
Madden, Frederick	1807	0	VA
Mading, John	1805	0	MA
Mahall, Walter	1807	0	MD
Maloy, Philip	1805	0	PA
Mandly, James	1809	0	MD
Mannery, Alexander	1817	0	MD
Marbery, Joseph C.	1817	0	MD
Marburg, Leonard	1809	0	MD
Marshale, John	1807	21	MD
Martin, Thomas	1809	0	MD
Mastin, William	1822	0	
Matheney, Thomas	1805	0	MD
Mayo, Mosses	1805	0	
Mazervey, Ephraim	1807	0	MA
McAfee, John, Jr.	1809	0	MD
McAlister, John	1822	27	VA
McAllester, Joseph	1822	0	
McCarty, James	1811	0	NY
McClish, Archibald M.	1805	0	VA

Name	Year	No.	State
McCoy, John	1811	0	MD
McDonald, Francis	1838	25	NY
McElwee, Thomas	1807	0	MA
McKoy, William	1805	15	DC
McLean, Thomas	1821	0	
Meggs, Thomas	1805	0	VA
Melvin, John	1822	0	ME
Melvin, Severn	1807	0	MD
Metcalf, John	1817	0	MD
Micou, John H.	1809	0	VA
Mifflen, Jonathan	1807	22	PA
Mifflin, Jonathan	1807	0	NY
Miles, Peter	1822	0	DC
Miller, Alexander	1805	0	NY
Miller, Riley	1809	0	VA
Mills, Ignatius	1807	0	VA
Mitchel, Samuel	1811	0	VA
Mitchell, John	1805	0	MD
Mitchell, Nathaniel	1820	17	RI
Mooney, Hugh	1838	42	DC
Moore, Henry	1807	0	VA
Moore, Thomas	1822	0	MA
Morris, Benjamin	1809	0	VA
Morrison, John	1809	0	MA
Moulds, William	1807	27	VA
Mudd, Joshua	1809	0	MD
Mullins, Spencer	1807	0	VA
Murray, Robert	1805	0	
Muskett, Henry	1809	0	MD
Myers, Daniel	1811	0	PA
Myrick, Benjamin	1807	0	MA
Neal, Benedict J.	1807	0	MD
Neal, William	1805	0	NC
Neale, James	1811	0	MD
Neale, John	1811	0	VA
Neale, Samuel	1811	0	NH
Neale, Samuel C.	1811	0	VA
Nelson, Jesse K.	1805	0	MD
Newberry, Henry	1805	0	MA
Newbery, Henry	1805	0	
Newton, William	1811	0	VA
Nickolls, Sturges	1807	0	CT
Noriss, Thomas	1822	0	
Norris, Ignatius	1805	0	MD
Norris, John R.	1811	0	MD
Norris, William	1809	0	MD
Norton, Matthew	1811	0	CT
O'Neil, Cornelius	1820	0	
Oakley, John	1809	0	MD
Oliver, Griffin	1807	0	VA
Olliver, James	1811	0	VA
Olliver, Walter	1811	0	VA
Orme, Archibald	1811	0	MD
Osborn, Ashar	1805	0	NY
Osbourn, John E.	1838	20	MD
Outen, Walter	1807	0	MD
Oversnau?, John	1805	0	NC
Page, John L.	1811	0	RI
Pailor ?, Thornton	1811	0	DC
Palmer, Eliel	1809	27	MD
Palmer, Richd.	1811	0	VA
Palmer, Thomas	1807	0	SC
Patten, John	1805	0	NY
Payne, John	1811	0	MD
Pearce, James	1809	0	VA
Pearce, Richard	1811	0	MA
Peasley, Ithram	1805	0	MD
Pecuse, Samuel	1809	0	MD
Pedley, Richard	1820	0	
Penn, Thomas	1805	0	PA
Peters, Collin	1805	0	DC
Pettit, George	1809	0	DC
Phelps, Jesse	1809	0	
Philips, John B.	1822	0	
Philips, John H., Jr.	1817	21	PA
Pickering, Mott	1811	0	VA
Pierce, Daniel	1807	0	PA
Plumer, Daniel	1817	0	MA
Pogue, William	1811	0	MD
Polland, John	1809	20	PA
Ponwelien, John	1811	0	SC
Pope, Edward	1809	0	VA
Potter, David	1821	33	MA
Powell, Posey	1807	0	VA
Powell, Thomas	1805	0	MA
Prichard, George	1817	0	MD
Pridanse, James	1807	0	MD
Pridanse, James	1807	17	
Prince, John	1805	0	VA
Pulley, Richard	0	0	
Railey, Lewis	1811	16	MD
Ramsay, Anthony	1811	0	DC
Randall, William	1817	0	
Ratliff, Robert	1805	0	MD
Reeve, Joseph	1809	15	VA
Reiley, William	1807	0	NJ
Renland, Samuel	1820	0	
Renland, Samuel	1820	0	
Rentro, Thomas	1805	0	MD
Rhodes, Charles	1805	0	RI
Richardson, Edward Gardner	1807	0	VA
Richardson, Jesse	1805	0	VA
Richs, George	1809	19	VA
Riddle, Jas. W.	1822	0	
Riddle, John H.	1811	0	PA
Rising, Thos. John	1811	0	MD
Roberts, John	1820	0	MD

Name	Year	No.	State
Roberts, John	1820	0	
Roberts, Richard	1811	0	MD
Roberts, Truman	1805	0	CT
Roberts, William	1807	0	NJ
Robinson, Charles	1809	0	MD
Robinson, James	1838	24	MA
Robinson, William	1805	0	ME
Robinson, Zephamih	1811	0	MA
Roe, Charles	1811	0	MA
Rook, William	1805	0	MD
Rook, William	1811	0	MD
Rose,AlexanderMoore	1807	0	VA
Rose, John	1807	0	
Rose, Thomas	1805	0	MD
Rowe, Cornelius	1809	20	PA
Ruckle, Jesse Lee	1838	0	MD
Rumney, John	1838	18	DC
Rust, Ewell	1820	0	VA
Sandford, Andrew	1807	0	VA
Scott, Henry	1807	0	
Scott, Joseph Day	1805	0	MD
Seidel, Francis	1809	0	MD
Selden, John	1822	0	MA
Select, Thomas	1809	0	CT
Shafer, Lewis, Jr.	1807	0	MD
Shallcross, William	1805	0	DE
Shanks, William	1808	29	MD
Sherman,Benjamin H.	1820	0	MA
Short, Silas	1811	0	VA
Shortbridge, John	1805	0	VA
Sillick, Thos.	1820	0	CT
Silvershorn, James	1811	0	VA
Simpson, Hanson	1809	0	VA
Skinner, George	1811	0	CT
Skinner, James W.	1809	0	VA
Small, John	1822	0	ME
Smith, Charles	1822	0	VA
Smith, Henry Adam	1805	0	PA
Smith, Hezekiah	1838	27	CT
Smith, John	1809	0	NY
Smith, John	1805	0	NY
Smith, John	1805	0	RI
Smith, John	1811	0	VA
Smith, John H.	1822	0	VA
Smith, Obadrat	1809	0	DE
Smith, Richard	1805	0	NY
Smith, Robert E.	1822	0	RI
Smith, Thomas	1807	0	VA
Smith, Thomas	1811	0	MD
Smith, William	1809	0	VA
Smith, William	1811	0	MD
Smoot, Charles	1807	0	VA
Smoot, Matthew	1809	40	MD
Smoot, Matthew	1809	0	MD
Snow, Charles	1808	0	MA
Soley, Nathaniel	1822	25	
Spicer, Thomas	1811	0	MD
Spilman, James	1805	0	VA
Sprey, Archibal	1811	0	RI
Stanton, Wm.	1809	0	MD
Stephens, Charles	1807	0	
Stephens, David	1809	0	MD
Stevens, Johnston	1811	0	MA
Steward, Archibald	1817	0	MA
Stillwell, John	1805	0	NJ
Stockdale, Thomas	1807	0	
Stone, Richard	1807	0	MD
Stone, William	1807	0	MD
Stranghan, Hiram L.	1811	0	VA
Sullivan, John	1822	0	
Sutton, William	1822	0	VA
Talbert, Levy	1811	0	VA
Taliaferro, John	1807	20	VA
Tarboe/Turboe,James	1805	0	MD
Tarlton, James	1807	25	MD
Tarlton, Richard	1811	0	MD
Tate, William	1804	16	MD
Tayler, William	1811	0	MD
Taylor, James	1811	0	MD
Taylor, John	1817	0	
Tebbets, James	1807	0	NH
Tebbs, Thomas	1805	0	VA
Thomas, Amos	1805	0	PA
Thomas, Edward	1805	0	MD
Thomas, Jonah B.	1811	0	MD
Thompson, Charles	1805	0	PA
Thompson, James	1811	17	
Thompson, James	1822	0	SC
Thompson, James	1811	0	MD
Thompson, Powell	1805	0	VA
Thornton, Thomas	1805	0	DC
Thrift, George	1805	0	VA
Thrift, William	1809	0	VA
Tiar, Charles A.	1809	0	MD
Toverill?, John	1811	0	VA
Trammel, John	1811	0	VA
Travers, Hes?	1807	0	MD
Triplet, Thomas	1817	0	MD
Troop, William	1811	0	VA
Tuffet, John	1817	0	
Tufts, Caleb	1811	0	MA
Turner, Vincent	1805	0	MD
Tyng, Janus H.	1822	0	MA
Vasse, James	1805	0	PA
Veith, Charles	1809	0	VA
Vieurs, James	1805	0	MD
Wade, Melvin	1807	0	MA
Walden, Thomas	1803	24	

Walker, James	1805	0	MD
Walker, Robert	1817	0	VA
Wallace, David S.	1805	0	DC
Ward, James	1820	0	
Ward, James H.	1822	0	NY
Wathen, Sabine	1811	0	MD
Watson, Dunham	1805	0	MA
Watson, Thomas	1822	0	DE
Watson, William Henry	1811	19	VA
Way, John	1809	0	MA
Webster, George	1811	0	NY
Welch, Edward	1807	0	PA
Welch, Walter	1809	0	VA
Weston, Benjamin	1805	0	NJ
Weston, John	1809	0	VA
Wharff, John	1809	0	MA
Wharton, Michael	1820	0	ME
Wharton, Thos.	1838	0	MD
Wherret, William	1807	0	MD
Whetlow, Reuben	1811	0	VA
White, John	1811	0	NC
White, Levin	1822	0	VA
Whiting, Warren	1809	0	VA
Wicker, Joel	1807	0	NC
Wigmore, John	1811	0	NY
Wilkinson, Henry	1811	0	VA
Williams, George	1811	0	NJ
Williams, Gifford	1811	0	RI
Williams, Isaac	1838	26	PA
Williams, John	1811	0	MD
Williams, John, Jr.	1805	0	SC
Williams, Moses	1821	32	ME
Williams, William	1805	0	VA
Williamson, Thomas	1822	0	
Willing, James	1807	0	MD
Willing, Thomas	1805	19	MD
Willis, James	1805	0	MD
Willkey, Cornell	1807	0	MA
Willson, Richard	1821	0	PA
Wilson, James	1805	0	MD
Wilson, John	1811	18	NJ
Wilson, Joseph	1807	19	
Wilt, Benjamin	1805	0	MA
Winset, Jas., Jr	1809	0	MD
Wise, Joseph	1807	0	DE
Wistt, John	1811	0	VA
Wolfe, Andrew	1805	0	MD
Wood, Henry	1820	0	
Wood, John	1822	0	MD
Wood, William	1805	0	VA
Woodward, Ruffus	1822	0	MA
Woollard, John	1809	0	VA
Wun, Joseph	1822	0	GA
Yeasley, Charles	1811	17	VA
Young, John	1811	0	MA
Young, John, Jr.	1809	0	VA
Young, Shubael	1811	0	MA
Young, Wm.	1805	16	VA
Zimmerman, ...nes ?	1811	0	VA
Zolkinhorn, Richard	1811	0	DC

This is to certify that Thomas Lawton, alias
Commings, son of Vina Lawton was born
in the Town of Swansey in the County of
Bristol & Commonwealth of Massachusetts
on the fifteenth day of April in the year
of our Lord One Thousand Seven hundred
& ninety four
A true Copy of Record
Swaney Jan'y 29. 1796.   attest John Mason Town Clerk

Proofs of Citizenship

Port of Newport, Rhode Island

There are 395 proofs of citizenship submitted by seamen applying for a Seaman's Protection Certificate in the port of Newport, Rhode Island, 1813 to 1817. The proofs are small documents, all written in longhand, most of which are refreshingly legible. This is particularly important since the name of the seaman is given only once on the face of the document.

The place and date of birth is given, and often the names of both parents and additional genealogically significant information. In the Weeden family, as successive sons went to sea, they are identified for example as Henry Weeden, fifth son of Peleg and Sarah Weeden.

A description of the seaman, his age, height, color of complexion, hair and eyes, is on the back of the proof.

There is one box of abstracts which cover 1814 to 1869, with gaps.

Proofs of Citizenship

Port of Newport, Rhode Island

<u>Data order: Name, Year, Age, State or Country</u>

Name	Year	Age	State/Country		Name	Year	Age	State/Country
Albro, Benjamin	1815	16	RI		Brownell, George W.	1815	17	RI
Albro, Thomas	1815	18	RI		Brownell, Paul	1815	47	RI
Allen, Samuel	1817	23	MA		Browness, Gardner T.	1815	19	RI
Allin, Beriah	1815	32	RI		Bruggs, Weston L.	1815	23	MA
Almy, Andrew	1815	20	RI		Bryer, Stafford	1815	17	RI
Almy, James, Jr. G.	1815	17	GA		Bullinggame, Rufus	1813	26	RI
Almy, Job	1815	17	RI		Bullock, John	1817	34	RI
Almy, William A.	1815	18	RI		Burroughe, Samuel	1815	21	RI
Ambrose,					Burroughs, Peleg	1815	18	RI
William Langley	1816	14	RI		Burroughs, William T.	1815	24	RI
Anthony, Benjaman	1816	19	RI		Bush, William A.	1815	20	RI
Anthony, Giles	1815	20	RI		Butts, John	1816	45	RI
Anthony, Jacob G.	1815	15	RI		Cahoone, Charles W.	1815	15	RI
Anthony, Nicholas B.	1816	12	MA		Capron, Gidion B.	1815	20	RI
Anthony, William	1815	23	RI		Card, Colonel C.	1815	25	RI
Austin, John	1815	19	RI		Carpenter, William	1815	24	RI
Ayleswort, Thomas	1816	35	RI		Cary, James	1815	17	RI
Aylesworth, Thomas	1815	35	RI		Cassady, Thomas	1815	29	naturalized
Babcoch, Cyrus	1813	21	RI		Castoff, Jeremiah F.	1815	17	RI
Babcock, William	1813	22	RI		Ceus, John L.	1815	18	RI
Backes,William Smith	1815	17	RI		Chace, Ezraae	1815	16	MA
Bailey,JamesAugustus	1815	17	RI		Chace, George R.	1815	23	MA
Bailey, John Warren	1815	19	RI		Chace, Isaac B.	1817	19	MA
Bakier, Sharanton	1815	20	NH		Chadwick, John	1815	20	RI
Ball, Gideon	1815	19	RI		Chase, Increase	1815	20	MA
Bangs, Dillingham	1815	19	MA		Chase, Jeremiah	1815	36	MA
Barker, Benedict S.	1816	20	RI		Chase, Jesse	1815	16	MA
Barlow, Thomas	1815	23	MA		Chase, Peter	1815	20	RI
Bartes, James	1815	18	MA		Chenovard,			
Bass, Thomas L.	1815	14	RI		John Michael	1815	19	CT
Bassett, Calvin	1815	21	MA		Childs, Abiel S.	1815	20	RI
Bead, Edmund	1815	17	MA		Christian, Jacob	1813	20	MA
Beaman, Thomas W.	1815	16	RI		Cisson, Samuel	1813	33	RI
Beebe, William	1815	22	CT		Clark, Benjamin	1816	41	RI
Bennet, William G.	1817	22	RI		Clark, Jesse	1815	17	MA
Bennett, Martin	1815	25	MA		Clark, Stephen	1815	23	RI
Berry/Perry, Simeon	1815	22	RI		Clarke, Banjamin	1815	19	MA
Bliffens, William R.	1815	17	MA		Clarke, Ebenezer	1815	18	RI
Bliven, Samuel	1815	23	RI		Clarke, Ebenezer, Jr.	1816	19	RI
Boss, Robert P.	1816	12	RI		Clarke, Joseph J.	1815	18	RI
Bowers, George	1815	18	MA		Clarke, Latham	1815	40	RI
Briggs, Amos	1815	18	RI		Clarke, Sherman	1816	19	RI
Briggs, Henry	1815	17	MA		Claskel, Thomas	1815	13	RI
Brigley, Joshua C.	1815	17	RI		Coggeshall, Charles	1813	30	MA
Brown, Clarke	1813	18	RI		Cole, Horace	1817	17	RI
Brown, David	1815	18	RI		Collins, Robert	1815	18	MA
Brown, Edward G.	1816	20	RI		Colvell, Thomas	1815	32	NH
Brown, Ezekiel	1815	21	SC		Congdon, George W.	1816	16	RI
Brown, Joseph	1813	21	CT		Congdon, John	1815	16	RI
Brown, Philip	1816	18	RI		Cook, Henry Hudson	1816	12	RI
Brown, Philip, Jr.	1815	18	RI		Cook, Job	1815	21	RI
Brown, Salisbury	1817	19	RI		Cook, John, Jr.	1815	15	RI
Brown, William	1817	24	RI		Cook, Joseph	1815	27	RI
Brown, William	1815	21	RI		Cook, William F.	1815	12	RI

Cooke, Charles C.	1815	16	RI
Cooper, Lodowick	1817	20	RI
Cooper, Thomas	1816	18	RI
Corey, Caleb	1816	33	RI
Corey, Daniel	1815	15	RI
Cornell, George, Jr.	1815	21	RI
Cornell, Robert	1815	21	RI
Cornell, Stephen	1815	18	RI
Cornell, Stephen	1814	16	RI
Cory, Caleb	1815	21	RI
Cottrell, Jeremiah	1815	12	RI
Cottrell, Samuel	1813	22	RI
Cozezens, Peter	1815	30	RI
Cranston, Samuel, Jr.	1815	24	RI
Croucher, David	1816	33	RI
Davenport,			
Charles Eleanezer	1816	22	RI
Davis, David	1815	19	MA
Davis, Justis	1815	21	MA
Davis, Nathan	1815	19	MA
Davis, Nathaniel G.	1813	20	RI
Davis, Peter	1815	28	RI
Davis, Samuel	1815	26	RI
Davis, Simeon	1815	25	CT
Dean, Henry Hope	1815	18	RI
Delphey, Samuel C.	1815	18	RI
Dennis, Darius	1815	16	RI
Dickinson, Washington	1815	15	SC
Dickson, Gordon	1815	33	Ireland
Dockhay, James R.	1815	17	RI
Dunham, Silas	1816	27	MA
Dunwell, Tennant	1815	17	RI
Dunwill, George	1813	21	RI
Dyre, Joseph W.	1815	18	RI
Easton, Banjamin	1815	32	RI
Easton, William	1815	19	RI
Eddy, Caleb	1816	17	RI
Eldridge, Henry	1815	27	RI
Elrad, Bowen	1815	20	RI
Evans, Hezekiah	1817	33	RI
Evans, Hezekiah	1815	30	RI
Finch, Henry Jakeways	1815	16	RI
Finch, James Boss	1814	11	RI
Finch, John	1815	27	RI
Fowler, Samuel	1817	16	RI
Fowler, Samuel C.	1817	21	RI
Fox, Philip	1815	22	MA
Freeman, Samuel	1813	22	RI
Gardiner, Hyman	1815	32	RI
Gardner, Nicholas E.	1815	17	RI
Gardner, Willet C.	1815	17	RI
Gardner, William	1815	19	RI
Gibbs, John	1815	18	MA
Gladding, Samuel	1815	17	RI
Gladding, William	1813	21	RI
Goff, Enoch	1815	22	MA
Goff, Robert	1815	25	MA
Goold, William	1815	17	RI
Gould, John	1815	19	RI
Gray, Samuel O.	1815	24	MA
Greene, Christopher			
Washington	1815	17	RI
Greene, Hazard	1813	24	RI
Greene, William	1815	17	RI
Grey, William	1816	19	RI
Grinnell, Billings, Jr.	1817	18	RI
Groves, Alexander	1817	21	RI
Guemey, John H.	1815	15	RI
Guiney, Thomas	1815	17	RI
Hadwen, Isaac	1817	20	RI
Hamilton, Isaac	1815	20	MA
Hammond, Benjamin	1815	17	RI
Hammond, Zenas L.	1815	18	MA
Hanson, Thomas R.	1815	17	NH
Harding, John	1815	21	RI
Hart, Charles	1815	21	RI
Hart, George S.	1816	14	RI
Hart, Jarvis Pinkney	1815	26	RI
Harvey, Lewis	1815	25	RI
Harzard, Bowdoin	1815	40	RI
Hathaway, Lot	1817	23	MA
Hathaway, Samuel	1815	22	MA
Hathaway, Samuel	1816	20	RI
Hathaway, William R,	1815	21	RI
Hatheway, Isaac	1815	20	MA
Hazard, George R.	1816	22	RI
Helmes, John R.	1815	15	CT
Holland, John	1815	20	RI
Honeywell, John M.	1815	22	RI
Hooper, George K.	1817	23	CT
House, John	1815	44	VA
Howett, Abraham	1813	20	NC
Hoxie,			
Freeman Mayberry	1814	23	RI
Hoxse, Gideon	1815	24	RI
Hoxse, Lodowick	1817	44	RI
Hoxsie, Joseph L.	1814	28	RI
Hudson, John	1817	18	RI
Hudson, Thomas, Jr.	1816	14	RI
Hunt, George	1815	21	RI
Hunt, William	1816	27	RI
Huntington, Edwar W.	1815	18	RI
Huntington, Joseph	1815	17	RI
Irish, George	1815	18	RI
Irish, Otis	1815	20	RI
Janner, John, Jr.	1815	16	RI
Janner, Palmer	1815	19	RI
Jeffers, James D.	1816	17	RI
Jeffers, Samuel, Jr.	1815	21	RI
Johnson, Jeremiah	1816	31	MA
Johnston, William H.	1817	16	PA
Jones, Gardner	1815	25	MA
Jonvet, William	1816	19	RI
Kaighor, Charles	1815	18	RI
Kielle, William	1815	20	NH
Langworthy, William	1815	18	RI
LaRoche, Benjamin	1817	22	RI
Lawson, Job	1815	19	RI
Lawton, Benjamin	1816	18	RI
Lawton, Jonathan	1815	20	MA
Lawton, Lewis D.	1817	17	RI
Lawton, Peleg	1816	22	RI
Lawton, Thomas	1816	20	MA
Lawton, Thomas	1815	30	RI
Lawton, Thomas H.	1815	19	RI
Lewis, Augustus	1815	22	RI
Lindsey, Jonathan W.	1813	34	RI
Linscott, Abraham	1817	28	MA

Name	Year	Age	State
Litchfield,			
Augustus Newman	1816	14	RI
Littlefield, William	1816	18	RI
Loch, Timothy	1815	18	RI
Lovett, Olney	1815	14	RI
Luther, Jonathan	1815	19	MA
Mackinzie, James	1817	33	RI
Manchester, Arnold	1817	18	RI
Marble, William	1817	17	RI
Martin,			
Frederick Stanley	1815	20	VT
Martin, Waite	1815	22	VT
McCarty, James	1815	19	RI
McClish, Thomas H.	1815	15	RI
Meuble, William	1815	15	RI
Millerd, John	1815	17	RI
Millerd, Welcome	1815	17	RI
Mitchell, Nicholas	1817	18	RI
Moody, Edward	1815	31	RI
Moon, Nathaniel	1817	25	NY
Moore, John	1815	28	NJ
Mores, WililamGardner	1815	19	RI
Morse, Gardner	1815	20	MA
Morton, ClothierPierce	1815	25	RI
Mumford,			
Augustus William	1817	14	RI
Murphey, Samuel	1815	14	RI
Murphy, John	1817	31	RI
Newbone, Nicholas	1816	20	RI
Newcomb, Edward C.	1815	18	MA
Newhall, Francis	1817	24	MA
Newman, JohnTopham	1815	17	RI
Nichols, George	1815	19	RI
Nichols, John	1813	18	MA
Nichols, William A.	1815	22	RI
Nicklye, Francis	1815	15	RI
Northrup, Smith	1815	30	RI
Norton, Elisha	1815	18	RI
Norton, Robert	1813	30	MA
Norton,			
William Spooner	1813	20	RI
Oakley, Samuel	1815	21	RI
Obrine, Samuel	1813	24	RI
Oman, William B.	1817	27	RI
Page, William	1815	14	RI
Palmer, William	1816	21	RI
Pawn, John	1817	23	RI
Peabody, Benjamin	1815	18	RI
Peabody, Nicholas	1815	21	RI
Pearse, Joseph M.	1817	19	RI
Peckham, Elisha	1813	22	RI
Perry, Christopher	1815	19	RI
Perry, James	1813	23	RI
Pickens, Dannis	1815	15	MA
Pickens, Samuel	1815	21	MA
Pickens, Samuel	1813	20	MA
Pierce, Daniel/David	1816	19	MA
Pinniger, John B.	1815	13	RI
Pitis, Thomas	1815	29	RI
Porter, Stephen	1816	19	MA
Potter, Aazon Buzz	1816	16	RI
Potter, John	1817	14	RI
Potter,			
Thomas Jefferson	1817	16	RI
Price, William, Jr.	1816	13	RI
Prior, Christopher H.	1813	19	RI
Randall, John	1815	22	NH
Rathbun, Samuel	1815	22	RI
Read, Caleb	1815	23	MA
Read, George	1815	20	RI
Reece, Thomas	1813	40	MA
Reynold, Abel, Jr.	1817	19	RI
Reynold, Daniel	1815	17	RI
Reynold, David G.	1817	16	RI
Reynold, Henry	1815	25	RI
Reynold, James	1817	19	RI
Reynolds, Allen	1815	22	RI
Reynolds, George W.	1813	17	RI
Rhodes, George C.	1815	21	RI
Robinson, Edward W.	1815	17	RI
Robinson, Samuel P.	1816	18	RI
Robinson, Samuel W.	1815	16	RI
Robinson,			
Stephen Ayrault	1815	16	RI
Robinson, Thurston	1815	21	RI
Robinson, William	1816	20	RI
Rose, Frederick	1817	29	Prussia
Scott, Edward	1815	15	RI
Scott, JohnCleaveland	1815	42	RI
Scott, Joshua A.	1815	21	RI
Seabury, George W.	1815	15	RI
Sheaeman, John, Jr.	1816	21	RI
Shearman, Richard	1813	21	RI
Sherman, Aalbert	1816	17	RI
Sherry, David	1813	21	CT
Sisson, Barney	1817	25	RI
Slocum, Ebenezer	1815	20	RI
Smith, Benedict	1817	16	RI
Smith, Henry	1816	28	CT
Smith, Nathaniel, Jr.	1817	19	RI
Smith, Westgate	1815	21	RI
Snow, James	1815	22	MA
Spalding, William	1816	17	RI
Spear, James, Jr.	1817	21	RI
Spencer, Job	1816	20	RI
Spink, Charles F.	1817	18	RI
Spooner, Jonathan	1815	16	MA
Squire, John	1815	33	CT
Stanhope, Charles R.	1816	12	RI
Stoddard, David	1813	26	RI
Stoddard, Isaac	1813	19	RI
Stoddard, Isaac	1817	24	RI
Stoddard, Salisbury Jr.	1817	19	RI
Strange, Charles, Jr?	1815	22	MA
Sumner, William	1813	22	MA
Swaney, William	1815	18	RI
Sweeny, Benjamin	1816	27	RI
Sweeny, John	1815	17	RI
Sweet, John	1815	17	RI
Sweet, John	1813	16	RI
Sweet, John	1815	18	RI
Swinburne, Joseph	1815	25	RI
Swinburne, Nathaniel	1815	18	RI
Tallman, John	1817	33	RI
Tanner, Job	1815	23	RI
Tansley, John	1815	23	MA
Taylor, Robert	1817	20	RI
Taylor, Thomas	1814	19	MA

Taylor, William Oliver	1815	16	RI
Tennant, Andrew M.	1817	18	RI
Tew, William C.	1816	42	RI
Thayer, George, Jr.	1813	19	MA
Thurston, William	1815	16	RI
Tillinghas, William C.	1815	16	RI
Tompkins, Isaiah	1816	19	RI
Turner, Gardner	1816	21	RI
Valentine, Lynde	1815	18	MA
Vaughan, George	1815	18	RI
Vinson, Samuel H.	1814	17	RI
Waite, George	1817	24	RI
Waldin, John	1815	15	RI
Wales, Luke	1815	28	RI
Wall, Benjamin	1813	17	RI
Wall, Benjamin	1813	0	RI
Wall, Benjamin	1816	18	RI
Wallace, John G.	1815	36	RI
Watson, Edward	1815	19	RI
Way, William	1815	29	RI
Weaver, Henry	1815	16	MA
Weeden, Benjamin	1816	17	RI
Weeden, Daniel	1816	23	RI
Weeden, Henry	1816	20	RI
Weeden, William P.	1815	19	RI
Weeden, William P.	1816	21	RI
Wells, Elisha C.	1815	17	RI
West, William	1815	15	RI
White, Edmund	1816	16	RI
White, James	1817	21	RI
White, Thomas P.	1816	17	RI
Wickham, Hezekiah	1815	27	CT
Wilbom, Thomas	1815	20	RI
Wilbour, Benjamin	1816	43	RI
Wilbur, John	1817	22	RI
Wilcox, Ishmiel	1815	24	RI
Wilkey, Peter C.	1815	18	RI
Willis, Edward, Jr.	1817	12	RI
Winchester, William	1815	17	CT
Wing, John	1813	28	MA
Wood, William	1815	18	RI
Woodman, Humphrey	1815	22	RI

State of Maine.

Sworn to at Rockland

this _Stewart_

of _June_ 185_5_ _day_

Before me

T. R. Osgood D'yCollector.

I _John D. Crabtre_ of _Rockland_ in the
County of _Lincoln_ and State of _Maine_
do testify and declare, that _Frank Crabtre_ now present,
was born in the town of _Bluehill_ and that he has an actual
residence in the State of _Maine_

John D. Crabtre

Oaths of Citizenship

Port of Rockland, Maine

Oaths of Citizenship for the Port of Rockland are unique in that they are bound by hand in one volume. The forms are printed three to a page, and the blanks are completed by the Customs Collector. The first pages, carefully written in 1855, are very legible. Later, the handwriting of a different official has deteriorated greatly.

The Rockland volume is filed with the Port of Bath registers and abstracts. Abstracts for the Port of Rockland cover the period 1857 to 1864 with gaps.

These Oaths of Citizenship give the seaman's name and place of birth, but no age or date of birth. All are witnessed, often by the father of the seaman.

Oaths of Citizenship

Port of Rockland, Maine

Data Order: Name, Year, State

Name	Year	State
Ackrow, Josiah	1859	ME
Allen, Charles	1857	ME
Archbold, Wm. C.	1859	
Babbidge, Augustus S.	1856	ME
Barker, George H.	1855	ME
Barrow, David	1855	NY
Barrow?, Jackson	1859	ME
Bartlett, William	1855	ME
Bassett, C. H.	1858	ME
Bastes, Daniel? B.	1859	ME
Bradbury, George	1855	ME
Brewer, Horace	1858	ME
Brown, Arthur K.	1858	ME
Brown, Edwin E.	1856	ME
Brown, James	1858	RI
Brown, Wm.	1858	ME
Brown, Wm. H.	1858	ME
Bunker, Theodore	1857	ME
Campbell, Joseph A.	1859	ME
Cates, Henry	1859	ME
Chase, Edward	1856	MA
Colleman, S. R.	1858	ME
Colson, Isaac	1855	ME
Condon, Joshua P.	1856	ME
Cotten, Joseph C.	1859	ME
Crabtree, Frank	1857	ME
Creamer, Silas	1857	ME
Crockett, Alex C.	1858	ME
Crockett, George W.	1855	ME
Crooker, William	1856	ME
Cutler, Charles S.	1859	ME
Davis, Amos	1859	MA
Davis, Benjamin W.	1856	ME
Daws, George M.	1856	ME
Deen?, S. B.	1858	ME
Dickey, William A.	1856	ME
Dodge, Charles H.	1858	ME
Doveler?, Henry?	1858	CT
Dunn, Peter	1855	ME
Eldridge, A.	1858	ME
Emery, Saml. A.	1858	ME
Flower, Horatio P.	1855	ME
Gardner, John	1856	NY
Graves, John, Jr.	1855	ME
Gray, Robert L.	1856	ME
Gray, Walter R.	1856	ME
Gray?, William	1859	ME
Green, Alva F.	1859	ME
Gregory, Weston	1856	ME
Hall, Joseph	1855	ME
Hall, Wm. R.	1859	ME
Hanley, Patrick	1859	ME
Hazeltine, William	1857	ME
Herbert, Francis	1858	DC
Higgins, James B.	1855	ME
Hing, Henry A.	1859	CT
Holmes, Charles	1857	ME
Holmes, Stillman	1855	ME
Jameson, James L.	1857	ME
Jones, Henry	1856	ME
Keen, Lucien B.	1858	ME
Kendall, George E.	1856	ME
Kennedy, Thomas	1857	ME
Kennison, Edward	1859	ME
Lash, Emerson W.	1856	ME
Lawless, John E.	1858	MA
Leach, Thomas W.	1858	ME
Long, Roscoe	1858	ME
Machens, Allen F.	1858	ME
Mahoney, James M.	1857	ME
Manchester, William	1855	NY
McComiskey, James	1855	ME
McGilvery, John	1855	ME
McKay, Adam	1855	ME
McKenze, John W.	1858	ME
Merrill, Edwin W.	1859	ME
Morang, Lebeas C.	1856	ME
Morang, Peter C.	1856	ME
Murray, John	1857	LA
Orton, Franklin A.	1858	ME
Owens?, Reuben	1858	ME
Palmer, John	1855	NJ
Patter, Stewart	1858	ME
Peine, Joseph	1858	ME
Perry, Oscar R.	1855	ME
Peters, Emerson	1857	ME
Porter, Charles	1859	ME
Pottle, Benjamin F.	1856	ME
Pottle, Frederic A.	1856	ME
Rhoades, Orris	1859	ME
Richardson, Owen	1858	ME
Robinson, Joseph	1856	ME
Rockliff, Jerem. P.	1859	ME
Sandford, Edward	1856	ME

Sansom, John	1858	MA
Sartell, Wm. C.	1859	ME
Shaw, George W.	1856	ME
Sheals, James	1855	NY
Simmons, Alvin	1859	ME
Simmons, Wilber L.	1855	ME
Sleefer, H. J.	1858	ME
Sleepe, B. F.	1858	ME
Small, James H.	1855	ME
Smith, Clinton P.	1855	ME
Smith, Coburn S.	1859	ME
Smith, D. K.	1858	MA
Smith, Franklin	1859	ME
Smith, Richard	1857	ME
Snow, Benjamin F.	1856	ME
Spencer, Roscoe F.	1858	ME
Squires, David	1857	MA
Stover, Ephraim S.	1856	ME
Sylvester, Albert	1859	ME
Tasko, David	1856	ME
Thayer, Samuel S.	1855	ME
Thurlo, George M.	1858	ME
Trim, E. M.	1858	ME
Trusworthy?, Simon	1858	ME
Turner, Tileston	1859	ME
Usher, Charles L.	1856	ME
Webster?, Genp?	1858	ME
Wileilf?, Joseph Le	1859	ME
Williams, Samuel	1855	ME
Willis, Charles E.	1856	ME
Wilson, Richard, Jr.	1855	ME
Wolcott, George	1858	ME
Wood, Charles	1857	ME
Worthly, Lucien	1858	ME
Wyman, Henry S.	1859	ME

I George Bruce of Salem in the County of Essex, laborer do solemnly swear, that, to the best of my knowledge and belief, John Bruce of Salem, my son was born within the limits of the United States, viz. at Salem in the State of Massachusetts County of Essex

George Bruce

So Help me God.

ESSEX, SS. December 21 1841

Then the above named George Bruce made oath to the truth of the foregoing, before me.

John Prentiss

Justice of the Peace.

Port of Salem, Massachusetts, Oath of Citizenship

Oaths of Citizenship

Port of Salem, Massachusetts

The 114 records for the Port of Salem are for 1811 and 1813, and two for 1798. About 20 of these records have no date and are found in a file folder entitled "1811 or 1813."

They do not provide a date or year of birth, and have no description of the seaman. The witness, who gives his name and trade, often is identified as a relative.

The National Archives hold fairly extensive abstracts of Seamen's Protection Certificates issued in the Port of Salem. They cover the years 1813 to 1869, with large gaps.

Oaths of Citizenship

Port of Salem, Massachusetts

Data order: Name, Year, State

Name	Year	State	Name	Year	State
Andrews, James	1811	MA	Lewis, Ebed	1813	MA
Andrews, Nathl.	1811	MA	Mackintire, John	1811	MA
Aspinwall, John	1813	MA	Mann, Perez, Jr.	1811	MA
Batchelder, Winthrop	1813	MA	Marsh, Allen	1813	MA
Becket, Benj.	1813	MA	Millet, Andrew	1813	MA
Birgas, William	1813	MA	Noyes, John E.	1813	MA
Bisbrown, Thomas	1813		Nutting, Joseph, Jr.	1813	MA
Bisbrown, Thomas	1813	MA	Odiorne, John B. H.	1811	NH
Boden, Wm.	1811	MA	Osgood, Thos. B.	1813	MA
Bowers, Amos	1813	MA	Peirce, John	1811	MA
Bray, Eleazer D.	1813	MA	Perkins, George	1813	MA
Brazier, William	1813	NH	Phippen, Nathl.	1811	MA
Breed, Bassett	1798	MA	Picket, Charles	1813	MA
Bright, Thomas	1813	MA	Picket, Josiah	1813	MA
Brown, Henry	1811	MA	Pierce, William	1811	MA
Brown, John	1813	MA	Pourland, Jos.	1813	MA
Brown, William	1813	MA	Preble, Joseph	1811	MA
Bruce, John	1811	MA	Presson, Saml.	1811	MA
Burnham, Joshua	1811	MA	Quimby, Daniel	1811	MA
Callum, Ebenenezer	1811	MA	Richards, George	1813	MA
Chamberlain,			Richardson, John	1813	MA
Benjamin P.	1813	MA	Robinson, John	1798	SC
Clark, David	1813	MA	Sawyer, Uri	1813	MA
Colman, William	1813	VA	Short, Philip	1813	MA
Courtis, Stacy	1813	MA	Silver, James, Jr.	1811	MA
Crowninshield, Jacob	1811	MA	Silver, Samuel	1813	MA
Curtis, David	1813	MA	Skerry, Francis	1813	MA
Danforth, Joseph	1813	MA	Smith, Christopher	1813	MA
Deland, John	1813	MA	Smith, John	1813	MA
Dennis, Wm., Jr.	1813	MA	Smith, William, Jr.	1811	MA
Dobbin, Hermes	1813	MA	Soley, Nathl., Jr.	1813	MA
Doggett, Seth	1813	MA	Stafford, Hensey	1813	MA
Douglas, George	1813	MA	Stoddard, Thos.	1813	MA
Dupar, John	1811	MA	Stone, George	1811	MA
Edmonds, John	1811	MA	Stone, James	1813	MA
Ellingwood,			Strout, Joshua	1813	MA
William Hilton	1813	MA	Swan, Samuel	1811	MA
Fowler, Isaac	1813	MA	Swasey, William	1813	MA
Frye, John N.	1813	MA	Swqsey, Samuel	1811	MA
Fuller, Benj.	1813	MA	Symond, Nathaniel D.	1813	MA
Galloway, Samuel	1811	MA	Symonds, Ephraim	1813	MA
Gardner, David	1811	MA	Symonds, Procter	1813	MA
Gardner, Thomas	1813	MA	Taylor, John	1811	MA
Gentlee, Thos.	1811	MA	Thomas, Benjamin A.	1811	MA
Glover, Edward	1811	MA	Treadwell, Saml.	1813	MD
Gomes, Emanuel	1813	MA	Trusk, Thomas	1813	MA
Gould, Thomas	1811	MA	Vans, John	1813	VT
Gould, William P.	1813	MA	Walden, David	1813	MA
Harrison, Jas. F.	1813	MA	Warthen, Lewis	1813	MA
Hill, Hugh, Jr.	1811	MA	Weare, Ebenezer	1813	MA
Hills, James	1813	NH	Webben, Theodore	1813	MA
Hood/Wood, Saml.	1811	MA	Wells, Aaron	1813	MA
Hoyt, David	1813	MA	Wells, Nathan	1813	MA
Humphries, William	1811	NH	Wendell, Abraham	1813	MA
Hutchinson, John	1811	MA	Wilson, George	1811	NH
Ingalls, Thomas	1813	MA	Wilson, Jona.	1813	MA
Johnson, Osmond	1813	MA	Wilson, Thomas	1813	MA
King, Thos	1811	MA	Woodward, John B.	1813	MA

Various Records
Relating to Seamen's Protection Certificates
Port of New Bedford, Massachusetts

Only 36 documents related to Seamen's Protection Certificates, 1801 to 1826, have been preserved for the Port of New Bedford. These documents, a mixture of proofs, applications, and certificates from other ports, probably submitted when the seaman applied for a new certificate, are in no order whatsoever. The single file is found in a flat box with Middletown registers. In the same box a file containing one certificate issued in the Port of Boston is found. Very likely, it was turned in in New Bedford when a new protection was sought.

According to the Location Register, abstracts of protections issued in this port 1815 to 1843 are held by the National Archives.

It is noteworthy that 9 of the 36 documents identify seamen as having a black, colored, mulatto, or yellow complexion.

None of the documents seems typical of this port, and no example is included with this index.

Oaths of Citizenship

Port of New Bedford, Massachusetts

Data order: Name, Year, Age, Color, State

Name	Year	Age	Color	State
Ally Moses M.	1809	16		MA
Andress, John	1803	19	b	DC
Anthony, Abraham	1815	18	c	MA
Ayres, Samuel M.	1814	0		PA
Bagly, Levin	1815	22	c	MD
Barry, John	1813	23	c	
Bell, Hartfield	1817	24	c	PA
Chase, Robinson	1815	19		MA
Church, James C.	1815	19		MA
Cooper, Abraham	1816	21	m	
Cuffe, Paul, Jr.	1810	17		MA
Curtis, Samuel	0	0		MA
Davis, Henry	1817	22	y	MD
Devol, John	1813	20		RI
Eldridge, Stephen	1815	16		MA
Fuller, James Cook	1820	15		
Howe, Nathan	1809	0		MA
Howland, Borden	1815	17		MA
Hurd, James G.	1830	0		CT
Jenkins, Eli, Jr.	1811	17		MA
Jenney, Edward A.	1819	19		MA
Johnson, Peleg	1810	0		MA
Jones, Joseph H.	1811	12		
Liverton, Jesse Merrcumber	1820	19		
Luce, Jaba	1815	17		MA
Luce, Edmund	1811	15		MA
Mason, Edward	1815	0		
Miller, Joseph	1817	0		CT
Page, Cato H.	1816	25	c	MD
Perry, Edward G.	1827	0		MA
Ryerson, Tunis	1807	0		NJ
Smith, John	1816	0		PA
Spellman, John	1820	25	c	NC
Tuttle, Jesse	1801	22		
West, Nathaniel T.	1811	14		
Williamson, Richard	1813	25		NC

30,

Custom House, Collector's Office,

District of Portsmouth,

Portsmouth, November 5 18 57. State of

I George Wingate of New Hampshire do solemnly swear, according to the best of my knowledge and belief, that James W. Wingate is a Citizen of the United States, and was born in Portsmouth State of New Hampshire.

George Wingate

Sworn to, before me, J. M. Edmonds

Collector.

Further description, such as scars, marks, &c.

has a mole on the upper lip —

Age, 18 years,
Height 5 ft. 5 inches,
Hair, dark
Eyes, dark
Complexion, dark

Proofs of Citizenship

Port of Portsmouth, New Hampshire

Only 22 proofs of citizenship submitted at Portsmouth in 1857-1858 for Seamen's Protection Certificates have survived and are preserved by the National Archives in Washington, D. C. This is an index to those few records.

It should be noted that these records are found in a box with records for the port of Bath, Maine.

All of these proofs are written on printed forms in legible handwriting. They give the seaman's name, his age at the time of application, place of birth, height, and color of eyes, hair and complexion.

There are numerous abstracts which span the years 1814 to 1868 with many gaps, and a register for the years 1796 to 1798 in a multi-purpose volume.

Proof of Citizenship
Port of Portsmouth, New Hampshire

Name	Year	Age	State
Anderson, George E.	1857	25	NH
Anderson, Horace	1857	18	NH
Barnes, Nelson	1858	16	NH
Briard, Levi	1857	21	ME
Bussard, Lewis A.	1857	54	DC
Cate, Henry Harrison	1858	17	NH
Davis, Alfred S.	1857	16	NH
Franklin, Harrison T.	1857	18	NH
Gillis, Robert	1858	24	ME
Gray, William H.	1858	23	ME
Gurney, Albert A.	1857	17	NH
Kehoe, Thomas	1858	25	NH
Langton, John B. F.	1858	19	ME
Lise, Francis P.	1857	23	NH
Preston, James W.	1857	14	NH
Smith, Geo. W.	1858	20	NH
Townsend, James W.	1857	20	NH
Townsend, John E.	1857	25	NH
Weeks, Charles A.	1857	16	ME
Whitehouse, George F.	1857	15	NH
Wingate, George W.	1857	18	NH
Young, William C.	1857	38	NH

Proofs of Citizenship

Port of New London, Connecticut

There is only a handful of proofs of citizenship from New London preserved in the National Archives. However, there are a number of abstracts and one register. These are a useful supplement to the actual proofs since they give the most essential information about a seaman, his name, age at time of application, and his place of birth.

In addition to the box containing the proofs, four Protection Certificates issued at New London, are found in a folder with a notation, "found among Bridgeport proofs." It is assumed that these Certificates were reported lost, a duplicate was issued in Bridgeport, and the original was subsequently found and turned in. Normally, the Certificate remains with the records of the port which issued the duplicate. For some reason, these became separated.

No illustration is given for this port.

Proofs of Citizenship

Port of New London, Connecticut

Name	Year	Age	State
Bartholomew, Samuel	1803	21	
Briggs, Willim	1803	16	
Button, Jesse	1803	0	CT
Dutton, William, Jr.	1803	0	CT
Harvey, Henry	1803	0	CT
Jeffery, Russel	1803	17	
Mildrum, John	1802	20	
Morgan, Alfred	1803	20	
Mullikin, James	1803	23	
Noble, Walter	1803	21	MA
Robbins, Joshua	1804	22	
Wheat, James	1799	18	
Williams, Nathan	1803	0	CT
Wright, David	1800	16	

Seamen's Protection Certificates

Certificates for these four seamen are found in a separate folder:

Name	Year	Age
Bailey, Jeremiah	1799	17
Hollomon, Benjamin	1799	17
Ranney, James	1801	18
Williams, George	1804	25

www.ingramcontent.com/pod-product-compliance
Lightning Source LLC
Chambersburg PA
CBHW061741270326
41928CB00011B/2324